Jostling Between
"Mere Talk" & Blame Game?
Beyond Africa's Poverty and
Underdevelopment Game Talk

Edited by

Munyaradzi Mawere

Langaa Research & Publishing CIG
Mankon, Bamenda

Publisher:
Langaa RPCIG
Langaa Research & Publishing Common Initiative Group
P.O. Box 902 Mankon
Bamenda
North West Region
Cameroon
Langaagrp@gmail.com
www.langaa-rpcig.net

Distributed in and outside N. America by African Books Collective
orders@africanbookscollective.com
www.africanbookscollective.com

ISBN-10: 9956-764-82-5

ISBN-13: 978-9956-764-82-2

© Munyaradzi Mawere 2018

About the Contributors

Munyaradzi Mawere is a Professor in the Simon Muzenda School of Arts, Culture and Heritage Studies at Great Zimbabwe University in Zimbabwe. He holds a Ph. D in Social Anthropology, Master's Degree in Social Anthropology, Master's Degree in Development Studies, Master's Degree in Philosophy and, a B. A (Hons) Degree in Philosophy. Before joining this university, Professor Mawere was a lecturer at the University of Zimbabwe and at Universidade Pedagogica, Mozambique, where he has worked in different capacities as a senior lecturer, assistant research director, postgraduate co-ordinator, and professor. He is an author of more than 50 books and over 230 academic publications with a focus on Africa straddling the following areas: poverty and development, African philosophy, society and culture, democracy, politics of food production, humanitarianism and civil society organisations, urban anthropology, existential anthropology, cultural philosophy, area studies, experimental philosophy, environmental anthropology, society and politics, decoloniality and African studies. Some of his bestselling books are: *Humans, Other Beings and the Environment: Harurwa (Edible stinkbugs) and Environmental Conservation in South-eastern Zimbabwe* (2015); *Theory, Knowledge, Development and Politics: What Role for the Academy in the Sustainability of Africa?* (2016); *Democracy, Good Governance and Development in Africa: A Search for Sustainable Democracy and Development,* (2015); *Culture, Indigenous Knowledge and Development in Africa: Reviving Interconnections for Sustainable Development* (2014); *Myths of Peace and Democracy? Towards Building Pillars of Hope, Unity and Transformation in Africa* (2016); *Harnessing Cultural Capital for Sustainability: A Pan Africanist Perspective* (2015); *Divining the Future of Africa: Healing the Wounds, Restoring Dignity and Fostering Development,* (2014); *African Cultures, Memory and Space: Living the Past Presence in Zimbabwean Heritage* (2014); *Violence, Politics and Conflict Management in Africa: Envisioning Transformation, Peace and Unity in the Twenty-First Century* (2016); *African Philosophy and Thought Systems: A Search for a Culture and Philosophy of Belonging* (2016); *Africa at the Crossroads: Theorising Fundamentalisms in the 21st Century* (2017); *Colonial Heritage, Memory and Sustainability in Africa: Challenges, Opportunities and Prospects*

(2016); *Underdevelopment, Development and the Future of Africa* (2017), and *Theorising Development in Africa: Towards Building an African Framework of Development* (2017); *African Studies in the Academy: The Cornucopia of Theory, Praxis and Transformation in Africa?* (2017); *GMOs, Consumerism and the Global Politics of Biotechnology: Rethinking Food, Bodies and Identities in Africa's 21ˢᵗ Century* (2017); and *Human Trafficking and Trauma in the Digital Era: The Ongoing Tragedy of the Trade in Refugees from Eritrea* (2017).

Mohammed Abubakar Yinusa is an Associate Professor and Lecturer in the Department of Sociology at the University of Ilorin in Nigeria. His area of specialisation is in Sociology of Development, Health and Wellbeing and Social Problems. He has published many journal articles and other such academic pieces in internationally acclaimed publishing outlets. Professor Yinusa has also attended conferences and presented various papers both locally and internationally.

Fidelis Peter Thomas Duri is a Senior Lecturer of History in the Department of Archaeology, Culture and Heritage, History and Development Studies at Great Zimbabwe University. He is a holder of a PhD in History from the University of the Witwatersrand in Johannesburg, South Africa. He has published a number of books and articles which focus on environmental history, socio-cultural dynamics, subaltern struggles, African border studies, and Zimbabwe's socio-political landscape during the colonial and post-colonial periods. In addition to reviewing a number of scholarly articles, he has also edited books such as *Resilience Amid Adversity: Informal Coping Mechanisms to the Zimbabwean Crisis during the New Millennium* (2016) and *Contested Spaces, Restrictive Mechanisms and Corridors of Opportunity: A Social History of Zimbabwean Borderlands and Beyond since the Colonial Period* (2017). He is also a member of the editorial boards of international journals which include the *Zimbabwe Journal of Historical Studies* and the *International Journal of Developing Societies*.

Johnson O. Olaniyi obtained his PhD degree in Political Science (specialising in Comparative Politics with special emphasis on

Electoral Studies-Psephology) from University of Ilorin, Ilorin, Nigeria. He is also a holder of a B.Sc. and M.Sc. degrees in Political Science from Nigeria's Premier University, University of Ibadan. Dr Olaniyi also holds a Postgraduate Diploma in Education (PGDE) Certificate which he obtained from University of Ilorin, Ilorin, Nigeria. He is currently a Senior Lecturer in the Department of Political Science, University of Ilorin, Ilorin, Nigeria, where he has been teaching core courses in Political Science since January, 1992. He is the immediate past Head, Department of Political Science, University of Ilorin, Ilorin, Nigeria and had previously served as the Sub-Dean, Faculty of Business and Social Sciences, University of Ilorin, Ilorin, Nigeria. He has served in different capacities as Electoral Officer in elections conducted in Nigeria by successive Election Management Bodies since 1977. He has authored two books; Introduction to Contemporary Political Analysis and Foundations of Public Policy Analysis; and co-authored a book; Introduction to Constitutional Development in Nigeria; which have all become reference points in Nigerian Universities. Furthermore, he has contributed chapters to some edited books both locally and internationally; and published widely in both national and international journals.

Takavafira Masarira Zhou is an environmental historian, a Lemba, trade unionist, and Human Rights defender. He is a holder of B.A. General, B.A. Special Honours in History, Masters in African History, Graduate Certificate in Education, and Doctoral Degree in Environmental History from the University of Zimbabwe. He was a Teaching Assistant in the History Department at the University of Zimbabwe (1991-1995), a History Lecturer at Mutare Teachers' college (2002-2004), and a part-time History Lecturer at Africa University (2002-2004). As a History Lecturer at Great Zimbabwe (2004-2008) he helped to transform the history subject area into the Department of History and Development Studies. He was a technical advisor (researcher) in Zimbabwe Constitution Select Committee (2010-2011) that produced Zimbabwe's new Constitution in 2013. He was also a member of the National Education Advisory Board (2009-2013) that among other things helped the then Ministry of Education, Sports, Arts and Culture in strategic planning, resource mobilisation and policy formulation during the period of Inclusive Government. Currently he is the president of the Progressive Teachers' Union of Zimbabwe, and treasurer of the Non Aligned Teachers' Unions of Southern Africa (ANTUSA). He has presented various papers at conferences in Zimbabwe, Africa, Europe and Asia. He has also published on African agriculture; white settler farming; environmental impact of mining in Zimbabwe; peace and security in Africa; History curricula changes in Zimbabwe; post-2016 Africa's developmental trends; teacher education; poverty, natural resources and underdevelopment in Africa; poverty, conflict and vulnerability in Africa; and general history and politics of Zimbabwe.

Caleb Oladokun Ogunkunle is a Senior Lecturer in the Department of Religions, Faculty of Arts, University of Ilorin, Ilorin, Nigeria. He had his Ph. D. from the University of Ibadan, Ibadan, Nigeria in Biblical Studies with emphasis in the Old Testament. He teaches Biblical Hebrew and Old Testament courses at both undergraduate and postgraduate levels at the University of Ilorin. He has supervised many undergraduate projects, a number of Master of Arts projects and three PhD theses. His areas of specialisation include: Biblical Studies, Biblical interpretation and Christian Theology. He contextualises his research papers on the Nigerian situation in general and the Yoruba ethnic group in particular. He is an ordained minister with the United Missionary Church of Africa. He is the current Chaplain- in- Charge of Chapel of the Light, University of Ilorin; an inter-denominational Chapel in the University.

Phillip T. D. Mazambara holds a PhD from Hamburg University in Germany. He is also a holder of a B.A (Hons) and Master of Arts in Religious Studies from the University of Zimbabwe. Since 2010, Dr Mazambara has been teaching New Testament and other related courses at Great Zimbabwe University. His research interests are but not limited to New Testament Studies, Political theology and linking Chivanhu and the Bible independent of European Christianity as a way of renaissancing autonomous ethnic African originality.

Odeigah, Theresa Nfam is a holder of a B.A Degree in History; M.A. (History), PGDE, and PhD (History). She is a lecturer in the Department of History and International Studies at the University of Ilorin, Kwara State, Nigeria. She is an Economic Historian specialising in the Niger Delta Region of Nigeria. She has published widely in scholarly journals in the area of economic history.

Nyasha Madzokere is a lecturer in the Department of Philosophy and Religious Studies at Great Zimbabwe University from 2007 to date. He lectures Old Testament Studies and Biblical Hebrew. He is widely published in the Bible and its contextual applicability to Zimbabwe with two books, eight book chapters and five refereed journal articles. He has travelled widely in Africa and beyond presenting papers at international conferences. He recently co-published a book chapter with Ephraim Matanda entitled: *'The Tarnished Jewel?' Post-Independent Zimbabwe Tag under the reign of Robert Mugabe.*

Kadiri Kehinde Kehinde lecturers in the department of Mass Communication in University of Ilorin, Nigeria. She has a PhD degree in Communication from University Utar, Malaysia. She specializes in health communication, photo journalism, public relations and advertising. She has several publications in both local and international journals and has attended several academic conferences within and outside Nigeria.

Tasara Muguti is a lecturer in the History, Archaeology and Development Studies Department at Great Zimbabwe University. He holds a Bachelor of Arts (Hons) in Economic History, a Master of Arts in African Economic History and a Graduate Certificate in Education, all obtained from the University of Zimbabwe. He is currently a registered PHD Student with UNISA. He has several published book chapters and journal articles to his credit. His research interests are in Indigenous Knowledge Systems, with special emphasis on African traditional medicine, land reform, human rights, democracy and many other topical issues on contemporary Southern African history.

Joseph Adesoji Oluyemi is a PhD Candidate in the Department of Sociology, University of Ilorin, Nigeria. His areas of specialization include Medical Sociology and Sociology of Development with special interests in Adolescent Health, Occupational health, Infectious diseases, Emerging diseases, Sexualities and issues in development.

Angeline Sithole holds a Bachelors of Arts Honours Degree in Economic history (from Great Zimbabwe University). She is currently pursuing a Master of Arts Degree in Development Studies with the same institution. Her research interests are in the areas of urban, environmental and women history.

Raji Abdulateef is a PhD Candidate and Lecturer II in the Department of Sociology, University of Ilorin, Nigeria. His areas of specialisation include Sociology of Development, Rural Sociology and Social issues.

Costain Tandi is a Graduate teacher for Advanced level History and Sociology as well as Head of Department (Humanities) at Rufaro High School in Chatsworth, Zimbabwe. He holds a Master of Arts Degree in Development Studies from Midlands State University; Bachelor of Arts 4th year Honours Degree in History from Great Zimbabwe University; Bachelor of Arts General Degree from the University of Zimbabwe; Graduate Certificate in Education from Great Zimbabwe University; An Executive Certificate in Project and Program Monitoring and Evaluation from the University of Zimbabwe; and An Executive Certificate in Project Management from the University of Zimbabwe. Tandi has six publications and his research interests include but not limited to Indigenous Knowledge Systems, Climate Change and Variability, Rural Poverty, Agriculture and Community Development.

Joseph Adejoke is a Consultant Clinical Microbiologist and Infectious Disease Physician. She is a Lecturer in the Department of Medical Microbiology at Bowen University, Iwo, Nigeria. Her area of specialization is in Sexually Transmitted infection especially with people living with HIV.

Atolagbe Emmanuel is a facilitator at the National Open University of Nigeria. He is currently running his PhD programme in Sociology at the University of Ilorin, Nigeria with specialization in medical Sociology. He has interest in industrial relations, industrial sociology, peace studies and intergroup relations and has several publications.

Orji Boniface Ifeanyi is a lecturer in the Department of History and Diplomatic Studies, Crown Hill University, Eiyenkorin, Ilorin, Kwara State Nigeria. Orji is a native of Oso Edda, in Afipko-South LGA Ebonyi State. He has BA and MA History from the University of Ilorin, and he is currently a PhD candidate at the same University of Ilorin, Kwara State. His areas of interest include History, Migration and Diaspora Studies, Gender Studies, Economic and Social History; Peace and Conflict Studies.

Table of Contents

Chapter 1

The Marginalisation and Impoverishment of Africa: Reversing the Causes and Consequences of Poverty in Africa

Munyaradzi Mawere

Introduction

Among other tragedies, Africa has over the years suffered a double tragedy – that of marginalisation and impoverishment (or dispossession) by the Global North – which aimed at suppressing and retarding the continent's development efforts and potentials. The consequence of this tragedy has been far-reaching and in fact disastrous for the people of Africa. It resulted in developmenticide of Africa's progress in all spheres. The effects of the tragedy remain printed in bold on the face of Africa even today. Only a reversal of such marginalisation and impoverishment – what I call here "developmenticide" – can heal the wounds of Africa and restore its long lost legacy and dignity. By developmenticide, I mean the development for conquest that the hegemonic powers of the Global North inaugurated and seeded in Africa to seal the latter's underdevelopment. For Africa, such a tragedy requires a complete reversal to ensure a North-South partnership and collaboration based on fairness, sustainability and mutual benefit. Development-wise, a reversal of developmenticide would seek to turn back the fortunes– the "stolen legacy" – of the continent of Africa as it would entail repatriation of the African riches that were stolen to Europe and U. S. during colonialism, establishment of a fair playing ground for all people of the world based on equality, and most especially creation of even development amongst all societies of the world. But how Africa was in fact impoverished and marginalised? More so, how can developmenticide in Africa be expurgated? There is need to discuss these questions, lest others would think that the story of Africa's impoverishment and marginalisation (or dispossession) is built on mythical towers and tirading efforts meant to tarnish the image of the Global North.

Talking of impoverishment and or dispossession, Walter Rodney was right to pen down his 1972 book *How Europe Underdeveloped Africa*, while talking of marginalisation, George James was apt to pen down his *Stolen Legacy*, depicting how African epistemologies and other such resources – material and intellectual – were unduly appropriated by the West and used to subjugate and marginalise the very people who should have optimally benefitted from the treasure of their fatherland and motherland, Africa. Both Rodney's and James' texts are a succinct summary of how, as a result of the unfair play of the Global North, Africa found herself in the jaws of both poverty and marginalisation.

To start with how Europe and indeed the Americas – a combination whose due to their geographical location vis-à-vis Africa I refer to in this book as "Global North" – Rodney convincingly argue that deliberately exploited Africa. This deliberate exploitation which reached its peak during the 19th and 20th centuries when Europe decided to colonise Africa, undoubtedly underdeveloped Africa in almost all spheres of life, that is, economically, politically, psychologically, spiritually and culturally. In fact, there was no human sphere of Africa that was spared by the nefarious imperialistic well calculated exploitations of Africa by Europe. From a politico-economic point of view, Rodney (1972: 115) notes, with respect to Africa, that "when one society finds itself forced to relinquish its power entirely, that is a form of underdevelopment". The society will have been politically and economically subjugated, which in fact leads to its underdevelopment. Thus, delivering his main argument from a historical materialist perspective, Rodney concludes that it is the European economic exploitation and power politics that resulted in Africa's poverty and marginalisation. This economic exploitation and political terrorism was facilitated by parochialised education which was not only instituted to compete with the existing 'formal' indigenous knowledge, but to destroy and substitute the indigenous education of the African people. All this was made possible by demonising everything that was African, including its indigenous epistemologies, modes of development, local forms of technology and science. Western education, thus, perpetuated the mythical incompetence of the indigenous people of Africa to contribute to the development of their own societies. Santos, Nunes and Meneses (2007: xix) capture this aptly when they note:

> the epistemological privilege granted to modern science from the seventeenth century onwards, which made possible the technological revolutions that consolidated Western supremacy, was also instrumental in suppressing other, non-scientific forms of knowledges and, at the same time, the subaltern social groups whose social practices were informed by such knowledges.

This certainly shattered the innovative and creative potentials of the African people. Rodney (1972: 4), summarises this domineering and subjugating tendencies of the colonial imperialists when he argues that "development during *colonialism* has always meant the increase in the ability to guard the independence of the social group and indeed to infringe upon the freedom of others-something that often came about irrespective of the will of the persons within the societies involved."

In a similar fashion, the Guyanese George James in *Stolen Legacy* (1954) shows how, for centuries, the world has been misled to believe that the source of the Arts and Sciences is the West with Socrates and Aristotle having been falsely idolised as the originators of science. He argues that Greek philosophy, religion and science originated in Africa, particularly ancient Egypt. In fact, for James, the ancient Greeks were not the original authors of Greek philosophy as the philosophy was mainly based on ideas, principles and concepts 'stolen' from ancient Egyptians – the 'Egyptian Mystery System'. This philosophy and all ideas which form the foundation of Greek civilisation were stolen during the time Alexander the Great invaded Egypt and captured the Royal Library at Alexandria and plundered it. Aristotle, who contributed to almost all disciplines, was the greatest beneficiary as he is said to have been present during the time of the invasion. He even later on established his school within the library. James notes that other Greek prominent philosophers like Pythagoras and Plato studied in Egypt. He also cites Greek sources such as Herodotus who describes the cultural debt of Greco-Roman society to Egypt to support the central argument in his book. James' mysterious death soon after the publication of his *magnum opus*, Stolen Legacy, most probably in the hands of racist 'white' scholars could in itself evidence that by arguing that Egyptian philosophy was African innovation that Western intellectuals had falsely attributed to the Greeks, he had struck below the belt of Western civilisation which verily rests on the pillars of Greek civilisation. Yet, for James as with many Africanists, the 'stealing' of African 'resources' by European imperialists which became more evident during colonialism, marked the beginning of African impoverishment while the nonacknowledgement of African ideas by ancient Western prominent scholars like Aristotle marked the beginning of the marginalisation of Africa.

I add that Africa's impoverishment and marginalisation has been ongoing since the birth of the trans-Atlantic slave trade. It never ended with the demise of colonial administration in Africa. As van Stam (2017: 6) notes:

> Most power structures we see, including in our academia, are the continuing of colonial structures, epistemologies and systems. Actually, in my assessment from the *colonialised* perspective, colonialism never ended! No, we live in super-colonial times, where not only we are continually shamed, brainwashed and usurped by the economic structures, but also, more and more, in the techno-social structures (e.g. by social media).

As this book is more concerned with the socio-economic development of Africa, particularly how its socio-economic predicament could be changed for the better, it is important to underscore that all the exploits, subjugation and marginalisation of the African people have had serious repercussions on the well-being, dignity and human development of the African people. However, I underline the need for a generative action – an action that goes beyond mere talk and blame game on problems that have haunted Africa for centuries now. Of course, the end result of Africa's experiences was marginalisation and impoverishment of the African people – a serious problem that continue to haunt Africans even today. The questions now are: "Is the impoverishment and marginalisation that Africa has suffered for centuries since the beginning of the trans-Atlantic slave trade through colonialism reversible? If yes, how can we *truly* change Africa's socio-economic and political situation after many years of both impoverishment and marginalisation? How can we go beyond mere talk and blame game on Africa's predicament?"

On the wheel of change: A quest for global political and socio-economic transformation

The questions raised in the section above are critical, yet difficult to answer. They are critical because speaking from a human right point of view, there is need, in the name of equality and justice, to level the ground for all peoples of the world. There is need to go beyond 'the mere talk' and blame game on Africa's predicament to proffer workable homegrown solutions that quest to transcend Africa's trepidations and problems of sorts. This calls for all communities of the world to recognise the realities of global inequalities and move swiftly in the most transparent manner to address Africa's predicament and its manifestations in the form of poverty and underdevelopment. It also calls for the urgency of fair partnership and collaboration in research and knowledge production between North and South to give both greater insight into global problems. This can only be possible when the ground is first levelled evenly for all players. This levelling of the ground should be extended to all spheres of life be that education, knowledge production and dissemination, politics, development, technology, religion or culture. More so, it has to start right at the global level for many of the factors within national boundaries such as national politics and economics depend on global politics. They are in fact dictated by global politics as multilateral agencies tend to draw up blueprints of development models and theories for emulation and implementation by their "weaker" Southern partners. This results in useless and unsustainable development packages as the "blueprints are often loaded with cultural and ideological content generated by the major powers' and

5

indeed 'the importing of these models that are allegedly universally applicable is one of the major causes of slow development in Africa" (Kasozi 2015: 88). This is because Africans tend to embrace only those development tenets that are not contrary to their beliefs and ways of life, and which are affordable to them and sustainable. What this entails is that while a change of attitude and *modus operandi* within national governments such as economic and political policies can impact the political and socio-economic terrain, their impact will be short-lived as long as there are no equal adjustments at the global level on how development models and knowledge are shared. Sustainable transformation, thus, should be supported by global policies and politics, but of course with the ultimate aim of advancing home-grown knowledge and solutions produced by scholars and researchers who have knowledge and experience of African conditions.

A guide through the book

Chapter 2 by Munyaradzi Mawere critically examines the role of Bretton Woods Institutions – the International Monetary Fund (IMF) and the World Bank (WB) –in either the promotion or eradication of underdevelopment and poverty in the developing world. While these two institutions have been labelled by some as "gods" of development in Africa, this chapter argues that the IMF and the World Bank have largely played a "paternalistic" role, disregarding contextual and circumstantial differentiations across the nations of Africa. This has stifled development and efforts to eradicate poverty form the face of Africa. Further, Mawere argues that the involvement of the World Bank and IMF in Africa's development has a long history littered with miscarriages of development or what he calls "developmenticide" and the suffering of the innocent ordinary people. So are the acts by many African rulers since Africa's independence. For these reasons, among others, Mawere argues that both African governments and the Bretton Woods Institutions are fallible, and therefore should take a thorough self-introspection gesture with the view to mend their differences which have often frustrated efforts towards development and poverty eradication in Africa.

Odeigah Theresa Nfam and Munyaradzi Mawere's Chapter 3 critically examines and determines if the Multinational Corporations in Africa (as elsewhere in the so-called developing world) have contributed in any positive way to the level of poverty – both socio-economic and environmental. Basing on the findings obtained in the Delta Region of Nigeria during research for this chapter, Nfam and Mawere argue that African states and continental resources such as minerals and land in general are constantly in a state of capture by Multinational Corporations and their foreign governments. In fact, for Nfam and Mawere, Multinational Corporations and their foreign governments operating in Africa have always been dangling the carrot of promoting African lives and environments even as they destroy, dispossess and impoverish African [human] peasants. They conclude that the poverty level in the Delta Region and by extension Nigeria, is the direct consequence of the manipulative, rapacious, oppressive, selfish, domineering and exploitatively pernicious tendencies of the Multinational Corporations operating in the region.

Through a critical interrogation of contemporary politics in Zimbabwe, Fidelis P. T. Duri's Chapter 4 lays bare poverty and shifting consumer dynamics in rural Zimbabwe between 2000 and 2008. While in this chapter Duri mentions that the dietary options during the referred period were largely "wild foods" in the sense that the animal and plant species were not domesticated and also did not constitute a regular part of their diet, he is quick to note that his chapter does not downplay the importance of wild foods, both flora and fauna, in human life. In fact, Duri hails the importance of wild foods during times of crisis and famine as he wittingly argues that besides providing dietary diversity, various plant and animal species from the wilderness remained of great medicinal and nutritional value to human beings during the 2000 to 2008 crisis. Making cross references to other studies in Africa, Duri reveals that many green leaves and fruits from the wilderness are rich in Vitamin C while most insects are rich in protein, fats and micronutrients that are required for the wellbeing of humanity. Yet, though important as such, Duri argues that "there is a problem when all communities in a country are forced by circumstances beyond their control such as chronic hunger to abandon their staple diet and settle for wild foods in order to survive" as was the case of Zimbabwe during the period 2000-2008 crisis. For him, such inexorable political, socio-economic and ecological disasters, which are largely a result of government's mismanagement of the economy should be avoided at all cost.

Takavafira Masarira Zhou's ground-breaking Chapter 5 grapples with the intricate and complex relationship between poverty and conflict as well as their subsequent ramifications on African states and communities. Although Zhou acknowledges that many of Africa's contemporary conflicts and cases of poverty are rooted in the colonial era, admittedly, "the correlation between poverty and conflict is captured in the familiar mantra that there can be no security without development, and no development without security". Zhou, however, remains careful to note that even with this obtaining reality, the relationship between poverty and conflict are complex and difficult to pin down with acute precision. Yet Zhou's central argument remains that poverty is as much a cause of conflict as it is a consequence of conflict such that the problem of poverty should always be viewed in a multi-dimensional manner, transcending economics to social, political and cultural spheres. Making reference to case studies around Africa – from Angola, Sierra Leone, Somalia, Central Africa Republic and Libya – Zhou concludes that if we are to overcome poverty we need to have a clear comprehension of the interaction and synergies of conflict and poverty.

In Chapter 6, Mohammed Y. Abubakar, Joseph A. Oluyemi, Joseph Adejoke, Raji Abdullateef, Kadiri Kehinde, and Atolagbe Emmanuel meticulously examine the impact of poverty on infant and maternal mortality rates in Nigeria and the lessons and insights drawn for Africa. As these authors explore the impact of poverty on infant and maternal health in Nigeria and in Africa in general, they anticipate that results from such a study would help to speak to and inform policy across the continent and beyond. To this anticipated result, the authors focus on the Nigerian healthcare system and policy implications for infant and maternal health to draw lessons and insights for Africa.

Costain Tandi and Munyaradzi Mawere's Chapter 7 unflinchingly explore the vulnerability and resilience of poverty in disaster-prone areas of the Global South in general and Africa in particular. Tandi and Mawere draw upon some of the factors and processes that have prevented human communities in ecologically vulnerable areas to escape from extreme poverty, even as some researchers view disasters as windows of opportunities for development. Tandi and Mawere thus argue that as extreme weather linked to climate change is increasing at a sporadic pace in the African continent, this is likely to cause more disasters in the future. Consequently, such disasters, especially those linked to drought, floods and hurricanes are likely to stand as the most important causes of impoverishment and vulnerability, set to undo progress on poverty reduction in Africa. As such, Tandi and Mawere urge Africa to take a front seat position as it negotiates climate change mitigation measures.

In Chapter 8, Caleb O. Ogunkunle uses the Biblical stories to explore the emergence of the cycle of poverty and traditional systems for poverty eradication in Yorubaland. More specifically, Ogunkunle draws on his personal knowledge of the Old Testament to interrogate the story of Ruth and Naomi in an exegetical fashion that allows him "to x-ray its import and exemplary implication of the family support system that has almost broken down totally in Yorubaland". As Ogunkunle himself notes, the purpose of the chapter "is to promote the revival of the traditional African value of 'I am because you are and since you are therefore I am', and what the Yorubas express as Ènìyàn ni aso mi (Human beings are my clothes- referring to protection and care)". In so doing, Ogunkunle advances the argument that Nigeria can draw insights and inspiration from the story of Ruth and Naomi "which in itself demonstrates the extent to which the Old Testament Jews and traditional Africans have affinity". Ogunkunle concludes his chapter by imploring the Yorubas and Africans in general to enliven and embrace the principle of "we-feeling" and corporate social existence as is the case in the Christian World.

Chapter 9 by Phillip T. D. Mazambara and Munyaradzi Mawere examines the concept of Mwariology and how it informs Heritage Studies and act as springboard for Africa's Development. For Mazambara and Mawere, the concept of 'Mwariology' should not only used to refer to the 'The-Human-Being-Who-Is' or 'Voice-Ultimate-Concept' in terms of protection seeking, applied to other spheres of human life such as education, Heritage Studies and development. This conceptualisation should stand because, Mazambara and Mawere argue, when the ethnic Zimbabweans talk of the Voice-Ultimate-Concept, they do not only seek protection but also guidance from their vulnerable situations, including situations of poverty and underdevelopment. Drawing on this understanding and the perspective of ethnic Zimbabweans, Mazambara and Mawere, thus, conclude that Mwariology is the springboard of societal development in Africa, and more specifically Zimbabwe, besides that it informs Heritage Studies.

In Chapter 10, Tasara Muguti and Angeline Sithole revisits the effects of land grabbing in sub-Saharan Africa by foreigners, and more specifically wealth nations and multinational institutions during the new millennium. The duo argues that "though land grabs have become a global phenomenon affecting Southeast Asia and Latin America, the Global South is the worst affected with 70% of the land grabs taking place in sub-Saharan Africa". They note one of the key drivers for Africa's attractiveness to land grabbing by foreigners as the perception by the latter that Africa has an abundance of idle land. For Muguti and Sithole, this perception and [land] grabbing of African lands by these foreigners and at times in conjunction with the ruling African elites, has not only resulted in diminished agricultural sovereignty and exacerbated landlessness among rural communities, but exacerbated the poverty situations and vulnerabilities of the African peoples.

Johnson O. Olaniyi's Chapter 11 examines the manifestations of the symptoms of poverty in the electoral behaviour of Nigerian political actors. Though focusing on poverty in general, Olaniyi is most interested in how the poverty status of political actors and candidates in Nigeria have had a negative bearing on the electoral process of the country over the years. Using a historical-cum – comparative research methodology and a theory of voting behaviour known as 'the rational choice theory', Olaniyi explains why an average political actor (especially those whose economic status are poor) in Nigeria (as elsewhere beyond) usually give paramount consideration to what s/he stands to gain from supporting a political party or candidate in any election. Olaniyi reveals that this scenario is clear manifestation of partisan politics which has begun rampant in Nigeria and other African countries since independence. He calls for a departure from such politics, which in no way quest to bring in real democracy, peace and development to Africa.

In Chapter 12, Fidelis Peter Thomas Duri uses the concepts of witchcraft, development and politicking to examine the power struggles within Zimbabwe African National Union Patriotic Front (ZANU-PF) and their poverty implications to Zimbabwe. He argues that the struggles for power and the counter-productive wrangles smeared with witchcraft beliefs, particularly witchcraft accusations which are sometimes instrumentalised as a transformative dynamic in contemporary political contestations within the Zimbabwe African Union Patriotic Front (ZANU-PF) – a party that dominated Zimbabwe's political landscape since independence in 1980 – are not only counter-productive but reverses the gains of development. To this end, Duri contends that power struggles constitute one of the major barriers to development and causes of poverty and underdevelopment in contemporary Zimbabwe since such struggles divert the attention of the ruling elite towards political survival instead of addressing the urgent socio-economic needs of the majority of the people.

In Chapter 13, ORJI Boniface Ifeanyi, using Nigeria as a case study, grapples with corruption and failures of various poverty alleviation programmes aimed at eradicating poverty. Basing on his findings, Ifeanyi reveals that the failure of the Nigerian government and the country's leadership to reduce poverty rate is largely a result of corruption and other such unethical and unprofessional practices. The authenticity of this claim holds, Ifeanyi argues, the very moment we realise that "in spite of *many* poverty alleviation programmes instituted by various administration, Nigeria still ranks 54th in Human Poverty Index (HPI), and is among the 20 poorest countries in the world with 70% of the population living below the poverty datum line as of 2003". This is because "those that are saddled with the responsibility of implementing the various programme, see it as opportunity of enriching themselves, thereby inflicting more poverty on the Nigerian populace".

Drawing on the critical analysis of the Biblical texts on Micah, Nyasha Madzokere's Chapter 14 examines the poverty situation in Zimbabwe in the 21st century. To do so, Madzokere draws on "the identity of Micah which takes two parallel positions namely: Hans Walter Wolf's Thesis which designates Micah as one of the elders of Moresheth and the rebuttal of Hans Walter Wolf's Thesis which tags Micah as the prophet for the Poor". Merging his biblical knowledge with discourses on poverty, Madzokere advances the argument that "social justice is a promoter of peace, abundance, equality and tranquillity whilst social injustice is a promoter of chaos, inequality, poverty and hunger". He thus, uses the biblical character of Micah and the poverty situation in Zimbabwe to draw lessons and inspiration from and champion a message of justice (*mispat*) to quell prevalent inequalities and injustices in the Zimbabwean society and beyond.

References

James, G. (1954). *Stolen legacy: Greek philosophy is stolen Egyptian philosophy*, University of Arkansas, Pine Bluff.

Kasozi, A. (2015). 'The status of research at three Ugandan universities', In: Halvorsen, T. & Nossum, J. (Eds). *Knowledge networks: Towards equitable collaboration between academics, donors and universities*, African Minds: South Africa.

Rodney, W. (1972). *How Europe underdeveloped Africa*, East African Educational Publishers: Nairobi, Kampala & Dar es Salaam.

Santos, B. D. S., Nunes, J. A. and Meneses, M. P. (2007). Opening up the Canon of Knowledge and Recognition of Difference, In: B. D. S. Santos (Ed.), *Another Knowledge is Possible: Beyond Northern Epistemologies*, Verso: London, pp. xix – 1xii.

Van Stam, G. (2017). 'Decolonising Science: Switching the Paradigm to 'Community', *Invited Address by The Science Faculty Teaching and Learning Committee to address the entire university community*, University of the Western Cape, Bellfore, Cape Town, 6 November 2017.

Chapter 2

Gods of Development or Perpetuators of Poverty and Underdevelopment in the 'Developing' World? Rethinking the Role of the World Bank and IMF on Africa's Socio-economic Development

Munyaradzi Mawere

Introduction

Development is not only multi-dimensional, but relative. So is poverty and underdevelopment. They are all fields which call for a multi-sectorial and multi-dimensional approaches as opposed to the mono-approach often used to deal with the phenomena. The multi-dimensional and multi-sectorial approaches to poverty are critical as no one organisation or group (or individual) can solely achieve development without the meaningful engagement and participation of all stakeholders. Development needs more than so-called architects of development: even those being assisted (or the poor on the ground) need to participate if meaningful development is to take place.

This chapter interrogates the role of Bretton Woods Institutions, particularly the International Monetary Fund (IMF) and the World Bank (WB) in the promotion of development and eradication of poverty in the developing world, especially in African countries. While these two institutions have been labelled as "gods" of development in Africa, this chapter argues that just like other Bretton Woods Institutions and tyrannical post-colonial African rulers (or the African elite group), the IMF and the World Bank have largely played a "paternalistic" role, disregarding contextual and circumstantial differentiations across the nations of Africa. In Africa, the role of indigenous communities and traditional leadership in the promotion of development and eradication of poverty and underdevelopment have been disregarded while tyrannical government rulers allowed to push forward their corrupt agendas, thereby assuming a paternalistic role in the whole development and poverty eradication mantra.

Further, the chapter argues that the involvement of the World Bank and IMF in Africa's development has a long history littered with miscarriages of development (or what I have termed "developmenticide") and suffering of the innocent ordinary people. This makes it suspicious if the institutions are really for the development of the so-called developing world countries such as Africa or were established to serve the interests of the empire (and sometimes those of a few African elites) and to stifle development anywhere outside the empire.

If these observations are seriously considered, then the need to rethink the role of these Bretton Woods Institutions – IMF and World Bank – and African elites becomes peremptory and urgent.

Purported role of the IMF and the World Bank

The Bretton Woods Institutions – IMF and World Bank – were formed after the second World War, which somewhat brought about the Great Depression of the 1930s (Kwagyang, Ghide & Haruna 2015). John Maynard Keynes (of Britain) and Harry Dexter White – the Chief International Economist at the US Treasury – were the intellectual founding fathers of the IMF and the World Bank (Ibid). In fact, the Bretton Woods Institutions were set at a meeting of 43 countries at Mount Washington Hotel in Bretton Woods, New Hampshire, USA from 1-22 July 1944 popularly known as the Bretton Woods Conference, with the aim to help rebuild the shattered post-war economy and to promote international economic cooperation (Bretton Woods Project 2015). It is common knowledge that the end of any international crisis such as the two World Wars – 1st World War (1913-1918) and 2nd World War – is often followed by a period of economic hardships of varying kinds. Such was the case with end of the 2nd World War. At the end of this war, nations of the Global North, led by the United States of America and Britain, sought to salvage their economies from the calamities and predicaments caused by the 2nd World War and subsequently by the

Great Depression. In his opening speech at the Bretton Woods Conference, Henry Morganthau had this to say:

> Bewilderment and bitterness resulting from the Depression became the breeders of fascism and finally of war. Proponents of the new institutions felt that global economic interaction was necessary to maintain international peace and security. The institutions would facilitate, in the creation of a dynamic world community in which the peoples of every nation will be able to realise their potentialities in peace (Kwagyang, Ghide & Haruna 2015: 49).

Thus, in their attempt to salvage the Global North economies, the USA and Britain, facilitated the establishment of multilateral institutions which was mandated to spearhead development and reconstruction among countries of the world devastated by the 2nd World War and the Great Depression. It is these circumstances which saw the birth of the Bretton Woods Institutions namely International Monetary Fund (IMF), the International Bank for Reconstruction and Development (IBRD) which was later renamed the World Bank (WB), and the International Trade Organisation (ITO) which was dormant up until the creation of the World Trade Organisation (WTO) in the 1990s. The ITO was later split into the General Agreement on Tariffs and Trade (GATT) and WTO.

Three points are worth noting right from the outset. First, the formation of the Bretton Woods Institutions by the Global North countries bear testimony to the fact that neither the USA nor Britain alone had adequate resources to single-handedly deal with the reconstruction and development needed after the grand destruction of the 2nd World War and the Great Depression. Both the USA and Britain saw the solution to the predicaments caused the war and the Great Depression as lying in the Bretton Woods Institutions. Second, of the forty-four countries that were represented at Bretton Woods Conference, Africa was represented by only 9 % of the total countries' delegates (Schuler & Bernkopf 2014). Third, since the United States of America and Britain initiated the formation of the Bretton Woods Institutions, their ideas and ideals dominated all proceedings during the Bretton Woods Conference, though

"America's plans were largely incorporated into the final documents of the IMF and WB" (Kwagyang, Ghide & Haruna 2015: 50). This explains the influence that the US has always exercised and indeed continue exerting on Bretton Woods Institutions even today. But one wonders the motive behind forming the Bretton Woods Institutions – IMF and the WB – as separate entities.

The answer to this lies in the fact that while the IMF and the WB were instituted as separate entities, their roles were always meant to be complementary. As aptly spelt out by Kwagyang *et al* (2015), on one hand, the IMF was given the mandate to promote international monetary cooperation and provide policy advice as well as technical assistance, and loans to help member states to build and maintain their economies at equilibrium. The loans provided by the IMF were to range from short-term to medium-term mainly taken from disbursements from a pool of quarterly contributions by member states. To ensure that the loans are not abused, IMF was also mandated to assist member states with policy design of different programmes to ensure that the concerned states overcome balance of payment problems, and also that long term sustainable development is guaranteed. On the other hand, the WB was given the mandate to promote long-term development initiatives and programmes in all its member states. This was to be done through the provision of financial (in the form of loan) and technical assistance needed by member states. The loans by the WB were to be funded from the issuance of "bonds" and contributions by member countries. Programmes that were mainly targeted to benefit from the WB long-term initiatives included but not limited to education, health, water and sanitation, electrification, and environmental conservation. All these sectors were targeted to benefit from the WB loans. Yet, though the IMF and the WB had distinct mandates to fulfil in the reconstruction of member states' economies, the two were right from the outset designed to complement each other towards rebuilding infrastructure, providing economic safety nets and promoting mutually beneficial business avenues and ethos. Such were the perceived roles that the Bretton Woods Institutions were purported to play equally in all their member states, regardless of their geographical location or race.

Bretton Woods Institutions and the African economies: Successes and failures

While the Bretton Woods Institutions have managed to salvage some countries from poverty and underdevelopment that had been inflicted by the 2nd World War and the Great Depression, other member states especially those of Africa have never mutually benefited from the programmes of the institutions. In fact, both success and failure stories of the Bretton Woods Institutions have been recorded in diverse areas. Helleiner (2006; 2009), for example, has pointed to the rapid growth and expansion of economies particularly after the 2nd World War, while the World Economic Situation and Prospects (2012) has underscored the liberalisation of and multilateralism in world economies. Furthermore, Driscoll (1996) has credited the WB and IMF with the minimum (or basic) international standards for doing business such as the Standard of Non-discrimination and Reciprocity Standard. More so, the proliferation of international economic institutions, bilateral and multilateral agreements, and international and national economic integrations, are largely a result of the WB and IMF policies.

However, the manner in which IMF and the WB have delivered their mandates has not been without criticism. Even those who believe that successes have largely been registered among member states of the Bretton Woods Institutions have admitted that dealing with new challenges, particularly those that the charters of the IMF and WB have not envisaged, has always been problematic. As enunciated by Action Against Bretton Woods (1994) and Dibie and Kawewe (2015), these new challenges include spiralling national debts, environmental degradation, unresponsive and incompetent governance, lack of respect for human rights, national political upheavals and civil unrest. While these situations are a reality in many countries of the world and the IMF and WB have tried to intervene in some cases, their intervention strategies and socio-economic and political impacts on nations which availed themselves for such assistance have been largely damaging to the extent that poverty, underdevelopment, inequality and human violations have amplified. It is for this reason that Harrison (1999: 39) describes the Bretton

Woods – Africa engagements as "...often a tragic story of the hopes, frustrations, efforts and failures, suffering and conflicts of thousands of people in Africa". In view of the IMF and WB, more failures than successes seem to have been registered in Africa. Both the IMF and the WB have in most instances interfered with economic policy programmes of the loan-receiving nations, availing assistance to African nations on the backdrop of stringent conditionalities. This interference has been quite visible in Structural Adjustment Programmes (SAPs) – one of the many 'developmental' programmes of the Bretton Woods Institutions in the late 1980s – which many governments, including Zimbabwe's embraced though deceived the public that it was homegrown (Chidzero 1990). What remains striking with respect to the IMF and the WB assistance to Africa is that the tenets of their programmes have almost been the same in all receiving nations in which "governments were required to cut public expenditure (including eliminating subsidies for food, medical care and education), raise interest rates (thus reducing access to credit), privatise state enterprises, increase exports, and reduce barriers to trade and foreign investment such as tariffs and import duties" (Ismi 2004: 5). The endorsement of these agreements at the initial phase was followed by two other stages namely implementation and evaluation. The World Trade Organisation (WTO) has played the policing role in the last two phases to ensure compliance with the rules of the "game".

The implementation of the policies highlighted above impacted negatively on the development of targeted economies, such that it was mainly at the implementation stage that SAPs were discontinued in many African countries. While African governments cited the zeal for Western Countries to experiment African economies with classical economic strategies on the basis of one size fits all philosophy and outcries of the African people as a result of the suffering and turmoil ignited by the SAPs, the Bretton Woods Institutions widely blamed African nations of non-cooperation. Contrary to accusations by African governments, the IMF and WB have cited non-compliance and adverse effects of the hugely uncontrolled phenomena like floods and droughts, as contributors to the failures of the IMF and the WB policies and strategies. What remains clear, however, is the fact that of the entire so-called underdeveloped world, Africa has been hardest hit by the Bretton Woods Institutions as cases of the successes of their programmes in the continent are very few if any. Despite billions of dollars pumped to Africa by donor agencies, African economies have in fact regressed into the chasms of poverty and underdevelopment. In the midst of all this, the Bretton Woods Institutions' Directorate declared at the turn of the new millennium that poverty "is the greatest challenge facing the international community' and to include on the WB lobby wall the inscription 'our dream is a world free of poverty" (William 2003: 361). Though there seem to be altruistic commitment to end global poverty and underdevelopment by the Bretton Woods Institutions, the facts remain – that poverty and underdevelopment are still far from being overcome, even in the face of the IMF and the WB policies and strategies. In fact, it remains written in bold that with the introduction of Structural Adjustment Programmes, many African states found themselves sinking in debts they never imagined before. Furthermore, member nations in arrears with the repayment of loans to the IMF and WB have often times been refused access to more loans. Worse still, the IMF and WB have in most instances interfered with economic policy programmes of the loan receiving nations as has been the case with SAPs. This has stifled local initiatives, thereby creating unrealistic and unsustainable economies.

More so, the assumption by the Global North that African socio-economic and political environments are homogeneous is grossly erroneous, yet it was the very assumption used as basis to impose SAPs on Africa. The reason why development failed to take off in Africa as a result of the Global North's initiatives was largely this overgeneralisation by the "gods" of development – IMF and WB – and their failure thereof to appreciate the fact that national circumstances require that each nation be treated on its own terms. The IMF and WB failed to take into account the level of development of each African state. For example, these Bretton Woods Institutions demanded imports in countries such as Zimbabwe, Zambia, Mozambique, Ghana and others where economies are export-driven (Dibie and Kawewe 2015). The net effect for this demand was indirect protection of the Global North industries against competition from African goods and services. Consequently, this suffocated industries in Africa leading to shortage of forex to sustain industry, mass unemployment, underemployment, dilapidation of institutional physical structures, break-down in health care system, fuel and transport challenges, and brain drain, among others. This disempowered Africa and sealed its industrial death, leaving the continent with no clear avenue at all to break the "culture of poverty" and underdevelopment. This means that economic austerity measures prescribed and enforced by the WB and IMF have always undermined Africa's capital development and its provision of social services and investment initiatives thereof. Thus, instead of helping African countries to become self-sustaining and self-sufficient, the IMF and WB made most African countries and their people to become welfare cases and "beggars" in the midst of plenty who lived on handouts and international donor community.

However, while the Bretton Woods Institutions have always blamed endogenous factors and African governments for choosing to remain poor (as a result of corruption, dependency syndrome, self-serving leadership, repressive laws, and poor planning) and uncompetitive despite an array of possibilities in the global world, African governments have blamed exogenous factors and undue interference in Africa's development patterns, therefore making development in Africa a contested terrain. Endogenous factors such as self-serving leadership and corruption are for example very difficult to dismiss when it comes to development discourse on Africa. Many African countries have been largely bloated such that they have qualified as oligarchies – governments run by a clique that is selected on political partisanship rather than merit. This has sealed the badge of corruption in Africa. Cases of corruption by the ruling African oligarchy are numerous to document. Mobutu Sese-Seko, for instance, is said to have accumulated an amount of US$5 billion while other military rulers like Thomas Sankara and Sani Abacha have maintained very huge amounts of money with Swiss banks (Didia 2015). Indeed, no country could expect development and progress under such shameless regimes which steal public funds on such a scale. In other countries like Uganda, studies have shown that in the 1980s, less than 30 % of the foreign aid meant to support primary education actually reached the intended beneficiaries (Ayittey 2002). The missing funds were stolen, wasted or re-apportioned to priorities identified by politicians and senior government officials. This state of affairs has been blamed on donor agencies which failed to monitor the use of their funds, but also there is no way African governments can be exonerated from Africa's corruption problem. African governments and rulers are in fact in the habit of protecting corrupt officials since they are part of their systems. During the time in which Robert Mugabe was president of Zimbabwe, for example, many corrupt senior government officials were spared the wrath of the law simply because they were part of Mugabe's corrupt government (see Mawere 2010; Didia 2015). Transparency International estimates that corruption in Zimbabwe in the past 37 years could have accounted for over US $60 billion (Mpofu, My Zimbabwe News 22 Dec 2017). As Mpofu further notes:

In 1980, Mr [Robert] Mugabe owned nothing except a few suits purchased in London from his favourable tailor. Today, he owns several luxury mansions in South Africa as well as homes in Hong Kong, Singapore, Malaysia and Dubai. In Zimbabwe, he owns a multimillion dollar home in Harare and at his village in the rural area. Nearly all these assets are in other people's names and that could be a problem for him and Zimbabwe in the future. His cash assets must run to billions…

On the other hand, elections were worn on the basis of politically motivated violence as was in the case of Zimbabwe's 2002 and 2008 elections. The same scenario obtained in Kenya in the 2007-2008 post-election violence and in the 2011 Spring Revolutions in North Africa – all which had serious repercussions on the general public and the national economy. All the realities also point to the fact that the laws in many African countries are applied selectively depending on one's status in the ruling parties. Such governance does not only erode the African countries' potentials to develop, but also keep them in constant conflict with the IMF and WB, which have a say in the day-to-day running of world economies. One point remains clear here, that both endogenous and exogenous factors are to blame for

Africa's poverty, underdevelopment and unsustainable development endeavours.

Bearing all this in mind, the point that the Bretton Woods Institutions are one of the key tools for achieving sustainable development is not only false but grossly misleading. This is compounded by weaknesses associated with the programme of sustainable development itself. The Brundland Report of 1987 published what has become the standard definition of sustainable development as "development that meets the needs of the present without compromising the ability of future generations to meet their own needs" (Desjardins, 2013: 74). The Brundland Report's definition of sustainable development can be criticised for being too anthropocentric – the only subjects referred to are humans. In fact, anthropocentrism is a view or theory which places humans at the centre of moral concern – only humans have moral value – such that only and only humans are accorded intrinsic value while nature is accorded instrumental value. This connotes that humans have no duties to rocks, rivers, vegetation or to 'nature' in general. As such, "some educational researchers have highlighted that the concept of sustainable development neglects our relationships with nature, and that as a consequence sustainability simply becomes a matter of human welfare" (Kronlid & Öhman, 2013: 36). In fact, while sustainable development is arguably the present generation's best approach to climate change and development discourse, the definition of such a significant approach, fails to consider, or even mention any non-humans or what others would call 'nature'. This is to say that, sustainable development's definition is too anthropocentric. I underline that, in view of climate change and underdevelopment, being too anthropocentric is problematic since it uses the same approach and thought processes that caused climate change and underdevelopment in the first place. Thus, using the same kind of thinking to mitigate climate change and underdevelopment respectively, is likely doomed to failure such that even the kind of sustainable development implied by the Bretton Woods Institutions still needs to be reimagined.

Conclusion

The Bretton Woods Institutions have, since their establishment, been hailed by some scholars, researchers and governments as gods of development. This characterisation, however, has been challenged by others as inappropriate especially when applied to the countries of Africa. Whatever the case, this chapter has shown that both African governments and the Bretton Woods Institutions are fallible and to blame as far as Africa's poverty and underdevelopment are concerned. However, it has been underscored that African governments need to take a leading role in the development of their people. At the same time, because of their incompatible needs and interests, both African governments and the Bretton Woods Institutions should take a thorough self-introspection gesture with the view to mend their differences which have often frustrated efforts towards development and poverty eradication in the continent. It should not be therefore business as usual for both Africa and the Bretton Woods Institutions. Rather, efforts should be unreservedly made to carve a new development path with clear and just beacons, whose colours and development agendas should not be shifted or masked to disadvantage either party.

References

Action Against Bretton Woods. (1994). Women for a just and healthy planet, *Economic and Political Weekly*, 29 (27): 1618.

Ayittey, G. (2002). Biting their own tails: African leaders and the internal intricacies of the rape of a continent, A Keynote Address at the International Conference of the Society of Research on African Cultures (SORAC), 7-9 Nov 2002, New Jersey.

Bretton Woods Project. (2015). What are the Bretton Woods Institutions? *Critical Voices on the World Bank and IMF*: USA.

Chidzero, B. (1990). Economic policy statement: Macro-economic adjustment and trade liberalisation, *Ministry of Finance, Economic Planning and Development*, Government Printer: Zimbabwe.

DesJardins, J. R. (2013). *Environmental Ethics: An Introduction to Environmental Philosophy*, (5th ed.), Belmont, Calif: Wadsworth.

Dibie, R. & Kawewe, S. M. (2015). The impact of Economic Structural Adjustment Programmes (ESAPs) on Africa: The Revived Bretton Woods System, *International Journal of Finance and Economics* 9 (4): 307-13.

Didia, D. O. (2015). *Ten reasons why sub-Saharan Africa has failed to develop economically: Can Africans succeed by themselves*, The Edwin Mellwn Press, USA.

Driscoll, D. D. (1996). The IMF and the World Bank How Do They Differ? *External Relations Department Publication Services International Monetary Fund*, Washington, D.C: U.S.A.

Harrison, G. (1999). *The World Bank and Africa: The Construction of Governance States*, Wessex Walter: USA.

Helleiner, E. (2009). The development mandate of international institutions: where did it come from? *Studies in Comparative International Development* 44 (3): 189–211.

Helleiner, E. (2006). Reinterpreting Bretton Woods: international development and the neglected origins of embedded liberalism', *Development and Change* 37 (5): 943–67.

Ismi, A. (2004). Impoverishing a Continent: The World Bank and the IMF in Africa, *A Report Commissioned by the Halifax Initiative Coalition (www.halifaxinitiative.org)*, USA.

Kronlid, D. O. & Öhman, J. (2013). An environmental ethical conceptual framework for research on sustainability and environmental education, *Environmental Education Research, 19*(1): 21-44.

Kwagyang, G. U., Ghide, H. B., & Haruna, A. L. (2015). Bretton Woods Institutions: Their evolution and impacts on the field of International Economic Law, *Journal of Law, Policy and Globalisation* 35 (2015): 48-55.

Mawere, M. (2011). *Moral Degeneration in Contemporary Zimbabwean Business Practices*, Langaa RPCIG Publishers: Cameroon.

Mpofu, M. (2017). The price of bad governance in Zimbabwe, *My Zimbabwe News – 22 Dec 2017*, Harare.

Schuler, K. & Bernkopf, M. (2014). Who was at the Bretton Woods? *Paper in Financial History*, Centre for Financial Stability: New York.

William, E. (2003). *The Effect of International Monetary Fund and World Bank Programmes on Poverty*, World Bank: USA.

World Economic Situation and Prospects 2012 (Sales No. E.12.II.C.2), pp. 33-36, United Nations; Available from http://www.un.org/en/development/desa/policy/wesp/index. shtml.

Chapter 3

The Impoverishment of Africa by the West's Multinational Corporations: A Case of Multinational Corporations in Nigeria's Delta Region

Odeigah Theresa Nfam & Munyaradzi Mawere

Introduction

In Nigeria's Delta Region and the whole of Africa continent, Multinational Corporations along with their mother countries – the emperors – have been allegedly labelled one of the causes of the continent's poverty and underdevelopment. In Nigeria, for example the inception of the East India Company and the Royal Niger Company in 1879, planted the first seed of poverty and underdevelopment in the Nigeria's Delta Region, heretofore referred to as the Delta Region. After the decolonisation of Nigeria in 1960, the British government and other European countries like French, Spain, Netherlands and Germany, among others, saw the large African market potential as one way of keeping a grip on Africa – through what has come to be known as neo-colonialism – while continuing the siphoning of the continent's resources through the use of Multinational Corporations (Caves, 1994).

The Delta Region has always been a place of great attraction for the Europeans fortune seekers because of the abundant raw materials that the region is endowed with. The Multinational Corporations have always had various platforms for reaching out to the African markets, especially in the production of oil and gas and in other sectors of the economy such as Nigeria Breweries, Sony, Toyota, Nestle, Peugeot Automobile and companies in construction engineering, as well as in communication and information technology (Gavin, 1973). Sadly, Multinational Corporations in the Delta Region have done more harm than good in the region. They have impoverished the Nigerians in the area and beyond on top of what they have reaped and siphoned out of the country to their mother countries. For this reason, Multinational Corporations in the Delta Region have been viewed by many critical scholars as more of agents of neo-colonialism than they are real agents of development (newsrescus.com, 2015). Through their unfair and unethical modus operandi, the Multinational Corporations have dominated the Delta Region economically, socially, culturally and even politically by creating differential economic outcomes between their home and host communities (Onodugo, 2012).

The perfidious nature of the Multinational Corporations in the Delta Region has also resulted in part, in the destruction of the ecosystem of the area, thereby making agriculture impracticable. The Multinational Corporations have in fact not only caused economic poverty, but also environmental poverty. The uncountable extraction activities of the Multinationals Corporations have, for instance, led to oil spills which have damaged the ecosystem and caused pollution in the region.

In view of the obtaining reality highlighted above, this chapter critically examines and determines if the Multinational Corporations in Africa have contributed to the soaring level of poverty – both socio-economic and environmental. Basing on the findings obtained during research for this chapter, we conclude that the poverty level in the Delta Region and by extension Nigeria, is the consequence of the manipulative, rapacious, oppressive, selfish, domineering and exploitatively pernicious tendencies of the Multinational Corporations operating in the region.

The genesis of Multinational Corporations and the birth of the 'seed' of poverty in the Delta Region

The Berlin Conference of 1884-85 and subsequent British conquest of Nigeria in 1885 were largely motivated by the enormous raw materials found in the Delta Region by the capitalists, who at that time had trading companies in the region (Ebegbulem, 2013). Right from the days of the industrial revolution in Europe, the Europeans unscrupulously evacuated raw materials to their home countries at the expense of their host communities (Aworom, 2013). This was done to enable Europe meet the great need for the commercial expansion at that time. The British Parliament realised that it would be difficult for any reasonable transaction to take place without adequate security for their trade and investments in the Delta Region (Bernardine, 2013). The modalities used in ensuring security for their investments reduced the possibilities of opposition and resistance from the indigenous people. This further subjugated the indigenous people both politically and economically since the terms of trade were unfavourable. The institution of the modalities was as a result of uncooperative attitude of the Nigeria's Delta Region people after realising the Multinational Corporations' exploitative machinations. The Nigeria's Delta men like Jaja of Opobo and Nana of Itsekiri were extensively aggressive towards these foreign Companies because of their exploitative tendency. It was during this period that eminent Britons established Joint Stock Companies to really exploit the Delta Region's resources (Eluka, Ndubuuisi, Uzoamaka, Anekwe, 2016).

Some of the notable Multinational Companies at that time were the River Niger Navigation and Trading Company, Company of African Merchants, the African Merchants of Bristol, the Anglo-African Company, the West African Company, the Merchants of London, and Liverpool Trading Company, among others (Rodney, 1972). Most of these companies got their subsidies from their home countries, which aided their trading activities in controlling and undermining the coastal trade in the region against the existing indigenous trading and economic activities (Eluka *et-al*, 2016).

The inordinate imperial ambition (or the undue interest) in the region gave room to the British government's recommendation of more companies being established in the Delta Region. Alexander Miller Brothers and Company and some other smaller companies were further established by the British capitalists, with full determination to exploit the African resource in this region. Most of these companies had their posts in Calabar, Akassa, and along the banks of the Niger and Benue rivers. Eventually, George Taubman Goldie amalgamated some of the different British companies to form the United African Company, and later the Royal Niger Company (Ugochukwu, Jurgen, 2008). These companies had remarkable business success because they had substantial assistance from their home government. Till today, George Taubman Goldie is seen as the founder of the Multinational Companies in Nigeria, because from inception he played a prominent role in the trading activities that took place in the Delta Region (Onimode, 1982). What has to be said loud and clear is that right from inception these mega conglomerates were exploitative as they dominated all economic activities in the region. The business monopoly that the British government created in favour of the Multinational Companies gave room for differential economic outcomes within the Nigerian society (Ozoigbo, Chukuezi, 2012). It also created fertile grounds for corruption and other such unscrupulous business activities in Nigeria.

In the quest for cheaply priced raw materials, the Royal Dutch Shell-British Petroleum Company, discovered oil in Oloibiri on the 15th of January, 1956 in Nigeria's Delta Region. This discovery attracted more oil companies such as Mobil in 1970, Chevron in 1961, Elfin 1962, and Agip Oil Company in 1962, among others. It has clearly been shown that since the exploration of oil in the Delta Region, the economy and trading activities of the indigenous people have suffered, while Multinational Corporations continue to enjoy enormous profits (Ejikeme, 2014). It is important to note that a scholar like Bade Onimode, who happens to be the author of the book: *Imperialism and Underdevelopment in Nigeria: The Dialectics of Mass Poverty,* has from as early as 1983 and over the years raised alarm on the exploitative character and cynicism of the Multinational Corporations in the region (Onimode, 1983). It is on record that the Multinational Corporations took advantage of their technology, production experience and business monopoly to export raw materials from Nigeria to developed countries rendering the people in the region impoverished (see for example, Stopfort, 1998: 12-13).

The Multinational Corporations by their very nature do not transfer technology to their host countries. Their technology was highly restricted, preventing their host communities from acquiring such technology or knowledge. According to Bode Onimode (1983), the patronage of the imperialists turned out to be a miserable disappointment to the African countries. The Multinational Corporations undermine the values of indigenous technology and have refused to introduce the advanced technology to their host communities as a result of their imperialistic character. For example, the indigenous machines take days to accomplish its production while the Multinationals technology takes less hours in producing their products (Osuagwu Ezie, 2013), yet the Multinationals are not ready to share their technology with the host communities.

Multinational Corporations and their Exploitation of Nigeria's Delta Region

Multinational Corporation is a business organisation that controls production of goods and services in more than two countries. Some of the powerful business mega conglomerates that came into Africa and 'seemingly' helped to abolish slave trade and introduce legitimate trade did that because of the associated economic benefits. They were more wolves in sheep's skin. As a result, they remained powerful, prominent, manipulative and exploitative during colonialism and even after African countries got their independence (www.encyclopedia.com, 2012). Due to its richness in oil and other such mineral deposits, Nigeria is one of the African countries heavily dominated by the Multinational Corporations. These are concentrated mainly in the Delta Region where over 85 percent of the oil exploration activities are carried out by these companies (Aworom, 2013).

To ensure that they affect the 'nerve' of the Nigerian economy and society as a whole, the Multinational Corporations in Nigeria's Delta Region have diversified their business. They are engaged in various business activities across various sectors such as health, telecommunications, exploration of oil, gas, manufacturing and construction engineering, among others. All these sectors have deprived Nigerians from engaging on indigenous manufacturing and other sectors that would have improved the lives of the people. The impoverishment of the Delta Region and its people came under various guises, one of which was the employment of highly skilled workers from the Multinational Companies' home countries even when there were skilled professionals in the host countries. This is done "to prevent the building of the capacity of the local people and prevent technology transfer as well as to provide employment opportunities for their home countries at the expense of their host countries" (Kadafa, 2012: 20). This is echoed by Osuagwu and Ezie (2013: 354) who had this to say:

> Some of the Multinational Corporations extract or cheaply bought raw materials and produce for their buyers who got their raw materials at ridiculously low prices from their host countries, but very aggressively marketed their finished products at exorbitant prices to the host communities. From inception scholars such as Eluke *et al*, 60, *in Multinational Corporations and Their effects on Nigerian economy*, have emphasised that, Multinational Corporations are exploitative to countries like Nigeria where lots of natural resources are found (Eloke, Ndubuisi, Anekwe, 1916: 60). Multinational Corporations have also been seen as agents of neo-colonialism and as ruthless exploiters of the host communities.

This is clear testimony that Mutational Companies in Africa, and the Delta Region in particular, are bent to exploit the African resources largely at the expense of the host communities who in fact should benefit most from resources in their communities. This realisation takes us to another level, where it might be important to understand and unpack possible factors responsible for unscrupulous exploitations in the Delta Region.

Factors responsible for the impoverishment of the Delta Region

There are many factors that led to the impoverishment of Nigeria's Delta Region by the Multinational Corporations operating in the area. Multinational Corporations by their nature and 'untamed' business ethics have pushed the local industries and production virtually into extinction, because of their very high technological muscle, aggressive marketing, and powerful advertisement strategies. The indigenous business men and women could not afford any of these and so they found themselves in a position of great disadvantage. In Nigeria, for instance in 2000, an indigenous Soda drinks company by the name Limca Nigeria Limited was established, but after a period of nine years of operation, the Coca Cola Company offered very stiff competition against the Limca forcing the indigenous company unproductive such that it eventually closed down (Nku, 2017). Today, Limca products are no longer found in the Nigerian market. The closure of Limca Nigeria Limited led to massive retrenchment of workers and the closure of other smaller companies who were doing business with Limca Nigeria Limited. This 'unfair' harsh business relationship or tactic had seen the collapse and closure of several small business enterprises in the Delta Region (Ozoigbo & Chukuezi, 2012) as elsewhere across the African continent.

Worse still, the activities of the Multinational Corporations such as those in the oil and gas sector result in environmental degradation making agriculture which is the primary occupation of the people rendered unviable (Collins, N. C. Ugochukwu & Jurgen Ertel 2012). The images below show some of the environmental degradation being inflicted by Multinational Corporations operating in the Delta Region:

Fig. 1: Vegetation destruction
Source: https://wwwtheguardian.com

Fig. 2: Oil spills
Source: https://wwwtheguardian.com

Fig. 3: Oil spills ejatlas
Source: org or www.google.com

Both the closure of indigenous companies and environmental degradation as a result of activities of Multinational Companies in Delta Region have eventually resulted in soaring unemployment, poverty and even criminality. What this tells us is the fact that the investments of the Multinational Corporations do not always result in development of their host countries mainly because their profits are repatriated to their home countries, and worse still the Multinationals discourage local capacity building. The influence of these mega conglomerates is pervasive to an extent that even if a country does not want their products, they corruptly influence the licensing authorities and other relevant agencies to ensure the registration and sale of their products and globalisation has even made it easier for the multinationals (Ezema & Azikiwe, 2010).

The Multinational Corporations have relegated the local communication companies to the periphery. In the past, the Nigeria Postal Agency was surviving generally well and the Telecommunication sector flourishing, but with the aggressive nature of the Multinational Corporations in the country, the Nigerian Telecommunications (NITEL) could not stand anymore. All these indigenous companies were retrenched and in fact directed to an oblivious chasm of inutility by the emergence of communication companies like MTN, among others. The coming on stage of these Mega Conglomerates in the telecommunication sector frustrated the efforts of the indigenous communication system. The banking sector was not spared by the overbearing effects of the Mega Conglomerates in the banking, finance and real estate industry. Some indigenous banks such as Oceanic Bank, were forced to close their doors after collapsing partly as a result of corruption in the banking and finance industry, but most importantly as a result of stiff competition from international banks in the country.

Coming back to the telecommunication sector, it is important to note that the Global System of Mobile Communications (GSM) revolution began in 2001 in Nigeria. This has positioned Nigeria as one of the fastest growing telecommunications nations in Africa. Since 2001, developments in the sector have become massive resulting in these companies exploiting the region and Nigeria at large (www.newsrescue, 2015). This has enhanced the growth of mobile phones in Nigeria, which have further relegated to the periphery the local communication technology that would have transformed the indigenous communication enterprises to the modern forms. The

35

Telecommunication Mega Conglomerates include companies like MTN, Etisalat, Airtel, DHL, UPS, Red Star Express, and Globacom Limited, among others which have taken over the functions of the Nigeria Postal Agency. The development of this technology has increased unemployment and subsequently poverty in the area. For instance, the subscription and the purchase of expensive handsets have put more economic demands on families while the closure of indigenous communication enterprises has resulted in mass retrenchment of workers. Air time for voice calls in Nigeria is very expensive and data bundles for internet access are not spared the high prices as well (Nwankwo, 2015).

We further note that the GSM Companies in Nigeria have brought about an upsurge in criminality in the Delta Region and Nigeria at large because of their initial sharp practice of not registering SIM cards purchased by customers. In Nigeria, the quality of GSM services remain poor, with internet access equally poor and network services generally attract higher costs (Ejikeme, 2014). Despite the relatively poorer services that the people in the Delta Region and Nigerians receive, the cost of services is said to be one of the highest in the world (Ossai, 2012) prompting some scholars to argue that these Mega Conglomerates have turned the region into a dumping ground because the quality of services of MTN and other telecommunication companies have not met with the needs of the people they profess to be serving.

Even in the aspect of payment of taxes to the government, these Mega Conglomerates have not been regular in their payments. They have tried under several guises to evade tax in collusion with corrupt local tax officials (Mbat, Ekong & Obioakpa, 2013). In Nigeria's Delta Region, the negative effects of operations of the Multinational Corporations where heavy trucks lift and transport oil to different parts of the country leading to deplorable roads among others have become very obvious (Odisu, 2015). Some of these Mega Conglomerates such as United Africa Company (UAC) operating in the beverages and food sector have dominated the food and beverages landscape of Nigeria's Delta Region for a long time (Okon, 2017). Through aggressive advertisement, they have changed the people's habits and lifestyle to the extent that foreign processed foods and beverages are preferred to the local indigenous food and beverages. These processed foreign beverages are more expensive, not health friendly, and have rendered indigenous food and beverages enterprises redundant thereby increasing poverty among the local people (Etta, 2017).

The marginalisation of the indigenous people of Nigeria's Delta Region by the management of the Mega Conglomerates is another way through which the Multinational Corporations are impoverishing the region. The Multinational Corporations ensure, through appropriate policies, that the top policy positions in the Corporations are reserved for the foreigners to see to it that their agenda remains focused and that a change does not occur (Peter, 2017). Corporate social responsibilities which are usually the hallmark of big companies and corporations abroad is paid lip service by the Multinationals in Nigeria's Delta Region. Even when educational institutions or health facilities are provided by the Multinationals in the region, the cost of accessing such services in these facilities is exorbitant and therefore the indigenous people cannot have access to the facilities provided (www.thisdaylive, 2016: 25).

More so, the powerful Mega Conglomerates exert some degree of political influence on governance of Nigeria's Delta Region as well as Nigeria as a whole. Multinational Corporations in Nigeria have been known to influence governance indirectly through [international] financial institutions or organisations (Wiil & Kolsted, 2010). During the period of military dictatorship in Nigeria, 1988-1993, for example, there was a lot of pressure on the regime at that time to liberalise trade, remove fuel subsidy and devalue the Nigerian currency. All this pressure was exerted by Multinational Companies, of course, largely indirectly through international financial organisations such as the World Bank and the International Monetary Fund (IMF). Where such pressure fails to work, Multinational Corporations in Nigeria have been known to make monetary donations to political parties that will be well disposed to them when the party takes over the rein of governance (Ighodalo, 2012).

Last but not least, Multinational Corporations in Nigeria's Delta Region have impoverished the region through their undue advantage in electricity power distribution. The Multinational Corporations are supplied regular electricity by the public electricity companies because they are able to pay high electricity bills which the small scale enterprises or smaller electricity consumers cannot afford to pay (Nwankwo, 2015). This gives them undue advantage over the indigenous small scale enterprises some of which are forced to shut down because of lack of electricity supply. Those small enterprises that are able to continue with their operations have had to purchase generators to provide electricity for their operations. This is also at a great cost as these generators are imported from foreign countries such as China and Japan, among others. Multinational Corporations that should have the capacity to generate electricity for their use and for the use of other indigenous industries have not bothered to do so because it is not their priority (Ahiuma, 2013). The developed countries using Multinational Corporations to indirectly control the economy have really affected almost all the economic sectors of Nigeria politically, economically, socially and culturally. Considering that mining in the Delta Region is around a century or so old, it is surprising that Multinational Corporations over the years have not been able to refine crude oil in Nigeria to improve the living standard of the people therein. Why oil continue refined outside Nigeria remains a mammoth question yet to be answered. It is, however, pertinent to note that the raw materials – such as crude oil – taken from Africa are eventually brought back to the continent as finished products. For example, in the Nigeria's Delta Region, the crude oil gotten from the region is being refined in foreign countries such as Germany and France and the Nigerians pay higher rates when purchasing the refined petrol (Odeigah, 2017). This prompts the conclusion that the presence of Multinational Corporations in Nigeria have not shown any sign of development except poverty and exploitation. Something, thus, really needs to be done to arrest this situation.

What Nigeria needs to do? A framework towards restoration, order and genuine development

Owing to the foregoing discussion, there is no doubt that Nigeria is undeservingly being deprived of its own precious resources – resources which in fact should benefit and propel the country's development. Something really needs to be done in order to restore order, sanity and foster development in the Delta Region and Nigeria in general!

The starting point towards such restoration is admission that Multinational Corporations in the Delta Region have done more harm than good to both the region's environment and the people's lives. The cause of existence and effects of these Multinational Corporations have created more poverty than development. To resolve this menace, there is need for the Nigerian government to be audacious and take-over or at least have more than half shares in all the Multinational Corporations in the Delta Region. This can be done by simply putting in place indigenisation policies that favour indigenous communities. Besides empowering the indigenous people, this move will afford the government an upper hand in decision making, operations and all developments that take place within the Multinational Corporations and the Delta Region as a whole.

Besides, there is need for the Nigerian government to push for quota system for all local communities in the Delta Region, whereby the Multinational Corporations will be 'asked'– whether they like it or not – to plough back to the local communities some of their profits. This could be done by persuading or 'forcing' the Multinational Companies to engage in development projects in the region (and even beyond) such as construction of schools, hospitals, roads, and rural electrification, among others. Such a system will do magic to the whole region in no time, especially if the companies are made to work on targets. This will allow Nigeria, and most especially, the local communities to realise profits and benefits from their resources.

More so, given that the Multinational Companies in the Nigeria's Delta Region have almost 80% exploration activities which undoubtedly have burdened and destroyed the ecosystem, resulting to environmental degradation, due to oil spills from unmaintained pipe lines, gas flaring pollution and the destruction of waterways, these companies, through national policy and governing laws, should be made to pay heavy compensation to their host communities regularly. This can be done through taxing of the Multinational Corporations, make them to engage in environmental cleaning campaigns, and more importantly ensuring that compensation to both the local communities and environment is done whenever an accident is caused by the Corporations.

Last but not least, the Multinational Corporations should be made to transfer their technology to host communities. This is critical considering that ideally Multinational Corporations should always act as agents of growth and development in their host countries by constituting a source of capital investment, technology transfer and providing employment to the people of their host countries. Sadly, in Nigeria, this is the opposite of what is on the ground as Multinational Corporations have failed to live up to their responsibilities to the extent that they are now seen as agents of exploitation (cf. Mbat, Ekong & Obioakpa, 2013) and neo-colonialism. Some of the Multinational Corporations like Guinness Nigeria Limited, Nigeria Bottling Company, and Nigeria Breweries, have put the palm wine and brewery local industry out of operation and even when they employ Nigerian nationals, they are usually engaged as casual or contract workers (Udensi, 2015: 107-110). This does not guarantee technology transfer, development and poverty eradication for the local communities.

Conclusion

From the foregoing discussion, it has come clear that the business character and philosophy of the Multinational Corporations in the Nigeria's Delta Region are that of impoverishment and incapacitation. This is so if one is to consider the magnitude of poverty that has been inflicted on the indigenous people of the Delta Region by the Multinational Corporations in the region. We have noted with concern that Multinational Corporations, due to their aggressive business tactics and unfair competition have led to the collapse of many indigenous small scale enterprises. They have, thus, promoted destitution and poverty instead of capacity building and development. Out of all these findings, we have come to the conclusion that Multinational Corporations in the Delta Region of Nigeria, as others elsewhere on the African continent, have never really been true agents of development of the host communities. Besides paying lip service to corporate social responsibility, they have not improved on the unemployment situation in the region. Neither have they alleviated the poverty situation of the people in the region, worse still to eradicate poverty from the face of Nigeria. We, have thus, suggested a number of ways to deal accordingly with Multinational Corporations in the Delta Region and by extension many other parts of the continent.

References

Ahiuma-Young V. (2013). Epileptic Power, a Major Challenge Facing Nigeria-TUC, www.vanguardngr.com, Accessed 26th July, 2017.

Anna Etta, 70+ years, Female, Famer, place of interview Calabar, Date of interview 21th July, 2017.

Articlesng.com, (2016). The Influence of Multinational companies in the Economic Development of Nigeria, Accessed 26th July, 2017.

Aworom Annang,. (2013). Multinational Corporations and Development in Nigeria, *African Journal of Culture, Philosophy and Society*, 3 (1): 63-65.

Aworom, Annang, (2013). Multinational Corporations and Development in Nigeria, *African Journal of Culture, Philosophy and Society*, pp. 63-66.

Bernardine, H. J. (2003). In Onodugo (2012). Multinational Corporations and Employment and Labour conditions of developing countries: The Nigerian Experience, *European Journal of Business and Social Science*, 1 (6): 69-74

Begbulem J. C. *et al*. (2013). Oil Exploration and Poverty in the Niger Delta Region of Nigeria: A

Critical Analysis, pp 280-281, Vol. 4, No. 3, Ijbssnet.com, Accessed 7th August, 2017.

Caves, R. E. (1974). Causes of Direct Investment: Foreign Shares in Canadian and United Kingdom Manufacturing Industries, *Review of Economic Statistics*, pp. 80-91.

Collins, N. C. Ugochukwu & Jurgen Ertel, (2012). Negative Impacts of Oil Exploration on Biodiversity Management in the Niger Delta area of Nigeria,. pp. 140-146. www.trandfonline.com. Accessed 20th July, 2017.

Collins, N. C. Ugochukwu & Jurgen Ertel, (2008). Negative Impacts of Oil Exploration on Biodiversity Management in the Niger Delta area of Nigeria, pp. 141-144.

Ebegbulem Joseph. C. Ekepe Dickson, & Adejumo Theophilus Oyime, (2013). Oil Exploration and Poverty in the Niger Delta Region of Nigeria: A Critical Analysis, *International Journal of Business and Social Science*, 4 (3): 277-289.

Ejikeme Jomobo Nwagwu, (2014). Unemployment and Poverty in Nigeria: A link to National Insecurity, *Global Journal of Politics and Law Research*, Vol. 2. No. 1.

Eluka, J, Ndubuisi-Okolo, Ndubuisi-Okolo Purity Uzoamaka, & Anekwe Rita Ifeoma, (2016). Multinational Corporations and Their Effects on Nigeria Economy, *European Journal of Business and Management* 18 (9): 59-66.

Emeka Ossai,. (2012). Why Africa (Nigeria) has Remained Underdeveloped? Way Forward.
http: //emekeossai.wordpress.com. Accessed 25th, July, 2017.

Emmanuel Okon, (2017). 68+ years, Male, Business man, place of interview, Uyo, Date of interview 10th July, 2017.

Gavin, R. J. And Betley, J. A. (1973). *The Scramble for Africa*, Ibadan University Press, Nigeria.

Ifeanyi J. Ezema & Namdi Azikiwe. L., (2010). Globalisation, Information Revolution and Cultural Imperialism in Africa; Implications for Nigerian Library and Information Professionals, https: //www.libr.org. Accessed 21th July, 2017.

Ighodalo, Akhakpe, (2012). Poverty and Sustainable Socio-Economic Development in Africa: The Nigeria Experience, *European Science Journal*, Vol. 8. No. 26, www.eujournal.org

Kadafa Adati Ayuba,. (2012). Environmental Impact of Oil Exploration in the Niger Delta of Nigeria, *Global Journal of Science Frontiers Research Environmental and Earth Science*, 12. (3): 20-26.

Mbat David, Enefioklbok, Ekong Daniel and Obioakpa (2013). Campus, ExxonMobil and Corporate Responsibility in Akwa-Ibom State, Nigeria: Past and Present, Vol. 3. No. 3. www.iiste.org Accessed 25th July.

Multinational Corporations in Nigeria: The Ultimate List-Nigeria Finder, 2017, nigeriafinder.com. Accessed 25 July, 2017.

nairaproject.com. (2017). A Critical analysis of the Role of Multinational Companies in Developing Countries, (The Nigerian Experience), .Accessed 16 July, 2017.

newsrescue.com, (2015). Multinational Corporations in Nigeria Economy: The Question and the Responses. Accessed 22 July 2017.

Nku Felix. (2017). 51+ years, Male, Ex-staff of defunct Limca Bottle Company PLC, place of interview Ilorin, Date 6th September, 2017.

Nwankwo Beloveth Odochi. (2015). The Politics of Conflict over Oil in the Niger Delta Region of Nigeria, A Review of the Corporate Social Responsibility Strategies of the Oil Companies, http://pabs.sciepub.com, Accessed, 6th July, 2017.

Odeigah, T. N. (2017). "Poverty in the Midst of Plenty": A Study of Poverty and Underdevelopment in Niger Delta Region of Nigeria, In: Munyaradzi Mawere (Ed). *Underdevelopment, Development and the Future of Africa,* Langaa RPCIG, Cameroon.

Odisu, T. A. (2015). The Nigerian State, Oil Multinationals and Environment: A Case Study of Shell Petroleum Development Company (SPDC), *Journal of Public Administration policy Research*, 2 (2): 27-28.

Onimode, B. (1982). *Imperialism and Underdevelopment in Nigeria:* The Dialectics of Mass Poverty, Zed Press, London.

Onodugo, V. A. (2012). Multinational Corporations (MNC) and Employment and Labour Conditions of Developing Countries: *The Nigerian Experience, European Journal of Business and Social Science,* 1 (2): 68-75.

Osuagwu, Godwin Onyewuchi & Ezie Obumneke, (2013). Multinational Corporations and the Nigerian Economy, *International Journal of Academic Research in Business and Social Sciences,* 3 (4): 359-366.

Ozoigbo, B. I & Chukuezi, C. O. (2012). The Impact of Multinational Corporations on Nigeria's Economy, *European Journal of Social Science,* Vol. 19, No 3. https://www.lap-publishing.com. Accessed 18th July, 2017.

Samson Peter, 59+ years, Civil servant, place of interview Calabar, Date of interview 21th July, 2017.

Stopford, J. (1998). *Multinational Corporations, Foreign Policy,* winter, pp. 12-13.

Tatum, M. "The Activities of Multinationals". Retrieved from www.wisegeek.com/what-is-a-multinationalcorporation.htm, Accessed 13th July, 2017.

Udensi Eugene Udoka. (2015). The Impacts of Multinational Corporations to the Nigerian Economy, *International Journal of Social Science and Humanities Research,* 3 (2): 107-110.

Walter, R. (1972). *How Europe Underdeveloped Africa,* Bogle-L'Ouverture, London.

Wiig A and Kolsted, I. (2010). Multinational Corporations and Host Country Institutions, A Case Study of CSR Activities in Angola, *International Business Review* 19 (2): 179-186. www.sciencedirect.com.

www.encyclopedia.com. (2012). "Underdevelopment and Persistent Poverty in the Niger Delta of Nigeria. A Constraint to Sustainable Development in the 20th Century, Neo-colonialism," New Dictionary of History of Ideas, , Accessed 13th of July, 2017.

www.grossarchieve.com, The Influence of Multi-National Corporations in Economic Development of Nigeria, (A Case Study of Guinness Nigeria PLC, Benin City), https://www.grossarchive.com, Accessed 25th July, 2017.

www.thisdaylive.com. (2016: 25). Accessed 5th July, 2016.

www.wewsrescue. Multinational Corporation in Nigeria's economy: the Question and Responses, (2015). Accessed 7th July, 2017.

Chapter 4

Foraging to Survive: Poverty and Shifting Consumer Dynamics in Rural Zimbabwe between 2000 and 2008

Fidelis Peter Thomas Duri

Introduction

By the beginning of the 21st century, Zimbabwe was already engulfed in a horrendous socio-economic crisis of unprecedented proportions characterised, among other things, by investor flight, deindustrialisation, widespread unemployment, underemployment, hyperinflation, abject poverty and human misery. The acute hunger that blanketed the country, and was most acute in the rural areas, condemned many ordinary Zimbabweans to a predatory life of hunters and gatherers.

During the period 2000-2008, when the socio-economic quagmire was most severe, the consumption patterns and choices of many rural Zimbabweans were drastically transformed as they increasingly survived on a broad range of wild animal and plant species neither for their nutritional and medicinal value nor because some of them were delicacies, but largely due to the gaping food insecurity that prevailed in the country. In this chapter, these dietary options are referred to as wild foods in the sense that, for many societies in Zimbabwe, the animal and plant species were not domesticated and also did not constitute a regular part of their diet.

This chapter does not downplay the importance of wild foods, both flora and fauna, in human life. In addition to providing dietary diversity, various plant and animal species from the wilderness are of great medicinal and nutritional value to human beings. Many green leaves and fruits from the wilderness, for example, are rich in Vitamin C while most insects are rich in protein, fats and micronutrients (Daudet, 2012; Mawere, 2015). There is, however, a problem when all communities in a country are forced by circumstances beyond their control such as chronic hunger to abandon their staple diet and settle for wild foods in order to survive. This was the case of Zimbabwe during the period 2000-2008 when most rural communities, whose staple is maize (Human Rights Watch, 22 January 2009), were forced scrounge for alternative sources of food in the wilderness due to severe food shortages emanating from the government's mismanagement of the economy and inexorable ecological disasters.

Historical evidence abounds that the pre-colonial ancestors of many societies in present-day Zimbabwe, mostly the Ndebele and the Shona, were Bantu-speaking people who produced food and domesticated animals (Chigwedere, 1980; Lee and Hitchcock, 2001). They are generally believed to have migrated into Southern Africa, including present-day Zimbabwe, and subdued indigenous hunter-gatherer societies such as the San during the first century AD (Lee and Hitchcock, 2001). In pre-colonial Zimbabwe, cereal grain crops such as millet and sorghum were the staple for most Bantu-speaking societies. Maize gradually replaced millet and sorghum as the staple food for many African communities in Zimbabwe during the colonial period, which lasted with the attainment of independence in 1980. In the Gutu District of Masvingo Province, for example, maize was first introduced during the 1940s (Schrimpf and Feil, 2012). Basing on the known and widely documented history of the Bantu past, wild foods are indigenous to Africa mainly because the plant and animal species from which they are derived are not exotic, but originated within the African continent. In dietary terms, these foods were largely supplements to the basic domesticated staples which were dominantly cereal grain crops such as sorghum and millet during the pre-colonial and early colonial times and maize from the later colonial period into the post-colonial era.

It should be emphasised, therefore, that the upsurge in the consumption of wild foods by many Zimbabwean rural communities for the greater part of the first decade of the 21st century was largely due to "lack of alternatives" and desperate attempts to "mitigate the consequences of insufficient agricultural production" (Maroyi, 2013: 6). In his study of the Chiweshe Communal Lands in northern Zimbabwe during the 1980s, Campbell (1987) also noted that wild fruits did not constitute a major part of the people's diet; they were only supplements in normal times but were mostly consumed during periods of food stress. Clarke (1983) and Lee (1979) reiterate that most rural communities largely utilise wild foods for purposes of famine relief in times of crisis.

It is the central argument of this chapter that circumstances which force people to abandon their staple food and alter their consumption patterns and choices constitute a humanitarian crisis and gross disregard of human rights because, as Daudet (2012: 20) asserts, "people have the right to choose, and to decide their food preferences by themselves." The chapter demonstrates that, for most Zimbabweans, depending on wild foods "is an indication of crisis" (*IRIN News*, 29 October 2008: 1). Answering the question whether wild foods are a solution to hunger and undernutrition, Daudet (2012: 24) said, "Certainly not. No wild food, especially taken alone, will be a magic solution to undernutrition as no food product will cover all nutrient needs."

Contextualising the hunter-gatherer in livelihood discourses

As Zimbabwe was besieged by an unprecedented socio-economic meltdown, most especially from the beginning of the new millennium, many poverty-stricken and famished rural communities were forcibly transformed into hunter-gatherers who survived largely by foraging for food from the wilderness. These developments had far-reaching implications on the consumption dynamics of most rural Zimbabweans. It is cogent from the onset to contextualise the concept 'hunter-gatherer' as a characterisation in livelihood discourses.

According to Kusimba (2005: 353), hunter-gatherer has been "the primitive baseline in models of cultural evolution and the wellspring of humanity's essential features." Daudet (2012: 20) also observes that "the gathered food plants tend to be poorly considered in many food systems, for example, being 'modern' is valued and 'modern foods' are preferred socially while gathered food plants are for 'savage people' or 'ancient people'." In 2008, Maud Muchuweti, a lecturer of Biochemistry at the University of Zimbabwe, confirmed that edible species from the wilderness are often dismissed by many contemporary Zimbabweans as "poor man's food" (*IRIN News*, 29 October 2008: 1). This widely-held negative characterisation is premised on the activities of many historic hunter-gatherer communities which largely involved foraging for food rather than producing it. As Lee and De Vore (1968) note, hunter-gatherer societies lack both predictable sources of food and tend to be itinerant and opportunistic in their survival pursuits. Consequently, they have no food reserves and live from hand to mouth by scavenging in the wilderness.

In addition, as Sadr and others (2003) state, hunter-gatherer communities have dietary variations and inconsistencies because they have no fixed location of food sources. Consequently, such communities tend to be peripatetic in their pursuits of livelihood (Berland and Rao, 2004). An example can be drawn from the ancient hunter-gatherer communities of central Ghana who had no fixed diet but fed on an assortment of foraged foods which included land snails, fruits, seed husks and the meat of various primates and reptiles (Kusimba, 2005). These views resonate with the Zimbabwean situation, especially from the onset of the new millennium when the majority of rural communities were forced to scrounge for food in the wilderness owing to persistent droughts and the disastrous socio-economic policies and mismanagement practices of the ruling Zimbabwe African National Union Patriotic Front (ZANU-PF) government under the leadership of President Robert Mugabe. As a result, it has been observed that in Zimbabwe from the beginning of the new millennium, it was mostly the poor people who depended on wildlife products for sustenance (Shava *et al* 2009). A study carried out by Maroyi (2013) in the Shurugwi District of Zimbabwe actually confirms that impoverished populations largely depend on the natural environment for daily food which includes insects, wild fruits and vegetables.

It would be misleading, however, to regard hunter-gatherers as static and unproductive stereotypes. As Bailey and Aunger (1989) argue, many hunter-gatherer communities, despite largely surviving from foraging, have the capacity to interact socially and economically with other societies. Kusimba (2005) also notes that hunter-gatherers have always interacted with food-producing communities during which they readily exchanged commodities and technologies, among other things.

These scholarly views are quite applicable to the Zimbabwean situation especially from the onset of the 21st century until 2008. As will be noted later in this chapter, many rural Zimbabweans did not become hunter-gatherers by choice. They are basically food-producers who were forced to scrounge for sustenance in the wilderness by circumstances beyond their control. Despite having been forcibly turned into scavengers instead of producers, they strove to produce food and interact with other communities in order to generate income under very difficult circumstances.

Zimbabwe's socio-economic paralysis, 2000-2008

This section explores Zimbabwe's socio-economic meltdown from the onset of the 21st century in order to provide the context in which the hunter-gatherer tendencies of procuring food by many Zimbabwean rural communities emerged and became prevalent. These developments had far-reaching implications on the dietary dynamics as well as consumption patterns and choices of many rural Zimbabweans. The socio-economic catastrophe, despite being aggravated by ecological calamities, was firmly rooted in the government's mismanagement of the economy and social services which culminated in chronic food shortages and grinding poverty of unprecedented proportions for most citizens.

Even though Zimbabwe's socio-economic degeneracy can be traced back to the early 1990s (Bond and Manyanya, 2002; Duri, 2016; Mawere 2011), the situation became worse from the year 2000 when the ruling ZANU-PF Party, which had been in power since independence in 1980 under Robert Mugabe's leadership, sanctioned the invasion of white-owned commercial farms with promises of redistributing them to the landless blacks (Bond and Manyanya, 2002; Raftopoulos, 2003). This move was largely motivated by political expediency given the fierce challenge that was being posed by the opposition Movement for Democratic Change (MDC), led by Morgan Tsvangirai, which had been formed in September 1999 with considerable funding from white commercial farmers (Raftopoulos,

49

2003; Richardson, 2005). Thus, the farm invasions were fundamentally a two-pronged political gamble meant to lure landless peasants from supporting the MDC and to prevent the white commercial farmers and their employees from becoming a viable constituency of the opposition (Hammar and Raftopoulos, 2003).

The late 1990s witnessed sporadic cases of intrusions into white commercial farms by land-hungry villagers in some parts of the country such as the Svosve (Mashonaland East Province), Nyamajura (Manicaland Province), Nyamandlovu (Matabeleland) and Nemamwa (Masvingo Province) (Madziyauswa, 2017). The ZANU-PF government, which was initially opposed the land grabs, changed its mind from late 1999 when the opposition MDC was formed with considerable funding from white farmers (Ibid). The widespread seizure of white commercial farms erupted on 26 February 2000 with the support of the government. By 8 March, approximately 400 farms had been grabbed without any compensation being paid (Meredith, 2002). As the invasions persisted, the number of confiscated farms rose to 1 500 in June 2000 (Meredith, 2002) and over 4 000 by August 2007 (*Financial Gazette*, 26 July-1 August 2007).

Even though some scholars contend that the land redistribution exercise resulted in an increase in agricultural production in areas that were put to good use (Scoones *et al* 2010), the same cannot be said about most parts of the country. To a great extent, the so-called Land Reform Programme laid the foundations of a severe and multi-layered socio-economic crisis that made Zimbabwe critically food-deficient, among other things. In most parts of the country, agricultural production fell drastically because many of the beneficiaries of the land redistribution exercise, the so-called 'new farmers' in public discourse, either lacked the requisite skills, adequate capital and even the enthusiasm to engage in commercial farming (Richardson, 2005). Consequently, over 50% of the seized farms were either unclaimed or neglected in 2005 (Ibid). The extent of commercial farmland under productive use therefore fell over the years from 200 000 hectares during the 1999-2000 season, 90 000 in 2000-2001 and 50 000 in 2001-2002 (Ibid). In addition, some of the outgoing white farmers either looted or damaged farming equipment and infrastructure thereby scuttling the prospects of economic recovery in the near future (Organisation for Economic Cooperation and Development, 2004). To aggravate the situation, many disinterested 'new farmers' and criminals looted property from unclaimed and underutilised farms. Some ZANU-PF supporters allegedly melted irrigation pipes and sold them as scrap metal or coffin handles (Godwin, August 2003). The country became critically food-insecure as a result of these chaotic developments. The production of maize, groundnuts, cotton, wheat, soya beans, coffee and livestock sank drastically from 50% to 90% during the period 2000-2003 (Richardson, 2005). As the production of basic food crops dwindled, the country began to depend on food imports from the year 2001 (*Reuters Alert*, 20 March 2007).

The farm invasions as well as numerous incidents of politically-motivated violence that became prevalent between ZANU-PF and opposition parties, particularly the MDC (Raftopoulos, 2003; Richardson, 2005), had several calamitous repercussions on Zimbabwe's socio-economic landscape. The violation of property rights through farm seizures and the insecurity posed by endemic political violence scared away investors resulting in deindustrialisation (Richardson, 2005). In early October 2000, for example, 24 firms in Zimbabwe's eastern city of Mutare had closed (*Manica Post*, 6 October 2000). By 2001, 700 companies had shut down countrywide (Richardson, 2005). In the manufacturing sector, production tumbled by 10.5% in 2001 and around 17.5% in 2002 (Richardson, 2005). Zimbabwe's foreign currency reserves increasingly became depleted, and continued as such, as a result of the drastic fall in the production of export crops, investor flight, deindustrialisation and the country's isolation from the greater part of the international community (Raftopoulos, 2003; Richardson, 2005).

Owing to foreign currency shortages, the government faced severe challenges when it came to the importation of food. In addition, revenue inflows (in the form of royalties and corporate tax) into government coffers dwindled considerably owing to investor flight and industrial closures. The government increasingly became bankrupt, and therefore incapacitated, to import basic commodities that were scarce thereby forcing the country to increasingly depend on donor agencies (United Nations, 11 September 2008). The critical shortage of basic commodities was compounded from June 2007 by a government directive which compelled manufacturers and retailers to slash the price of goods by 50%. This triggered serious nationwide shortages of staple foods and other basic commodities as the few remaining factories either scaled down or ceased production in defiance (*Zimbabwe Times*, 23 July 2008).

Another catastrophic effect of farm invasions, investor flight and industrial closures was widespread unemployment. As far as the land seizures were concerned, many former farm workers lost their jobs after the new owners failed to take them up or fully utilise the land (Sachikonye, 2003). At Kondozi Farm, in eastern Zimbabwe, for example, more than 20 000 workers lost their jobs following the invasion by riot police and ZANU-PF supporters on 19 July 2005 (Poverty Reduction Forum Trust, 2013). Statistics from the General Agricultural and Plantation Workers Union of Zimbabwe (GAPWUZ) indicated that employment for its members had decreased from 500 000 in 2000 to 200 000 in 2008. Consequently, GAPWUZ's membership slumped from 150 000 before the farm seizures to only 25 000 in 2008 (Chikwanha, 4 May 2014). According to the Internal Displacement Monitoring Centre, a Geneva-based human rights group, approximately one million farm workers were left jobless during the period 2000-2010 due to the farm seizures (Zimbabwe Human Rights NGO Forum, 2010). These developments also condemned to destitution, millions of dependants of former farm workers who constituted about 20% of the total population of Zimbabwe (Sachikonye, 2003).

The farm invasions and industrial closures left more than 300 000 workers out of the country's formal labour force of 1.3 million unemployed by the close of 2000 (Hammar and Raftopoulos, 2003). The formal unemployment rate skyrocketed over the years to 70% in 2002, over 80% in September 2008 (United Nations, 11 September 2008) and 94% in early 2009 (Chiriga, 16 April 2011; *Mail and Guardian*, 29 January 2009).

Predictably, the Zimbabwean economy degenerated into a state of paralysis. The economy shrunk by 5% in 2000, 8% in 2001, 12% in 2002, and about 18% in 2003 (Organisation for Economic

Cooperation and Development, 2004). As the country became bankrupt, the government began printing paper money thereby fuelling inflation. The Zimbabwean dollar lost 99% of its value as the annual inflation rate soared from about 20% in mid-1996 to 100% at the end of 2001 (Bond and Manyanya, 2002). It rocketed to 117% in May 2002, 145% at the close of 2002, 269% in April 2003, and to over 500% in July 2003 (International Monetary Fund, July 2003). In November 2005, it rose slightly to 502.4% (*Reuters Alert*, 20 March 2007). In September 2006 the inflation rate hovered around 1 200% (*Reuters Alert*, 20 March 2007). In March 2007, Zimbabwe's annual inflation rate of 1 700% became the world's highest (*Reuters Alert*, 20 March 2007). The annual inflation rate hiked to more than 4 500% in May 2007 (Ndlela, 26 July-1 August 2007), 66 212.3% in December 2007, 100 580.2% in January 2008, 165 000% in February 2008, 355 000% in March 2008 (*Zimbabwean on Sunday*, 18 May 2008) and 11 000 000% in September 2008 (United Nations, 11 September 2008).

The Zimbabwean currency became virtually worthless as a result of hyperinflation. The prices of basic commodities shot up. The hyperinflationary conditions made it very difficult for ordinary Zimbabweans, most of who were unemployed, to afford the costs of procuring basic commodities, which increasingly became scarce due to farm invasions and deindustrialisation, whenever and wherever they became available. In April 2007, for instance, the average family basket consisting of transport, food, accommodation, water, electricity, health, education and clothing for a family of six people cost Z$1 482 324 or the equivalent of US$59 on the parallel market, using the exchange rate of Z$25 000 to US$1, which was far above the average monthly salary of low-income earners (World Food Programme, April 2007). Thus, the prices of basic commodities were beyond the reach of many Zimbabweans, including those who were still employed.

Even though Zimbabwe's socio-economic crisis particularly from the onset of the new millennium was largely human-made, the plight of many ordinary Zimbabweans was exacerbated by persistent droughts. The 2001-2002 drought was the worst to hit Zimbabwe in a decade. The droughts persisted late into the decade and the government declared 2007 a drought year after crops, particularly maize, were a complete write-off in many parts of the country (*Reuters Alert*, 20 March 2007).

From early 2009, there was some improvement in the socio-economic and political conditions in Zimbabwe as a result of the formation of the Government of National Unity (GNU) (*Thomson Reuters Foundation*, 13 July 2014). The GNU, which became operational from February 2009, comprised ZANU-PF and two MDC factions led by Morgan Tsvangirai (MDC-T) and Arthur Mutambara (MDC-M). Mugabe remained President, Tsvangirai became the Prime Minister and Mutambara, the Deputy Prime Minister. The new political arrangement helped to reduce incidents of overt political violence and inflows of food aid and basic commodities from the international community improved considerably. In addition, the multi-currency fiscal regime introduced by the GNU significantly alleviated the hyperinflationary challenges and greatly improved the living conditions of many Zimbabweans (Ibid).

It should be noted that the negative socio-economic developments that prevailed during the period 2000-2008 made Zimbabwe to become critically food insecure resulting in chronic hunger for many citizens. The next section pays particular attention to the severe food shortages that critically eroded the livelihoods of many citizens, a considerable number of who increasingly resorted to hunting and gathering in order to survive.

The vanishing staple: Chronic hunger in Zimbabwe between 2000 and 2008

A combination of factors such as droughts and the government's mismanagement of the economy from the onset of the new millennium made Zimbabwe to become critically food insecure. The situation became desperate as the staple maize and other basic commodities became scarce. It should be noted, however, that the number of people on the verge of starvation tended to fluctuate upwards or downwards over the years depending on the quantities of food that were brought in by the donor community as well as those that were sometimes availed by the government.

Communal maize production fell by 60%, from 1.091 million tons in the period 2000-2001 to 315 000 tons in 2003 (Richardson 2005). In May 2002, about 25% of Zimbabwe's 12 million people were starving (Flanagan, 26 May 2002). In the Masvingo Province, for example, food shortages reached critical levels to the extent that more than two million people were urgently in need of food aid (Bara, 2 May 2002). By July 2002, an estimated 7.8 million people, including 5.4 million children, were faced with hunger (SMH, 12 July 2002). In September 2002, the United Nations stated that about six million Zimbabweans were in need of emergency food aid (Ruhanya, 9 September 2002). Child malnutrition resulting from severe food shortages was also estimated at 8% countrywide (*Daily News*, 11 September 2002). In May 2003, the country had no official grain reserves and people in the rural and urban areas who had some disposable income formed long queues to purchase grain and maize meal at exorbitant prices (Church World Service, 24 July 2002). By the close of 2003, an estimated 6.7 million Zimbabweans were food insecure (Mushita and Mpande, 2003; Schrimpf and Feil, 2012). During the 2003-2004 season, five million Zimbabweans were critically food deficient (Amnesty International, October 2004; Solidarity Peace Trust, November 2004).

The limited quantities of food which the government managed to procure locally and abroad through the Grain Marketing Board (GMB), a state-owned company with the sole monopoly to import and distribute grain supplies in the country, were often politicised as the ruling party privileged its supporters while famishing opposition sympathisers. While threatening opposition supporters in early 2002, Abednico Ncube, a ZANU-PF government minister, for example, said, "As long as you value the government of the day you will not starve...You cannot vote for the MDC and expect ZANU-PF to help you...You have to vote for ZANU-PF candidates...before the government starts thinking your entitlement to this food aid" (Meredith, 2002: 231). Also speaking in August 2002, at a time when an estimated 50% of Zimbabwe's population was in a state of starvation, Didymus Mutasa, a senior ZANU-PF politician, clearly articulated the government's position on the manner in which food aid was distributed: "We would be better off with only six million people, with our own people who support the liberation struggle. We don't want all these extra people" (Meredith, 2002: 231; Solidarity Peace Trust, November 2004: 2).

The GMB increasingly became defunct due to a number of factors. GMB silos were virtually empty since the year 2000 due to the drastic fall in agricultural production following the invasion of commercial farms. In addition, owing to hyperinflation and several financial constraints the country was experiencing, the GMB increasingly lacked the capacity to buy adequate supplies of grain either abroad or locally from the few remaining productive farmers. Many of the few local farmers who managed to produce some surplus grain avoided the GMB and took their produce to the black market where buying prices were much more competitive. The GMB was also plagued by corruption as some of their meagre stocks were either sold on the black market by senior managers or given to ZANU-PF politicians and supporters. Attempts by the Reserve Bank of Zimbabwe (RBZ) to provide small-scale farmers with inputs in an effort to resuscitate food production through Operation *Maguta* (Food Security) from early 2008 did not yield much as the project largely benefitted senior ZANU-PF officials and war veterans (Human Rights Watch, 22 January 2009).

The collapse of the GMB clearly illustrates the Zimbabwe government's inability to alleviate the plight of its hungry citizens. Instead, the government aggravated the situation when, on 4 June 2008, it imposed a blanket ban on all operations on non-governmental organisations, except those that were engaged in HIV/AIDS-related activities, after accusing most of them of using food aid to mobilise support for the opposition MDC (Human Rights Watch, 22 January 2009; *IRIN News*, 3 September 2008). This was a morally insensitive move given that over four million people were desperately in need of food aid in May 2008 (Nhemachena, 2014). As the food situation became more desperate, the ban was lifted on some non-governmental organisations on 29 August 2008, but subject to strict operational conditions (Human Rights Watch, 22 January 2009; *IRIN News*, 3 September 2008).

Despite the lifting of the ban, the donor community was always overwhelmed by the number of starving Zimbabweans in need of emergency food aid. Data released by the United Nations World Food Program (UNWFP) on Zimbabwe in October 2008 indicated that the proportion of people who had gone for a full day without eating anything had risen from 0% to 13%, while those who afforded only one meal a day shot up from 13% to 60% since 2007 (Dugger, 22 December 2008). During the same month, the UNWFP stated that more than two million people were desperately in need of food relief (*Zimbabwe Situation*, 16 October 2008). In December 2008, more than 75% of Zimbabweans were living in abject poverty (Nsingo, 20 January 2009). In addition, approximately 30% of Zimbabwean children under the age of five years were undernourished (Human Rights Watch, 22 January 2009; Nsingo, 20 January 2009). For the greater part of the first decade of the new millennium, maize was unavailable in most shops and where it was available at the black market, it was charged against the United States dollar. In November 2008, for example, a 20-kilogramme bucket of maize-meal cost US$20 at a time when teachers were earning an average of US$4 per month (Human Rights Watch, 22 January 2009).

This section has examined the severe food crisis in Zimbabwe from the onset of the new millennium up to the end of 2008. In addition to the general shortage of basic commodities, the section has demonstrated how many ordinary Zimbabweans increasingly failed to access maize, their staple food, as the crisis worsened. It should be noted, however, that the impact of natural disasters, such as droughts, could not have been so severe on the ordinary people had the ruling ZANU-PF party not embarked on political expediency at the expense of the economy. As noted earlier in this chapter, some of the government's blunders which caused severe food shortages, chronic hunger and starvation included the sanctioning of the invasion of commercial farms, economic mismanagement, scaring away investors, suspending the activities of non-governmental organisations and "the immoral use of food aid" (Solidarity Peace Trust, November 3004: 2). Having embarked on such disastrous policies, the government largely failed to procure food for most of its hungry citizens thereby forcing most of them to eke livelihoods by foraging wild foods.

Foraging wild vegetal species for survival

As a coping mechanism to the severe food crisis, "various famine foods were consumed by people, for example, some fruits and wild plants, several of which were unpalatable, poisonous or of little nutritional value, demonstrating the level of desperation in times of famine" (Schrimpf and Feil, 2012: 24). During the ensuing struggles for survival, "jackals, baboons and goats competed with villagers for roots and wild fruits" (*Daily Mail*, 20 November 2008). This section dwells on the foraging of wild vegetal species for food by many hungry rural Zimbabweans as they sought to avert starvation. The major vegetal foods they gathered from the wilderness included fruits, berries, leaves, tubers, bark and roots of trees.

The fierce competition for wild fruits can be demonstrated in the case of Monkey Oranges (*matamba* in Shona; *umkhemeswane* in Ndebele; botanical name, *Strychnos spinosa*) which cannot be safely eaten until they ripen. Hungry villagers who came across a tree with some *matamba* which were about to mature but could not be safely consumed were not guaranteed of getting them when they ripened. One common strategy of securing the fruit ahead of other people, and even wild animals that fed on it, as *The Daily Mail* (20 November 2008: 1) noted, was to "pick the fruit and cover it with donkey or cow dung, leaving it in the sun to hasten ripening."

In some parts of Matabeleland South Province in May 2002, many children spent most of their time ransacking bushes in search of wild fruits, roots and berries (Flanagan, 26 May 2002). The most popular wild fruit which most villagers in the province survived on was the *mabubatsa*, a long, brown fibrous pod. *Marula* nuts gathered from the bush were another important source of food for many people in the province (Ibid).

By September 2002, wild fruits and tubers had become the major source of food for many villagers in the Musana Communal Areas in the Mashonaland Central Province (*Daily News*, 9 September 2002). In the Chireka Village, for example, villagers routinely scrounged for *manyanya* (wild tubers) and Mobola Plums (*hacha/shakata* in Shona; *umphafa/umkhuna* in Ndebele*)*, wild fruits from the *Muchakata* tree (botanical name, *Painari curatellifolia*) (Ibid). Alice Chikoto, a 64-year-old woman from Chireka Village, told the *Daily News* (9 September 2002) that, together with her eight grandchildren, they usually woke up in the morning and travelled for about 10 kilometres to the Murembe Hills where they gathered Mobola Plums that donkeys also fed on. They pounded the fruits in a mortar and mixed with water to eat as porridge. They also dug up nearby mountains and forests for *manyanya* roots which they boiled and used as relish during the three sadza meals that they could only manage every week.

Similarly, by August 2008, it had become daily routine for many desperately hungry villagers in the Gwanda District of Matabeleland North Province to wake up at dawn and scour the surrounding bushes in search of edible wild fruits to eat (Gumpo, 20 August 2008). The baobab trees that grew wild in many parts of the district were virtually their only source of food. The villagers firstly crushed the shell of baobab fruits (*mawuyu* in Shona; *umkhomo* in Ndebele and Tonga; botanical name, *Adansonia digitate*) in order to extract their seeds which are coated by crumbs of clotted white powder. The crumbs were pounded into a fine powder which was mixed with fresh milk or water. The resultant mixture was a meal for many Gwanda villagers. When the baobab fruits were offseason, most villagers resorted to the roots of trees. Most of the roots were taken from a tree popularly known by the local Ndebele people as *amagontsi* or *umtopi* (botanical name, *Boscia albitrunca*). The roots were pounded into a porridge-like paste which served as the main meal for many villagers (Ibid).

In the Nharira Village of Mashonaland East Province in September 2008, most villagers survived from eating a wild fruit that grew in abundance in the area during the dry season (*IRIN News*, 3 September 2008). In processing the wild fruit, its pulp was separated from the hard seed by pounding it with pestles. More often than not, as *IRIN News* (3 September 2008: 1) observed in the area, "Villagers have been competing for the wild fruits with baboons and monkeys, sparking conflict between people and animals." Janet Chagwiza, a 70-year-old Nharira woman, stated that the wild fruit was an important source of sustenance in the area. She said, "This fruit has become our staple food. We do not have mealie-meal (maize-meal) and our vegetable gardens have been overwhelmed by the daily demand, leaving whole villages in this area to depend on wild fruits" (Ibid: 1).

Reports abound that by September 2008, many people from the chronically food-deficient Nyaminyami communities in the Zambezi Valley were surviving by scavenging for tree roots known as *makuri* (Williams, 26 September 2008). The *makuri* are yellow, stringy apple-sized tubers with a bitter taste (Ibid). Some consumers complained of health ailments after eating the tubers. As one 15-year-old boy stated in September 2008: "We have to dig the roots because we have nothing to eat. It has been like this for many months. I have stomach pains and diarrhoea after eating this. They do not taste good but I have to eat them" (Ibid: 1). These revelations were confirmed by Sarah Jacobs, an official of Save the Children, a British-based charity organisation, who had this to say: "It (*makuri*) has got no nutritional value whatsoever. Its taste is disgusting and it also has a parasite which attaches to it which is toxic. This is all they have to eat. You see babies eating it and toddlers eating it, and it is not digestible. It creates terrible stomach pains" (Ibid: 1).

In some villages of Matabeleland South Province during October 2008, many poverty-ravaged people were "working shoulder-to-shoulder with baboons" in search of wild foods such as berries because "there was no food, other than wild fruits" (Dixon, 3 December 2008: 1). In the Lupane District, for instance, many villagers were going for "as long as five days without eating anything solid" and were surviving on wild fruits and roots from edible local plants and trees (Dube, 31 October 2008: 1). As Dumezweni Sibanda, a 77-year-old male villager, moaned: "There is no food and people are surviving like animals. There is nothing to eat and we are competing with baboons and donkeys for fruits that are in season" (Ibid). Many villagers were surviving on a variety of wild fruits that included *umkhuna* (wild cork fruit), *umkhemeswane/matamba*, *umgwadi*, *inkelo* and *umsosobiyane. Inkelo* is a dried hard-shelled nut from the wild *marula/umganu* tree (*Sclerocanya birrea*) which grows in the more arid areas of southern and western Zimbabwe. In the Ndengwende Village of Lupane District in late October 2008, scores of children carrying sacks full of these wild fruits which, apparently, "had become the staple food," were a common sight (Ibid).

Sethule Ndlovu, a 65-year-old villager, also confirmed in October 2008 that scavenging for food in the wilderness had become a vital livelihood option for most people in the Lupane District (Dube, 2008). He said that they were surviving on the roots of the *umjumbula* (cassava) tree, which grows wild in the district. He explained that villagers pound the root into powder which they used to make sadza. Some villagers pounded baobab fruits and boiled the powder to prepare porridge which they ate either in the morning at breakfast or in the afternoon for lunch (Ibid). He added, "We are surviving on wild fruits and the children are the ones who spend the whole day looking for the fruits in the bush and they no longer go to school as they were collapsing of hunger at school" (Dube, 31 October 2008: 1). During the same month, in the Nyanga District of Manicaland Province, many villagers were reportedly surviving on wild fruits such as Monkey Bread (*masekesa* in Shona; botanical name, *Piliostigma thonningii*), *matamba*, *matohwe* and *hacha* (*Zimbabwe Situation*, 16 October 2008).

In the Matabeleland North Province in October 2008, most villagers were also reportedly subsisting on fruits and okra-like vegetables which grew in the wilderness (*Irin News*, 29 October 2008). As Samuel, Ndlovu, a man from Dakamela Village, told *IRIN News* (29 October 2008: 1): "Every day, we eat the wild fruits that are available in the bush, but the fruits are not good to eat every day. And school children are no longer going to school but spend the whole day looking for the wild fruits."

Throughout 2008, Tonga children in the Siachilaba Village of Binga District in Matabeleland North Province were reportedly spending most of their time gathering baobab fruits and a variety of tubers which included *makuli* (botanical name, *Ipomoea shirambensis*) and *bbonga* (botanical name, *Raphionaeme monteiroae*) (Manyena, Fordham and Collins, 2008). The powder of the baobab fruit (*umkhomo*) was often mixed with goat milk or water to make *mulondo*, a thick yoghurt-like mixture, which they drank. Children were mostly assigned foraging tasks because of their mobility (Ibid).

A similar generation-based pattern in the division of labour was also prevalent in the Mhondoro District where children played prominent roles in foraging for food during the same period. As

Yeukai Chirinda, a 13-year-girl from the district, stated: "We go out early in the morning and return in the evening, looking for wild fruits and gathering leftovers from shopping centres, some of them as far away as 30 kilometres. We are helping our parents in these difficult times. If we do not do that, there will not be anything to eat" (*IRIN News*, 3 September 2008: 1).

By mid-2008, *umkhuna/hacha* had become the staple for many starving families countrywide (*Zimbabwean*, 24 October 2008). In December 2008, as Dugger (22 December 2008: 1) observed at the Jirira Village near Harare, the capital city:

> No food aid has reached the village…So, each morning, people rise before the sun and stumble from their huts…to fill metal pails with the small, foul-smelling *hacha* fruit. Those who arrive as dawn breaks find the fruit has already been picked clean…The sweet, fibrous, yellow pulp of the fruit has become the staple of the villagers' diet. The fruit is now infested with tiny brown worms. Nevertheless, the women peel it, crush it and soak it in water. Some of the worms float to the surface and can be skimmed off. The mashed ones they eat…

In the Wedza District of Mashonaland East Province in early December 2008, there were numerous accounts of "people fighting with each other and even with wild animals like warthogs just to take some food back to their children" (Dixon, 3 December 2008: 1). Similarly, during the same month in President Mugabe's home district of Zvimba, villagers were reportedly "fighting with donkeys for wild fruit to eat" (Bakwa, 10 December 2008: 1). McDonald Lewanika, the leader of the Crisis in Zimbabwe Coalition, a human rights organisation, summed up the situation when he said, "People have been reduced to hunters and gatherers who have to look for wild food to survive" (Dixon, 3 December 2008: 1).

All these cases illustrate the desperate situation of food insecurity which many Zimbabwean villagers endured for the greater part of the first decade of the 21st century. Given the scarcity and unaffordability of basic commodities in general and the staple maize in particular, many famished Zimbabweans encroached into the habitats of wild animals in an effort to salvage livelihoods. During the process, fierce contestations for resources became banal not only among human beings, but also with wild animals whose habitat the hungry villagers often violated as hunger gnawed.

As severe hunger ravaged the country, the roots and bark of trees became a regular part of the diet for most rural communities, particularly during times of the year when most of the locally-available fruits were offseason. In September 2008, Save the Children captured the pathetic experiences of impoverished Nyaminyami communities in the Binga District "where the only food available are roots riddled with toxic parasites and rats" (Williams, 26 September 2008: 1). In the same district, "every available man, woman and child spent every waking hour searching for edible roots, leaves, berries and the very bark of the trees" (Kriel, 2 January 2009: 1).

In October 2008, Esnath Nyoni, a woman from the Lupane area of Matabeleland North Province, also informed *IRIN News* (29 October 2008) that they were surviving on porridge made from ground roots of the cassava tree into which she squeezed the sweet juice of wild fruits to improve the taste. She added that some families which had limited maize-meal economised by mixing it with ground cassava tree roots. She acknowledged that the taste was not appetising but those with livestock mixed the porridge with sour or fresh milk to improve the palatability of the meal.

In addition to subsisting on wildlife products such as fruits and insects, some impoverished but enterprising Zimbabweans sold some quantities as they sought to generate income in a harsh socio-economic dispensation. These initiatives qualify Morrison and Junker's (2003) conceptualisation of hunter-gathers as forager-traders. This conceptualisation, which is also supported by scholars such as Bailey and Aunger (1989), Kent (2002) and Kusimba (2005), dismisses the notion of hunter-gatherers as static and monocultural in terms of survival options. Instead, they acknowledge that even though hunter-gatherers were basically foragers, they often opened up to innovations and interacted socially and economically with other communities in an effort to widen their livelihood options. In addition, as Terrell and others (2003) argue, human livelihood initiatives should be analysed by a subsistence spreadsheet where a broad range of food-producing, food-getting and income-generating activities are considered. In the Masvingo Province, for example, scores of villagers flooded the Harare-Beitbridge Road selling wild fruits they had picked from the bush to travellers in an effort to salvage livelihoods. Their major targets were travellers aboard buses, private vehicles and haulage trucks. The wild fruits they sold included *mazhanje*, *matamba* and *matohwe* (Maramba, 8 December 2015). Similarly, in the Binga District, many Tonga villagers sold *Nchenje* fruits to travellers and visitors at various shopping centres along the Binga-Cross Dete Road (Zikhali, 29 August 2016).

There were, however, some notable tragic consequences of surviving on wild vegetal species. As already noted earlier in this chapter, some people suffered from health ailments such as diarrhoea after consuming some plant species. In some cases, some people actually died after eating poisonous plant species. In many cases, the young generation was more vulnerable since they were not familiar with the vegetal species that are toxic. As Themba Dlomo, a villager from Lupane District, told *IRIN News* (29 October 2008: 1): "This is now the time when the elderly, who have survived in previous droughts, play a crucial role, as the young people have no idea which trees have edible roots and which ones do not."

In early September 2008, in the Nharira Village of Mashonaland East Province, two grandchildren of Janet Chagwiza, a 70-year-old woman, reportedly died from overfeeding on a wild fruit that grew abundantly in the area during the dry season (*IRIN News*, 3 September 2008). According to the same source, the wild fruit had virtually become the staple food in the area owing to the prevailing socio-economic hardships and inexorable droughts. Health officials at a local hospital where the two children had been rushed for emergency treatment indicated that the wild fruit can cause severe constipation if consumed in excess. According to Janet Chagwiza, her two grandchildren were buried in a single pit because "people here no longer have the energy to dig graves" due to chronic hunger (*IRIN News*, 3 September 2008: 1).

In mid-October 2008, Sifiso Dube, 15-year-old boy, was choked to death after eating the nut of the *umkhuna/hacha* wild fruit at a village in the Sivalo area of the Midlands Province, at a time when acute food shortages had forced many families to survive on tree leaves, wild roots and fruits. He was buried on 20 October 2008. Collin Mantiya, the local headman, confirmed the boy's death and stated that several mishaps had taken place in the village when some people fell ill after eating poisonous wild fruits (*Zimbabwean*, 24 October 2008).

This section has illuminated how wild vegetal species increasingly became central in the dietary considerations and income-generating pursuits of many rural Zimbabwean communities during the period 2000-2008. This dramatic shift in consumption and entrepreneurial dynamics was not out of choice, but was necessitated by the agency and resilience of people encapsulated by poverty and hunger to improvise avenues of extricating themselves from such a predicament. The section has also articulated how the wilderness became a fiercely contested space as human beings often clashed among themselves and with animals over limited food resources. It now becomes apparent that the dividing line between the livelihood pursuits of human beings and wild animals, as well as their consumption behaviour and choices, increasingly became blurred as socio-economic hardships worsened.

Rising dependence on wild animal species for livelihoods

A broad range of fauna from the wilderness has been part of the diet of many African societies since the pre-colonial era with some species such as insects being critical supplements (Dzerefos, 2014; Mawere, 2014). During the colonial and post-colonial periods, however, anti-poaching laws which criminalised unlicensed hunting were instituted (Duri, 2017). After independence, for example, the Zimbabwean government passed the National Parks and Wildlife Act, Chapter 20: 14, which outlawed unlicensed hunting (Duri, 2017; Kuvirimirwa 2013; Laiton, 27 August 2014; *New Zimbabwe*, 17 April 2015). All hell broke loose from the year 2000 when this piece of legislation was frequently violated as hungry villagers sought livelihoods from the wilderness. While some wild animal species supplemented the diets of many African societies since the pre-colonial period, a considerable section of Zimbabwe's rural population came to depend almost entirely on them for food and income as socio-economic hardships gnawed. One notable departure from the longstanding consumption behaviour of many rural Zimbabwean communities, which clearly illustrates the magnitude of their plight, was the eating of rats and other animal species that were not usually eaten since historical times.

As livelihood options increasingly became exhausted, unlicensed hunting, which is criminalised under Zimbabwean law, became an important source of food for most starving rural communities. In fact, many hungry villagers became predators of wild animals as they sought to survive against the odds. Hunger-stricken villagers sometimes sneaked into game ranches and conservancies to slaughter animals for food. In May 2002, for example, wildlife officials reported that an estimated 600 000 wild animals had been killed in various parts of the country since the year 2000. This resulted in the decimation of 60% of wildlife in privately-owned game parks and conservancies. Some of the animals killed were protected species such as black rhinos. While animals such as black rhinos were killed for their highly-valued horns, many other wildlife species were slaughtered by hungry villagers for subsistence or commercial sale in order to make ends meet owing to the severe socio-economic environment that prevailed in the country (Goddard, 21 May 2002). Johnny Rodriguez, an official of the Zimbabwe Conservation Task Force, bemoaned these developments: "Unless the government restores law and order, we can ultimately kiss Zimbabwe's wildlife goodbye" (Ibid: 1). In October 2003, Michael Wines, a *New York Times* journalist, also lamented:

> …Thousands of hungry families…have turned to poaching as their prime source of food and income. Private wildlife programs have been all but destroyed. Precise figures do not exist. But by estimates from several conservationists, former landowners and opposition politicians, as many as two-thirds of the animals on Zimbabwe's game farms and wildlife conservancies have been wiped out (Wines, 25 October 2003: 1).

In late October 2003, there were reports that 40% of the big-game animals had been poached or unlawfully hunted down countrywide. Some local conservationists, however, stated that hunters mainly targeted impalas for food and killed most of them using snares (Wines, 25 October 2003). During the three-month period stretching from August to October 2003, the anti-poaching units of Born Free, a conservation organisation operating in Zimbabwe, found more than 1 400 wire snares in the Gwayi Valley Conservancy (Ibid). By June 2006, Gourlays Ranch in Matebeleland had been emptied of its 6 000 animals, 50 of which were the endangered black rhinos that were probably killed by poachers for their horns (SOS Rhino, 7 June 2006). This pitiful scenario was aptly captured by Roberts (2009: 1):

A country that is battling with starvation, cholera and 90% unemployment now faces an extra challenge. Zimbabwe's starving millions are targeting wildlife...as a source of food and income. There have always been poachers who have no qualms about killing elephants and rhinos for their tusks, mainly for the Chinese market, where they are bought for their supposed aphrodisiac and medicinal powers. But now, the anti-poaching units who patrol hundreds of square miles of Zimbabwe's game parks are reporting that hungry locals are targeting the animals for their meat. The hungry are chasing and killing all the animals - elephant, zebra, giraffe... The people lay their traps on the paths that lead to the animals' watering holes...The trees and bushes are festooned with crude loops of wire torn from telephone lines and fashioned into cruel snares which catch and cripple the animal...

Even those wild animals that were not hunted down for meat since historical times became vulnerable to hunger-stricken sections of the population. In September 2007, for example, the police restrained a group of hungry villagers from slaughtering and eating a giraffe that had strayed into the outskirts of Harare. The large giraffe was believed to have strayed into the Seke District on the southern margins of Harare from nearby farms. Wildlife authorities rescued the giraffe after the police had restrained the villagers from "killing it for the pot" (*News24 Archives*, 22 September 2007: 1).

The scrounging for rodents in order to survive also attests to the magnitude of the Zimbabwean crisis. While many African societies supplemented their diets with rodents such as mice since the pre-colonial period, some Zimbabwean villagers came to entirely depend on them for food in an effort to surmount the challenge of hunger. In September 2002, for example, there were reports of some hungry communities surviving on mice in many rural areas of Zimbabwe (Refugees International, 4 September 2002).

On 12 December 2006, Machivenyika Mapuranga, Zimbabwe's ambassador to the United States, argued that there was nothing unusual about feeding on rodents since mice in particular were a delicacy in the diet of most indigenous Zimbabweans since the pre-colonial period. He said, "The eating of the field mice - Zimbabweans do that. It is a delicacy. It is misleading to portray the eating of field mice as an act of desperation. It is not" (Koinange, 19 December 2006: 1). These sentiments should be viewed in the context of desperate damage-control mechanisms and political grandstanding by an official from the ruling ZANU-PF party to downplay the magnitude of a horrendous food crisis and absolve the government of any blame for instigating and failing to handle it. Joram Nyathi (22 January 2007: 1), a *Zimbabwe Independent* journalist, accurately captured the situation by stating that, in Zimbabwe, "mice (are) no delicacy but (a) saucy sign of poverty."

In September 2007, mice hunters were blamed for the fire that destroyed an old movie set of a mythical African town known as Tongala that had been set up by Western filmmakers near Harare (*News24 Archives*, 22 September 2007). The mythical town had been constructed for the movie *King Solomon's Mines* which featured American stars such as Sharon Stone and Richard Chamberlain (Ibid). Similarly, by November 2008, in the Doma Communal Lands, many pastures had been burned by villagers "to scare rabbits and rodents into traps" (*Daily Mail*, 20 November 2008: 1).

Rats also became part of the starvation diet of some villagers as conditions of food insecurity worsened in many parts of Zimbabwe. This marked a drastic shift in the consumption dynamics of some rural people given that most African societies in present-day Zimbabwe did not eat rats since the pre-colonial period (Jonasi, Interview: 2017; Vengesai, Interview: 2017; Yeukai, Interview: 2017). In December 2006, for example, Elizabeth, a mother of six from the

Midlands Province, blamed the government for the horrendous food crisis which forced most villagers to feed on rats:

> Look what we have been reduced to eating? How can my children eat rats in a country that used to export food? I cannot remember the last time I ate real food. We cannot afford anything anymore. We are now just eating these rats to survive. This is a tragedy (Koinange, 19 December 2006: 1).

For some hungry and impoverished Zimbabweans, the foraging of certain species of insects became a vital livelihood pursuit. It should be noted, however, that entomophagy, the practice of eating insects by human beings (Dzerefos, 2014), is not peculiar to Zimbabwe. In 2008, for example, at least 1 400 insect species were recorded as human food worldwide (Durst and Shono, 2010). While insects are basically dietary supplements in many societies worldwide, some Zimbabwean rural communities subsisted on them during the period 2000-2008 as the food security situation deteriorated rapidly. It was not out of choice that a wide variety of insects also became a regular constituent of the starvation diet of many rural Zimbabwean families. For many villagers during the year 2008, "crickets, cicadas and beetles also can make a meal" (*Associated Press*, 19 November 2008: 1; *Daily Mail*, 20 November 2008: 1). As Dugger (22 December 2008: 1) observed at Jirira Village near Harare in December 2008: "Destitute villagers pull the shells off crickets, then toss what is left into a hot pan."

Given the high levels of unemployment and poverty that prevailed in the country, some villagers also sold quantities of insects in order to generate income to meet other basic needs. In some cases, insects were bartered in exchange of basic commodities that were scarce in most shops as a result of investor flight, deindustrialisation and industrial closures. In the Masvingo Province, particularly in Bikita District, for example, many villagers earned livelihoods by selling small edible stinkbugs locally known as *harurwa* (*Enconsternum delegorguei*). Many women and children sold the bugs at major business centres such as Nyika Growth Point, Maregere Business Centre, Mupamawonde Business Centre, Chikuku Business Centre, Bikita

Business Centre, Makuvaza Business Centre, Zaka Growth Point and Gutu Growth Point (Mawere, 2014). In 2003, in the Bikita District, the Norumedzo community, comprising 30 villages, got between Z$20 million and Z$26 million (US$3770 to US$4900) annually from selling the bugs with each household average amounting to an estimated Z$1 million (US$190) per annum (Mapendembe, 2004).

Some wretched but enterprising Zimbabweans also ventured into the wilderness where they harvested Mopani/Mopane worms (*madora/mashonja* in Shona, *amacimbi* in Ndebele and *mahonja* in Kalanga) which they either sold to generate income or bartered in exchange of critically scarce commodities such as the staple maize. The Mopane worm is the large caterpillar of the *Gonimbrasia belina* species, commonly known as the Emperor moth (Banda and Zimela, 22 March 2012; *Xinhua News*, 2 May 2017). The worms are named after the Mopane/Mopani tree (*Colophospermum mopane*) whose leaves they feed on after hatching in summer (Dyke, 4 May 2008; Mhlanga, 13 August 2016; *Xinhua News*, 2 May 2017). The Mopane tree grows in hot, dry, low-lying areas whose altitude ranges between 200 metres and 1 150 metres above sea level (Dyke, 4 May 2008). In Zimbabwe, the worms are mainly found in the southern regions where Mopane trees abound (*Xinhua News*, 2 May 2017). In early May 2008, villagers in the Mangwe area of Matabeleland North Province were reportedly earning a living by selling Mopane worms which are considered a delicacy in the region (Dyke, 4 May 2008).

Quelea birds, known scientifically as *Quelea lathamii* (Mpala *et al* 2015), also became an important source of income for some Zimbabweans, particularly in the Hwange District of Matabeleland North Province and in the Lowveld areas of Manicaland Province. In the Manicaland Province, quelea birds are popularly known as *ngozha* or 'little chickens' and are mostly found in the Lowveld, especially in areas of the Chimanimani and Chipinge Districts (Masau, 21 July 2012; Saunyama, 16 November 2013). The little birds fly in large groups, often in millions (Masau, 21 July 2012), and feed on small grains such as sorghum, millet and wheat (Saunyama, 16 November 2013). During the evening, villagers trapped the birds in nearby bushes using thick glue, known as *urimbo* in the Shona language, and wide nets. In some cases villagers who used nets caught more than 500 birds in a single swoop. After harvesting, the birds are deep-fried and then spiced with chili, salt and other ingredients (Masau, 21 July 2012; Saunyama, 16 November 2013). As socio-economic challenges besieged the country, many people from the drought-stricken Lowveld areas of Manicaland Province such as Tanganda, Chakohwa, Wengezi and Birchenough Bridge, survived through selling quelea birds at local business centres and in various parts of the country (Masau, 21 July 2012; Saunyama, 16 November 2013). Similarly, in the Hwange District of Matabeleland North Province, many villagers also depended on quelea birds for sustenance (Mpala, Sibanda, Dlamini and Sibanda, 2015). These pursuits exemplify James Scott's (1985) 'weapons of the poor' analysis in which the marginalised sections of societies, including the peasants, often improvise strategies of survival that may depart from established or conventional practices and sometimes benignly defy or challenge the dominant authority or discourses.

Conclusion

This chapter has shown how, between 2000 and 2008, Zimbabwe's socio-economic crisis, which can largely be blamed on the government's shortcomings, but aggravated by ecological calamities, precipitated drastic shifts in the consumption dynamics of many rural people. The farm invasions from the year 2000 triggered a multiplicity of calamitous developments that ruptured Zimbabwe's socio-economic landscape resulting in many citizens experiencing severe food shortages. The ravaging impact of the ecological disasters could have been mitigated by the government through effective food security programmes. Instead, the food relief provisions which the government sometimes instituted were rendered futile by undercapitalisation, corruption, politicisation and outright negligence, among other ills. This left many rural Zimbabweans dependent on donor agencies, most of who were always overwhelmed by the ever-increasing levels of hunger and poverty in the country.

The debilitating socio-economic meltdown, epitomised by chronic hunger and abject poverty, severely compromised the consumption patterns and dietary options of many marginalised sections of the population. The new consumer regime, which was largely sustained through hunting and gathering, was necessitated by the agency of many impoverished Zimbabweans to urgently address challenges of food insecurity, particularly the scarcity of the staple maize and other basic consumer needs, unpredictability of food sources, and inconsistencies in dietary options, among other things. Given these life-threatening challenges as well as the government's lack of capacity, competence and commitment to effectively address them, foraging from the wilderness became a realistic alternative to securing livelihoods for many wretched Zimbabweans.

This chapter does not in any way downplay the importance of wild foods to human life since pre-colonial times. It acknowledges that indeed, the contribution of wildlife species to the food, health and nutritional security of human beings in history cannot be doubted. As far as the daily food needs of most African societies were concerned, the chapter has noted that wild foods largely served the purpose of supplementing the staple which initially comprised sorghum and millet, and later, maize. Between 2000 and 2008, however, most rural Zimbabweans experienced unprecedented socio-economic hardships, characterised by severe food shortages, which forced them to depend almost entirely on wild foods that, historically, had not been their staple.

The rising dependence on wild foods only serves to manifest the resilience and innovation on the part of impoverished Zimbabwean rural communities to salvage sustenance in times of debilitating crises. They had very limited options of survival, given the rugged socio-economic terrain that was brought about by the ruling ZANU-PF's prioritisation of political survival at the expense of the economy and the ravages of unpredictable climatic conditions. Their quest to produce food was often frustrated by natural disasters, coupled with the government's inability and incapacitation to provide irrigation equipment and subsidised farming inputs, among other things. Despite subsisting almost entirely on hunting and gathering for food, some enterprising Zimbabweans generated income from selling various animal and plant species obtained from the wilderness, thus demonstrating their determination to utilise the natural biophysical environment in order to survive against the odds.

It should be noted, however, that scavenging from the wilderness, a livelihood option that became prevalent during the period 2000-2008, is not environmentally sustainable because most wildlife species such as animals, fish and vegetation were rapidly depleted. Thus, in an attempt to avert hunger, foraging pursuits generated an environmental catastrophe. In addition to the ravages of persistent droughts, wildlife resources became scarcer and fiercely contested as too many people and even wild animals converged on them. Another notable dimension of the multi-layered Zimbabwean crisis, therefore, was the vicious struggle between and among human beings and wild animals over increasingly shrinking resources. The fierce contestations between human beings and wild animals became inevitable given that the two parties now had a lot in common in terms of sources of food which they accessed through foraging, limited dietary options, both of which they sought to outcompete each other in order to survive, and, consequently, similar consumption patterns and behaviour which were largely opportunistic and predatory.

References

Amnesty International (October 2004). *Zimbabwe: power and hunger - Violations of the right to food*, London: Amnesty International.

Associated Press (19 November 2008). 'Hungry Zimbabwe: If you rest, you starve,' Available at: http://www.nbcnews.com/id, Accessed 19 May 2017.

Bailey, R. and Aunger, R. (1989). 'Net hunters versus archers: Variation in women's subsistence strategies in the Ituri forest,' in: *Human Ecology*, Volume 17, pp.273–297.

Bakwa, P. (10 December 2008). 'Failing Zimbabwe: Rural roundup,' Available at: http://news.bbc.co.uk/2/hi/africa/7771184.stm, Accessed 16 May 2017.

Banda, I. and Zimela, Z. (22 March 2012). 'Zimbabwe: Mopani worms disappearing from rural diets,' Available at: http://www.ipsnews.net, Accessed 21 May 2017.

Bara, E. (2 May 2002). 'Zimbabwe's famished fields,' Available at: http://news.bbc.co.uk/2/hi/africa/1964548.stm, Accessed 15 May 2017.

Bond, P. and Manyanya, S. (2002). *Zimbabwe's plunge: Exhausted nationalism, neo-liberalism and the search for social justice,* Trenton: Africa World Press.

Campbell, B.M. (1987). 'The use of wild fruits in Zimbabwe,' in: *Economic Botany,* Volume 41, Number 3, pp.375-385.

Chigwedere, A.S. (1980). *From Mutapa to Rhodes, 1000-1890 AD,* London: Macmillan.

Chikwanha, T. (4 May 2014). 'Land seizures leave farm workers destitute,' Available at: www.dailynews.co.zw, Accessed 2 June 2015.

Chiriga, E. (16 April 2011). 'Unemployment still high in Zimbabwe,' in: *The Daily News,* Harare: Zimbabwe.

Church World Service (24 July 2002). 'Zimbabwe drought,' Available at: www.churchworldservice.org, Accessed 16 May 2015.

Clarke, J.M. (1983). 'A socio-ecological study of a rural community in the northern Sebungwe,' Master of Science thesis, Harare: University of Zimbabwe.

Daily Mail (20 November 2008). 'The desperate plight of scavenging, starving families as Zimbabwe self-destructs,' Available at: http://www.dailymail.co.uk/news/article-1087911, Accessed 12 May 2017.

Daily News (9 September 2002). 'Villagers scrounge for wild fruits, roots as hunger bites,' Available at: http://www.africafiles.org/article.asp?ID=562, Accessed 15 May 2017.

Daily News (11 September 2002). 'Hunger takes toll in Zimbabwe's rural schools,' Harare: Zimbabwe, Available at: http://www.africafiles.org/article.asp?ID=562, Accessed 15 May 2017.

*Daudet, A. (2012). *Wild foods and their potential for undernutrition prevention,* Paris: Action Contre la Faim (ACF).

Dixon, R. (3 December 2008). 'Hunting and gathering- and starving in rural Zimbabwe,' Available at: http://articles.latimes.com, Accessed 15 March 2017.

Dube, L. (31 October 2008). 'Villagers resort to wild fruits as food shortages worsen,' in: *The Zimbabwe Independent*, Harare: Zimbabwe, Available at: https://www.theindependent.co.zw, Accessed 15 May 2017.

Dugger, C.W. (22 December 2008). 'In Zimbabwe, survival lies in scavenging,' in: *New York Times*, Available at: http://www.nytimes.com, Accessed 15 May 2017.

Duri, F. P. T. (2016). 'Defining the Zimbabwean crisis during the new millennium', in: F.P.T. Duri (ed.) *Resilience amid adversity: Informal coping mechanisms to the Zimbabwean crisis during the new millennium*, Gweru: Booklove Publishers, pp.22-49.

Duri, F.P.T. (2017). 'Development discourse and the legacies of pre-colonial Shona environmental jurisprudence: Pangolins and political opportunism in independent Zimbabwe,' in: M. Mawere (ed.) *Underdevelopment, development and the future of Africa*, Bamenda: Langaa Research and Publishing Common Initiative Group, pp.435-460.

Durst, P.B. and Shono, K. (2010). 'Edible forest insects: Exploring new horizons and traditional practices', in P.B. Durst, D.V. Johnson, R.N. Leslie and K. Shono (eds.) *Forest insects as food: Humans bite back: Proceedings of a workshop on Asia-Pacific resources and their potential for development, 19-21 February 2008*, Chiang Mai, Thailand, Bangkok: Food and Agriculture Organisation of the United Nations, pp.1-4.

Dzerefos, C.M. (2014). 'The life history, use and socio–economics of the edible stinkbug *encosternum delegorguei (hemiptera: tessaratomidae)*, in South Africa,' PhD thesis, Faculty of Science, University of the Witwatersrand, Johannesburg.

Financial Gazette (26 July- 1 August 2007). 'Price blitz devastates Zimbabwe's rural economy,' Harare: Zimbabwe.

Flanagan, J. (26 May 2002). 'Starving children scavenge for berries as famine sweeps Zimbabwe,' Available at: http://www.telegraph.co.uk/news/worldnews, Accessed 15 May 2017.

Goddard, J. (21 May 2002). 'Poachers wiping out wild animals in Zimbabwe,' in: *The Globe and Mail*, Available at: http://www.theglobeandmail.com/news/world, Accessed 21 May 2017.

Godwin, P. (August 2003). 'A land possessed,' in: *The National Geographic Magazine*, pp.100-114.

Gumpo, O. (20 August 2008). 'Hungry Zimbabweans forage to survive,' Available at: https://iwpr.net/global-voices, Accessed 19 May 2017.

Hammar, A. and Raftopoulos, B. (2003). 'Zimbabwe's unfinished business: Rethinking land, state and nation,' in: A. Hammar, B. Raftopoulos and S. Jensen (eds.) *Zimbabwe's unfinished business: Rethinking land, state and nation in the context of crisis*, Harare: Weaver Press, pp.1-47.

Human Rights Watch (22 January 2009). *Crisis without limits: Human rights and humanitarian consequences of political repression in Zimbabwe*, Available at: www.hrw.org/report, Accessed 16 May 2017.

International Monetary Fund (July 2003). *Zimbabwe: 2003 Article IV Consultation – Staff Report*, Washington: International Monetary Fund.

IRIN News (3 September 2008). 'Zimbabwe: Wild fruits instead of food aid,' Available at: http://reliefweb.int/report/zimbabwe, Accessed 15 May 2017.

IRIN News (29 October 2008). 'Zimbabwe: Survival recipe book,' Available at: http://reliefweb.int/report/zimbabwe, Accessed 16 May 2017.

Jonasi, N. (26 February 2017). Interview at Sherukuru Business Centre, Mutasa District, Zimbabwe.

Kent, S. (ed.) (2002). *Ethnicity, hunter-gatherers and the other: Association or assimilation in Africa*, Washington DC: Smithsonian Institution Press.

Koinange, J. (19 December 2006). 'Living off rats to survive,' Available at: http://edition.cnn.com/2006/WORLD/africa, Accessed 15 May 2017.

Kriel, M. (2 January 2009). 'Villagers in Binga, Zimbabwe, eat roots, berries, leaves and the bark of trees,' Available at:

http://www.digitaljournal.com/blog/1706, Accessed 13 May 2017.

Kusimba, S. B. (2005). 'What is a hunter-gatherer? Variation in the archaeological record of Eastern and Southern Africa,' in: *Journal of Archaeological Research*, Volume 13, Number 4, pp.337-366.

Kuvirimirwa, F. (7 October 2013). I want my pangolin back: Man tells cops, in: *The Herald*, Harare: Zimbabwe.

Laiton, C. (27 August 2014). 'Man jailed nine years for pangolin possession,' in: *The Newsday*, Harare: Zimbabwe.

Lee, R.B. (1979). *The Kung San*, Cambridge: Cambridge University Press.

Lee, R.B. and De Vore, I. (1968). 'Problems in the study of hunter-gatherers,' in: R.B. Lee and I. De Vore (eds.) *Man the hunter*, Chicago: Aldine, pp.3-12.

Lee, R.B. and Hitchcock, R.K. (2001). 'African hunter-gatherers: Survival, history, and the politics of identity,' in: *African Study Monographs*, Supplement 26, pp.257-280.

Madziyauswa, T. (2017). 'Fetishisation of knowledge: A case of patriotic history in Zimbabwe,' in: A. Nhemachena and M. Mawere (eds.) *Africa at the crossroads: Theorising fundamentalisms in the 21st century*, Bamenda: Langaa Research and Publishing Common Initiative Group, pp.199-221.

Mail and Guardian (29 January 2009). 'Zimbabwe's Unemployment skyrockets,' Available at: www.mg.co.za/index, Accessed 6 May 2015.

Manyena, B. Fordham, M. and Collins, A. (2008). 'Disaster resilience and children: Managing food security in Zimbabwe's Binga District,' in: *Children, Youth and Environments*, Volume 18, Number 1, pp.302-331.

Mapendembe, A. (2004). 'The role of non-timber forest products in forest conservation and rural livelihoods: The case of the edible stinkbug (*Encosternum delegorguei*) in Ward 15 of Bikita District, Zimbabwe,' Unpublished Master of Science thesis, University of Zimbabwe.

Maramba, G. (8 December 2015). 'Starving Zimbabwe villagers selling wild fruits for survival,' Available at: http://www.voazimbabwe.com, Accessed 15 May 2017.

Maroyi, A. (2013). 'Use of weeds as traditional vegetables in Shurugwi District, Zimbabwe,' in: *Journal of Ethnobiology and Ethnomedicine*, Volume 9, Number 60, pp.1-10.

Masau, P. (21 July 2012) 'Women sell "little chicken" for survival,' in: *The Standard*, Harare: Zimbabwe, Available at: www.thestandard.co,zw, Accessed 22 May 2017.

Matikiti, R. (2007). 'Environmental management: Karanga eco-theology in Charumbira Communal Lands,' in: *Swedish Missiological Themes*, Volume 95, Number 3, pp.217-228.

Mawere, M. (2011). *Moral degeneration in contemporary Zimbabwean business practices*, Bamenda: Langaa Research and Publishing Common Initiative Group.

Mawere, M. (2014). 'Forest insects, personhood and the environment: *Harurwa* (edible stinkbugs) and conservation in south-eastern Zimbabwe,' Unpublished PhD thesis, Faculty of Humanities, School of African and Gender Studies, Anthropology and Linguistics, Department of Social Anthropology, University of Cape Town.

Mawere, M. (2015). *Humans, other beings and the environment: Harurwa (edible stinkbugs) and environmental conservation in south-eastern Zimbabwe*, Cambridge: Cambridge Scholars Press.

Meredith, M. (2002). *Mugabe: Power and plunder in Zimbabwe*, New York: Public Affairs.

Mhlanga, L. (13 August 2016). 'Not just another can of worms,' in: *The Chronicle*, Bulawayo: Zimbabwe, Available at: www.chronicle.co.zw, Accessed 25 May 2017.

Morrison, K. and Junker, L. (2002). *Forager-traders in south and south-east Asia: Long-term histories*, Cambridge: Cambridge University Press.

Mpala, C. Sibanda, P. Dlamini, M. and Sibanda, B. (2015). 'Are quelea birds really a menace? Innovative use of indigenous knowledge systems in the harvesting and utilisation of quelea, *Quelea quelea lathamii,* in Hwange District of Matabeleland North Province,' in: *International Journal of Agricultural Sciences*, Volume 5, Number 3, pp.476-486.

Mushita, T.A. and Mpande, R.L. (2003). 'Linking food security, relief, rehabilitation and development by civil society institutions in

Southern Africa,' in: *Masvingo Workshop Report*, Germany: Diakonie Emergency Aid (DEA).

Ndlela, D. (26 July-1 August 2007). 'Last inflation data released in April,' in: *The Financial Gazette*, Harare: Zimbabwe.

New Zimbabwe (17 April 2015). 'Pangolin causes stir at Gweru courts,' Available at: http://www.newzimbabwe.com/news, Accessed 16 March 2016.

News24 Archives (22 September 2007). 'Giraffe "for the pot" saved,' Available at: http://www.news24.com/Africa/Zimbabwe, Accessed 8 June 2017.

Nhemachena, A. (2014). 'Knowledge, *chivanhu* and struggles for survival in conflict-torn Manicaland, Zimbabwe,' Unpublished D.Phil. Thesis, University of Cape Town.

Nsingo, E. (20 January 2009). 'Zimbabwe now a factory of poverty,' Available at: http://www.ipsnews.net, Accessed 16 May 2017.

Nyathi, J. (12 January 2007). 'Zimbabwe: Mice no delicacy but saucy sign of poverty,' in: *The Zimbabwe Independent*, Harare: Zimbabwe, Available at: http://allafrica.com/stories, Accessed 16 May 2017.

Organisation for Economic Cooperation and Development (OECD) (2004). *African economic outlook 2003-2004: Country studies: Zimbabwe*, Paris: OECD.

Poverty Reduction Forum Trust (2013). 'Study of poverty in Manicaland: The case of Mutare rural,' Research paper, Harare: Poverty Reduction Forum Trust.

Raftopoulos, B. (2003). 'The state in crisis: Authoritarian nationalism, selective citizenship and distortions of democracy in Zimbabwe,' in: A. Hammar, B. Raftopoulos and S. Jensen (eds.) *Zimbabwe's unfinished business: Rethinking land, state and nation in the context of crisis*, Harare: Weaver Press, pp.217-41.

Refugees International (4 September 2002). 'Zimbabwe: Survival strategies in the face of starvation,' Available at: http://reliefweb.int/report/zimbabwe, Accessed 15 May 2017.

Reuters Alert (20 March 2007). 'Zimbabwe says drought will worsen food shortages,' Available at: www.alertnet.org, Accessed 16 February 2017.

Richardson, C. J. (2005). 'The loss of property rights and the collapse of Zimbabwe,' in: *Cato Journal*, Volume 25, Number 3, pp.541-565.

Roberts, S. L. (15 April 2009). 'Massacre of the innocents: How starving families slaughter Zimbabwe's wild animals just to put food in their mouths,' Available at: http://www.dailymail.co.uk/news/article, Accessed 15 May 2017.

Ruhanya, P. (9 September 2002). 'Depoliticise food aid, Catholic bishops say,' in: *The Daily News*, Harare: Zimbabwe, Available at: http://www.africafiles.org/article.asp?ID=562, Accessed 15 May 2017.

Sachikonye, L. (2003). 'The situation of commercial farm workers after land reform in Zimbabwe,' Report prepared for the Farm Community Trust of Zimbabwe, Harare: Farm Community Trust of Zimbabwe.

Sadr, K. Smith, A. Plug, I. Orton, J. and Mutti, B. (2003). 'Herders and foragers on Kasteelberg: Interim report of excavations, 1999–2002,' in: *South African Archaeological Bulletin*, Volume 58, pp.27-32.

Saunyama, J. (16 November 2013). 'Quelea birds invade Christmas Pass,' in: *The Newsday*, Harare: Zimbabwe.

Schrimpf, B. and Feil, P. (2012). *Traditional food crisis coping mechanisms: A regional perspective from Southern Africa*, Stuttgart: Diakonisches Werk der EKD.

Scoones, I. Marongwe, N. Mavedzenge, B. Mahenehene, J. Marimbarimba, F. and Sukume, C. (2010). *Zimbabwe land reform programme: Myths and realities*, Woodbridge: James Currey.

Scott, J. C. (1985). *Weapons of the weak: Everyday forms of peasant resistance*, London: Yale University Press.

Shava, S. Donoghue, R. Kransky, M.E. and Zazu, C. (2009). 'Traditional food crops as a source of community resilience in Zimbabwe,' in: *International Journal of African Renaissance*, Volume 4, pp.31-48.

Sithole, D. (4 May 2008). 'Zimbabwe: Villagers earn a living selling *mopane* worms,' in: *The Zimbabwe Guardian*, London: United

Kingdom, Available at: http://allafrica.com/stories, Accessed 21 May 2017.

Solidarity Peace Trust (November 2004). *No war in Zimbabwe: An account of the exodus of a nation's people*, Johannesburg: Solidarity Peace Trust.

SMH (12 July 2002). 'Theft, prostitution on rise as hunger bites Zimbabwe,' Available at: www.smh.com.au, Accessed 19 May 2015.

SOS Rhino (7 June 2006). 'Hunger drives rural people to hunt wild animals,' Available at:
http://www.sosrhino.org/news/rhinonews060706a.php,
Accessed 19 May 2017.

Terrell, J. Hart, J.P. Cellinese, N. Curet, A. Denham, T. Kusimba, C. Kusimba, S.B. Latinis, K. Oka, R. Palka, J. Pohl, M. Pope, K. Williams, P.R. Haines, H. and Staller, J. (2003). 'Domesticated landscapes: The subsistence ecology of plant and animal domestication,' in: *Journal of Archaeological Method and Theory*, Volume 10, pp.323–368.

Thomson Reuters Foundation (13 July 2014). 'Zimbabwe crisis,' Available at: www.trust.org, Accessed 10 May 2015.

United Nations (11 September 2008). 'Southern Africa: Mozambique-Zimbabwe: The commodities life line,' Available at: www.allAfrica.com, Accessed 22 April 2017.

United States Government (2014). *CIA World Fact Book 2014*, Washington DC: Central Intelligence Agency Publications.

Vengesai, L. (27 February 2017). Interview at Watsomba Business Centre, Mutasa District, Zimbabwe.

Williams, D. (26 September 2008). 'Children in Zimbabwe who are being forced to eat rats to survive while Mugabe enjoys five-star hotel service,' Available at:
http://www.dailymail.co.uk/news/article, Accessed 15 May 2017.

Wines, M. (25 October 2003). 'Zimbabwe's woes are bringing grief to its wildlife, too,' in: *The New York Times*, Available at: http://archive.kubatana.net/html/archive/wild, Accessed 21 May 2017.

World Food Programme (April 2007). *Mobility, HIV/AIDS and livelihoods: An assessment of informal trade activities on the Mozambique-Zimbabwe border*, United Nations: World Food Programme Southern Africa in collaboration with FEWSNet and SIMA.

Xinhua News (2 May 2017). 'Feature: A worm that sustains many Zimbabwean families,' Available at: http://news.xinhuanet.com/english, Accessed 21 May 2017.

Yeukai, V. (26 February 2017). Interview at Sherukuru Business Centre, Mutasa District, Zimbabwe.

Zikhali, Z. (29 August 2016). 'Hungry villagers compete for wild fruit with baboons,' Available at: http://www.radiovop.com/index.php/national-news, Accessed 16 May 2017.

Zimbabwe Human Rights NGO Forum (2010). *The land reform and property rights in Zimbabwe, Volume 1*, Harare: Zimbabwe Human Rights NGO Forum.

Zimbabwe Situation (16 October 2008). 'War veterans block donation,' Available at: www.zimbabwesituation.com, Accessed 19 May 2017.

Zimbabwe Times (23 July 2008). 'Mozambique tightens screws on Zimbabwe,' Available at: www.thezimbabwetimes.com, Accessed 12 June 2015.

Zimbabwean (24 October 2008). 'Boy chokes to death on wild fruit nut as Zimbabwe hunger worsens,' Available at: http://thezimbabwean.co, Accessed 16 May 2017.

Zimbabwean on Sunday (18 May 2008). 'Inflation rockets to 355 000%: Prices double each week,' London: United Kingdom.

Chapter 5

Poverty, Conflict and Vulnerability in Africa

Takavafira Masarira Zhou

Introduction

This chapter examines the intricate and complex relationship between poverty and conflict, their subsequent ramifications on African states and communities. While acknowledging that many of today's conflicts and cases of poverty are rooted in the colonial era, the thrust of this chapter is on the post-colonial period. Admittedly, the correlation between poverty and conflict is captured in the familiar mantra that there can be no security without development, and no development without security. Yet sound as this may be, the links between poverty and conflict are somewhat complex and difficult to precisely pin down. It is, however, my argument that poverty is as much a cause of conflict as it is a consequence of conflict. The problem of poverty is viewed in a multi-dimensional manner, transcending economics to social, political and cultural issues. Poverty causes conflict when grievances are not handled properly, with the poor people becoming restive, staging an uprising, questioning government altogether and joining rebel groups. On the other hand, conflict brings poverty in as much as it brings destruction, violence, and hatred. As such, poor societies are at risk of falling into no-exit cycles of conflict in which ineffective governance, societal warfare, humanitarian crises, and the lack of development perpetually chase one another. Brief case studies from Angola, Sierra Leone, Somalia, Central Africa Republic and Libya are used to reflect the two way association in which poverty leads to conflict and poverty is a product of conflict. While acknowledging the challenge of a one-size fits all conflicts, the chapter argues that a clear comprehension of the interaction and synergies of conflict and poverty is necessary in order to provide possible remedies. To this effect, the chapter proffers not only peace, good leadership, conflict management and prevention, but also good governance, judicious management of resources, poverty alleviation and reduction of inequality, as pre-requisites for sustainable development in Africa.

While violent conflict is not confined to the Global South, a disproportionate number of conflicts take place in poor countries. Of the nineteen countries ranking lowest on the UNDP Human Development Index (2017) - Ivory Coast, Djibouti, Gambia, Ethiopia, Mali, Democratic Republic of Congo (DRC), Liberia, Guinea-Bissau, Eritrea, Sierra Leone, Mozambique, South Sudan, Guinea, Burundi, Burkina Faso, Somalia, Chad, Niger and Central African Republic – all are from Africa and none of these countries has escaped civil conflict since independence. Many other African countries – such as Angola, Libya, Sudan, Uganda, Rwanda, Lesotho, Zimbabwe and others, have also been experiencing civil conflict, wide spread poverty and poor economic growth while others where growth has been poor and poverty increasing also face the risk of civil conflicts. As such, more than half of the countries in Africa are affected by internal and regional conflicts. The poor people increasingly live in the contexts of insecurity. There has been lack of clarity in academic circles on the links between poverty, conflict and development. Traditionally, poverty has been restricted to development studies, anthropology and economics. Conflict has been a major concern of conflict and peace studies, international relations and political science. However, the various academic disciplines have recently begun to converge (under the rubric of multi-disciplinary approach) around cutting-edge issues of poverty and conflict. There has been limited historical research which examines the nature of relationship between poverty and conflict. It is within this framework that this chapter examines the nature of the relationship between poverty and conflict as well as effects of such a conjunction. Poverty and conflict are treated as inseparable spheres of historical inquiry. Conversely, development in Africa needs to be attuned to the links between the two in order to respond to the challenges of growing conflict and chronic poverty. Political economists (Collier 2006; Collier and Hoeffler 2001) argue that greed (opportunities for predatory accumulation), rather than grievance (generated by poverty and social exclusion) tends to cause violent conflict. Rather than framing the 'greed-grievance' debate in 'either-or' terms, this chapter unravels the interaction and synergies between the two. An attempt is also made to use a human needs theory in which poverty is viewed as a result of basic human needs, which lead to reactions that result in conflict.

Conceptions of poverty and conflict

Admittedly, poverty is simply a condition of lack, whereby people do not have access to basic necessities of life. It is characterised by inadequate shelter, that is, improperly constructed, overcrowded, and lacking in basic services such as water and sanitation, as well as homelessness. Ramlogan (2004: 140) asserts that "poverty, in its most extreme form, is the condition that exists when people lack the means to fulfil basic human needs, adequate and nutritious food, clothing, housing, clean water, and health services." Similarly, Narayan *et.al* (2000: 4-5) define poverty as multidimensional deprivation that "includes hunger, illiteracy, illness and poor health, powerlessness, voicelessness, insecurity, humiliation, and lack of access to basic infrastructure." Poverty, therefore, undermines people's liberty to make decision over and shape their own lives; it robs them of the chance to decide on matters of basic importance to them. In essence, it is the lack of power, choice and lack of material resources that it is often said, beggars have no choice, poverty makes one a beggar. Power, opportunities and security, and the lack of them, are closely linked. As propounded by Restrepo *et.al.* (2008), empowerment and opportunities can reduce insecurity while lack of security reduces the ability to make use of opportunities.

Different conceptualisation of poverty implies the use of different indicators for measurement; which may lead to the classification of different individuals and groups as poor and require different policy solutions for poverty reduction. Poverty can be understood from four basic dimensions: the monetary approach, the capabilities approach, social exclusion and the participatory approach. Shukla (2008: 27) posits that poverty is "the state of one who lacks a usual or socially acceptable amount of money or material possessions." Whatever definition one uses, scholars and lay persons alike normally believe that the effects of poverty are harmful to both individuals and society. The father of modern economics, Adam Smith (1776), saw in impoverishment not just a lack of access to the basic human needs to maintain a decent life, but also a social handicap. Social exclusion, or marginalisation, thus becomes a key aspect to get a real grasp of what poverty is. As such, poverty is about being an active member of society taking part in social, economic and cultural life of your country. One of the renowned researchers on the topic, Sen (1982), has given a more appealing meaning of poverty that completes Adam Smith's approach. In the broadest sense, it means survival but also contribution and participation to social daily activities. In this context, the identification of poor people in Africa first requires a determination of what constitutes basic needs. Arguably, as much as poverty is multi-dimensional it is more often than not now associated with lack of economic development, immiseration, marginalisation and diseases. Therefore, thinking about what poverty means nowadays is becoming intimately linked to pathways to help poorer countries to develop their economy so as to uplift the livelihoods of their respective people.

Goodhand and Hulme (1999) posit that conflict is a struggle between individuals or collectives over value or claims to status, power and scarce resources in which the aims of the conflicting parties are to asset their values or claims over those of others. Conflict in this chapter, is viewed as any violent activity that is capable of disrupting peace, development and stability in any country or community. As propounded by Justino (2006: 1), "violent conflict is a multi-dimensional phenomenon, covering a range of intensities of violence from riots to war." In this chapter, my focus is on militarised violence, although it is recognized that distinctions between war, predatory violence and crime are becoming increasingly blurred. Conflict management or resolution is not about preventing conflict but about supporting institutions which are able to manage conflict in an inclusive and nonviolent manner. This requires sound leadership, which is lacking in most conflict prone areas. Aigbe (2014: 8) defines conflict generally as "an interface among interdependent people who recognise contrary goals and who expect interference from the other party if they attempt to achieve their goal." Conflict could also be viewed as a triangle with structure, attitudes, and behaviour as its vertices. Within this framework, structure refers to the conflict situation, the parties, and the conflict of interest among them. According to Galtung (1996), conflict arises where the parties come to have conflict of interest, which is often referred to as incompatible interests, values or goals. Galtung uses the term attitudes to refer to the propensity for the parties to see conflict from their own point of view, to identify with own side, and to diminish the concerns of others. Behaviour entails gestures and communications, which can convey either aggressive or provocative intent. Admittedly, when a conflict turns into open fighting with at least 25 clash related deaths per year, then it is classified as armed conflict. These are conflicts that exist between governments (inter-state) or between governments and armed groups within states or between opposing armed groups (intra-state).

Collier (2000) and Rasheed (2003) argue that intra-state conflict is the current foremost form of conflict globally and Africa in particular. The political economy of conflict has also emerged to illuminate essentially 'complex political emergency' or hybrid conflicts that combine transnational and internal characteristics. Duffield (2000) and Reno (2000) link the spread of 'complex political emergency' to the related process of the declining power of the nation state and the intensification of transnational commerce. The end of Cold War era and the impacts of globalisation have led, particularly in the South, to a decline in the competence and capacity of the nation state. Duffied (2000) argues that the South has entered an era of weak states often with multiple and overlapping centres of authority. Arguably, as much as warlords in Africa may act locally, they think globally. The value of political economy perspectives is that they highlight that conflict may serve important functions and confer benefits on certain groups and individuals, though causing poverty and misery to the common people. Clausewitz (1832: 87) viewed traditional nation-state war as "the continuation of politics by other means." Similarly, Keen (1998: 7) views internal wars as "the continuation of economics by other means."

The conflating causes of conflict and poverty

As reflected in the preceding section, conflict and poverty are different phenomena which plague many societies in Africa and beyond. The impact of one on the other has been the subject of much research and debate alike. It is imperative to address the correlation between conflict and poverty and vice versa in order to show their impact on African societies and communities. The correlation between poverty and conflict is complex with some scholars arguing that conflict causes poverty, while others argue that it is poverty that causes conflict. It is, however, my argument in this chapter that poverty is both a cause and consequence of conflict. As such, the nexus is two way: poverty leads to conflict as conflict leads to poverty as reflected below.

How conflict causes poverty?

There is general consensus among scholars that conflict causes poverty (Abdullah 1997, Ahmed 2014, and Aigbe 2014). Admittedly, this is not a new phenomenon as images of famine, pestilence, death and war riding together has been invoked in times of crisis through the ages. There are direct and indirect costs that emanate from conflict. The direct effects that include battlefields deaths, disablement and displacement have long term effects on societies. As Goodhand (2000: 13) argues, "chronic poverty is likely to increase due to higher dependency ratios caused by an increased proportion of the old, women and disabled in the population." In several wars in Africa, many more people have died as a result of lack of basic medical services, damage to rural life, transport and collapse of the state, than from direct battlefield. Indeed, the cost of conflict in terms of human and property loss, and the damage done to social infrastructure are enormous, for instance, the human cost of conflict in DRC from the 1990s to the 21st century was between 4 to 5.4 million lives (Zhou, 2017). Collier (2007) postulates that civil war tends to reduce growth by around 2.3% per year, so the typical seven-year war leaves a country around 15% poorer than it would have been without occurrence of war. The World Bank (2007) estimates that countries that have endured a war take an average of 11.1 years to regain pre-conflict per capita income levels. Justino and Verwimp (2006), Hoeffler and Reynal-Querol (2003) posit that national income dwindle and poverty deepens during period of conflicts such as civil war. By employing household panel data, Justino and Verwimp's (2006) study reveals that about 20% of Rwandan population stepped into poverty following the Rwandan genocide in 1994, and around 26% of the sample entered into extreme poverty. Arguably, that conflict impacts on poverty in any economy is widely and generally accepted, both during and after conflict situations, and the negative consequence on development is evident.

There are other works that have contributed greatly to a better comprehension of how conflict affects politics, economies and societies. Studies that focus on macro-level economics include, among others, Duffield (2000), Collier (2000, 2006), Reno (2000), Ross (2004) and Ikejiaku (2012). Those whose thrust is on micro-level entitlements, vulnerability and coping strategies include, *inter-alia*, Wanyande (1997), Keen (1998), Richards (1996) and Ahmed (2014). These works reflect that the impacts of wars vary according to the nature, duration, phase of the conflict, and the background economic and social conditions. However, chronic internal wars are likely to produce chronic poverty. This particularly applies to collapsed states, war lord type conflicts (like Somalia since the early 1990s, Sierra Leone in the years 1991-2000, Liberia in the years 1989-1996, Libya since 1911, and South Sudan since 1912) where the purpose of war was/is to make money for the elite group and the combatants ensured/ensure that it lasted/last long enough in order to acquire more money. It is the conviction of Gurr *et.al.* (2001: 13) that "poor societies are at risk of falling into no-exit cycles of conflict in which ineffective governance, societal warfare, humanitarian crises, and the lack of development perpetually chase one another." Above all, as many of today's wars in Africa are regionalised, the costs are often widely spread with neighbouring countries suffering from the spill over effects. The conflict in Somalia has effects in East Africa particularly in Kenya and Ethiopia; while conflict in eastern DRC has had effects in Rwanda and Uganda. Conflict in Libya has effects in North Africa, while conflict in Central Africa Republic has effects on DRC and Cameroon (News Day, 25 July 2017). Conflict in South Sudan is no exception as it has effects in Ethiopia and elsewhere.

In light of the above discussion Goodhand's (2001) assertion that in Mozambique war was the 'mid wife' for wide social change is untenable. The claim that war has contributed to the emergence of a thriving local economy is a tissue of misrepresentation as the so-called 'barefoot entrepreneurs' are a testimony to the poverty and misery still inherent in Mozambique. Above, all conflict in Mozambique in the 21st century has continued to militate against peace, security and development concerns in Mozambique. Rather than contributing to the emergence of moral economies, conflicts in Africa have contributed to predatory economies. Arguably, a sole focus on destruction, poverty and people as victims, to a large extent, provides a true reading of the effects of conflict in Africa. As such, the political, economic and social dimensions of conflict in Africa lead to poverty. It is, therefore, imperative to link poverty and conflict.

Poverty causes conflict

While there is general consensus among scholars that conflict causes poverty, the premise that poverty causes conflict is debatable. Modern conflicts are intricate phenomena that usually lug short term and long term factors into play, including a sudden economic slowdown in the face of rising expectations, external shocks and state crises. Debate is raging over whether poverty is a permissive or casual factor; a structural cause, a trigger or an accelerator of violent conflict. As much as I acknowledge that conflicts are products of complex set of factors or events and mutate over time, it is my argument that poverty is an important factor among the multi-causal factors behind conflict. Indeed, poverty and underdevelopment is the tap-root of conflict in different parts of Africa, including the violence in DRC, CAR, Somalia, Sudan and South Sudan. At any rate, poverty is multi-dimensional and goes beyond economics to include social, political, and cultural issues. Fundamentally, uneven development processes lead to inequality, exclusion and poverty which generate growing grievances, particularly when poverty coincides with ethnicity, religion, language or regional boundaries. These underlying grievances may detonate into open conflict when triggered by external shocks or mobilised by conflict entrepreneurs. Much as poverty per se may cause conflict, it is noteworthy that extreme horizontal inequalities are a source of grievance which is used by leaders to mobilise followers and legitimate violent action.

An analysis of the conflict-grievance nexus needs to be based on a careful reading of history. Many of today's conflicts are rooted in colonial era and post-colonial development strategies, which led to the marginalisation of the rural and urban poor. Goodhand (2001) traces the roots of the 1994 Rwanda crisis back to the failed developmental policies pursued in previous decades. Zhou (2017) has shown that in countries which have high value resources, for instance oil and minerals as in the case of Nigeria and DRC respectively, inequitable resource extraction and distribution and the local environmental 'terrorism' have led to growing tension. As such, environmental degradation and resource scarcity, while perhaps not the crux of conflict may become a significant aggravator or trigger for violence. The link between poverty and conflict, and the impact on development in Africa has been captured by Austin (1999) who posits that Africa, particularly Sub-Saharan Africa is an all too appropriate region in which to consider the relationship between poverty and conflict because, besides being the poorest region of the world in terms of average incomes in the 1980s and 90s, it has been the most plagued by civil strife. Austin further notes that the campaigns against colonial or white-minority regimes are over but the region has recently been characterised by many examples of other forms of civil strife because of poverty.

A considerable number of scholars have linked poverty and inequality in many African countries to political violence. In Kenya for example, where Kikuyu benefited from the colonial policies, Kimenyi and Ndung'u (2002) argue that poverty, struggles over increasing land rights and limited business credit programs after independence, caused antagonism and violent conflict against the Kikuyu from other poorer communities, leading to their expulsion from Masai-land immediately after independence. Humphreys and

Habaye (2003) asserts that poverty and inequality were part of cardinal factor in the Casamance conflict in Senegal. It is Isichei's (1987: 194-208) conviction that recession in Nigeria in the late 1970s caused poverty and, unemployment arising from poverty doubled to more than 20 percent before the Maitatsine rising started. Hungry, unemployed and poor Nigerian youths were extensively used in this conflict. It is within this context of poverty and misery that Isichei (1987: 194) has called the Maitatsine rising, "a revolt of the disinherited". Weinstein and Francisco (2003) have shown how rapid deterioration of economic conditions in Mozambique contributed to poverty during independence, and led to the civil conflict. In Sierra Leone, a chronic shortage of employment opportunities in the period 1991-2000 was matched by a contraction in educational opportunities and in these circumstances many youths turned to rebellion as a kind of 'short cut' to wealth as well as status (Keen, 1998; 2005).Similarly, Copson (1994) contends that when guerrillas join a rebel group, they may obtain food and clothing, as well as opportunities for identity, recognition, advancement and accesses to some facilities that are normally unavailable to them in urban slums and in farming communities common in most poor African society. Conversely, the participants in many of Africa's violent demonstrations and, some wars in recent years have been stimulated by the inherent poverty, inequality and underdevelopment in their respective communities or countries.

More (2000) posits that there is a close link between bad governance and poverty. Politically underdeveloped states are too independent of their citizens. Not only are they able to raise revenues through 'unearned income such as mineral resources or foreign aid but they also have few incentives to provide public goods for their citizens. At any rate, rulers of 'shadow states'(failing states) use patronage and clientelism as instruments of political control and in fact seek to make life less secure and more materially impoverished for subjects. As Reno (2000: 4) puts it:

> ...a shadow state ruler will minimise his provision of public goods
> to a population. Removing public goods, like security or economic
> stability that are otherwise enjoyed by all, irrespective of their economic

or political station, is done to encourage individuals to seek the ruler's personal favour to secure exemption from these conditions.

Although not all African states are shadow states, in many parts of Africa large numbers of people are excluded from the benefits of development, in part, as a result of conscious state policies. A case in point is the withholding of food assistance to people from Matabeleland and Chipinge in the 1980s by the government of Zimbabwe in order to starve the respective people into 'obedience' (Zhou and Makahamadze, 2012). Similarly in South Sudan, the movement and flow of humanitarian aid continues to be co-opted by parties to the conflict and appropriated in the interests of the military objectives. The South Sudan National Security Service has repeatedly blocked the delivery of humanitarian supplies to Kajo Keji in Central Equatorial state, thereby, denying potentially lifesaving assistance to a population that it considers supports the opposition (News Day, 10 August 2017).The nexus between remote rural areas, poverty and conflict deserves further examination. It is noteworthy that many conflicts in developing countries originate from and are fought out in the border regions that have historically suffered from collapse of social contract and consequent marginality, limited voice and hard core poverty. Conflicts in eastern Democratic Republic of Congo in the period 1996-2017 have clearly been linked to differential development and patterns of exclusion particularly of the areas bordering Rwanda and Uganda (Zhou, 2017). Historically, such border areas have had an ambiguous relationship with the state and an attraction for potential insurgents. Conflict entrepreneurs have been able to mobilise around a discourse of grievance. Above all, the weak presence of the state in such remote areas has made it easier for insurgents to mobilize and establish launch pads for acts of destabilisation.

It is noteworthy that a long term crisis of underdevelopment, of economic and social exclusion, may be aggravated by short term shocks. Keen (1998) argues that poverty and poor social services can fuel conflict 'from below', just as it feeds into 'top down' violence. Cederman *et.al.* (2013) argue that in countries endowed with resources but with high poverty levels, grievances are exacerbated by inequalities, unemployment, poor resource access and labour migration, among many other reasons. Although stressing an economic determinism over grievance related causes of war, Collier and Hoeffler (2001: 2) argue that "rebellion occurs when grievances are sufficiently acute that people want to engage in violent protest." Stewart (2010: 7) contends that much as both vertical and horizontal inequalities may lead to war, horizontal inequalities are more likely to cause violent conflict because "when cultural differences coincide with economic and political differences between groups, this can cause deep resentment that may lead to violent struggles." Historically, marginalized sections of the population have been likely to turn to organized conflict.

A case that illustrates the importance of a coincidence in political, economic and social incentives and interests in provoking war is the Nigerian Civil War (1966-70), which resulted in the deaths of hundreds of thousands of people. According to Stewart (2010), the Igbos and Yorubas, the most educated groups, initially shared many of the high-level posts in the new federation. The coup d'état of July 1966, led by Lieutenant-Colonel Murtala Mohammed, a northerner, resulted in the exclusion of the Igbos from power and established an increasingly anti-Igbo climate. The religious differences between traditionalists Igbo and Muslin northerners also came into play. It is the conviction of Nafziger (1973) that amidst widespread anti-Igbo sentiment and the subsequent attacks, many Igbo migrated to their home region in the eastern part of Nigeria and became a powerful lobbying group for an independent Biafra, in which they now had vested economic and cultural interest. Economic, cultural and political exclusion was further compounded by fear that without political power in the Nigerian Federation, there would be an increasingly detrimental distribution of oil revenues – by then the most vital source of government revenue. It is also noteworthy, as Nafziger (1983) argues, that the oil revenues promised an independent Biafra relative wealth. By and large, political, economic and socio-cultural deprivations tend to produce mass grievances that make mobilisation for war possible.

Evidently, conflict brings poverty in as much at it brings destruction, violence and hatred. On the other hand, poverty is a cause of conflict. Where grievances are not handled properly, poor people who are restless will stage an rising (as was the case in Egypt and Tunisia), questioning government altogether and joining rebel groups. However, at the root of conflicts always lie multi-faceted factors: inequality of political, social, economic and cultural opportunities among different groups, lack of democratic governance and effective leadership, absence of civil society and mechanism for non-violent conflict management. Although some scholars such as Nelson (1998) and Goodland (2001) understand the correlation of poverty and conflict as indirect at best, I have provided enough historical evidence on the association between poverty and conflict. As much as the association between poverty and conflict is a complex one, a common thread that has emerged from my analysis is that violent conflict affects the poor disproportionally. Poverty and inequality, on the other hand, cause and feed conflict as the lack of opportunities for the people make them restive and more prone to engage in risky behaviour, with leadership less likely to solve social conflicts in a peaceful manner. While there are, therefore, clearly links between poverty and conflict, it is noteworthy that the transiently poor are more likely to engage in rebellion than the chronically poor. The chronically poor tend to be the least organised and most passive group in society. Conversely, relative rather than absolute poverty appear to be more critical in terms of building up grievance which leads to conflict. Case studies from Angola, CAR, Libya, Sierra Leone and Somalia further unravels the intricate and complex relationship between poverty and conflict, and their subsequent effects on African states and communities.

Angola

Angola is a country endowed with resources but riddled by conflict for many years (1975-2002) with the consequent dwindling of national income and deepening of poverty. Over this period poverty, inequalities, unemployment, poor resource access and labour migration, among many other reasons, generated enough grievances that fuelled conflict, lawlessness and violations of human rights in Angola. The conflict-poverty nexus, therefore, generated state failure, ineffective and illegitimate governance, imbalance of power and opportunities, the theft of national wealth by a small, self-declared elite, the repression of opposition, rights and freedoms, as well as destruction, excessive loss of human life and the pauperisation of the generality of Angolans. Admittedly, Angola is one of Africa's most resource rich countries representing sub-Saharan Africa's second largest oil producer and the world's fourth largest producer (in value) of diamonds. The country is also fortunate to possess a wealth of other natural resources including minerals, water, forestry and fisheries (Tvedten, 1997). After 14 years of fighting, Angola attained independence from Portugal in 1975, but before people enjoyed the new thaw, the country relapsed into one of Africa's most protracted civil conflicts.

Indeed, Portuguese colonial rule ended in Angola in 1974. However, conflict quickly arose and the Total Movement for the Liberation of Angola (MPLA) with Cuban and Soviet Union assistance drove its rivals the National Front for the Liberation of Angola (FNA) and the National Union for the Total Independence of Angola (UNITA) from the capital, instigating a civil war for 27 years (James, 2011). Labour and energy that could have been put to productive use in tapping and harnessing resources such as diamonds and oil for sustainable development was wasted in war in the period 1975-2002 with the consequent destruction of crops, herds, villages and towns. The government (dominated by MPLA) controlled oil fields, while the rebel group (UNITA) sustained itself for years through illegal diamond mining. Green (1994) and Tvedten (1997) have shown how war in Angola led to the militarisation of society, undermined democratic institutions and government's ability to alleviate poverty. As such, after Portuguese colonial rule had drained Angola's resources through slavery and exploitation, in independence period, Angola became a Cold War staging ground, and its attempts to democratise collapsed as both the government (supported by Cuba, Soviet Union and China) and rebel movement, UNITA, supported by United States, took the country back to war thereby exacerbating poverty. For the poor in Angola, taking up the gun became a rational livelihood strategy. A similar effect ensued in the Liberian civil war (1989-1996), and as Kapusckinski (2001: 28) notes "the law in force here is: whoever has weapons eats first." Tanca

(1993) and Fernando (1998) argue that external intervention aggravated conflict and chronic poverty in Angola. Growing insecurity encouraged speculative activities rather than investment in production and employment and attracted 'rogue' foreign companies such as the diamond companies which had a high tolerance of risk and exacerbated conflict in Angola. Conflict led to capital flight, loss of Foreign Direct Investment and increased poverty.

Using impoverished youth that turned to UNITA rebel group as a kind of 'short cut' to wealth and status, Jonas Savimbi launched a catastrophic new war in the period 1992-93 and came close to seizing power as 70% of the country came under his control. Ross (2004) argues that the government responded by selling off future exploitation rights to both oil fields (still under government control), and diamond areas (some of which were under rebel control) to fund a counter-offensive. Peleman (2000) and Vines (1999) reflect how in one contract, the government paid a private military services company with a share of contested diamonds, to recapture the diamonds fields near the DRC border. Arguably, both the UNITA rebels and the government used poverty, foreign companies, and diamond and oil resources to prolong the war in Angola. Ross (2003) reflects that UNITA sold several billion dollars' worth of diamonds in the 1990s. Meger (2016) argues that during this period the MPLA controlled oil fields yielded the governing group more than US$3.3 billion annually. Instead of ploughing such resource wealth into development both MPLA and UNITA oiled their war machines. In fact, it were these oil interests that enabled the MPLA regime to establish a 'private diplomacy' with foreign investors and much stronger states that backed her battle against UNITA. These foreign actors had an interest in ensuring the maintenance of MPLA governance and assisted the regime in the conduct of warfare and diplomacy. By 1998, Angola was producing 760,000 barrels of oil per day, 70% of which was exported to the United States, making Angola the sixth-largest provider of oil to the United States (Meger, 2016). Oil export accounted for 87% of MPLA's formerly recorded revenue. This economic relationship played an important role in the maintenance of conflict, as each country or corporation involved in the trade of either diamonds or oil benefitted.

The heavy investment and wastage of resources in war by MPLA and UNITA, coupled with foreign companies' looting of diamonds and oil, is a clear testimony of how conflict caused poverty in Angola. Global Witness reports (1999, 2002, 2004) have shown how the Angolan civil war provided a cover for the full scale looting of the country's oil and diamonds money by national and international business and political elites, typified by the Angolagate 'arms-to-Angola' scandal that broke in France at the end of 2000. Angolagate is the story of how a legitimate exercise in self-defence by the MPLA government against UNITA turned into a conspiracy to rob the country of its oil and diamonds money through overpriced military procurement, kickbacks and mortgaging of future oil reserves and diamond mines for ready cash in the form of oil/diamond-backed loans. According to Global Witness (2002), an average of US$1.7 billion went missing each year from 1997-2001 from the Angolan treasury. That government officials siphoned US$8.5 billion at a time the international community was struggling to raise the US$200 million required to feed the one million Angolans dependent on aid each year, speaks volumes of the paradox of plenty and callousness and economic banditry nature of MPLA ruling elite. The ruling elite did not only profit from the brutal civil war, but they also ensued that Angola became heavily indebted. According to Global Witness (2004: 8), " at the end of 2001, the country owed about US$9.6 billion to foreign creditors, or 129% of its average annual export income. Of this debt, US$4.8 billion (i.e. half) is in arrears." As with the arms procurement, the restructuring of the country's debt appears to have been exploited to covertly move more of the nation's wealth through opaque offshore accounts.

When the devastating effects of the war are added, it becomes glaringly clear that conflict in Angola was an excruciating curse. By the end of the protracted war, more than a million people had died, 4 million had been displaced, and more than 500,000 Angolan refuges had fled to neighbouring countries. Much of the country's economy had collapsed, infrastructure had been destroyed and institutions weakened or no longer functioning (Global Witness (2004). Poverty was rampant, while hunger, disease, and starvation were wide spread. The landmines and unexploded bombs littered the countryside, and remain a danger to humans and animals to this day. The prolonged war in Angola was also rife with human rights abuses. During the war, child trafficking, prostitution, pornography, and sexual slavery were rampant. Meger (2016) estimates that 30,000 girls were kidnapped during the war, and even in 2003, after the end of the conflict; an estimated 5,000 to 8,000 underage girls remained 'married' to UNITA soldiers. In the context of the war, women regularly experienced rape and other forms of sexual violence and abuse at the hands of both the state armed forces and rebels, though the statistics available suggests that prior to the mid-1990s, the former were a lesser evil than the latter, but thereafter the latter were a lesser evil than the former. Women suspected of supporting UNITA were subjected to rape and sexual violence while held in MPLA detention centres. Meger (2016: 109) further asserts that in the months prior to the peace accord, reports emerged of government forces "attacking women in their homes, while they worked in the fields, near military camps, or during searches of their homes."

When a separatist group emerged in a diamond resource-rich area of northern Angola (Cabinda region) and complained of their exclusion from political power and wealth generated in their homeland, government forces responded by an orgy of sexual abuse whose tentacles even extended to Congolese migrants living in the area. In all, more than 3,000 women were victims. Sexual violence against male detainees in Angola by state forces has also been reported during the war. Sexual violence in Angola fits the pattern of rape as a weapon of war, amplified by some armed groups to generate political instability for the purpose of economic gain (Cohen, 2016). Sexual violence in Angola is grouped by Meger (2016) within the same pattern of this orgy in DRC, Sierra Leone, Liberia, South Sudan (inter-alia) as very highly prevalent, occurring predominantly in the field, and perpetrated by both rebel and state actors. In this scenario, civil wars are often resource driven and take place in the context of state failure or a high degree of political instability. While the use of various forms of sexual violence by UNITA forces, such as sexual slavery, forced recruitment, and rape, fostered mass population displacement and instability that facilitated their control of natural resources, sexual violence perpetrated by the state against women in their homes and near military camps, and against men in detention is more reflective of counter insurgency tactics aimed at punishing real and imagined UNITA supporters and sympathisers.

Chronic conflict in Angola caused intergenerational exclusion. This did not suddenly change after the 2002 peace settlement. Post conflict Liberia also continues to experience the same problems of political and economic exclusion that contributed to the 1989-1996 conflict in the first place. Similarly, Keen (1998) contends that the end of Sudan's first civil war in 1972 did not produce a political system that remedied the underdevelopment of the south or the marginalisation of significant groups in the north. Neither has the independence of South Sudan in 2011 brought a remedy to conflict, poverty and underdevelopment of the new country. In spite of the 2002 peace agreement, the criminalised war economy merely became a criminalised peace economy and continued to benefit a few elites in collusion with multi-national companies at the expense of the poverty and immiseration of the generality of Angolans. According to Pacheko (2001) and Tvedten (2017), the central highlands region was the most affected by the war and is the most vulnerable to food insecurity. The province of Huambo, northern Huila and parts of Bie were the core of the conflict, and most of the combatants on both sides came from these areas. The region is subject to intense population pressure, with an estimated two thirds of the country's population concentrated there, most of them living in extreme poverty. Due to migration and deaths in the war there are now more women than men. Households who are headed by women are amongst the poorest and are weaker. Without male assistance to farm and cultivate land the families that are headed by women face drastic problems to produce food which makes them even the poorest and destitute (Tvedten, 2017). Environmental decline is accelerating, while impoverished soils, poor farming practices and competition for farmland combine to diminish productivity and aggravate food insecurity. Arguably, the effects of conflict are, therefore, felt for many years after the fighting ended, and many of those who were chronically poor during the war have remained so during the peace. As put forward by Green (1994: 45), "the end of any war is not the end of its costs. In one sense the costs do not end until levels of output per capita, infant mortality, access to basic services, food security and poverty alleviation are achieved which correspond to those that would have been predicted in the absence of war."

Angola has reportedly experienced rapid economic expansion over the period 2003 to 2008 supported primarily by high global oil prices and increased oil production with an average growth rate in gross domestic product (GDP) of some 17%. Following sharp drops in GDP due to the global economic crisis of 2008-2010, the country has experienced a return to growth driven primarily by an increase in oil prices as well as public investment programme targeting non-petroleum sectors. Growth in GDP over the 2015-2020 years was projected to range between 6.4 to 6.9%. As such, Angola is reported to have made remarkable progress in rebuilding infrastructure to emerge top in the ranking of performance in Sub-Saharan Africa (UNECA, 2016: 11). Yet, even when oil abundance produces high growth, it often benefits only a few corrupt elites rather than translating into higher living standards for most of the population. Despite having one of the world's highest rates between 2003 and 2010, its score on human development index remained a miserable 0.49, and its infant mortality rate was lower than the sub-Saharan African average. From the 2016 figures available (UNDP, 2016), Angola is ranked 150th out of 188 countries on the HDI, which is reflective of the exceptionally poor scores in terms of education and health indicators. Poverty, underdevelopment, and inequality remain prevalent throughout much of the country, with 94% of households in rural areas categorised as poor. Other factors reflecting current conditions include that, 30% of the population is illiterate and only 54% of enrolled children complete primary education; 42% of the population does not have access to safe water; only some 30% of people have access to government health facilities; life expectancy marginally improved from 48.6 to 51 years and is therefore among the lowest in the world; and the child mortality rate is 167/1000 (UNICEF, 2015; World Bank, 2016; Tvedten, 2017). Tvedten (1997) argues that the colonial legacy and decades of post-colonial war turned Angola into one of the poorest countries in the world, despite considerable oil resources, huge hydro-electric potential, vast fertile agricultural lands, and some of Africa's most productive fishing waters. Arguably poverty in Angola is mainly due to its civil war and the length of time it lasted.

Even in the post-war era the economy of Angola has remained heavily inclined to oil production at the expense of agriculture and manufacturing sectors. Oil still represents 95% of all exports and accounts for 79.5% of fiscal revenues. As Ross (1999: 301-302) argues:

> ...resource industries were unlikely to stimulate growth in the rest of the economy, particularly if foreign multi-nationals dominated resource extraction and were allowed to repatriate their profits instead of investing them locally. Resource exporters would be left with booming resource enclaves that produced few 'forward' and 'backward' linkages to other parts of the economy.

Despite that agriculture has been identified as a priority area in the poverty reduction strategy, budget allocations remain very low. Prior to independence, Angola was self-sufficient in all key food crops (except wheat) and was an exporter of cash crops, in particular coffee and sugar. A working irrigation system for banana estates and sugarcane existed before the war, but the protracted civil war, neglect and lack of money, ruined the scheme (Tvedten, 1997). Crops and farm animals were also stolen or damaged with the consequent decline of farming and food production. Conversely, the war and lack of investment severely impacted on both sectors of food production and cash crops and reduced the country to dependency on food imports and food aid since 1990. Worse still corruption and economic banditry perpetrated by oil companies in cohorts with elites have continued unabated in Angola. Much of the oil that Angola ships to China is via a company called the China International Fund. Its trading prices are not public (*The Economist*, 2013) under the rubric of business secrecy and government's desire for confidentiality, which in essence is tailor-made to conceal looting and capital flight.

It is true that Angola embarked on a rebuilding process after the war, but the question now is how much the rebuilding process will benefit the majority of Angola's people, most of whom live in abject poverty? The development of roads, bridges, power and water supplies will benefit the entire country, but the provision of education, health care, hospitals, housing, and jobs are needed if the interior is to develop and if the wretched conditions there are to improve. The Diamond Industry Annual Review (2005) highlighted the building of schools, rehabilitation of health clinics and hospitals, installation of hydroelectric power plants and sanitation system, and inauguration of agricultural projects as benefits that a growing diamond industry was bringing to the process of reconstruction (Gordon, 2005). The same report also noted that, "Government investment – very low in a diamond producing former war zone – needs to be increased. The expenditures by mining companies are little more than a drop in an ocean of need" or an island of development in a sea of backwardness. Diamond mining has also caused environmental degradation, characterised by deforestation, soil erosion and pollution, which have impoverished the soil and when combined with poor farming practice and competition for farmland, cumulatively diminish productivity and aggravate food security and poverty. The relationship of mining and poverty is clear, although how much soil erosion is a cause of poverty and how much poverty is a cause of soil erosion is not clear.

By law mining companies in Angola are expected to invest in local development in their region, including infrastructure, schools, agriculture and medical posts. Gordon (2005) points out that improving local facilities for workers and their dependents is an obvious necessity, but the policy for social development is not integrated across the mining areas. Investment is local and limited, and efforts beyond a company's own immediate staff may be little more than a 'hearts and minds' operation. Diamond mining companies justify their limited involvement in social development by claiming that they provide benefits in the form of taxes to the government, and employment and its benefits to the local community. But these benefits are clearly localised. A broader strategy on the part of diamond mines' corporate social responsibility is needed if benefits are to be fairly spread across the mining regions. Allais (2007) and US Child Labour and Forced Labour Reports

(2015) have shown the diamond industry's curse of regularly employing children as an easy source of cheap labour thereby pushing them deeper into abject poverty. It was not until 2014 that Angola accepted rampant child labour in diamond mines. Many a times government officials were dismissive of the deleterious effects of diamond mining positing that, "We do not recognise the country you have described" to human rights defenders (Gordon, 2005).

Undoubtedly, civil war in Angola dramatically slowed the country's development process as it generated poverty and incapacitated the Angolans' ability to tap and harness natural resources for betterment of their livelihoods. The exploitation of oil and diamonds not only financed and motivated military operations beyond their Cold War and South African context, but also affected the legitimacy of the government and the economy. This conjunction of politics, geography, and military strategies sustained – and was sustained by – financial flows linking fighters and war profiteers to markets in industrialized countries. Angola starkly illustrates devastating effects of conflict, revenue misappropriation, state corruption and poverty. As such, so few corrupt government officials have continued to get a larger share of the oil and diamond wealth than the majority of the Angolan people. While most Angolans suffer devastating poverty, oil and diamond income, has enabled top government officials of the ruling MPLA to become filthy rich. Indeed economic banditry, plundering and looting have generated wealth for the few, and poverty for the many. Angola's oil money threatens to remain as out of reach for the Angolan people as the oil platforms themselves. The greatest reward from natural resources known in Angolan history is poverty, underdevelopment, indebtedness and instability.

Central Africa Republic

Since gaining independence from France in 1960, poverty has been a cause and product of conflict in Central Africa Republic. Not surprisingly, the country has failed to achieve substantial economic development and has considerable foreign debt. With more than 80 different ethnic groups, the CAR represents a truly multiethnic country. Progress has been hampered by corruption, external interference, civil war, insecurity and macroeconomic decisions such as the reduction of public expenditures in the past. The country has seen numerous coup d'états, rebellions and brutal regimes since independence. Poverty manifesting itself in form of denial of choices and opportunities, violation of human dignity, lack of basic capacity to participate effectively in society, shortage of food, absence of education and health facilities, unemployment, insecurity, powerlessness and exclusion of individuals, households and communities must be viewed both as a result of conflict and trigger and accelerator of conflict. Faced with such challenges it has been easy for conflict entrepreneurs to induce the soldiers, workers and youth into rebellion thereby leaving CAR people more susceptible to violence, living on marginal or fragile environments, and without access to clean water or sanitation.

David Dacko, became the first president of the Central African Republic in 1960, following the death in a plane crash of Barthélemy Boganda, who had led the independence movement. According to Kalck (2005) although Dacko relied domestically on setting up the elite of various ethnic groups as a governing committee known as MESAN (Movement for the Social Evolution of Black Africa), the country largely remained under French control in external affairs. Its economy decline rapidly, while the national debt constantly increased. It was such economic decline that the army commander, Jean-Bédel Bokassa, used as a *cassus-belli* to seize power in a staged coup in 1965 (Lentz, 2014). Bokassa introduced a brutal and dictatorial regime, abolishing the constitution, dissolving parliament, suppressing opposition and finally crowning himself Emperor of the Central African Empire in 1976 in an extravagant ceremony. Corruption, ineptness, nepotism, frivolity and lavishness saw the government debt soaring. When salaries and scholarships could no longer be met, discontent grew. France overthrew Bokassa after he brutally suppressed student protests in 1979, and restored Dacko as president (Kalck, 2005: 102). His return was not well received however, and he had to rely on French paratroops to defend his presidency. André Kolingba, appointed by the president as chief of staff of the armed forces in 1981, used this enduring instability to displace Dacko in a bloodless coup the same year.

Kolingba suspended the constitution and ruled with a military junta until 1985. With the fall of the Berlin Wall in 1990 calls for democracy became louder throughout the country. The outbreak of riots, when salaries could not be paid once again, induced Kolingba to finally give in to demands for a more pluralistic political system. However, he was not successful in the 1993 election and thus Ange Félix Patassé, a cousin of Bokassa's principal wife, became the first democratically elected president since the country's independence (International Business Publication USA, 2007). Patassé's government was characterized by civil unrest. During his mandate he was confronted by three army rebellions and several lootings in Bangui, which had severe consequences on the infrastructure of the capital. Even though under Patassé's rule the country had been forced to rely on peacekeeping troops under the UN mission, he was re-elected president in September 1999 (International Business Publication USA, 2007). In 2003 his government was overthrown by a rebellion led by François Bozizé, formerly his army chief of staff. Kalck (2005: 33) asserts that Bozizé admitted: "I took power with Chad's help". Admittedly, Bozizé's seizure of power would have been impossible without the support of Chadian forces as four fifths of the troops that captured Bangui were Chadian. As such, the increasing military presence of Chad as well as the continuous French tutelary influence meant that the CAR was on the verge of becoming a 'vassal state'. Nepotism reached worrying levels: more than 20 members of parliament belonged to Bozizé's direct family, including his wife, his sons and cousins (International Crisis Group, 2007). Arguably, since 1960 the country has faced a series of events leading to political instability emanating from poverty of leadership, government ineptness, external interference, corruption and poverty. It is within this framework that the removal of four of the seven presidents, referred above, by unconstitutional means, namely coups d'état with close familial connections, must be fully comprehended.

The country's conflicts are not primarily of a religious nature (Pastoor, 2013), but also stem from a deeper level of tension, that is, ethnic patronage; after all, Kolingba, Patassé and Bozizé considered themselves Christians. Yet, Kolingba favoured his own ethnic group - the Yakoma, while his successor Patassé explicitly dismissed the

Yakoma. Instead he rewarded his supporters from north western parts of the country, predominantly Sara-Kaba, with governmental positions. Bozizé, in turn, privileged the Gbaya (Arieff, 2014). A distinctive urban bias, especially towards the capital Bangui (which is in the south), adds to the large number of disparities. This becomes particularly evident in the area of government expenditure: Bangui, home of 30% of the Central African population exhausts nearly 90% of state spending (Arieff, 2014). This has generated grievances from people outside the capital, particularly in the North. Due to a lack of state authority in large areas outside of the capital Bangui, the country is often referred to as a phantom state. Ethnic conflicts in the northern CAR as well as the presence of the notorious Lord's Resistance Army (LRA) in the south continue to exacerbate insecurity and poverty. With more than 60% of the CAR's inhabitants being under the age of 24 its average population is very young (International Crisis Group, 2007). While this could represent a great dividend, it also remains challenging as the literacy rate among those aged 15 and over is low and poverty very high thereby making them susceptible to violence and rebellion.

Although from the very beginning the CAR has been an extremely fragile state, the conflict that started in 2012 is considered the worst the country has ever experienced. Indeed in 2012, a wave of violence swept through the CAR as Seleka rebels clashed with anti-Balaka militias. In the seemingly senseless bloodshed scholars, politicians and journalist struggled to account for the conflict's origins. Lombard (2017) argues that the conflict was more than a straight-forward religious clash between Christians and Muslims. Instead, she traces the roots of the conflict to the fears of spiritual insecurity and a social breakdown that drove inter-communal violence. Placing the uprising within its broader social, cultural, and historical context Lombard reveals the complicated roles played by marginalized rural youth, local political leaders, and the global community in sustaining the conflict. What is clear, however, is that the conflict fits within the broader synergy of poverty, unemployment, corruption and external influence. The Seleka were a rug-tag group loosely united by poverty, unemployment and hatred of Bozize and swept into power with the assistance of Chadian and

Sudanese forces. Bozize was overthrown by the rebels in March 2013 following which the Seleka rebel leader, Michael Djotodia declared himself President. His reign was short lived as the unprecedented orgy of violence pitting the Seleka and anti-Balaka, coupled with international pressure forced him to resign in 2014. French and UN forces restored some semblance of order that led, first to an interim government and election in March 2016 that ushered in the current President, Faustin-Archange Touadera. As much as a complex interplay of conflict and poverty has produced poverty and conflict in CAR, Lombard (2017) has given a new dimension and historicity to this multi-dimensional nexus. She argues that during the colonial period the French colonial government decided that rather than administer or develop institutions in the country, they would lease it out to private companies to run to their own profit. That kind of concessionary dynamic remain very much the case, and, if anything, has intensified. Lombard further argues that, rather than being viewed as a failed state, CAR reflect an intensification of the whole way of operating that has existed, for many years. Both in the colonial era and now, this way of operating has not been a boon to Central Africa.

What is undeniable is that poverty has fuelled coups, internal armed conflict, generalised violence and human rights violations that have intermittently led to destruction, loss of human life and internal displacement in Central Africa Republic. Poverty and conflict have also aggravated the effects of natural hazards. The state lacks authority and capacity to provide services in the provinces. A climate of widespread impunity has allowed armed groups to proliferate. In 2011 the IDMC (Internal Displacement Monitoring Centre) estimated that 6% of the entire population was either internally displaced or living as refugees in neighbouring countries (World Bank, 2017). With the outbreak of the crisis that began in December 2012, thousands of civilians became victims to unspeakable atrocities, and about 2.4 million, corresponding roughly to half of the country's population, was left in need of humanitarian aid. Even after the restoration of relative peace by the end of 2014, 650,000 people were still internally displaced and more than 290,000 had fled to neighbouring countries for refuge (Internal Displacement

Monitoring Centre, 2014). Findings of the International Displacement Monitoring Centre (IDMC) show that internal displaced people faced diverse threats to their physical and moral integrity, including killings, massacres, rape and recourse to survival sex. Family ties were disrupted by displacement, leaving displaced people with disabilities, single women and mothers, older displaced people and unaccompanied children more vulnerable. Women and children trafficking that is done for forced prostitution or labour is caused by war, poverty, and flawed or non-existent birth registration systems. Flower (2004: 11) argues that "poverty aggravates already desperate conditions caused by conflict, discrimination, and repression, and unregistered children are easy to move between countries because they never formally acquire a nationality." Arguably, conflict in CAR has forced hundreds of thousands to flee their homes and villages thereby making them vulnerable and taking them further away from educational and health care resources.

Many years of armed conflict have profoundly affected children in the Central African Republic: thousands have lost their parents in the civil conflict, have found themselves recruited as child soldiers or traumatized by the levels of violence they have been exposed to. The recruitment of minors in the ranks of armed groups continues to be a common phenomenon in the Central African Republic (SOS, 2016). Education system in Central African Republic is also a major factor that encourages poverty. Only 50% of the children in CAR are enrolled in primary school. The other 50% lacks in opportunity to receive even the most basic education because of violence, poverty, or also because there are no teachers, facilities or materials with which to operate a school. In some of the zones deeply affected by armed conflict, only 14% of children are able to attend school. The average Central African adult had no more than 3.5 years of schooling. Tens of thousands of children never attend school at all. Five in ten Central Africans are not able to read and write (IDMC, 2014).

By and large, despite being rich in resources such as diamonds, uranium, timber, gold and oil, the CAR is the poorest country in Africa and extensively relies on foreign donors and the help of NGOs. The country is ranked 188th (out of 188 countries) in the United Nations Human Development Index (1916), which assesses health, education, standard of living, child welfare, and other factors. Roughly 90% of the population lives in crippling poverty, without access to food, sanitation and decent housing. In rural areas, clean water is often not available, which abets the spread of numerous diseases. Around 40% of the population lack access to regular meals. Life expectancy of its meagre population of 4.9 million is 51.5 years (UNDP HDI, 2016). The major threat to the people there is HIV. People are at very high degree of risk to many other fatal diseases like malaria, hepatitis-A, malaria and rabies. As estimated in 2002 there were fewer than 3 physicians and 9 nurses per 100,000 people (Whiteside, 2002). The infant mortality rate continues to be extremely high at 112 per 1,000 live births. The main reason that led to the deterioration of basic health services in the country is political instability and civil conflicts, thus weakening the national response to diseases or epidemics. Poverty, on the other hand, has combined with other factors to feed conflict as lack of opportunities has made people restive and more prone to engage in conflict or to be mobilised for a war. Arguably, the absence of peace has militated against development and corroded development structures in CAR. At any rate, there is no development in war, but only destruction.

Libya

While acknowledging that civil wars are caused by highly complex social processes that greatly depend on the historical and regional context, the outbreak of the Libyan civil war in 2011 must be understood as a hybrid conflict that combined internal characteristics stemming from poverty and regional and global interests. The situation in Libya in 2011 did not conform to the conditions of greed-based rebellion as put forward by Collier and Hoeffler (2001). In regard to grievances, several can be identified. Both vertical inequalities: economic grievances, lack of political rights, and the lifestyle of Gadaffi's children, as well as horizontal inequalities: regional and ethnic differences. The combination of grievances seems to have acted as a powerful propellant for a violent rebellion. Yet, sound as this appears, most of these had been present for at least a decade without causing a rebellion. It is, therefore, imperative to look at, what fostered people to overcome what Lichbach (1994) calls 'the rebel's dilemma'; and government decisions and external factors that collectively fostered the demise of the Libyan regime. The Libyan war seems to have been interplay of brutal regime, 'resource curse' and poverty acted upon by internal and external forces.

Libya became independent as a state in 1951. A military coup in 1969 overthrew King Idris 1. The coup leader Muammar Gaddafi ruled the country from the Libyan Cultural Revolution in 1973 until he was overthrown and killed in the Libyan Civil War of 2011 (Paegeter, 2012; Martinez, 2007). Since then, Libya has been unstable. In the second Libyan Civil War ongoing since 2014, two authorities initially claimed to govern Libya: the Council of Deputies in Tobruk, and the 2014 General National Congress (GNC) in Tripoli, which considered itself the continuation of the General National Congress, elected in 2012. After UN-led peace talks between the Tobruk and Tripoli governments, a unified interim UN-backed Government of National Accord was established in 2015, and the GNC disbanded to support it (Boeke and Zuijdewijn, 2016). Parts of Libya remain outside of either government's control, with various Islamist, rebel, and ethnic militias administering some areas.

It is Ross's (2003: 19) conviction that conflicts are products of complex set of factors or events, be it "poverty, ethnic or religious grievances, and unstable governments." The Libyan war (2011-present) can be fully comprehended in form of vertical grievances in terms of Gadaffi's defective political system of sultanism and patronage, economic position of the population and behaviour of Gadaffi's family. Horizontal grievances also emanated from differences between and among ethnic groups in Libya. Admittedly Libya lacked political pluralism as political power was vested in the hands of the regime. A system of Gadaffism was operative as Gadaffi was the only person who could make political decisions, with regional political bodies merely rubber-stamping such decisions and, therefore, rendered ineffective. Libya was an authoritarian police state without political parties, and thus violated the legal rights of all those that opposed it. Not surprisingly, opposition to the regime was kept low through fear of victimisation. According to Simons (2003), responses to protests were violent, and prisoners faced torture and executions. As much as these measures guaranteed the regime's grip on power for a long time, they also generated widespread resentment. Pargeter (2012) contends that in a country that traditionally valued a sober lifestyle, the Gadaffi children exhibited their Western luxuries to the whole population and further exacerbated resentment.

The Libyan society suffered under the economic policies of the Gadaffi regime. In the 1990s, international sanctions were imposed on Libya that mainly hit the poorer citizens. Worse still, the sanctions regime was abused by the rich class, who managed to sell off food allowances and gained unique access to foreign products (Pargenter, 2012). Public services were eroded. Consequently, the gap between the poor and the rich widened and a shocking contrast between richness and poverty ensued. Pargenter (2012) shows how this was aggravated by the removal of subsidies in 2003, thereby further embittering Libyans. Compante and Chor (2012) argue that the combination of poor employment opportunities and the fact that education levels strongly increased prior to 2011 can be seen as a major source of vertical economic grievance, as it was impossible for citizens to work on the level that they were trained for. As such, economic grievances generated by poverty were crucial, and thus validate poverty as a cause of conflict. It is noteworthy that conflict in Libya was/is characterised by regional division. Horizontally, the east had been the centre of resistance against Gadaffi. During the 1990s, Benghazi had been the centre of an Islamist uprising against the regime. As propounded by Pargeter (2012), Gadaffi's response was to keep the East in a 'constant state of underdevelopment', in order to make it feel what it entailed to challenge the regime. Arguably, the Gadaffi policies towards the East generated enough resentment for a protracted rebellion. Warshel (2012: 735) argues that in 2001, 76% of the citizens in Benghazi felt alienated from the political process and sought change. Not surprisingly, it was the East that finally rose up against the regime, with Benghazi as its most important city.

Gadaffi had long played ethnic differences in Libya. Initially he played out the different ethnic groups against each other, with three ethnic groups as the main pillars under his regime. According to

Martinez (2007), after an attempted coup by the Warfalla ethnic group in 1993, the Libyan leadership comprised entirely members of Gadaffi's own ethnic group, the Gadaffa. Such patronage ensured their loyalty to the regime. Consequently, other people had no viewpoint at representation or improving its position and were kept on restraint through coercion. Lacher (2011) argues that ethnic loyalties shaped allegiances during the revolution, although they were less important than regional divisions. All in all, all the factors considered above, played a role in fostering resistance against Gadaffi regime. Collectively, they exuded Gadaffi's regime as brutal and illegitimate, and certainly for those in the East and from outside Gadaffi's ethnic group, as a regime that delighted in poverty and suffering of the generality of Libyans. This was certainly conceivable in light of the regime's use of poverty as an instrument of control in eastern parts of Libya. The centrality of Benghazi in the Libyan war confirms that conflicts in developing countries originate from and are fought out in the regions that have historically suffered from collapse of social contract (appropriate state-people relationship) and consequent marginality, limited voice and hard core poverty.

Indeed, a rebellion is a collective action problem. Lichbach (1994) calls this 'Rebel's Dilemma': the challenge that people generally do not participate in protests. Rational actors would always weigh the costs and benefits of protesting, and in most cases when the costs are high would decide not to protest. A possible explanation as to why protest gained momentum in Libya in 2011 is the unique regional context. The early Arab Spring protests showed that the autocratic regimes were not all powerful in cracking down on dissidents, lowering the opportunity costs for protest. Above all, the American led coalition interventions in Libyan war from 2011, partly influenced by America's attempts to establish friendly government in Libya that would guarantee her access to Libyan oil resource wealth, guaranteed rebel success.

That 'rogue militias' continue to hold sway in Libya long after the demise of Gadaffi regime seem to validate Collier and Hoeffler (2001)'s economic incentive and poverty for continuation of violence, that is, benefits from control over oil resources and taking up a gun as a rational livelihood strategy, respectively. With the outbreak of war, rebels swiftly moved to control oil reserves in order to control resources necessary for war. However, such a desire was quickly superseded by the desire to make quick profits from oil resources (Boeke, and Zuijdewijn, 2016). Suffice to say it cannot be disproven that poverty and the prospect of an economic incentive were reasons that fuelled violence. As of now, the state has collapsed with various former generals-cum-warlords, Islamist, rebel, and tribal militias administering some areas. Infrastructure has been destroyed, economy shattered and life has deteriorated to worse levels than during the Gadaffi era. In 2010 Libya was ranked number 53 out of 169 countries on UNDP Human Development Index (2010). It was ranked the highest in Africa, with the lowest infant mortality rate, highest life expectancy of over 73 years. The war in Libya has seen her ranking going down on UNDP Human Development Index (2016) to 102 out of 188 countries. The increase in education under Gadaffi regime, played an important role in allowing the revolution against Gadaffi to take flight (Pargeter, 2012), but that education has been rendered useless in attempts to bring peace in Libya. At any rate even its relevance is being challenged by warlords, Islamists and rug-tag ethnic militias. The collapse of the 'Big man' (Gadaffi), poverty and greed have reduced Libya to continued warfare/violence, lawlessness and destruction; economic disarticulation and marginalisation of the generality of the populace. While poverty generated grievances seem to have played an important role in the outbreak of conflict in 2011, currently greed and poverty seem to be fuelling conflict in Libya.

Sierra Leone

Sierra Leone epitomises the conjunction of civil war, poverty and poor growth, and is indicative of one of the most dramatic cases of development failure in Africa. Admittedly, poverty in Sierra Leone is as much a cause of conflict as it is a consequence of conflict. At independence in 1961, the country's development prospects looked encouraging. The country had a renowned educational system; a rich and diversified natural resource base comprising diamonds and other minerals, and abundant agricultural and marine resources; tourist attractions; and a seemingly stable democracy. However, coups, kleptocracy and political repression, ethno-regional divisions, mismanagement of diamond resources, civil wars and poverty, have typified people living in misery, slavery and limited liberty in a resource rich country.

Sierra Leone became Africa's first modern state created by British philanthropists from 1787 to the early 19th century through a combination of freed slaves (Creoles) in present day Freetown (Province of Freedom) and other indigenous ethnic groups in the hinterland. Though Freetown and the hinterland became British colony and protectorate in 1808 and 1896, respectively, Sierra Leone gained independence in 1961. Majority rule politically vanquished the Creoles, while rivalries intensified between indigenous ethnic groups initially united against the Creoles. The Sierra Leone People's Party (SLPP) ruling since independence came to be perceived as biased towards the Mendes in South-Eastern regions and other small ethnic groups. The Temnes and other small ethnic groups in the Northern regions rallied around the All People's Congress (ACP) which won the controversial elections in 1967 (Hirsh, 2001). A military coup prevented the ACP from forming a government. The military staged another coup in 1968 to instate Sikasa Stevens whose personalized, brutal, and corrupt dictatorship in the period 1968-1985 reduced the country to a pariah state. His hand-picked successor, General Joseph Momoh's weak administration accelerated the collapse of the state with the consequent launch of a rebel war from 1991 by the Revolutionary United Front (RUF) backed by warlord Charles Taylor from neighbouring Liberia (Gberie, 2005). Coups and bloody civil war raged on in Sierra Leone between 1991 and 2002 and further plagued the country into poverty and underdevelopment of development. The country's unpleasant history globally, is associated with slave trade, bloody civil war, poverty and diseases.

One of the basic factors causing poverty within Sierra Leone has been lack of democratic pluralism as government has been characterised by either one-party rule or military rule. Above all, since the departure of colonial rule, successive governments have been corrupt and extremely incompetent in the provision of most basic needs. These needs were fundamentally usurped for government officials. As pointed out by Ridell (2005: 126), Sierra Leoneans "were not just neglected, uninvolved, or would catch-up later in the nation's development. They were actively exploited or 'ripped off', and had been for roughly a hundred years – first by colonialism and then by the policies, plans, and programmes of the government of independent Sierra Leone." Stevens practiced kleptocracy for self-enrichment and to induce loyalty. He engineered a perverse attitudinal shift among the populace, institutionalising the self-seeking ethos "oosie tie cow nar dae ee go eat" – a cow grazes wherever it is tethered. As stressed by Davies (2000), unchecked state-sponsored corruption ensued, practiced through a patrimonial system of rational favours; public theft; illicit payment and bribes; administrative allocation of scarce basic commodities; and manipulation of access to diamond and other natural resources, and rents from economic distortions in foreign currency, financial and commodity markets. The judiciary, civil society, local government bodies and above all the military, as agencies of restraint and institutions that could pose a challenge, were destroyed or vitiated by Stevens.

Stevens also paralysed the crucial corporate diamond sector by promoting illicit mining on the corporate Sierra Leone Selection Trust (SLST) territory and everywhere else. He and his associates masterminded the theft of the SLST's November 1969 monthly diamond haul valued locally at US$3.4 million and resold it for US$10 million in Europe (Hirsh, 2001). Subsequently, he nationalised the SLST and encouraged rampant looting of its diamonds, thereby leading to the collapse of corporate mining in the 1970s. Indeed, the regime of the first president of Sierra Leone, Siaka Stevens, was infamous for its inordinate level of corruption. His ethos and survival strategy induced economic and political atrophy. Megalomaniac venality, kleptocracy and its economic complements of massive market distortion; excessive seigniorage and unsustainable foreign borrowing, *inter-alia*, inflicted huge welfare costs. Manipulation and looting of diamond resources led to the collapse of official diamond exports and criminalisation of economic activity which in turn eroded the tax base and government control of the economy, weakening the state and crippling its capacity to provide basic social services and security. Arguably, Stevens appropriated a vast amount of government revenue for his personal gain, and along with fellow government officials, lived in luxury while the people went hungry. As Ridell (2005) argues, he used up most of the financial resources that were meant for his state and people with the effect that poverty and underdevelopment reigned, and has continued within Sierra Leone. Not surprisingly, after a moderate rate of 2.5% in the 1960s, per capital GDP growth declined to 0.06 in the 1970s, turned negative -0.9% in the 1980s and deteriorated further to -8% in the 1990s (UNDP-Freetown, 1996). By 1989 over 80% of the population lived below the poverty line of US$1 a day; while out of 160 countries, Sierra Leone ranked bottom on the UNDP Human Development Index (UNDP, 1991, 2001). It was undoubtedly, this poverty that triggered civil war in Sierra Leone in 1991, which raged until 2002.

Growing poverty, unemployment, and disillusionment among youth, and government's use of socially deprived youth motivated with drugs and often-false promises of employment to unleash violence produced the recruitment base for rebel movement. By the late 1980s Sierra Leone's marginalised youth constituted a very large pool of potential rebels. Perceiving the corrupt and repressive government system as the source of their predicament, they became increasingly rebellious, spreading anti-government agitations. As Abdullah (1997) posits, poverty and political repression radicalised university students (government's main source of opposition), and some of them left in 1987 for military training in Libya to overthrow the APC, leading to the formation of the rebel movement. It is noteworthy that the pool of marginalised young men was a significant driving force behind the conflict. Conflict was mobilised by the educated but jobless youth which is an indicator that education without economic opportunities led to increased grievances. While there were, therefore, clear links between poverty and bottom up violence, it is noteworthy that it was the transient poor (educated youth), rather than the chronically poor who became the backbone of the rebel movement in Sierra Leone. Conversely, groups which suffer sudden changes in wealth and status are likely to mobilize and be mobilised, particularly when exclusion overlaps with group identity. Yet even to the chronically poor, taking up the gun became a rational livelihood strategy or a guarantee to a meal. Conflict entrepreneurs in Sierra Leone appear to have had an extremely nuanced understanding of community dynamics and how social capital could be mobilised for perverse outcomes. The ethno-regional divisions generated distributional grievances. As Gberie (2005) asserts, in the location of development projects the APC apparently discriminated against the south-eastern regions, the country's breadbasket producing virtually all exports – diamonds, rutile, bauxite, cocoa and coffee, which factor was used to mobilise such areas against the government.

During the civil war (1991-2002), diamond mining areas became contested areas pitting rebels on one hand, and pro-government combatants and 'junior' mining companies exchanging arms and mercenary services to the government for mining concessions on the other. Both the government and rebels financed arms deals by trading in conflict diamonds. Diamonds, therefore, played a direct role in the rebel war and hostility among citizens. The alluvial and geographically-dispersed nature of Sierra Leone's diamonds, economic distortions and exploitation policy encouraged crime – illicit mining and smuggling – and violence as a corollary, resulting in a large body of destitute, desperate and lawless illicit miners known as san-san boys. Many of them including the RUF field commander, General Mosquito, joined the rebellion expecting to access the illusory diamonds that had attracted them to the mining areas. The value of 'conflict diamonds' exported by the RUF was estimated at US$20-70 million a year for some years (USAID, 2001; Gberie, 2005). Recruitment into the military based on loyalty to the government and the APC eroded morale and discipline which prolonged the rebel war by producing a weak government military response to it. Above all, with the collapse of central government and its inability to fully control the behaviour of its officials and employees, rebels were frequently able to trade diamonds for weapons from the very government commanders and soldiers who were supposed to be fighting them. Conversely, diamonds produced a war-prolonging congruence of interests among the belligerents who sometimes mined diamonds peaceably side by side, attacking civilians to keep them off.

Civil war had far reaching consequences and entrenched unprecedented poverty and misery in Sierra Leone as well as borrowing environmental capital from future generations with no prospects of paying back. Not only did it entrench poverty and violence in Sierra Leone, but it also led to the rise of a one-armed banditry plunder, looting and wrecking of natural wealth; destruction of villages, infrastructure and towns; insecurity, rape and permanent suffering of the general populace that became a nut between brigand crackers. Coulter (2009: 114) argues that the war reduced women to nothing but units of domestic production and reproduction as mere homemakers or bush wives serving rebel militia members' sexual needs. Even after the war, women could/can hardly join the workforce, and could/cannot contribute to pulling the country out of the quagmire of economic failure, which in essence is a waste of human capital. In a global world that recognises gender equity, this degradation of women keeps Sierra Leone from developing as a nation. The civil war claimed 25000-75000 lives and displaced nearly half of the country's population (USAID, 2001). The war and consequent concentration of labour on illicit diamond economy, constrained agriculture and turned Sierra Leone from a net exporter to a net importer of rice and dependency on food aid. The post-conflict government urban bias policy has further constrained agriculture and other rural economic activities, undermining growth and entrenching poverty. War and mining also took a heavy toll on infrastructure and environment. Roads, building, bridges and farm land were destroyed, while mining pits were not reclaimed, thereby causing land degradation, environmental terrorism and increased poverty, that cumulatively have continued to affect the people of Sierra Leone to the present day. The destruction of infrastructure during the war and subsequent failure to develop an alternative rural road transport network further marginalised rural Sierra Leone and pushed the general populace into permanent poverty.

The diamond industry, one of the main sources of revenue for the Sierra Leonean government, has brought significant income to the country, but the top-down effect is virtually non-existent; lower class and rural citizens still experience exploitative labour relations, environmental degradation and persistent poverty within mining communities (Le Billion and Levin, 2009: 695). The contrast between the supposed right to health and actual exploitation is particularly stark in the diamond-rich Kono District around the regional capital of Koidu. As Le Billio and Levin further argue, Kono is both the richest and poorest part of Sierra Leone. This is where the civil war started in 1991 and is reflective of how conflict has caused inter-generational exclusion. The criminalised war economy has merely become a criminalised peace economy. The mining operations create lots of dust and people suffer from headaches, water eyes and respiratory disorders. Outside the town, new homes are built, but there is no land for farming to provide a livelihood. The massive domestic violence perpetuated against women and children since the war is even worse where thousands of people have been compulsorily resettled. Many of the thousands of frustrated young men who felt they had no prospect and were recruited by RUF in the 1990s with the hope of bettering their prospects are now frustrated, hopeless and poor old men. Above all, external factors such as a decreased demand for diamonds worldwide has thrown many Sierra Leoneans out of jobs into poverty. Brown (2005) has shown that the trade in conflict diamonds by militia men and government elites earned them personal revenue of about US$7.5 billion. Such money could have been judiciously used to alleviate poverty in a peaceful and corruption free country, rather than enriching government officials and militia rebels.

By and large, due to civil war and consistent corruption within government, Sierra Leone is still embroiled in poverty and has one of the lowest GDP figures: as of 2010, it was $900, even less than previously war-torn countries such as Rwanda (Central Intelligence Agency, 2010).Undeniably, there has been limited progress in post war Sierra Leone. As was the case during the civil war, the government tends to sign contracts that absolve managers of private-sector companies from any social responsibility. The result is modern day slavery and massive environmental damage. Not surprisingly, diamond, gold and rutile mining continue to raise only a few people's living standards at the expense of the suffering of the general populace. The government hardly levies export taxes, thus forsaking state revenues in favour of fast private profit. Private interests have continued to take precedent over social service for the ordinary people. Arguably, the complex interplay of poverty and conflict in Sierra Leone has ensured that that the majority of people today lead marginalised lives with scarce access to clean water, electricity or employment. Not surprisingly, in the UNDP Human Development Index (2016) Sierra Leone ranks 179 out of 188 countries with a life expectancy of 51.3% at birth. Indeed poverty in Sierra Leone is as much a cause and consequence of conflict. Conflict has been closely associated with mismanagement of diamond resources that induced severe and economic social dislocations, constraining agricultural and overall economic growth; entrenching poverty; and fostering crime, violence and civil war.

Somalia

Somalia is a typical case study that reflects poverty as a cause and consequence of conflict. Poverty was the driving force of the Somalis against Said Barre's brutal regime, yet after deposing him in 1991 Somalia descended into barbaric lawless that has caused poverty and misery in the country up to now. The Somalis are ethnically homogeneous, but their plight under and after colonial rule bore testimony of the capriciousness of colonial boundaries. Artificial colonial boundaries cut across their ethnic ties so that they ended in five countries, British Somaliland, Italian Somaliland, Ethiopia, Kenya and Djibouti. Ayittey (1999) states that the nation of Somalia was formed and granted independence in 1960 when the British Protectorate and the Italian Trust were joined, while the rest of the Somali people were left in Ethiopia, Djibouti, and Kenya. It is for this reason that the flag of Somalia depicts five-pointed stars to manifest the unity of all Somalis disjointed in five locations. The civilian administration that assumed power after independence became hopeless and corrupt, and was overthrown in a bloodless coup by Major-General Mohammad Said Barre who turned to Soviet Union for tutelage in the period 1970-1977. However, when Soviet Union refused to assist Barre's quest for the completion of the independence of all Somalis under the umbrella of Greater Somali (Woodward, 1996), he turned to United States despite his socialist rhetoric.

Barre's socialist policies were an economic disaster. The International Monetary Fund (IMF), summoned in 1980, called for market oriented economic policies, devalued the Somali shilling, and sale of unprofitable state enterprises. After eight years of government zigzag and posturing, a frustrated IMF pulled out in 1988 declaring Somalia ineligible for further borrowing (Ayittey, 1999). It is important to note that for the period between 1965 and1988, living standards remained stagnant despite receiving substantial amount of foreign aid poured into the country. GDP per capita grew at a miserable 0.3% per annum, with the consequent dubbing of Somalia as "the Graveyard of Aid" (*New Africa Yearbook*, 1991-1992: 303). Ayittey (1999: 53) shows that in 1984 "$15 million flowed out of Somalia." Arguably, with the soaring of corruption in Somalia, foreign aid just replaced capital outflows. The misguided socialist policies did not increase food production. Rather, it reduced food production with the consequent increase of consumer goods. By the late 1980s, therefore, Somalia was experiencing the dilemma of poverty (Rena, 2007). The increased poverty erupted into grievances and demonstrations against Barre's ineptness and despotic rule.

Rather than addressing the plight of the general populace, Barre's regime became increasingly corrupt, and torture, mass executions, pillage, and carnage increasingly became the regime's signatures. The dropping of bombs on demonstrators, their instant executions and imprisonment were a clear act of a declaration of war by the regime on its own people. In 1990 a human rights organization, Africa Watch, charged Barre's regime with "responsibility for the deaths of 50000 to 60000 civilians since hostilities broke out between the government and rebels from the Somali National Movement." Africa Watch further noted that "Entire regions have been devastated by military engaged in combat against its own people, resembling a foreign occupation force that recognizes no constraints on its power to kill, rape or loot" (*Africa Report*, 1990: 10). With increasing poverty, a bullet to the head and a diet of starvation from Barre's regime, many young desperate and unemployed youths swelled the ranks of two rebel movements, the United Somali Congress and Somali National Movement, and with massive support from the suffering civilians were able to overthrow Barre in January 1991. No sooner had rebels overthrown Barre, than wide differences and factions emerged among the rebels. Not only did they battle for presidency but they further started to divide Somalia. As Ayittey (1999: 34) argues, "the country, in the process of removing Barre, had already been devastated – reduced to an ash heap of charred buildings and burned-out vehicles, with decomposing bodies littering the streets. Yet educated barbarians were waging a fierce battle to determine who would be president, totally unconcerned about the plight of their people."

The demise of Mohamed Said Barre in Somalia in 1991 led to a total collapse of government and incessant fighting. It left a power vacuum that has been filled by competing non state military actors. As much as the Somali people fought against Barre's tyranny, democratic institutions and processes were never developed and a systematic redistribution of power, wealth and status to military actors has ensued. The country has relapsed into conflict that has aggravated destruction and poverty. Up to now there is no strong government in Somalia or services provided to a considerable number of poor people thereby leaving the young unemployed Somalis susceptible to joining radical Islamist group for a living. By and large, in situations where there are limited sources of livelihood, joining military groups is considered as a necessary survival strategy. Somalia has over the years experienced the law of the jungle, terrorism and increased vulnerability. An estimated 300,000-400,000 people died in the 1991 civil war while more than 1.4 million were displaced (Kidane, 2011). Many more people continue to die from the effects of war such as lack of basic medical services, the destruction of rural life and transport and collapse of state, than from direct battlefields deaths. Above all, war has produced a chronic state of uncertainty that retards development. Society cannot progress because fear and uncertainty are ever stronger than the desire for improvement. War has also created a serious food crisis in Somalia and crippled the fragile government's response to food crisis. In 2011, drought led to famine in which 250,000 people died from hunger and related diseases, including cholera (News Day, 4 August 2017). Arguably, there is less resembling a long term silver lining, as long as conflict and poverty are inherent in Somalia. Without peace, the people of Somalia have been unable to achieve the levels of co-operation, inclusiveness and social equity necessary to solve national challenges, let alone empower national institutions needed to regulate the challenges.

Africa's Development path in the 21st century

Admittedly, the chapter has shown the multi complex and dimensional linkages of poverty and conflict which ultimately retard development in Africa. It is within this context that I proffer not only the establishment of durable peace, good leadership, conflict management and prevention, but also good governance, judicious management of resources, poverty alleviation and reduction of inequality, as pre-requisites for sustainable development in Africa. Fundamentally, African states must promote the interconnectedness of sustainable development and peace. Along this thrust it is imperative to promote sustainable development and peace building along three core dimensions of economy, society and environment. Economic sustainability entails maximising society's wellbeing, economic equity, and eradicating poverty through the creation of wealth and livelihoods, equal access to resources and optimal and efficient use of natural resources. Socio-political sustainability means promoting social equity and uplifting the welfare and quality of life by improving access to basic health and education services, fulfilling minimum standards of security and respect for human rights, including the development of diversity, pluralism and grassroots participation. Environmental sustainability entails the enhancement and conservation of the environment and natural resources for present and future generations. As Zhou (2012) argues, sustainable development discourse upholds the three mutually reinforcing pillars of economic development, social development and environmental protection. Sustainable development can, therefore, address the factors that cause or exacerbate inequality, conflict and violence, and mitigate risk of conflict and prevent a relapse of conflict dynamics. Above all, it can transform socio-economic environmental system so that they sustain progress and equitable opportunity.

The case studies on Angola, CAR, Libya, Sierra Leone and Somalia have shown that the absence of mechanisms for peaceful transfer of political power, and for the resolution of conflicts are among major factors that have caused political violence, civil wars and poverty in Africa. Carnage and chaos often result from a mad grab for power centralised at the capital. The long-term solution would involve the decentralisation or diffusion of power and the adoption of power-sharing arrangements; namely democratic pluralism. Indeed there are too many dictators in Africa and this has affected development in the continent. The democratic reform process, which gathered momentum after the collapse of communism in 1989, has stalled. Wily autocrats quickly learned new tricks to beat back the democratic challenge by inflating voter rolls, manipulating the electoral rules, and holding fraudulent elections to keep themselves in power, as in Algeria, Angola, Burundi Cameroon, Congo, DRC, Egypt, Kenya, Mozambique, Sudan, Uganda, and Zimbabwe. Arguably, very few countries have given their people the right to change leaders through the ballot box. The most lethal practice of African leaders is the propensity to perpetually hold onto power. The fatality of an iron grip on power has been demonstrated several times in African politics, from the late Somalian ruler, Said Barre and the late Libyan ruler, Muammar Gaddafi, to Angola's Eduardo Do Santos, Burundi's Pierre Nkurunziza, Cameroon's Paul Biya, Rwanda's Paul Kagame, the DRC's Joseph Kabila, Zimbabwe's Robert Mugabe, Uganda's Yoweri Museveni, Gabon's Bongo dynasty, and Gambia's recently deposed ruler, Yahya Jammeh (Zhou and Machenjera, 2017). With a continued hold on power, leaders start to get a false sense of ownership of a nation, while in reality they are just but citizens mandated with a term to govern a country. Evidently, African leadership is squarely to blame for the stagnation, decay, conflict and backwardness in the continent. Falola (1996: 13) has vividly captured how African leaders are a stumbling block to development. "There is no effective way of changing regimes. Rulers refuse to relinquish power and the military uses violence to perpetuate itself. Political coercion and repression replace democracy. Life presidents have emerged, with a notion that a leader should possess a state and government", he stated. Africa must rid itself of dictatorial, egocentric and one armed bandit leaders so as to foster sustainable development. Such development ensures inclusivity, a balanced quality of life, and goes beyond immediate economic returns.

For this to become a reality, African leaders must play pivotal and committed roles to establish good governance, craft and entrench participatory economic policies, educate the young, establish a generation hostile to corruption, invest in farming and animal husbandry, improve the status and varieties of export items, and be cautious in dealing with foreign aid and support. Admittedly, the employment of peace is a major instrument to avert poverty and conflict in Africa (Zhou, 2016). Peace is the best preventive measure for conflicts, as it paves the way for dialogue, co-operation and compromise, ultimately making it the best framework for development. It follows, therefore, that there is no development without peace, and there is no peace without all-inclusive growth and raising quality of living - for all. Creating employment opportunities, protecting the most vulnerable and empowering people and communities, as well as establishing mechanisms for environmental protection will ensure that African states eradicate poverty and conflict. Elsewhere (Zhou, 2017), I argue that leaders must ensure good stewardship of resources and distribute them fairly, equitably through the system of equal opportunities to serve the working majority of the population. The political commitment to avert conflict through a transparent and accountable process of institutionalised democratisation, trust building, coalition building and developing the culture of settling conflicts through negotiation are indispensable mechanisms to curb problems in Africa. For Africa to be free from poverty and conflict, states should be truly democratic with leaders pursuing egalitarianism. Ekwo (2012: 13) argues that democracy based on freedom of expression, freedom of the press, open government, transparency, accountability and genuine commitment to change will guarantee Africa's growth and development. Above all, the exercise of democratic rights is supportive to economic objectives through revealing where remedial action is needed, thereby applying pressure on government to swiftly respond. Sadly, those in power in Africa are at best prepared to be accountable only to themselves and care little about the notion of popular democracy. Over-centralisation of decision making processes facilitates fraud, which affects not only the governance of the state but the management of the country's entire economy. Conversely, leaders must become democratic and acquaint themselves with the realities of economic dynamics in order to remedy conflict, poverty and underdevelopment inherent in Africa.

African states should unambiguously accept the defective colonial boundaries in order to promote peace and security and in turn eradicate poverty and conflict. The case study on Somalia has shown how the artificial colonial borders in East Africa cut across Somali ethnic ties so that they ended up in five different countries. It is a historical fact that artificial borders contributed to the Ethiopian-Eritrean war of 1998-2000 and North-South Sudan war of 1983-2011. It is, however, noteworthy that the artificial borders are not the tape-root of conflict in Africa. People of Africa traditionally have paid little attention to borders. They move when the need arises, border or no border, as attested to by the movement of refugees. At any rate even the creation of new boundaries between Ethiopia and Eritrea and the independence of South Sudan from Sudan in 2011 did not eradicate poverty and conflict in the respective countries. Above all, lamenting over artificial colonial borders that Organisation of African Union (OAU) – now African Union (AU) – accepted is illusory. The politics of exclusion has been the source of Africa's chronic political instability, civil strife, wars and chaos. Where the ruling elites had the foresight and wisdom to agree to and implement real democratic reform and power sharing, they saved not only themselves but their countries as well. Examples of such cases include Benin, Malawi, Mali, and South Africa (Zhou and Machenjera, 2017). But where benighted rulers and hardliners refused/refuse to share or relinquish power, those excluded had/have no choice but to seek to overthrow the system or to secede. It can, therefore, be argued that internal factors such as poverty of leadership, poor governance and parochialism have far more contributed to political instability, wars, destruction, poverty and underdevelopment than artificial borders. Arguably, an unambiguous acceptance of defective colonial boundaries by African states will certainly enhance peace, security and stability that can in turn foster development and improvement of livelihoods in Africa.

The role of women in African socio-economic and political sphere is minimal, and in some cases as evidenced by Sierra Leone and CAR non-existent. Although women play a crucial role in development, their status in African countries does not reflect their contribution. Colonialism and patriarchy have reduced women to units of production and reproduction. Conflicts in Africa, as shown above, have greatly affected women and children, and in essence ensured that they have become the poorest of the poor. Anunobi (2002) relates the limited investment in agriculture in Africa to dominance of the sector by women and states' reluctance to empower them, with the consequent aggravation of food shortages, poverty and conflict. The majority of women employed outside agriculture are found in the informal sector which is punctuated by low earnings, lack of social protection and vulnerability. Kevane (2014) argues that gender equality and equity in general, and tapping and harnessing of women power and authority in particular, can generate peace, harmony and sustainable development in Africa. He thus provides a gendered cogent analysis of underdevelopment and development in Africa. Arguably, enhancing the status of women would go a long way toward overcoming population and food production challenges and, therefore, help boost economic growth and development. The key to accomplishing women status is to ensure that they have greater influence on social, economic and political issues. As such, women participation is crucial and indispensable in alleviating conflict, poverty and supporting the economic and political endeavours. Given Africa's critical economic and political problems, it appears increasingly obvious that suppressing the talents and skills of women to protect men's privileges is an enormous waste of human resources that Africa with its vast potential can no longer afford. It is therefore imperative to empower women to become drivers of continental peace and security, sustainable development and prosperity. Arguably, inclusive political institutions in support of inclusive economic institutions and gender equity are key ingredients that can foster sustained prosperity.

Education is also an important fulcrum for development and must be promoted and expanded by African leaders in order to enhance peace building, democracy, development and control of population growth in Africa. Arguably, education plays a crucial role in enhancing awareness about the advantages and disadvantages of population increase, democracy, peace, poverty alleviation, responsibility and rights. All in all, the immediate task of leadership in Africa is to restore hope. Leadership in Africa has the additional challenge of proving that Africans can on their own (as Africans) resolve conflicting issues of governance and politics in their national domains in particular. Dictators in Africa must begin to realise that the perennial rule of the 'Big Man', once an African norm, is increasingly becoming unfashionable.

Conclusion

By and large, the links between poverty and conflict are complex and difficult to precisely pin down. There is clearly no single explanatory framework and one directional, mono-causal explanation is analytically and practically vapid and not useful. The chapter has provided a balanced assessment which argues for a two-way causality – poor countries have a greater disposition to conflict, and poverty is also an outcome to conflict. Even when conflict gives way to fragile peace, control over natural resources and their revenues often stays in the hands of a small elite and is not used for the broader development of the country. Evidently, where ever conflict occurs, the society is seriously affected, because it derails developmental gains with the consequent high level of poverty. As such, poverty, inequality, scarcity of resources and external economic forces can have a major destabilising effect on political stability. Similarly, configurations of poverty and bad governance, as evidenced in Angola, CAR, Libya, Sierra Leone and Somalia, result in conflict. Poverty is, therefore, central to the dynamics of conflict in Africa and is both a cause and consequence of conflict. Conversely, social strife and revolutions are not brought out by the conspiratorial or malignant nature of man; rather revolutions are derived from poverty and distributive injustice. When the majority of people are poor and have no hope of ameliorating their condition, they are bound to be restive and seek recompense through violence. No regime can hold stability and peace together when it is created on a sea of poverty. It is for this reason that African leaders must take a leading role in a campaign against poverty, conflict, resource curse, and foster good stewardship of resources, peace, security and sustainable development. Peace conditions development, just as development conditions peace. All in all, peace and security, responsible leadership, good governance, good stewardship and fair distribution of resources, gender equity and education can foster sustainable development in Africa, which in turn can improve mutual trust and cooperation and eventually diminish poverty and conflicts. Evidently, African states must adopt comprehensive approaches to development and provide practical solutions to complex needs of fragile environments where poverty and conflict must be addressed simultaneously.

References

Abdullah, I. (1997). 'Bush Path to Destruction: The Origin and Character of Revolutionary United Front (RUF/SL)', *African Development*, 22 (3/4): 45-76.

Africa Report, (1990). March/April.

Anunobi, F. (2002). 'Women and Development in Africa: From Marginalisation to Gender Inequality', *African Social Science Review*, 2(2): 41-63.

Allais, F.B. (2007). *Children's work in Angola: An overview*, UNICEF, December.

Ahmed, A. (2014). 'Poverty and conflict trap in Somalia', Opinion on Somalia Current.

Aigbe, O. A. (2014). 'Conflict and Poverty in Africa: The Effects of Natural Resource and Leadership', Paper presented at the International Conference on Governance, Peace and Security in Africa, Ekpoma-Institute for Governance and Development: Ambrose Alli University.

Angola, (2015). *Human Rights Report 2015*, United States Department of State, Bureau of Democracy, Human Rights and Labour.

Arieff, A. (2014). *Crisis in the Central African Republic*, Congressional Research Service.

Ayittey, G. N. B. (1999). *Africa in Chaos*, St Martin's Griffin: New York.

Boeke, S. and Zuijdewijn, J. (2016). Transitioning from Military Interventions to Long Term Counter-Terrorism Policy: The Case of Libya, 2011-2016, Australian National University.

Brown, P. P. (2005). *'Sierra Leone: Blood Diamonds'*, http://www.worldpress.org/Africa/*2193* .*cfm. accessed 10 August 2017*.

Campate, F. R. and Chor, D. (2012). 'Why was the Arab World poised for Revolution? Schooling, Economic Opportunities, and the Arab Spring', *Journal of Economic Perspectives*, 26(2): 167-188.

Cederman, L. *et.al.* (2013). *Inequality, Grievances, and Civil War*, Cambridge University Press: New York.

Central Intelligence Agency, (2010). *'The World Facebook – Country Comparison: GDP Per Capita (PPP)'*, CIA The World Facebook.

Clausewitz, C. (1832). *On War*, [edited by Howard, M and Paret, P. 1984], *Princeton University Press: New Jersey*.

Cohen, D. K. (2016). *Rape During Civil War*, Cornell University: New York.

Collier, P. (2000). 'Doing well out of war: An economic perspective', In Berdal, M. and Malone, D.M. (EDs), *Greed and Grievance: Economic Agendas of Civil Wars*, Lynne Rienner Publishers: London, 91-112.

Collier, P. and Hoeffler, A. (2001). 'Greed and Grievance in Civil War', *Centre for the Study of African Economies Working Paper, Oxford University Press: Oxford*.

Collier, P. (2006). Economic Causes of Civil Conflict and their Implications for Policy, Oxford University Press: New York.

Collier, P. (2007). The Bottom Billion: Why the Poorest Countries are failing and what can be done about it, Oxford University Press: Oxford.

Copson, R. W. (1994). *African Wars and Prospects for Peace*, M.E. Sharpe: Armonk.

131

Coulter, C. (2009). *Bush Wives and Girl Soldiers: Women's Lives through War and Peace in Sierra Leone*, Coenell University Press: London.

Davies, V. A. B. (2000). 'Sierra Leone: Ironic Tragedy', *Journal of African Economics*, 9 (3): 349-69.

Duffield, M. (2000). 'Globalisation, Trans-border Trade and War Economies', In: Berdhal, M. and Malone, D.M. (EDs), *Greed and Grievance: Economic Agendas of Civil Wars*, Lynne Rienner Publishers: London, 69-89.

Ekwo, E. (2012). 'Media, Governance and Africa's Agenda for Development', *The Global African Diaspora Parliamentary Summit*, May 22-23, Pan African Parliament: Johannesburg: 1-14.

Falola, T. (1996). 'Africa in Perspective', In Ellis, S. (ED), *Africa Now: Peoples, Policies and Institutions*, James Currey Ltd: London: 3-19.

Fernando, A. G. (1998). *The Origins of Angolan Civil War: Foreign Intervention and Domestic Political Conflict*, Macmillan: London.

Fowler, J. (2004). UNICEF: Human Trafficking in Africa Fuelled by War, Economic Hardship, and Lack of Birth Registration, Associated Press.

Galtung, J. (1996). *Peace by Peaceful Means: Peace and Conflict, Development and Civilization*, International Research Institute: London.

Gberie, L. (2005). *A Dirty War in West Africa: The RUF and the Destruction of Sierra Leone*, Indiana University Press: Bloomington.

Global Witness, (1999). *A Crude Awakening*, GW, December.

Global Witness, (2002). *All the Presidents' Men*, GW, March.

Global Witness, (2004). Time for Transparency: Coming clean on oil, mining and gas, GW, March.

Goodhand, J. (2001). 'Violent Conflict, Poverty and chronic Poverty', *Chronic Poverty Research Centre Paper 6*, Chronic Poverty Research Centre.

Goodhand, J. and Hulme, D. (1999). 'From Wars to complex Political emergencies: Understanding Conflict and Peace-building in the new World disorder', *Third World Quarterly*, 20(1): 13-26.

Gordon, C. (2005). Diamond Industry Annual Review: Republic of Angola 2005.

Green, R.H. (1994). 'The Course of the Four Horsemen: The Costs of War and its Aftermath in Sub-Saharan Africa', In Macre, J. and

Zwi, A. (EDs), *War and Hunger: Rethinking International Responses to Complex Emergencies*, Zed: London, 37-49.

Gurr, T. *et.al.* (2001). *Peace and Conflict 2001. A Global Survey of Armed Conflicts, Self-Determination Movements and Democracy*, Centre for International Development and Conflict Management: University of Maryland, U.S.

Hirsh, J. L. (2001). *Sierra Leone: Diamonds and Struggle for Democracy*, Lynne: Boulder.

Hoeffler, A. & Reynal-Querol, M. (2003). 'Measuring the Cost of Conflict', Unpublished Manuscript, Centre for the Study of African Economies, Oxford University: Oxford.

Humphreys, M. & Habaye, M. (2003). 'Senegal and Mali'. Paper Prepared for Case Study Project on Civil War: New Haven, Connecticut.

Ikejiaku, B.V. (2012). 'Poverty-Conflict Nexus: The Contentious Issue Revisited', *European Journal of Sustainable Development*, 1(2): 127-150.

Internal Displacement Monitoring Centre, (2014). Central African Republic: amid extreme poverty and state fragility, more robust response needed, http: www.internal-displacement.org, accessed 19 August 2017.

International Business Publication USA, (2007). *Central African Republic Foreign Policy and Government Guide*, Business Publications: Washington, DC.

International Crisis Group, (2007). 'Central African Republic: Anatomy of a Phantom State', http://www.crisisgroup.org/en/regions/africa/centralafrica/ce ntral-african-republic/136-central-african-republic-anatomy-of-a-phantom-state.aspx> [accessed 30 April 2014].

Isichei, E. (1987). 'The Maitatsine Rising in Nigeria, 1980-1985: A Revolt of the Disinherited', *Journal of Religion in Africa*, 17(3): 194-208.

James, W. M. (2011). *A Political History of the Civil War in Angola*: 1974-1990, Transaction Publishers: Piscataway.

Justino, P. (2006). *On the Links between Violent Conflict and Chronic Poverty: How much Do We Really Know*, Institute of Development Studies (IDS), University of Sussex: Brighton.

Justino, P. and Verwimp, P. (2006). 'Poverty Dynamics, Conflict and Convergence in Rwanda', Working Paper No. 16, Households in Conflict Network, Institute of Development Studies: University of Sussex Brighton.

Kalck, P. (Ed). (2005). *Historical Dictionary of the Central African Republic*, 3rd ed, Scarecrow Press: Lanham.

Kapusckinski, R (2001). *The Shadow of the Sun*, Alfred A. Knopf: New York.

Keen, D. (1998). 'The economic functions of violence in civil wars' Adelphi Paper, International Institute of Strategic Studies, London.

Keen, D. (2005). *Conflict and Collusion in Sierra Leone*, Palgrave Macmillan: Basingstoke.

Kevane, M. (2014). *Women in Development in Africa: How Gender Works*, Lynne Rienner Publishers: London.

Kidane, M. (2011). Critical Factors in the Horn of Africa's Raging Conflict, Discussion Paper, Nordiska Africainstitute: Uppsala.

Kimenyi, M. and Ndung'u, N. (2002). 'Sporadic Ethnic Violence: Why has Kenya not experience full-blown civil war?' Prepared for Case Study Project on Civil War: New Haven, Connecticut.

Lacher, W. (2011). 'Families, Tribes and Cities in the Libyan Revolution', *Middle East Policy*, 18(4): 140-154.

Le Billion, P. and Levin, E. (2009). 'Building Peace with Conflict Diamonds? Merging Security and Development in Sierra Leone' *Development and Change*, 40 (4): 693-715.

Lentz, H. M. (2014). *Heads of States and Governments since 1945*, Routledge: London.

Lichbach, M. I. (1994). 'Rethinking Rationality and Rebellion: Theories of Collective Action and Problems of Collective Dissident', *Rationality and Society*, 6(1): 8-39.

Martinez, L. (2007). *The Libyan Paradox*, Hurst and Company: London.

Meger, S. (2016). *Rape Loot Pillage: The Political Economy of Sexual Violence in Armed Conflict*, Oxford University Press: Oxford.

Nafziger, E. W. (1973). 'The Political Economy of Disintegration in Nigeria', *Journal of Modern African Studies*, 11 (4): 505-536.

Nafziger, E. W. (1983). *The Economics of Political Instability: The Nigerian-Biafra War*, Westview Press: Boulder.

Nelson, Joan (1998). 'Poverty, Inequality and Conflict in Developing Countries', *Rockefeller Brothers Fund Project on International Security*.

Narayan, D. *et.al.* (2000). *Voices of the Poor: Can Anyone Hear Us?*, Oxford University Press: New York.

New Africa Yearbook, 1991-1992.

News Day, 2017. 10 August.

News Day, 2017. 4 August.

Pacheko, F. (2001). 'Rural Communities in Huambo', *Community and Reconstruction in Angola*, Development Workshop Occasional Paper, No. 1.

Pargeter, A. (2012). *Libya, the Rise and Fall of Quddafi*, Yale University Press: London.

Pastoor, D. (2013).Vulnerability Assessment of the Christians in the Central African Republic, World Watch Unit-Open Doors International.

Peleman, J. (2000). 'Mining for Serious Trouble: Jean-Raymond Roulle and His Corporate Empire Project', In Musah, F. and Fayemi, J.K. (EDs), *Mercenaries: An African Security Dilemma*. London: Pluto Press.

Ramlogan, R. (2004). *The Developing World and the Environment: Making the case for Effective Protection of the Global Environment*, University Press of America: New York.

Rasheed, D. (2003). 'Poverty and Conflict in Africa: Explaining a Complex Relationship', Experts Group Meeting on Africa-Canada Parliamentary Strengthening Program, Addis Ababa.

Rena, R. (2007). 'Trends and Determinants of Poverty in the Horn of Africa – Some Implications', *Journal of Social Development. An International Journal*, 7(1): 65-77.

Reno, W. (1995). *Corruption and State Politics in Sierra Leone*, Cambridge University Press: Cambridge.

Reno, W. (1998). *Warlord Politics and African States*, Lynne Rienner: Boulder.

Reno, W. (2000). 'Shadow States and the Political Economy of Civil Wars', In Berdal, M. and Malone, D. M. (EDs), *Greed and*

Grievance: Economic Agendas of Civil Wars, Lynne Rienner Publishers: London, 43-68.

Restrepo, J. *et.al*. (2008). 'Study of the relationship between Conflict and Poverty and its relevance for the Swedish cooperating strategy with Columbia', *Final Report*.

Richards, P. (1996). *Fighting for the Rainforest: War, Youth and Resources in Sierra Leone*, James Curry: Oxford.

Riddell, B. (2005). 'Sierra Leone: Urban-Elite Bias, Atrocity and Debt', *Review of African Political Economy*, 32 (103): 115-133.

Ross, M. L. (2003). 'The Natural Resource Curse: How Wealth Can Make You Poor', In Bannon, I. and Collier, P. (EDs), *Natural Resources and Violent Conflict: Options and Actions*, World Bank Publications: Washington D.C.: 17-42.

Ross, M. L. (1999). 'The Political Economy of Resource Curse', in *World Politics*, 51 (2): 297-322.

Ross, M. L. (2004). 'How do Natural Resources influence Civil War? Evidence from thirteen cases', *International Organisation*, 58(1): 35-67.

Sen, A. (1982). *Poverty and Famines: An Essay on Entitlement and Deprivation*, Oxford University Press: Oxford.

Shukla, G. (ED), (2008). 'Poverty', *Encyclopaedia Britannica*.

Simons, G. (2003). *Libya and the West: From Independence to Lockerbie*, Centre for Libyan Studies: Oxford.

SOS, (2016). Children's Villages in Central Africa Republic, http: www.SOS-childrensvillages.org/where-we-help/Africa/central-africa-republic, accessed 10 August 2017.

Stewart, F. (2010). 'Horizontal Inequalities as Causes of Conflict: A review of CRISE findings', *Centre for Research on Inequality and Human Security and Ethnicity*, No.1.

Tanca, A. (1993). *Foreign Armed Intervention in Internal Conflict*, M. Nijhoff Publishers: Boston.

The Economist, (2013). Business in the Democratic Republic of Congo, 18 May.

Tvedten, I. (1997). *Angola: Struggle for Peace and Reconstruction*, Westview Press: Boulder.

Tvedten, I. *et.al*. (2017). 'Rural Poverty in Malanje, Angola', Chr. Michelsen Institute (CMI Report 2017.)

UNDP, (1991). *Human Development Report 1991*, Oxford University Press: Oxford.

UNDP, (2001). *Human Development Report 2001*, Oxford University: New York.

UNDP, (2010). *Human Development Report 2010*, Oxford University: New York.

UNDP, (2016). *Human Development Report 2016: Human Development for Everyone, UNDP: Washington.*

UNDP. (2017). *Human Development Index,* UNDP: Washington.

UNDP-Freetown, (1996). *National Human Development Report for Sierra Leone 1996*, UNDP: Freetown.

UNECA, (2016). *Greening Africa's Industrialization: Economic Report on Africa*, UNECA.

UNICEF, (2015). *Situation Analysis. Children and Women in Angola*, UNICEF: Luanda.

USAID, (2001). 'Sierra Leone: Conflict Diamonds', *Progress Report on Diamond Policy and Development Programme*, Office of Transition Initiatives: USAID.

Vines, A. (1999). *Angola Unravels: The Rise and Fall of Lusaka Peace Process*, Human Rights Watch: New York.

Wanyande, P. (1997). 'State driven Conflict in the Greater Horn of Africa', Revised Paper presented at the USAID Organised Workshop on Conflict in the Great Horn of Africa, 21-23 May, Methodist House: Nairobi.

Warshel, Y. (2012). 'Political Alienation in Libya: Assessing Citizens' Political behaviour'. *Journal of North African Studies*, 17(4): 734-737).

Weinstein, J. and Francisco, L. (2002). 'External Actors as Source of War in Mozambique', Paper Prepared for Case Study Project on Civil War: New Haven, Connecticut.

Whiteside, A. (2002). 'Poverty and HIV/AIDS in Africa', *Third world quarterly*, 23(2): 313-332.

Woodward, P. (1996). *The Horn of Africa: State Politics and International Relations,* I. B. Tauris Publishers: London.

World Bank, (2007). *Global Monitoring Report 2007*: 44-45, www.worldbank.org/gmr2007, accessed 12 August 2017.

World Bank, (2016). *Republic of Angola. Poverty and Social Impact Analysis*, World Bank: Luanda.

World Bank. (2017). The World Bank in Central African Republic, htpp://www.worldbank.org/en/who-we-are, accessed 20 August 2017.

Zhou, T. M. (2012). 'Environmental Mining in Colonial Zimbabwe: A Case Study of Mberengwa District, 1894-198', *D.Phil. Thesis*, History Department, University of Zimbabwe.

Zhou, T. M. and Makahamadze, T. (2012). *Asset or Liability? The Leadership of Mugabe in Independent Zimbabwe*, Lambert Academic Publishing: Saarbrucken.

Zhou, T. M. (2016). 'Envisaged Trends in Post-2016 African Development Agenda and their Impact on World Economic System', In Marongwe, N. and Mawere, M. (EDs), *Politics, Violence and Conflict Management in Africa: Envisioning Transformation, Peace and Unity in the Twenty-First Century*, Langaa Research & Publishing CIG: Bamenda: 199-232.

Zhou, T. M. (2017). 'Poverty, Natural Resources "Curse" and Underdevelopment in Africa', In Mawere, M. *Underdevelopment, Development and the Future of Africa*, Langaa Research & Publishing: Cameroon: 279-346.

Zhou, T. M. and Machenjera, P. (2017). 'Colonialism, Poverty and [Under-]development in Africa', In: Mawere, M. *et.al* (EDs), *The African Conundrum: Rethinking Trajectories of Historical, Cultural, Philosophical and Developmental Experiences of Africa*, Langaa Research & Publishing: Cameroon: 33-96.

Chapter 6

The Impact of Poverty on Infant and Maternal Mortality Rates in Nigeria: Some Lessons and Insights for Africa

Mohammed Y. Abubakar; Joseph A. Oluyemi; Joseph Adejoke; Raji Abdullateef; Kadiri Kehinde; & Atolagbe Emmanuel

Introduction

In the recent years, Nigeria has experienced massive increase in infant and maternal mortality rates as a result of the prevailing poverty rocking the country (Adamu, 2005, Ucha, 2010 and USAID, 2012). Poverty, which is sometimes determined by the level of income and expenditure people are predisposed to (Oduro and Aryee, 2003) as well as individual's social interactions and state of mental well-being, is deeply entrenched in the Nigerian Society. Incidentally, many infant and maternal deaths could be averted if, basic necessities of life such as, balanced diet, social security, and good healthcare services, among others could have been affordable by many.

With nearly two-thirds of Nigeria's population living below the poverty datum line, and surviving on less than one dollar per day (Ejikeme, 2014), many Nigerians cannot afford to pay for quality health care services while many cannot afford three square meals per day (UNESCO, 2015). This poses a serious challenge to majority of the poor who consequentially are incapacitated to access basic health services while many languish in hunger, malnutrition and fatalities particularly children and women of reproductive age thus, resulting in high mortality among the people.

It is against this backdrop that, this chapter explores the impact of poverty on infant and maternal health in Nigeria. It is anticipated that results from such a study as this would help to inform and address similar situations across Africa and beyond. The chapter further examines the concept of poverty as it relates to the Nigerian context. It focuses on the Nigerian healthcare system as well as infant and maternal mortality in the country. The policy implications for infant and maternal health in Nigeria are also broadly enumerated alongside with the lessons and insights for Africa and the recent measures embarked upon to reduce infant and maternal mortality in Nigeria.

Poverty in Nigeria

Poverty is a multi-dimensional phenomenon that entails social, economic, political and mental elements of the society (Mawere, 2017). Nigeria with a population of over 140 million people and a nominal Gross Domestic Product of about 207.11 billion Dollars and per capita income of 1,401Dollars (Salami, 2011), has, majority of the population enmeshed in the net of absolute poverty due to faulty economic policies and unsustainable poverty alleviation programmes of successive governments (Ejikeme, 2014). A huge percentage of its population live below 2 dollars per day and as such, insufficient money to pay for medical expenses serves as a barrier for treatment (Jeorge, 2014).

According to Garba (2006), the world's per capita income as of 2003 was 7,140 Dollars, however, when this is compared to Nigeria's per capita income of 290 Dollars, it makes Nigeria one of the poorest countries in the world behind countries like, Togo with 270 Dollars, Rwanda with 220 Dollars, and Mali with 210 Dollars per capital income respectively. Also, other indicators of development such as life expectancy, for which Nigeria is ranked 155th out of the world's 177 countries, and infant mortality, for which Nigeria is ranked 148th among 173 countries, were consistent with Nigeria's low rank in income per capita (CIA, 2009).

Based on these statistics, Nigeria has been classified as amongst the poorest nations in the world, a situation which can be described as a bewildering paradox given the vast resource base of the country. Unfortunately, Bayelsa State which is regarded as one of the highest measures of welfare per capital income in Nigeria, has a poverty incidence of 26.2 per cent between 1995 and 2006, which is still below the leading areas in Greater Accra, Ghana with 2.4 per cent,

Douala, in Cameroun Capital with10.9 per cent and Boateng in South Africa with 19.0 per cent (World Bank, 2008).

Geographic Zone	Absolute Poverty %	Relative Poverty%	Dollar per day
North-Central	59.9	67.5	59.7
North-East	60.0	76.3	69.1
North-West	70.0	77.7	70.4
South-East	58.7	67.0	59.2
South-South	55.9	63.8	56.1
South-West	49.8	59.1	50.1

Figure 1: Incidence of Poverty by Zone in Nigeria
Source: National Bureau of Statistics (2012)

The state of the Nigerian Healthcare System

Health care provision in Nigeria is the responsibility of the three tiers of government, i.e. the Federal, State and Local government while the private sector also play along (Aktah, 1991). The Federal government controls the affairs of the teaching hospitals and other tertiary hospitals, the State government oversees the activities of the general hospitals and other secondary health facilities while, the Local government sees to the affairs of the primary health centres all around the country. Unfortunately, despite Nigeria's strategic position as the giant of Africa, and her position in the League of Nations globally, Nigeria is still underserved in the healthcare spheres when compared to other sectors (Health Reform Foundation of Nigeria, 2010; Asangansi & Shaguy, 2011).

In May 1999, the Nigerian government created the National Health Insurance Scheme, the scheme encompasses government employees, the organized private sector as well as the informal sector. The health insurance scheme however could only apply to a few people such as government employees and those working in private firms who were privileged to enter into contracts with private health care providers (Ogundipe, 2011). As such, only a few people who fall within these categories could benefit from the scheme. The nation's poor healthcare delivery has however, been blamed on rising cost,

141

limited financial resources, inefficient health systems as well as the huge burden of diseases.

Also, several challenges have been reported within the health sector, especially in training, funding, employment, and deployment of the health workforce (Adeloye, David, Olaogun, Auta, Adesokan, Gadanya, Opele, Owagbemi and Iseolorunkanmi, 2017). For example, despite the high volume of human resources for health available in the country, Nigeria still cannot effectively deliver essential health services to her teeming population (Akinsete, 2016 and World Health Organization, 2017). While majority of her workforce is concentrated in urban centres (Awofeso, 2010).

As at 2010, reports have it that, the number of Nigerian trained doctors practicing in the United States and the United Kingdom stood at 2,392 and 1,529 respectively while the ratio of doctors to patients available in the country to offer health care services to the people only stood at, 39 per 100,000 people (Ogbom-Egbulem, 2010). Reports also have it that, some of the best doctors in the world who have made remarkable contributions in the field of medicine come from Nigeria (Akande, 2015), while many of the hospitals, especially government owned hospitals in and around the country, are in bad shape (Akor, 2015).

Sad to also know that, modern diagnostic procedures like, Magnetic Resonance Imaging (MRI), Computed Tomography (CT) scans common and affordable in many developed countries for instance are not affordable to many in Nigeria, as they are exclusive preserved of the rich (John, 2016). Some government owned hospitals even refer patients to private laboratory and diagnostic centres for their laboratory examinations and investigations which are not easily affordable (Mekwunye, 2016).

Also, the Nigerian health system has recently experienced numerous incessant industrial strike actions involving doctors, nurses and allied healthcare workers as a result of various demands and unhealthy rivalry among health professionals in the system (Olatunji, 2013; Hassan, 2013; Okafor, 2013; Premium Times, 2014; Obi, 2014; Ibeh, 2015 and Ehanire, 2016). This has however, been identified as a major contributor to the country's poor health indices which has brought untold hardship to many families and patients across the country (Ogbebo, 2015). This causes several avoidable deaths, complications and outgoing medical tourism (Adepimpe, Owolade & Adebimpe, 2010).

In addition to this, the Nigerian health system in recent times has also had to deal with the high incidence of various diseases. Aside from malaria which has been prevalent among many in the country from time immemorial, the system have had to deal recently with other emerging diseases such as HIV/AIDS, Ebola and Lassa fever which has posed a major strain on the system.

Figure 2: *Picture showing a dilapidated health care facility in Nigeria*
Source: *The Guardian, 2016*

Consequences of Poor Health System in Nigeria

Infant Mortality in Nigeria

One of the consequences of poor health facilities in Nigeria is the problem of infant mortality. Infant mortality refers to deaths of young children, typically those less than one year of age. According to the (CIA World Fact Book, 2017), infant mortality rate in Nigeria as at 2017 is 71.2 deaths/1,000 live births. However, many of infant death recorded are as a result of poor maternal health and poor care at time of delivery (NDHS, 2003). Like the grown-up population, many children also lack access to safe water and sanitation, which typically leads to several diseases that causes death in infancy (Ucha, 2010).

Infectious conditions such as septicaemia, pneumonia and meningitis account for the greatest proportion (42%) of deaths within the first month of life while delivery-related complications, such as, asphyxia and birth trauma account for 32%, and pregnancy-related complications such as eclampsia, malaria, anemia, and malnutrition for the remaining 26% of neonatal deaths (Khashu, Narayanan, Bhargava and Osiovic, 2009).

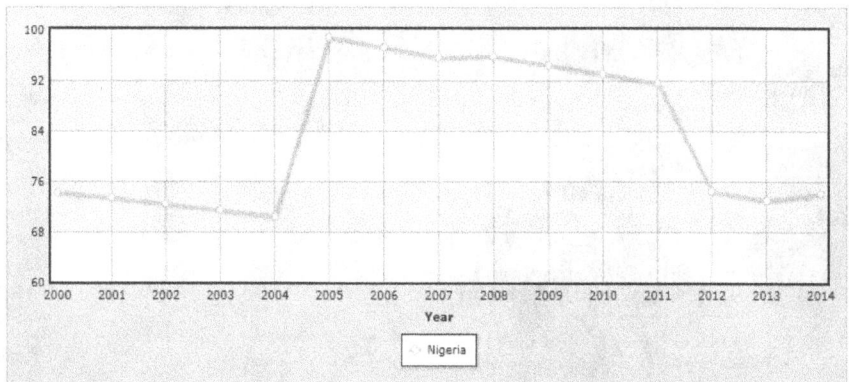

Figure 3: *Graph Showing Infant mortality rate in Nigeria (deaths/1,000 live births)*
Source: *CIA World Fact book, 2015*

Maternal Mortality in Nigeria

Another major consequence of poor health system in Nigeria is the problem of maternal mortality. Maternal mortality has been defined by birth (Yaukey and Anderton, 2001) as, female deaths associated with pregnancy, labour and the puerperium, the period immediately following child-delivery. It has also been defined as, the death of a woman while pregnant or within 42 days of termination of pregnancy, irrespective of the duration and site of the pregnancy, from any cause related to or aggravated by the pregnancy or its management, but not from accidental or incidental causes. (Lale and Mile, 2005)

The (World Health Organization, 2004) categorised maternal death into two major groups namely: direct and indirect obstetric death. Direct obstetric death are those maternal deaths that, result from obstetric complications of the pregnant state (pregnancy, labour and the puerperium) from interventions, omissions, incorrect treatment, or from a chain of events resulting from any of the above while indirect obstetric death are those maternal deaths that result from previous existing disease or disease that developed during pregnancy and which was not due to direct obstetric causes, but was aggravated by the physiological effects of pregnancy.

According to a (Ifijie, 2016), approximately 830 women die from preventable causes related to pregnancy and childbirth every day and a high percentage of all maternal deaths occur in developing countries, including Nigeria. In terms of the maternal mortality ratio, Nigeria is ranked eighth in Sub-Saharan Africa behind, Angola, Chad, Liberia, Niger, Rwanda, Sierra Leone and Somalia (Akinrinola, Sedgh, Okonofua, Imarhiagbe, Hussain and Wulf. 2009). This is as a result of the endemic nature of poverty in the country which limits peoples' access to basic services like health.

Research conducted in some locations in Nigeria has shown a drastic decline in hospital births apparently as a result of the country's deepening economic crises (National Population Commission, 2004, Adamu, 2005 and USAID, 2006).This explains why the life time risk of a woman dying as a result of pregnancy or child birth in the county is high. Poverty also limits peoples' access to food and balanced diet, thereby causing hunger and malnutrition which is found to increase vulnerability to serious and chronic illness, mental retardation and early death, especially among women of reproductive age and infants (Wermuth, 2003).

Measures Embarked upon by Government to Reduce Infant and Maternal Mortality in Nigeria

(a) Policy on Infant and Young Child Feeding in Nigeria
The National Policy on Infant and Young Child Feeding in Nigeria introduced in 2005 advocates the following policy statement for infants in Nigeria:

- The policy shall be known and referred to as the "National Policy on Infant and Young Child Feeding in Nigeria".
- . The Policy reaffirms government's commitment to optimal feeding of all children from birth, as a public health measure, and the

implementation of the global strategy for infant and young child feeding for improved child survival.

- Exclusive breastfeeding for the first six months of life shall be promoted and strengthened.
- In all population groups, breastfeeding shall be protected, promoted and supported, unless medically contra-indicated, on case-by-case basis and this should be in line with the provision of the Code of Marketing of breast milk Substitutes.
- All public and private places of employment shall be actively encouraged to provide crèches and establish flexible nursing periods during the working hours.
- Exclusive breastfeeding for the first six months of life shall be followed by the introduction of complementary foods that are safe, appropriate, locally available and nutritionally adequate, with continued breastfeeding for up to two years and beyond. The timing of introduction of complementary foods shall be from six months of life, except otherwise medically indicated.
- All individuals especially women of child bearing age shall have access to confidential voluntary counselling and testing to ascertain their HIV status and thus facilitate informed decision on infant feeding options.
- Mothers who are found to be HIV negative shall be counselled to breastfeed exclusively for six months, followed by complementary feeding with safe, appropriate, locally available and nutritionally adequate foods while continuing breastfeeding for up to two years and beyond. Such HIV negative mothers shall be encouraged to maintain their HIV status.
- Mothers who do not know their HIV status shall be counselled on confidential voluntary testing and the need to know their status, while encouraging them to adopt the feeding advice for mothers that are HIV negative.
- Mothers diagnosed and certified HIV positive shall be counselled on possible feeding options.
- . Government shall endeavour to train health and community workers to promote, protect and support optimal infant and young child feeding in all situations including emergencies and large displacement of persons, among others.

- In situations where the mother cannot breastfeed, caregivers/mothers shall be counselled and supported to practice replacement feeding of choice e.g. wet nursing, infant formula feeding, home prepared formula feeding.
- In cases of donations of commercial milk formulae during emergencies or to orphanages, they shall be given to only those who need them and for as long as they are required. Donations shall conform with the National Code on Marketing of breast milk Substitutes.

(b) Policy on Maternal Health in Nigeria

According to the Federal Ministry of Health (2001). The following are the policies national reproductive health policy and strategy to achieve quality reproductive and sexual health for all Nigerians:

- All tiers of Government hereby agree that the reproductive health of the people does not only contribute to better quality of lives but, is also essential for the sustained economic and social development of the nation.
- The people of Nigeria shall participate individually and collectively in the planning, implementation and evaluation of their reproductive health care.
- The Government and people of Nigeria affirm that the National Policy on Reproductive Health shall be complementary to the National Health Policy and its strategies to achieve health for all Nigerians;
- Government shall establish a sustainable framework to regulate and facilitate the implementation of the reproductive health policy, strategy and interventions;
- She shall promote the Reproductive Health Concept throughout the country using a multi-sectorial approach within the broader context of macro-economic policies;
- Review and update relevant policies, laws, strategies and programmes to encompass the broad spectrum of reproductive health issues in a coherent and integrated manner, with particular attention to priority-setting;

- Ensure compliance by all tiers of government and individuals with all relevant treaties, policies and laws supporting the attainment of the highest level of reproductive health irrespective of age, sex, ethnicity, religion and socio-economic status;
- Protect reproductive tights through the creation of an enabling legal environment by, the amendment and repeal of all laws contradicting reproductive rights principles and the enactment of appropriate legislation;
- Protect the rights of all people to make and act on decisions about their own reproductive health free from coercion or violence, and based on full information within the framework of acceptable ethical standards;
- Formulate and enforce legal instruments to support activities aimed at eliminating the practice of female genital mutilation and other forms of harmful practices such as gender-based violence especially sexual violence and rape, through intensified focus on public education and involvement of health care providers in the recognition and management of the Problems
- Ensure access of the public to scientifically proven preventive and curative reproductive health conditions including HIV/AIDS and protect them from unproven claims.
- Remove all forms of barriers that limit access to comprehensive, integrated and qualitative reproductive health care;
- Adapt health facilities to the new concept of reproductive health as part of primary ,health care through expansion and strengthening of outreach efforts at community level;
- Establish appropriate mechanisms for the review of relevant curricula and training manuals of schools of medicine, nursing and health technology in order to incorporate reproductive health concepts, principles, strategies and methodologies;
- Sustain and increase support to appropriate training of all cadres of health personnel (including various categories of community health workers) in reproductive health;
- Establish an enabling environment for all cadres of service providers through support for continuing education, constant supervision, provision of incentives and removal of all barriers to the delivery of quality reproductive health care including counselling

- Develop and encourage use of technologies and methodologies appropriate to effective delivery of quality reproductive health care at all levels;
- Promote access to information on family planning and provide wide choices of contraceptive methods including surgical methods and encourage the development of new initiatives for identifying and solving logistical problems at all levels;
- Provide comprehensive (including referral), client-oriented reproductive health services that are of good quality, equitably accessible, affordable and appropriate to the needs of individual men and women, families and communities, especially under- served groups such as adolescents and youths, persons with disability, underprivileged populations and people living with HIV/AIDS (PLWHA);
- Lower the risk of maternal and perinatal deaths through improved access to Emergency Obstetric Care (EOC) and post-abortion services;
- Develop appropriate, culture- and gender- sensitive information, education and communication materials in support of reproductive health so as to enhance the adoption of healthy reproductive health behaviour and lifestyles;
- Promote male involvement and support for reproductive health programmes in its entity;
- Remove all institutional and legal barriers, including barriers to education for girls, that prevent women from becoming equal partners in decision-making and development;
- Ensure that young people have the information, skills and means to prevent unwanted pregnancies, HIV/AIDS and other sexually transmitted infections;
- Develop appropriate criteria and guidelines to provide support for the development of minimum packages of reproductive health services appropriate for delivery at various levels of health care as well as for programmes and activities based on priority needs;
- Promote and support research relevant to reproductive health;
- Recognise and support the role of professional bodies, non-governmental organisations, CBOs, the private sector, international

bilateral and multilateral agencies in reproductive health programmes;

- Promote collaboration, partnerships and networking among all stakeholders in reproductive health projects and programmes;
- Establish mechanisms to co-ordinate all reproductive health activities in order to facilitate the mobilisation of resources for effective joint prioritisation, planning and implementation of the various components of the Reproductive Health Strategy;
- Provide adequate funding of reproductive health programmes through increased and timely financial contributions, judicious and transparent use of funds available to the programmes.
- Establish mechanisms for monitoring the quality, cultural acceptability, gender-sensitivity, comprehensiveness of, accessibility to, reproductive health information and care, particularly at community level using selected indicators within the broader framework of the National Health Management Information System;
- Strengthen the institutional capacity of the national health management information systems in order to adequately address reproductive health needs; Support the production, storage, retrieval and distribution of relevant literature/reports on reproductive health programmes and activities.

Unfortunately, despite attempts made in the past aimed at reducing infant and maternal mortality in Nigeria, such attempts, especially by the Federal and state governments, have generally not proved very successful in achieving the desired results. However, some promising results have recently begun to be recorded through some policy initiatives by a few State governments. In Anambra state for example, the state house of assembly approved a bill in 2005, guaranteeing free maternal health services to pregnant women (Shiffman and Okonofua, 2007). In Kano state, the state government included in its budget a line item for free maternal health services. Also in Jigawa State, state and local budgets have provided funds for the upgrading of obstetric care facilities in hospitals, the recruitment of obstetricians and gynaecologists and the provision of ambulances at the local level to transport pregnant women experiencing delivery complications to health facilities (Mojekwu and Ibekwe, 2012).

In addition, the Lagos State Government, in an effort stem the tide of maternal and child deaths recently set up five Maternal and Child Care centres (MCCs) fully equipped and well-staffed to provide a wide spectrum of care including family planning, ante- and post-natal care to facilitate safety of women during child delivery. The MCCs are located in Surulere, Ikorodu, Isolo, Ifako-Ijaiye, Ajeromi, Alimosho, Ibeju-Lekki, Epeand Badagry among others (Sunday Punch, 2012). One recent initiative that seems to be successful is the Ondo State Government initiative known as Abiye. This initiative in the rural communities in Ondo State, uses mobile phones to save lives of indigent pregnant women.

According to the World Bank (2008), 51.6 per cent of Nigerians live in rural areas, most of who are cut off from modern medical facilities, making pregnant women vulnerable to readily preventable adverse outcomes. Most of these adverse outcomes result from delay in seeking care, getting to health centres when care is sought, receiving care on getting to the health centre, and referring patients to more advanced centres when necessary. In the Ondo State initiative, pregnant women go for antenatal care at primary health care centres where each one is given a mobile phone. The pregnant women are put in government prepaid, caller-user groups and tracked by trained personnel so the pregnancy is monitored. Calls to the healthcare personnel are toll free (Sunday Punch, 2011) primarily because the lines are toll free the delay in seeking care is minimised to almost zero. The programme also takes care of the delay in reaching health centres since ambulances are stationed to bring in the pregnant women when they call. In emergencies, the health personnel go on motorcycle with a First Aid box. If it is something they can't handle, the women are taken to the general hospital.

Some Lessons and Insights for Africa

• One of the lessons that have been learnt from the Nigerian experience of infant and maternal health is that the Nigerian government should have done all in her capacity to improve the standard of living of the Nigerian people. Since majority of the people in the country live below poverty datum line (Ejikeme, 2014) and as such cannot afford the basic necessities of life in which health services is included. This could have been done by raising the standard of living of the people, reducing inflation, creating employment opportunities for the teeming population and provision of basic amenities that make life comfortable for the people. This would have gone a long way in reducing to the barest minimum the incidences of infant and maternal death among the people.

• Another lesson learnt from the Nigerian experience is that, government and other relevant agencies should not have undermined the infant and maternal health facilities for the teeming population. According to (Akinsete, 2016) The Nigeria government has not been able to provide quality health care to her populace due to inadequate basic infrastructure and obsolete medical equipment. Many of the health facilities in and around the country, especially government owned hospitals are arguably in bad shape (Akor, 2015).If this has been done, many of the infant and maternal deaths could have been averted and many lives could have been saved. Therefore any government that wants a healthy nation should not undermine the health of her citizenry.

• Furthermore, another lesson that could be learnt from the Nigerian experience for Africa is the issue of provision of Health Insurance that did not cover all (Ogundipe, 2011). Health insurance scheme in the country would have covered all categories of people including infants and women of reproductive age. This would have afforded many the opportunities to access infant and maternal health services and many infant and maternal deaths would have been averted. This is because it has been argued that, many of those who find themselves in this predicaments could not actually afford to pay for quality health services (UNESCO, 2015) and as such, would have been saved from infant and maternal mortality.

• In addition, rigorous and wider dissemination of infant and maternal health would have been provided both in English language and other local languages in the country, in order for the teeming population to access infant and maternal health information. This is because, information is key to health seeking behaviours and favourable health outcomes (Godlee, Pakenham-Walsh, Ncayiyana, Cohen, & Packer, 2004), it is imperative for individuals to be equipped with the right information on their health. (Fischetti,2011) has also argued further that, the more educated a woman is, the better they are able to make decisions concerning on their reproductive health like, prenatal care, basic hygiene, nutrition and immunization which are vital to reducing infant and maternal mortality.

- Lastly, the Nigerian government would have invested more on the health system to make the system more attractive for both patients and health workers by increasing the percentage of the budgetary allocation for the heath sector to meet the minimum requirement of the Millennium Development Goal. According to (Alabi, Adams, chime, Abu and Aiglomudu, 2010), less than 1% of GDP in Nigeria was allocated to health care provision and about 2% of government oil revenue was allocated to health sector between 1981 and 2006. This low financial commitment will only result in inequality in access to health care resources and since majority of Nigerian is poor and pay for their health care out of their pocket money may be left of health care provision (Ehikioya and Mohammed, 2013).

Confronting the infant and maternal mortality problem in Nigeria: Some recommendations

Improved Standard of Living
Standard of living refers to the level of wealth, comfort, material goods and necessities available to a certain socioeconomic class in a certain country. This may include among others, factors such as income, quality and availability of employment, class disparity, poverty rate, quality and affordability of housing, hours of work required to purchase necessities, gross domestic product, inflation rate, amount of leisure time every year, affordable (or free) access to quality healthcare, quality and availability of education, life expectancy, incidence of disease, cost of goods and services, infrastructure, national economic growth, economic and political stability, political and religious freedom, environmental quality, climate and safety.

The standard of living is closely related to quality of life (Investopedia.com). In Nigeria, widespread and severe poverty is a reality. It is a reality that depicts a lack of food, clothes, education and other basic amenities. Severely poor people lack the most basic necessities of life to a degree that it can be wondered how they manage to survive. However, one of the main effects of poverty is poor health, as is reflected in Nigeria's high infant mortality and low life expectancy. It has been found that malnutrition causes increased vulnerability to serious and chronic illness, mental retardation and early death (USAID, 2002). Poor people in Nigeria face several health issues as they lack basic health amenities and competent medical practitioners. Most children do not have the opportunity of being immunized and this leads to certain physical defects in some of the children. Their health has become low priority and as they have little or no choices, they live with whatever they are provided with, whether healthy or not (Uchua, 2010). This makes many vulnerable to illness and diseases and as such, stands the risk of death.

Provision of Adequate Healthcare Facilities

The nation's poor healthcare delivery has been blamed on rising cost, limited financial resources, inefficient health systems as well as the huge burden of diseases (Obinna, 2011). Government and other relevant agencies in Nigeria should of a matter of urgency address the problem of dilapidated structures and obsolete medical equipment rocking the system if medical tourism must be encouraged in Nigeria. According to Parma (2015), most of the government owned hospitals in the country are ill equipped and in a dilapidated state. With disability adjusted life expectancy (DALE) of 38.3 years and the rank of 187 in the World Health Report 2000, the performance of the Nigerian health system is said to be worse than many sub-Saharan countries (WHO, 2008). There has been many cries from various quarters on the deplorable state of the system and the need for rapid improvement (Onyedika-Ugoeze, 2017). The poor state of the system is traceable to several factors especially the gross under-funding of the health sector and shortage of skilled medical personnel at the primary health care level (Uneke, Ogbonna, Ezeoha, Oyibo, Onwe, Ngwu, and Innovative Health Research Group, 2007).

Massive Recruitment of Health Care Professionals

Among the many challenges facing the health system in Nigeria, is acute shortage of competent health care providers. Nigeria is a major health-staff-exporting nation, accounting for 432 out of a total of 2000 nurses that emigrated out of Africa between April 2000 and March 2001 (Nnamuchi, 2007). As a result of inadequate infrastructure and poor compensation packages, a sizeable number of physicians, nurses and other medical professionals are lured away to developed countries in search of fulfilling and lucrative positions (Rafiu, 2002 and Awofeso, 2008). Nigeria continues to export health-care professionals to the developed world. Many factors contribute to the trend of this brain drain in the 21st century. Some of these factors include better training ground and work environment and higher wages. It is therefore important for the Nigerian government to address the issue of shortage of health workers in the system in order to avert increase infant and maternal mortality in the country.

Equitable Distribution of Health Care Professionals

Related to brain drain is the problem of geographical distribution of health care professionals. There is a disproportionate concentration of medical professionals in urban area while access to medical personnel is readily available in cities; rural dwellers often have to travel considerable distance in order to get treatment (Uneke, Ogbonna, Ezeoha, Oyibo, Onwe, Ngwu, and Innovative Health Research Group, 2007). Health workers in underserved areas usually have motivational problems at work which may be reflected in a variety of circumstances but common manifestations include: (i) lack of courtesy to patients; (ii) failure to turn up at work on time and high levels of absenteeism; (iii) poor process quality such as failure to conduct proper patient examinations, and (iv) failure to treat patients in a timely manner (Hargreaves, 2002; Nnamuchi, 2007 and Chankova, Nguyen, Chipanta, Kombe, Onoja, Ogungbemi, 2007).

Furthermore, doctors and nurses are reluctant to relocate to remote areas and forest locations that offer poor communications with the rest of the country and few amenities for health professionals and their families. Urban areas in Nigeria are more attractive to health care professionals for their comparative social,

155

cultural and professional advantages. Large metropolitan centres in the country offer more opportunities for career and educational advancement, better employment prospects for health professionals and their family, easier access to private practice, lifestyle-related services and amenities (Chankova, Nguyen, Chipanta, Kombe, Onoja and Ogungbemi, 2007). Unfortunately, majority of Nigerians live in the rural areas (Nbanasor, Nwachukwu, Agwu, Njokwu, Onwumere, 2013).Whereas, the nature of poverty in Nigeria is overwhelmingly a rural problem (Federal Office of Statistics, 1994). Hence, the need for policies and programmes with poverty reduction mandate put in place to improve the productivity and income earning potential in the rural areas.

Improved Health Insurance Scheme

Health financing is a core necessity for sustainable healthcare delivery. Access inequalities due to financial restrictions in Nigeria; significantly affect disease rates and health statistics in the country. According to (WHO, 2008), health financing is fundamental to the ability of health systems to maintain and improve human welfare. Despite this, financial inclusion with regards to healthcare is relatively poor within sub-Saharan countries, Nigeria inclusive (Palmer *et al*, 2004). Unfortunately, the National Health Insurance Scheme which was launched in 2005 (Onwujekwe *et al* 2009) can be applied to a few instances. Health care provided by government through this scheme is channelled to government employees and private firms entering contracts with private health care providers (Ogundipe, 2011).

According to World Bank data, as at 2010, 62% of Nigerians lived on less than 1.25 Dollars a day (The World Bank 2014). In a country where the majority percentage of the people are classified as living under the global poverty level, the inability of people under a certain social stratus to access healthcare is worrisome and an obvious, important public health problem (Chukwudozie, 2014). Amaghionyeodiwe (2009) maintains that the access to health services by populations remains very low. This shows that there has been very little impact of the NHIS on reducing finance-related health inequality in the country. Therefore, inadequate health financing is one of the major obstacles in the path of the eradication of disease in

African countries including Nigeria (African Union, 2007). For these reasons, it is understood that people who fall at the bottom of the socioeconomic gradient are far more susceptible to raking up health costs. Therefore, an effective, functional health insurance system is key to ensuring accessibility to health services across the population (WHO 2014).

Improved Employment Opportunities

Unemployment is a major factor contributing to poverty in Nigeria. There is a strong correlation between unemployment and poverty. When people are unemployed, their source of livelihood depletes over time. The cost of living becomes high and the standard of living goes down. Many graduates in Nigeria wander the streets without anything reasonable to do for a living (UNDP, 2009) The government is capable but unwilling to provide jobs for them. Employment in Nigeria is usually not based on merit but depends on how connected you are with people that have power. This leaves many highly qualified people in poverty as seemingly no one cares to know what they are capable of achieving. These people are missing out on the income they would have gotten if they were employed. The number of quality jobs in the economy is low and many government resources are misallocated.

Free Health Care Services for Infant and Maternal Cases

In the absence of a well-structured health insurance system, the government should provide free health services through its free community-based primary healthcare services. The scope of the programme should cover free registration and consultation for all, free treatment of children aged 12 years and below, free treatment of adults aged 60 and above and free ante-natal care. Other area which should also be extended to mother and child to prevent mortality include Intermittent Preventive Treatment (IPT) of malaria, insecticide treated nets (ITN) and routine drugs for pregnant women in public health facilities.

Adequate Health Education for Mothers

The single biggest factor, by far, in reducing the rate of death among children younger than five is greater education for women. Women with more education tend to have smaller families, in part because of increased employment opportunities and better knowledge about contraception; fewer children in a family improve the chances that an infant will survive. More education also helps women make better decisions about many health and disease factors such as prenatal care, basic hygiene, nutrition and immunization which are vital to reducing the leading causes of death in children under five (Fischetti, 2011). Of all health indicators, maternal mortality reveals the greatest gap between rich and poor women, both between and within countries. Health experts agree that the interventions needed to avert much of the burden of maternal death. However, it has become increasingly clear that the success of these interventions depends on the capacity of the health system and the role play by mass media in each country to deliver quality care as well as creating awareness and especially in girls' education, family planning, good roads, and available transport for emergencies. There is no gain saying in the fact that mass media especially radio and television have a lot of responsibilities in the effort to reduce maternal mortality in our society. Apart from the responsibility of the mass media to entertain, it is also the priority of the mass media to educate, enlighten, sensitizing of varieties of issues which health is not an exceptional.

Conclusion

This chapter has explored the impact of poverty on the infant and maternal mortality in Nigeria. The chapter examined the concept of poverty as it relates to the Nigerian context. It looked at the Nigerian healthcare system as well as infant and maternal mortality in Nigeria. The policies on infant and maternal health in Nigeria were also broadly enumerated alongside with recent measures embarked upon to reduce infant and maternal mortality in Nigeria and some lessons from the Nigerian experience. Some of the recommendations to the problem of infant and maternal mortality in Nigeria as it relates to poverty in the country enumerated in the chapter include: Improved standard of living, provision of adequate healthcare facilities, massive recruitment of health care professionals, equitable distribution of health care professionals, equitable distribution of healthcare professionals, improved health insurance scheme, free healthcare services for infant and maternal cases and adequate health education for mothers.

References

Adamu, Y. M. (2005). Patterns of maternal morbidity and mortality in Kano State: A Geographical analysis. *Journal of Social and Management Sciences.* Vol 9 (Special edition): 196 – 221.

Adebimpe, W.O, Owolade, O.A., Adebimpe, M. A. (2010). Health worker's perception of the use of strikes as a tool for dispute resolution in Lagos State, Nigeria. *J Soc Sci Public Policy.* 2010; 2: 19–23.

Adeloye, D., David, R. A., Olaogun, A. A., Auta, A., Adesokan,A., Gadanya, M., Opele,J.K., Owagbemi, O., and Iseolorunkanmi, A. (2017). Health workforce and governance: thecrisis in Nigeria. *Human Resources for Health* 15: 32. Available from: https://link.springer.com/content/pdf/10.1186%2Fs12960-017-0205-4.pdf.Accessed 05/10/2017.

Adesanya T. (2008). *Nigerian Doctors in North America.* Available at: www.journalism.ryerson.ca/online/hubbub/hogs/tadesanya3.htm. Accessed 17/08/2-17).

Afolabi, A. (February 25, 2015). *Child mortality in Nigeria.*Available online from: http://www.fitila.ng/child-mortality-nigeria/. Accessed 6/10/2017.

Africa Union, (April 2007). Africa Health Strategy 2007 - 2015 *Strengthening Of Health Systems For Equity And Development In Africa.* In: African Union Conference Of Ministers Of Health South Africa: African Union. 27

Aigbokhan, B. E. (2000). *Poverty, Growth and Inequality in Nigeria: A Case Study of African Economic Research Consortium (AERC).* Nairobi, Kenya.

Akande, L. (March 1, 2015). *Nigerian Doctors Separate Conjoined Twins in U.S.* The Guardian Newspaper. Available at: http://allafrica.com/stories/201503021482.html. Accessed 30/09/2017.

Akhtar, R. (1991). *Health Care Patterns and Planning in Developing Countries,* Greenwood Press. pp 264.

Akinrinola,B., Sedgh, G., Okonofua, F., Imarhiagbe, C., Hussain R., and Wulf, D. (2009). *Barriers to Safe Motherhood in Nigeria.* New York: Guttmacher Institute. Available on line at: www.guttmacher.org p. 3.Accessed 5/10/2017.

Akinsete, E. (March 7, 2016). PPPs: The Antidote to Nigeria's Healthcare Infrastructure Deficit. Available at: http://www.lexology.com/library/detail.aspx?g=9d3ea77f-78ce-48d0-ad70-f9d6e999779a. Retrieved on 6/10/2017.

Akor, O. (December 7, 2015). *Nigerian health sector: Challenges new ministers should address.* Available at: http://www.dailytrust.com.ng/news/health/nigerian-health-sector-challenges-new-ministers-should-address/123157.html Retrieved on 4/10/2017.

Alabi, A., Adams, O. O., Chime, C.C., Abu, S. O, and Aigomududu, E. E. (2010). How to Make Public Spending Pro-poor in Nigeria. Policy Brief. Poverty and Economic Policy Network (PEP), Canada. Available online from: http://www.pepnet.

Amaghionyeodiwe, L., (2009). Government healthcare spending and the poor: evidence from Nigeria. *International Journal of Social Economics* 36: 220–236. 4.

Asangansi, I., & Shaguy, J. (2009). *Complex Dynamics in the Socio-technical Infrastructure: The Case with the Nigerian Health Management Information System.* Proceedings of the 10th International Conference on Social Implications of Computers in Developing Countries. Available at: http://www.ifip.dsg.ae/Docs/dc17_Asangansi finalv3.pdf. Accessed on29/09/2017.

Awofeso, N. (2008). Managing brain drain and brain waste of health workers in Nigeria. WHO. Available from: http://www.who.int/bulletin/bulletin_board/82/stilwell1/en/. Accessed 17/08/2017.

Awofeso, N. (2010). Improving health workforce recruitment and retention in rural and remote regions of Nigeria. *Rural Remote Health*. 10: 1319.

BBC NEWS February 13,2012 .*Nigerians Living in Poverty Rise to Nearly 6%*. Available from: http://www.bbc.com/news/world-africa-17015873. Accessed 08/8/2017.

Chankova. S., Nguyen, H., Chipanta, D., Kombe, G., Onoja, A. & Ogungbemi, K. (2007). *Catalyzing Human Resources Mobilization: A look at the situation in Nigeria*. Abt Associates Inc. Global Health Council Annual Conference, Washington DC

Chukwudozie, A. (2014). Inequalities In Health: *The Role of Health Insurance In Nigeria*. Available online from: https://www.researchgate.net/publication/284513775_Inequalities_In_Health_The_Role_of_Health_Insurance_In_Nigeria. Accessed 17/08/2017.

CIA. (2009). *The World FactBook*. Washington, D.C.

CIA World Fact book, (July 9, 2015). *Graph Showing Infant Mortality Rates in Nigeria*.
http://www.indexmundi.com/g/g.aspx?c=ni&v=29. Accessed 08/10/2017.

Egbujo, U. (June 27, 2015). *Our Rickety Hospitals and a Health System in Shambles*. Available at:
http://www.vanguardngr.com/2015/06/our-rickety-hospitals-and-a-health-system-in-shambles. Retrieved on 30/09/2017.

Ehanire, O. (July 18 2016). *FG to Revamp 10,000 Primary Health Care Centres Nationwide*. Available online- in Thisday at:
http://www.thisdaylive.com/index.php/2016/07/18/fg-to-revamp-10000-primary-health-care-centres-nationwide-2/.Retrieved on 6/10/2017.

Ehikioya and Mohammed, (2013). Determinants of Public Health Care Expenditure in Nigeria: An Error Correction Mechanism Approach. international Journal of Business and Social Science Vol. 4 No. 13; Available online from:
http://www.ijbssnet.com/journals/Vol_4_No_13_October_2013/24.pdf. Accessed i08/10/2017.

Ejikeme, J. N. (2014). Unemployment and poverty in Nigeria: a link to national insecurity. *Global Journal of Politics and Law Research*

161

Vol.2, No.1, pp.19-35. Available from: http://eajournals.org/wp-content/uploads/Unemployment-and-Poverty-in-Nigeria-A-Link-to-National-Insecurity.pdf. Accessed 8/8/2017.

FAO. (2006). *The State of Food Insecurity in the World 2006*. Washington D.C.

Federal Office of Statistics. (1994). *National Consumers Survey*. 1985/86 1992/93.FOS publication Lagos, Nigeria.

Federal Ministry of Health. (2001). *National reproductive health policy and strategy to achieve quality reproductive and sexual health for all Nigerians*. Available from: http://www.youth-policy.com/Policies/Nigeria%20National%20Reproductive%20Health%20Policy%20and%20Strategy.pdf. Accessed 14/08/2017.

Federal Office of Statistics. (1992). *Nigeria Demographic and Health Survey*, 1990 Lagos.

Fischetti, M. (July 7, 2011). *Female Education Reduces Infant and Childhood Deaths. Smarter Maternal Decisions Prevent Leading Causes of Mortality*. Available from: https://www.scientificamerican.com/article/graphic-science-femaleeducationreduces-infant-childhood-deaths/. Accessed 17/07/2017.

Garba, A. (2006). *Alleviating Poverty in Northern Nigeria*. A paper presented at the Annual Convention of Zumunta Association, Minneapolis, MN, USA. July 28-29.

Godlee, F., Pakenham-Walsh, N., Ncayiyana, D., Cohen, B, Packer, A. (2004). Can we achieve health information for all by 2015? Lancet.364: 295–300 Available from: http://image.slidesharecdn.com/nigerian-states-budget-analysis140908031316phpapp01/95/nigerian-states-budget-analysis-4-638.jpg?cb=1410146092. Accessed 08/10/2017.

Hargreaves, S. (2002). Time to Right the Wrongs: Improving Basic Health Care in Nigeria. *The Lancet* 359: 2030.

Hassan, J. (September 23, 2013). *JOHESU strike: issues, resolution and lessons* Daily Independent (online). Available at: http://www.dailyindependentnig.com/2013/09/johesu-strike-issues-resolutions-and-lessons/. Retrieved on 2/10/2017.

Health Reform Foundation of Nigeria (HERFON). Available at: http://www.herfon.org/ Accessed on 28/09/2017.

Ibeh, N. (2015). *Nigerian health workers call off strike.* Premium Times. http://www.premiumtimesng.com/news/top-news/176152-nigerian-health-workers-call-off-strike.html. Retrieved on 4/10/2017.

Ifijeh, M. (March 24, 2016). *Reducing Maternal, Child Mortality in Nigeria.* Available online from: http://www.thisdaylive.com/index.php/2016/03/24/reducing-maternal-child-mortality-in-nigeria/. Accessed 5/10/2017.

Jeorge, S. (July 15, 2014). *Over 120 million Nigerians live on less than two dollars per day* Available online from: Read more at: https://www.vanguardngr.com/2014/07/over-120-million-nigerians-live-on-less-than-two-dollars-per-day/. Accessed 3rd October 2017.

John, P. (2016). *The Plight of the Nigerian Doctor 2.* Available at: https://www.medicalworldnigeria.com/2016/07/the-plight-of-the-nigerian-doctor-2#.WAocv9IrJH0.Retrieved on 2/10/2017.

Khashu., Narayanan, Bhargava and Osiovic. (2009). *Prenatal Outcomes associated with Preterm Birth a 33 to 36 weeks gestation,* A pop. Based cohort study, 123 (1): 109- 113.

Krieger, N. (2002). A Glossary of Social Epidemiology. Epidemiological Bulletin, *Pan-American Health Organization.* Vol. 23 No. 1, March.

Lale S, and Mile, I. (2005). *Maternal mortality in 2005; estimates* developed by WHO, UNICEF, UNFPA and the World Bank. WHO library Cataloguing.

MacDorman, M. F. and Mathews, T. J. (2009). *The Challenge of Infant Mortality, Have We Reached a Plateau,* Public Health Reports, 124.

Mathews, T.J and MacDorman, M. (2010). Infant Mortality Statistics from 2006 Period linked Birth/infant Death data set, *Nathvitalstat.* Rep, 30; 58 (17): 1-31.

Mawere, M. (2017). *Theorising Development in Africa: Towards Building an African Framework of Development.* Langaa RPCIG, Cameroon.

Mekwunye, E. (June 7 2016). *The Death Camps Called Government Hospitals in Nigeria!* Read the Story of How Ekene Lost His Dad. Available at: https://www.bellanaija.com/2016/06/the-death-camps-called-government-hospitals-in-nigeria-read-the-story-of-how-ekene-lost-his-dad/. Retrieved on 6/10/2017.

Mojekwu, J and Ibekwe, U. (2012). Maternal Mortality in Nigeria: Examination of Intervention Methods. *International Journal of Humanities and Social Sciences.* Vol 2 No1. Availablefrom: http://ijhssnet.com/journals/Vol_2_No_20_Special_Issue_Oc tober_2012/13.pdf.Accessed 17/08/2017.

Nigerian Demographic and Health Survey. (2003). *Factors Responsible for High Infant and Mortality Rate in Nigeria.* Available from: http://articlesng.com/factors-responsible-high-infant-maternal-mortality-nigeria/. Accessed 06/10/2017.

National Health Insurance Scheme. (2014). *National Health Insurance Scheme* .Abuja, Nigeria. Available from: http://www.nhis.gov.ng/. Accessed 18/07/2017.

National Population Commission. (2000). *Nigeria Demographic and Health Survey,*1999.

National Population Commission. (2004). *Demographic and Health Survey,* 2003, Calverton, Maryland: National Population Commission and ORC Macro.

National Population Commission. (2004). *National Population Commission and ORCMacro.*

National Policy on Infant and Young Child Feeding in Nigeria. (2005). *Policy Statements. Federal Ministry of Health Nutrition Division, Abuja.* Available from: http://www.africanchildforum.org/clr/policy%20per%20count ry/nigeria/nigeria_infantfeeeding_2005_en.pdf.   Accessed 15/08/2017.

Mbanasor, J. A.; Nwachukwu, I. N.; Agwu, N. M.; Njoku, M. S. E.; Onwumere, J. (2013). Analysis of income inequality and poverty dynamics among rural farm households in Abia State, Nigeria. *International Journal of Food and AgriculturalEconomics* Vol.1 No.2 pp.99-105.Availablefrom: https://www.cabdirect.org/?target=%2fcabdirect%2fsearch%2 f%3fq%3ddo%253a%2522International%2bJournal%2bof%2b Food%2band%2bAgricultural%2bEconomics%2522. Accessed 17/08/2017.

Nigeria Bureau of Statistics. (2012). *The Nigeria Poverty Profile 2010. Report of the National Bureau of Statistics* Harmonized Nigeria Living Standard Survey (HNLSS).

Nnamani, C. (May 18, 2005). *Nigeria: Nnamani Wants Adequate Funding of Health Sector.* Available online on Thisday Newspaper at: http://allafrica.com/stories/200505190303.html. Retrieved on 17/07/2017.

Nnamuchi, O. (2007).*The right to health in Nigeria.* Law School, University of Aberdeen. Draft Report December 2007. Available from: http://www.abdn.ac.uk/law/hhr.shtml. Accessed 17/08/2017.

Nwaobi, G. C. (2003). *Solving the Poverty Crisis in Nigeria: An Applied General Equilibrium approach.* Quantitative Economic Research Bureau. Gwagwalada, Abuja.

Nwaokoro J. C., Ibe, S. N. O., Ihenachor, C. A., Emerole, C. O., Nwufo, R. C., Ebiriekwe, S. C., http://article.sciencepublishinggroup.com/html/10.11648.j.sjp h.s.2015030501.22.html#reference_15. Accessed 14/07/2017.

Obi, P. (2014). *BREAKING NEWS…At last, NMA calls off strike.* This Day Live. http://www.thisdaylive.com/articles/breaking-news-at-last-nma-calls-off- strike/187230/. Retrieved on 2/10/2017.

Obinna, C. (2011). *Why Nigeria's healthcare delivery system is poor, by SON chief.* Available from: http://www.vanguardngr.com/2011/12/why-nigerias-healthcare-delivery-system-is-poor-by-son-chief/.Accessed 08/08/2017.

Ogbebo, W. (July 13, 2015). *The Many Problems of Nigeria's Health Sector.* Available at: http://leadership.ng/features/446619/the-many-problems-of-nigerias-health-sector. Retrieved on 4/10/2017.

Ogbum-Egbulem, (April 5, 2010). Nigeria Health Facts. *Nigerian Health Journal.* Available at: nigerianhealthjournal.com/? p=182. Accessed on 22/09/2017.

Ogundipe, S. (December 25, 2011). *Mandatory health insurance: Access to good health on the horizon.* Available from: https://www.vanguardngr.com/2011/12/mandatory-health-insurance-access-to-good-health-on-the-horizon/.   Accessed 08/10/2017.

Ogwumike, F.O. (2001). *An appraisal of Poverty Reduction Strategies in Nigeria.* Central Bank of Nigeria Economic and Financial Review, vol. 39 No.4

Ojo, E. O. (2008). *Imperatives of Sustaining Democratic Values.* In Ojo, E. O (ed), Challenges of Sustainable. Democracy in Nigeria (pp. 3-24). Ibadan: John Archers Publishers Limited.

Olatunji, S. (June 25, 2013). *Resident doctors begin warning strike on Wednesday.* The Punch Newspaper. Available at: http://www.punchng.com/news/resident-doctors-begin-warning-strike-on-wednesday/. Retrieved on 2/10/2017.

Olokor, F. (2013). *NMA suspends warning strike' The Punch Newspaper.* Available at: http://www.punchng.com/news/nma-suspends-warning-strike/.Retrievedon 2/10/2017.

Okpe, I. J. and Abu, G. A. (2009). Foreign Private Investment and Poverty Reduction in Nigeria (1975-2003). *J. Soc. Sci.,* 19(3), 205-211.

Olowa, O. W. (2012). Concept, Measurement and Causes of Poverty: Nigeria in Perspective. *American Journal of Economics;* 2(1): 25-36. Available from:
http://article.sapub.org/10.5923.j.economics.20120201.04.html. Accessed 08/8/2017.

Oloyede, B. B. (2014). Effect of Poverty reduction programmes on economic Development evidence from Nigeria. *Arabian Journal of Business and Management Review* (OMAN Chapter) Vol. 4, No.1. Available from:
http://www.arabianjbmr.com/pdfs/OM_VOL_4_(1)/3.pdf. Accessed 08/8/2017.

Omotola, J. S. (2008). Combating Poverty for Sustainable Human Development in Nigeria: The Continuing Struggle. *Journal of Poverty,* 12(4), 496-517.

Onwuliri, V. A. (2015). Risk Factors Associated with Infant Mortality in Owerri Metropolis, Imo State, South eastern Nigeria. *Science Journal of Public Health Volume* 3, Issue 5-1,September 2015, Pages: 64-71.Available:

Onyedika-Ugoeze, N. (May 7, 2017). *Nurses, midwives decry poor state of Nigeria's health* facilities. Available online from The Guardian News at: https://guardian.ng/news/nurses-midwives-decry-poor-state-of-nigerias-health-facilities/. Accessed 17/08/2017.

Palmer, N., Mueller, D. H., Gilson, L., Mills, A. and Haines, A. (2004). Health Financing To Promote Access In Low Income Settings-How Much Do We Know? *Lancet,* 364 (9442), 1365-1370. Available from:
https://www.researchgate.net/publication/284513775_Inequalities_In_Health_The_Role_of_Health_Insurance_In_Nigeria, Accessed Aug 17, 2017.

Parmar, H. (March 7, 2015). *The Fledgling Nigerian Healthcare Market.* Available from: https://www.linkedin.com/pulse/fledgling-nigerian-healthcare-market-hemraj-parma. Accessed on 17/07/2017.

Population Reference Bureau. (2006). *Population Data Sheet.* Washington D.C.

Premium Times. (2014). *Fresh strike looms as doctors warn Nigerian government.* Available at:
http://www.premiumtimesng.com/news/157478-fresh-strike-looms-doctors-warn-nigerian-government.html. Accessed on 2/10/2017.

Raheem, L. (July 25, 2017). *Doctors bemoan poor health facilities in Ogun.* Available online from The Sun at:
http://sunnewsonline.com/doctors-bemoan-poor-health-facilities-in-ogun/. Accessed 17/08/2017.

Rank, M. R., Yoon, H., & Hirschi, T.A., (2003). *Two Theories of Poverty.* Available from: http://www.demos.org/blog/7/28/14/two-theories-poverty. Accessed 18/08/2017.

Raufu, A. (2002). Nigerian health authorities worry over exodus of doctors and nurses. *BMJ;* 325: 65.

Rey, E and Couturier, A. (1994). Prognosis of Pregnancy in Women with Chronic Hypertension, *Am. J. Obstet Gynecol,* 171 (2): 410-416.

Salami, C. G. E. (2011). Entrepreneurship and Youth Unemployment in Nigeria: The Missing Link, *Global Journal of*

Management and Business Research, Volume 11 Issue 5 Version 1.0, April.

Scholer, S. J., Hickson, G. B., and. Ray, W. A. (1999). Socio demographic factors identify US infants at High risk of Injury Mortality, *Paediatrics* 103 (6): 1183-1188.

Sen, A. K (1994). *Social Exclusion and Social Security: Three Paradigms*, International Institute for Labour Studies. Discussion Paper Geneva.

Shiffman, J., Okonofua, F. E. (2007). The state of political priority for safe motherhood in Nigeria, *BJOG* Vol.114: 127-133.

Sunday Punch. (December 25, 2011). *Abiye Safe Delivery*, Vol. 17, No. 19670, pp 18, 19.

Sunday Punch. (February 5, 2012). *Surulere Gets Maternal and Child Care Centre*, Vol. 18, No. 19676, p66.

The Guardian, (April 1, 2016). On the poor state of public hospitals. Available online from: https://guardian.ng/opinion/on-the-poor-state-of-public-hospitals/.Accessed 08/10/2017.

Ucha, C. (2010). Poverty in Nigeria: Some Dimensions and Contributing Factors, *Global Majority E-Journal* 1 (1): 46-56.

Uneke, C., Ogbonna, A., Ezeoha, A., Oyibo, P., Onwe, F., Ngwu, B. & Innovative Health Research Group. (2007). The Nigerian Health Sector and Human Resources Challenge. *The Internet Journal of Health*. Vol 8 No 1 . Available online from: http://ispub.com/IJH/8/1/6444#.Accessed 17/08/2017.

United Nations Children's Fund. (2000). *The State of World's Children*, UNICEF, New York.

United Nations Development Programme. (2000). *The Commitments to Poverty Reduction. in Overcoming Human Poverty:* UNDP Poverty Report. Available. from:
http://www.undp.org/povertyreport/exec/english.htmlhttp://www.undp.org/povertyreport/chapters/chap1.html.

UNDP. (2009). *Human Development Index Report.* UNDP, Nigeria-UNDAF II 2009-2012.

United Nations Educational, Scientific and Cultural Organisation. (November 11, 2015). *Poverty.* Available from: www.unesco.org.Accessed 28/07/2017.

United States Agency for International Development. (2002). *Youth and HIV/AIDS*. Available from: http://www.usaid.gov/pop_health/aids/TechAreas/youthhand hliv/youth `factsheet.html.

United States Agency for International Development. (2006). *Strategic Statement*, P 9.

Vogel, J. R. (1993). *Financing Health Care in Sub-Saharan Africa.* Greenwood Press, pp 1-18

Vogel, J. R. (1993). *Financing Health Care in Sub-Saharan Africa.* Greenwood Press, pp 101-102.

Wermunt, L. (2003).*Global inequalities and Human Needs: Health and Illness in an Increasing Unequal.* World.Person Education Inc.

World Bank. (1999). *Nigerian Consultations with the Poor.* Report of the Global Synthesis Workshop September 22-23.

World Bank. (1996). *Taking Action for Poverty Alleviation in Sub-Saharan Africa.* Report of an African Task Force, May 1, World Bank, Washington D.C.

World Health Organisation. (2008). *WHO Country Cooperation Strategy:* Federal Republic of Nigeria 2002-2007. World Health Organization Regional Office for Africa Brazzaville.

World Health Organisation. (2008). *Health Systems Financing: Toolkit on Monitoring Health Systems Strengthening.* The World Health Organisation.

World Health Organisation. (2008). *Factsheet, Maternal Mortality.* Department of Making Pregnancy Safer.

World Health Organisation. (1991). *Maternal Anthropometry for Prediction of Pregnancy.* Outcome: Memorandum for a USAID/WHO/PAHO Mother Care Meeting, Bulletin of the World Health Organization, 69: 523-532.

World Health Organisation. (2004). *Maternal mortality in 2000*: Estimate developed by WHO, UNICEF and UNFPA: Department of reproductive health and research WHO, Geneve.

World Health Organisation. (2008). *Health Systems Financing: Toolkit on Monitoring Health Systems Strengthening,* The World Health Organisation.

World Health Organisation. (2014). *Best Days Of Public Health Are Ahead Of Us.* World HealthOrganization. Available. from:

http://www.who.int/dg/speeches/2012/wha_20120521/en/.Accessed 17/07/2017.

World Health Organisation. (2017). *Global Health Workforce Alliance Health Workers for ALL and all foe Health Workers*. Nigeria. Available from:
http://www.who.int/workforcealliance/countries/nga/en/.
Accessed 05/10/2017.

Chapter 7

The Geography of Poverty and Disaster Risks in Africa: Challenges and Prospects for Development

Costain Tandi & Munyaradzi Mawere

Introduction

This chapter explores the vulnerability and persistence of poverty amongst the human communities in the disaster-prone areas of the Global South in general and Africa in particular. It draws upon some of the factors and processes that have prevented human communities in ecologically vulnerable areas escaping from extreme poverty, even though some researchers view disasters as windows of opportunities for development. Extreme weather linked to climate change is increasing at a sporadic pace in the African continent. This is likely to cause more disasters in the future. Such disasters, especially those linked to drought, floods and hurricanes, among others, can be the most important cause of impoverishment and vulnerability, set to undo progress on poverty reduction.

In Africa, countries such as the Democratic Republic of Congo, Ethiopia, Kenya, Sudan, Nigeria, Uganda and Mozambique are at high risk of disaster-induced poverty, mainly because of their geographical location and poverty situations. This being the case, disaster risk management should be a key component of poverty reduction efforts, focusing on protecting livelihoods as well as saving lives. This is so because climate change and exposure to natural disasters threaten to derail international efforts to eradicate poverty. As temperatures continue to warm, quite a significant number of African countries face the growing risks linked to more intense or lengthy droughts, extreme rainfall, and flooding and severe heat waves – risks that threaten lives and livelihoods, as well as the hard-won gains made on poverty reduction in recent decades.

Most countries in the Global South have already witnessed an increase in the frequency and severity of natural disasters over the years. Such prevalence of natural hazards has disrupted social and economic systems in affected regions and has produced massive costs in terms of human casualties, epidemics, disabilities, physical capital and income losses, dislocations, and lower accumulation of human capital. The combination of these impacts is expected to hinder development in the short-term and very likely to extend its negative effects in the long run.

While the occurrence of given natural disasters is largely exogenous, the impact that they have on the population is not. It is for those families living along rivers or in steep slopes, and in housing with inappropriate walls or roof, that natural disasters represent the biggest risk. In such cases, poverty exacerbates the potential effects of natural disasters. At the same time, the loss of crops, animals, assets, current and future human capital due to natural disasters threaten the living standards of affected families, often translating into a permanent loss of income and consumption. In other words, natural disasters can increase the incidence of poverty and perpetuate low income growth trends for the most vulnerable. Likewise, low levels of income can amplify the effects of natural disasters that could be relatively less severe otherwise.

It is worth mentioning that natural hazards have been happening since time immemorial and have taken part in shaping any community, both its existence and [potential] mortality. Cutter (2007) observes that in the contemporary times, human communities are getting increasingly subjected to the natural hazards culminating into disasters, claiming a large portion of life and property. If we look into the recent trend of natural disasters, it can be strongly argued that in the coming years the number, frequency and impact of natural disasters will be increasing at a tremendous pace. According to Tomkins *et al* (2002), this compels us to think that physical event is equally responsible for poverty and vulnerability as is the social construct of the given community which is exposed to it. In this scenario, a disaster free world can only be a valid argument when disaster warning/prediction, preparedness, and management are priority concerns in disaster prone regions (Oxfam, 2007).

As a gesture to think with those living in disaster-prone areas and out of the realisation that natural disasters as with poverty know no boundary, we seek to examine the spatial distribution of these phenomena – what we call the geography of disasters and poverty in Africa. This examination is premised on the assumption that disaster and poverty are more often than not viewed as bed fellows that are linked to each other. They co-exist with each other. More so, the chapter seeks to draw insights on both the challenges and opportunities that arise as a result of disasters and poverty.

Disasters and natural hazards in Africa

Hazards can be defined as natural events which pose threat to the natural environment and human population who are part of the environment. They can be divided into natural and anthropogenic hazards. Understanding the severity of hazards is usually essential for risk analysis and planning for resilience-building as there is evidence of the linkages between hazards and the resilience of rural communities. Additionally, understanding the spatial distribution of the effect of hazards unravels part of the reasons why communities and households need to build resilience.

While disaster can be a serious disruption of the functioning of the community or society, it essentially involves widespread human, material, economic or environmental losses and impacts that exceed the ability of the affected community or society to cope using its own [available] resources. Disasters are often described as a result of the combination of exposure to natural hazards, vulnerability of the resident human population and insufficient capacity or measures to reduce or cope with the potential negative consequences. Disaster impacts may include loss of life, injury, disease and other negative effects on human physical, mental and social wellbeing, together with damage to property, destruction of assets, loss of services social and economic disruption and environmental degradation (Oxfam, 2007). Disaster risk reduction refers to the conceptual framework of elements considered with the possibilities to minimise vulnerabilities and disaster risks throughout a society, to avoid (prevention) or to limit (mitigation and preparedness) the adverse impacts of hazards, within the broad context of sustainable development.

Lopez (2008) states that, disaster risk management includes both disaster risk reduction (prevention, preparedness and mitigation) and humanitarian and development action (emergency response, relief and reconstruction). The major aim of any disaster risk reduction programme is to reduce vulnerability and create more resilient individuals and communities. Understanding the reasons for vulnerability of a community to natural disasters can help us fill the gap between vulnerability and resilience. Assessing the economic, social, political, cultural, institutional, and psychological factors along with natural hazards perceptions of the exposed population, could lead to more effective interventions and practical adaptation strategies to enhance the ways people deal with natural hazards.

Natural disasters such as floods are the most costly and wide reaching of all natural hazards. Most importantly, they are responsible for up to 50,000 deaths and adversely affect some 75 million people on average worldwide every year (Nott 2006). Besides increasing poverty, floods have precipitated the outbreak of disease in most parts of the world. In Africa, malaria and typhoid outbreaks after floods have become a common phenomenon akin to fashion. As Nott further reminds us, floods have also caused poverty through physical damage to property. This includes the cost of damage to goods and possessions, loss of income or services in the floods aftermath and clean-up costs. Some impacts of floods are intangible and are hard to place a monetary figure on. Intangible losses also include increased levels of physical, emotional and psychological health problems suffered by flood-affected people.

Besides, natural hazards tend to hit communities in the Global South especially the least developed countries, increasing their vulnerability and setting back their economic and social growth, sometimes by decades or even centuries. The floods have led to loss of human life, destruction of social and economic infrastructure, degradation of already fragile ecosystems and increase in poverty levels. Ariyabandu and Wickramasinghe (2005) opine that some groups are more vulnerable to floods than others. Vulnerability is not always translatable to poverty, but the poor tend to be the most vulnerable due to their lack of choices. The influences of both poverty and development process on people's vulnerability to disaster are now well established. Interestingly, class, ethnicity, gender, disability and age are some of the factors affecting people's vulnerability. As Ariyabandu and Wickramsinghe have further noted, because vulnerability plays such an important part in why natural hazards become human disasters, it is worth spending time to examine the characteristics of vulnerability. Conditions of vulnerability are a combination of factors that include poor living conditions, lack of power, exposure to risk and the lack of capacity to cope with shocks and adverse situations.

Poverty is not equal to vulnerability but being poor makes people more vulnerable to disasters because poor people lack the needed resources (physical, social and knowledge based) to prepare accordingly for and respond to such threats and shocks as natural hazards. Poor people often get locked in a cycle of vulnerability. Due to their poverty situations, they become vulnerable. Because they are vulnerable, they are at great risk in the face of any striking [natural] hazard, leading to disaster. Close analysis of disaster impact shows that the vulnerability of men and women to disaster, their capacities, and the options available to them differ in character and scale to their gender (Ariyabandu and Wickramasinghe 2005). When severe floods occur in areas occupied by humans, they can create natural disasters which involve the loss of human life and property plus serious disruption to the on-going activities of large urban and rural communities. Flood losses are therefore essentially human interpretations of the negative economic and social consequences of natural events. The impact of the flood hazard will, in part be determined by the magnitude of the events and the duration of the event.

According to Hanson *et al.* (2007), reducing poverty is one of the great challenges facing the world. Over half of the world's poor live in rural areas. Poverty of these populations normally worsens when natural hazards destroy vital infrastructure in their communities. Economic losses and impacts in such areas have remained extremely high such that they constitute a large developmental challenge. This calls for the need for new types of strategies in order to cope with the financial burden posed by hazardous events in poor communities of the world.

We have already noted that in Africa, Mozambique is one of the countries with high risks of disaster strike. Most parts of Mozambique are seriously threatened by floods. Lives and property are often threatened by annual flood events which impose a substantial socio-economic burden on the communities. The areas have experienced increased flooding owing to their geographical location, poor [sand/clay] soils, dense and increasing population. Borrows and De Bruin (2006) indicated that among natural catastrophes, flooding has claimed more lives than any other single natural hazard. In the decade 1986 to 1995, flooding alone accounted for 31% of the global economic loss from natural catastrophes and 55% of the casualties (Ibid). Considering the effects of increase in global warming, the damaging effects of flooding are likely to become more frequent, more prevalent and more serious in the future.

Parker (2000) notes that because floods frequently destroy crops, livestock and property, food shortages are not uncommon in the aftermath. For example, in the Sudanese floods of 1988, an acute food shortage was immediately reported. Floods may affect food availability in a number of ways, which include food stocks being damaged or transportation of food being disrupted by floods as a result of other areas such as towns being cut off from supply sources and have inadequate food stocks. The flood that hit Sudan in 1988 is a good example of an extreme flood event which resulted in serious food shortages. The sudden and unexpected flow of water of the White and Blue Nile due to unprecedented torrential rain caused serious property damage and human sorrow that many Sudanese can hardly forget.

According to OCHA (2008), the cumulative number of people affected by rains and floods in 2007 in Southern Africa was more than 194,103 persons. This included 60,995 in Malawi (mostly as a result of damage to property and crops), 94,760 people in Mozambique (all were evacuated into resettlement camps); more than 16,680 in Zambia (1,890 persons in temporary accommodation, the rest in host families); and 15,168 in Zimbabwe. An estimated additional 4,000 people had been affected in Lesotho and another 2,500 persons in Swaziland. In 2008, thousands of people were affected after flash floods submerged hundreds of hectares of farmland in the north-eastern region where the floods displaced hundreds of families in the region. The farmland which supported some 1,200 farmlands had their livelihoods and food security disrupted (IRIN 2008). Theron (2007) indicated that at least 20 countries in Africa were seriously affected by floods. These countries included Algeria, Berlin, Burkina Faso, Cote d'Ivoire, Ethiopia, Gambia, Ghana, Guinea, Kenya, Liberia, Mali, Mauritania, Nigeria, Rwanda, Senegal, Sierra Leon, Sudan, Togo and Uganda.

Floods have always had several socio-economic and political implications which cause a wide range of complex issues. Some of the immediate consequences include the displacement of people, the destruction of infrastructure such as houses and roads, damage to forms and crops and loss of livestock and other such valuable property. The destruction of roads and other infrastructure delay on-going development initiatives and political processes (Theron 2007). For Theron, the immense damage to farms, crops and livestock cause long-term food insecurity. The Ivory Coast flooding, for example, occurred very close to harvest time making the loss even greater, since farmers did not have much food stored from the previous harvesting season.

More so, floods have caused serious loss of soil fertility which lessen future harvests (Ibid). In the long-term, affected areas had to deal with the spread of infections and water borne diseases, cholera, dysentery and diarrhoea which increased the need for safe drinking water and the provision of water purification tablets. Theron further observed that the displacement of people and damage to infrastructure disrupts African societies in their development effects and impact on the achievement of almost every Millennium Development Goal, for example, damage to schools in Uganda left at least 100,000 children out of school.

A study conducted on poverty, vulnerability and the impact of flooding in the Limpopo Province of South Africa argue that while disasters may affect everyone and play an important role in increasing vulnerability, poor people are made more vulnerable from a web of circumstances that make them prone to the effects of disasters (Khandlhela and May 2006). In this study, the researchers established that the varying impacts of floods on households and the community

177

at large show that vulnerability to the effects of a flood disaster is indeed an outcome of the interaction between socio-economic and political processes. It is in view of such observations that Adamson (1983) have argued that extreme events such as floods over Southern Africa have always resulted in loss of life, massive damage to property, crops and livestock and disrupted communications. The risk of such events at any given point in southern Africa may be small but their occurrence within the total sub-continental space have remained quite frequent at least historically.

The impact of disasters on household welfare

In most countries of the world, natural hazards such as floods, droughts, and extreme temperatures have the high likelihood of increasing their frequency or intensity as a result of climate change. The exposure, vulnerability, and lack of adaptive capacity of poor people puts them at higher risk. This means that from a household perspective, natural disasters can represent a multifaceted shock to welfare. There are three categories of impact on an individual or household's welfare. These include physical integrity, assets and income (Khandlhela and May 2006). Adverse effects are usually combined and occur at a time when individuals are out of their familiar environment such that community solidarity is unlikely made available and public services severely disrupted. These factors contribute to the intensification of the overall adverse impact on human welfare. Even if the physical event experienced by the community might be the same, there is certainly an idiosyncratic aspect to its impact. This is so given that not all households and individuals are equally affected, but the way they are affected will depend on their degree of vulnerability, perception of risk, and capacity to mitigate risk and cope with the consequences of the disaster (Ibid).

The direct impacts of disasters on the victim's physical integrity include fatalities, injuries, sickness and violence. Fatalities are a direct and immediate effect of the disaster, as buildings collapse and flows of water, mud or debris carry people and their properties away. Fatalities, which constitute a permanent shock to a household's

178

welfare, leave some individuals orphaned and widowed at a time when community and extended family solidarity might not be available (cf. Khandlhela and May 2006). In addition to fatalities, disasters can have various adverse effects on an individual's physical integrity. First of all, disasters can cause grave or permanent injuries that can provoke a fall in income and an increase in health-related expenditures. Sickness and violence can also accompany disasters, depending on the quality of the management of a disaster situation. Earthquakes, storm surges and floods tend to destroy water distribution or contaminate water supply, leading to increased risks of water-borne diseases in the aftermath of a disaster. The stagnation of waters following a flood is also a factor in the increase of certain endemic diseases such as malaria and malaria – diseases which are common during and after flooding. Unsanitary and crowded shelters, which are a common feature in many developing cities of Africa – can also promote the easy outbreak and spreading of diseases. At the same time, individuals are more likely to become victims of violence during and after disasters because of looting, the gathering of population in shelters, and the breakdown of family units and solidarity. Case studies report an increase in violence, rape, child abuse and prostitution in temporary shelters, which usually regroup the poorest and most marginalised members of a community (see for example, IRIN 2008; OCHA 2008; Khandlhela and May 2006).

Natural disasters can also affect household welfare through homelessness, as well as the loss of productive assets and income. Over the past 30 years or so, an estimated 148 million people have required immediate assistance during a period of emergency for basic survival needs such as food, water, shelter, sanitation and immediate medical assistance (OCHA 2008). Household assets such as housing and income-generating assets can be damaged or destroyed by disasters. Housing is likely to be destroyed by earthquakes, high winds, volcanic eruptions and landslides, while damages in times of flood might be more limited and null in the case of droughts, with disasters estimated to have made 2.5 million people homeless between 1990 and 1999 (Ibid). The partial or total loss of income-generating assets (shops, factories, crop, cattle, arable land, forests, and so on) is also a consequence of disasters. In the case of agricultural income-generating assets, the loss might be temporary or permanent. This is floods make land unsuitable for agricultural production until waters recede, while hurricanes might wash out arable land or permanently increase its salinity through storm surges and flash floods.

The effect of disasters on employment, though, is still largely unknown, since no study has looked into their impact on open unemployment and underemployment can never be doubted. In this chapter, we however note that the impact of disasters on unemployment depends primarily on the degree of destruction of income-generating assets and the period of disruption of flows of goods and services. The frictional unemployment generated by a disaster results in a long-term reduction of income especially where alternative sources of employment are not available inside or outside of the affected area and the reconstruction efforts are limited due to a combination of factors which include poverty and slow execution by donors and national governments. This frictional unemployment is likely to threaten human development, thereby resulting in poverty.

Poverty and human development

Poverty is not a newly born concept. It has a long history across the world societies and in Africa in particular. During the past few decades, a number of attempts has been made to try to reduce the world poverty level. It was found out that the phenomenon of poverty is directly connected to the development paradigms of the world such that many, if not all, development attempts focus on poverty alleviation and eradication. Thus, poverty is considered as a key concept. This should not be confused to mean that human development is a rise in national income level. Instead, human development is not only a rise or fall of national income level of a country. Besides, poverty is not only a lack of income. Both, poverty and human development have many dimensions which need to be thoroughly understood if we are to understand human development at any given time.

The concept of human development and human poverty was introduced by the UNDP's Human Development reports between

180

1990 and 1997. The Human Development Report of 1990, for example, defined human development as the process of enlarging people's choices. These choices were identified as infinite and change over time. In addition to that, human development was noted to have two dimensions: the formation of human capabilities — such as improved health, knowledge and skills — and the way people make use of their acquired capabilities — for leisure, productive purposes or being active in cultural, social and political affairs.

At the same time the report defines poverty as the inability to attain minimal standards of living. The World Development Report (2000; 2001) likewise conceptualise poverty as the deprivation of well-being. But what precisely is deprivation? This needs to be unpacked for us to have a clear understanding of what it means to be poor.

In view of the question raised above, we note that the voices of the people identified [by themselves or otherwise] bear eloquent testimony to its meaning. To be poor is to lack! It is to be hungry – to lack food, to lack shelter and clothing, to be sick and not cared for, to be illiterate and not schooled, to oppressed and lack freedom – be it of choice or what a view. But for the poor, living in poverty can be more than this. Poor people are practically vulnerable to adverse events out of their control. They are often treated badly by the institutions of state and society and excluded from voice and power in those institutions. This understanding of poverty broadens the whole scope of poverty as it shows us the multidimensionality of poverty. Thus, although poverty has been discussed mostly in relation to income, other dimensions such as the social, cultural, political, and environmental should always be accounted for. World poverty incidence is said to have decreased from 28 percent of the global population in 1990 to 21 percent in 2001 (World Development Report 2001). Also, people's living standards have risen dramatically over the last decades, of course with regional and even national disparities at a high level across many world communities.

From a human development perspective, poverty means the denial of choices and opportunities for a tolerable life. According to the Human Development Report 1997, poverty is not only lack of material well-being, but it is also about the denial of opportunities and choices most basic to human development – to lead a long, healthy, creative life and to enjoy a decent standard of living, freedom, dignity, self-esteem and the respect of others (UNDP 1997). Poverty in the human development perspective has many dimensions such as short life, illiteracy, exclusion and lack of material means and all these dimensions can overlap in different combinations. These things are related to the capability approach, which was introduced by Amartya Sen (1999). Further the Human Development Report from 2005 says human development is about freedom. It is about building human capabilities — the range of things that people can do, and what they can be. But this freedom can be restricted if they are poor, ill, illiterate, discriminated against, threatened by violent conflict or denied a political voice. All these are about people's capabilities.

To measure Human Development and Human Poverty there are often two main indexes introduced by the UNDP namely Human Development Index (HDI) and Human Poverty Index (HPI). To measure HDI, three main elements are considered by the UNDP. These are longevity, knowledge, and decent living standards. To calculate the former, three main elements, life expectancy at birth, adult literacy rate and GDP per capita are used. And the HPI measures deprivation in basic human development in the same dimensions as the HDI. The variables used are the percentage of people expected to die before the age of 40, the percentage of adults who are illiterate, and overall economic provisioning in terms of the percentage of people without access to health services and safe water and the percentage of under-weight children under five (cf. UNDP 1997). One point that remains critical is that HDI is often affected by disasters. So is the HPI. Thus, there is need to understand the nexus between HPI and [natural] disasters.

The nexus between natural disasters and poverty in Africa

Poverty is a plague afflicting, directly or otherwise, people all over the world in their various aspects of human conditions such as physical, moral and psychological. The World Bank (1993) defines poverty as increased vulnerability to environmental degradation or

182

loss of access to natural resources, employment, property and essential services. This assertion, mainly due to its realisation of loss, creates a link between natural disasters and poverty. At the same time, it suggests that natural disasters are forces that can aggravate poverty.

However, the relationship between poverty and exposure to risk is not linear. Causality runs in both directions: poor people sometimes choose to settle in risky areas where land is available or affordable; and living in risky areas may make people poorer when hazards destroy assets and livelihoods (Ibid). Yet, poor people are not always more exposed; for instance, flood-prone coastal or river areas benefit from low transport costs that attract firms and opportunities, and the wealthier populations in a country. In these cases, rich people may be the ones most exposed. In-depth analyses find no systematic overexposure of poor people to floods at the national level, although poor people are often the most exposed within a city or a region (Winsemius *et al.* 2015).

Amongst the natural disasters that ravage the nations of the world are severe droughts, fire outbreaks, floods, earthquake, windstorm and hurricane. Most of these disasters take place in the Global South where there is inadequate risk management mechanism as a result of poverty. According to Freeman *et al* (2003), the [poverty] situation makes these poor countries to experience heavy casualties with disproportionate numbers of deaths, displacements and damage to infrastructure and property. The adverse impacts also range from human casualties, epidemics, disabilities, dislocations and direct damages on critical infrastructure and physical capital to potential losses in income, drops in consumption and reductions in human capital (Jakobsen 2012).

The vulnerability and fatality of natural disasters depend on the location of the occurrence, the type of structure affected and the level of response to disaster management. The vulnerability of those living in risk prone areas is perhaps the single most important cause of disaster casualties and damage. The fact that the poor often live in areas that are at high risk to natural disaster means they also live in poorly built shelters that are easily damaged in the event of a disaster. Worse still, they live with few or no early warning programmes, thereby contributing to the severity of disaster casualties and damages.

Natural disasters are of growing interest to development economists especially in African countries (Jakobsen, 2012). They are increasing alarmingly owing to global warming. There are many types of natural disasters, such as earthquake, tsunami, volcanic eruption, cyclones, tornadoes, river-bank erosion, floods, and drought. Countries in the Global South are the most frequent victims of natural disasters, many of which have a major negative impact on the society. Besides, injuries and the loss of lives, the next point of negative impact is the economy, which is reflected in the Gross Domestic Product. Again, in such instances, marginalised people will bear most of the burden, and for whom there is usually no publicly funded social safety net. An added dimension of the negative impact is the significant costs of repairing and replacing the damaged infrastructural facilities like transportations, communications, bridges, culverts, and buildings. These crises undermine the overall operations of government, the private sector, and civil society.

Studies have shown that there are about ten billion US dollars flood losses all over the world every year (Freeman, Keen, & Mani, 2003; Jakobsen, 2012). It is important to note that this vulnerability turns into poverty when the poor people do not have access to resources. Due to recurrent natural disasters in most parts of Africa, this issue of resources produce other vulnerabilities like food insecurity, unequal resource distribution between different socioeconomic groups, gender gap, violence against children and women, downgraded social mobility, and decrease income generating employment opportunities. Therefore, the vulnerability occupies the lack of capability, which reproduces the multi-dimensional poverty conditions. The multidimensional characteristics of poverty indicate the lack of economic, human, political, socio cultural and protective capabilities, which create other problems of equity, property right, and the lack of good governance. Recurrent natural disasters are the major causes of these major poverty conditions. These problems incorporate the social, cultural, political, economic and environmental dimensions. For example, when people do not have economic opportunities, they exploit forest resources. Poverty vulnerabilities vary with location, age, gender, class, ethnic and racial identity, community strength, and the nature of power structure.

Besides, the link between natural disasters and poverty suggests that natural disasters are a force that can aggravate poverty in the Global South (Freeman, Keen, & Mani, 2003; Jakobsen, 2012). Developing countries such as those of Sub-Saharan Africa like are especially vulnerable to natural disasters both because of a high frequency of events and a lack of measures to prevent disaster harm (Freeman *et. al.* 2003). As a result, damages as a percentage of GDP and deaths resulting from disasters are much higher in these countries (Freeman *et al.*, 2003; Henderson, 2004).

Natural disasters can contribute to poverty in a number of ways. One of the most obvious ways is the loss of immediate income from labour due to deaths or injuries. If the deceased played an important role in providing productive labour within the household or earning labour income, this can exert immediate pressure on the household's ability to maintain consumption or accumulate assets. According to Thanh, *et al* (2006) an injury increases the probability of falling into poverty and decreases the likelihood of escaping poverty. Another important mechanism linking natural disasters to poverty is infrastructure. Freeman (2000) describes how infrastructure destruction can be an important creator of poverty. The poor are often extremely dependent on infrastructure for access to labour and goods markets (Freeman *et al.*, 2003).

Besides, damage to health or education infrastructure could have long-term impacts on the ability of the poor to invest in human capital, making poverty more persistent. Another effect that needs special attention is the influence disasters have on poverty and consumption through the destruction of assets (Berloffa & Modena, 2013; Dercon, 2004; Jakobsen, 2012; Mechler, 2009; Morris, *et al.*, 2002; Narayan, 2003). Disasters have been found to destroy assets and negatively affect asset investment (Carter, Little, Mogues, & Negatu, 2007). A number of studies point out that for the poorest households, disasters have a large impact on essential consumption. These impacts often have a disproportionate impact on the poor (Carter, *et al.,* 2007) and are more significant for those who have restricted access to labour markets, insurance, credit markets, or have existing loans (Berloffa & Modena, 2013; Carter, et al., 2007; Dercon, 2004; Jakobsen, 2012; Morris, *et al.*, 2002; Sawada & Shimizutani, 2008; Shoji, 2010). Traditional consumption-smoothing theory suggests that households will use assets to support consumption following a negative shock, but an asset poverty trap can reverse this behaviour for those near the poverty trap threshold (Berloffa & Modena, 2013; Carter, *et al.*, 2007; Dercon, 2004; Jakobsen, 2012; Morris, *et al.*, 2002; Shoji, 2010). The lack of credit access means using assets to support consumption would result in the household being trapped in poverty. As a result, households which already have lower consumption from the disaster reduce consumption further to avoid liquidating assets.

In developed countries, insurance and formal government aid play a large role in supporting communities following a disaster (Coffman & Noy, 2011). The presence of efficiently distributed aid on a sufficient scale could prevent disasters from having any noticeable impact on poverty. In developing countries, such transfers are often less significant compared to total losses and are often informal (Carter, *et al.*, 2007; Morris, *et al.*, 2002), focusing on family, religious, and other social groups. Large disasters may draw inflows of foreign aid, while regular smaller-scale disasters such as those experienced by Zimbabwe, do not attract the same level of foreign attention due to the low risks they carry.

IPCC (2007), notes that the social and economic consequences of natural disasters in Africa and across the globe have reiterated the need to place more attention to natural disaster as part of the global poverty agenda. It is important to note that there is mounting evidence that global climate change is increasing the recurrence and virulence of climatic hazards such as hurricanes and floods in many parts of the world. Natural disasters such as floods are now a common occurrence in many parts of Africa. Many countries in Africa, depending on their geographic location and geophysical characteristics, regularly experience natural disasters of geological and hydro-meteorological origin. These natural disasters always have a considerable impact on the lives and livelihoods of the people. Studies have shown that disasters are widely acknowledged to affect disproportionately the poorest in a community as they have relatively higher sensitivity to disaster events compared with communities of higher development status (Berloffa & Modena, 2013; Carter, *et al.*, 2007; Jakobsen, 2012; Shoji, 2010). Recurrent disasters increase the vulnerability of the poor. At the same time, increasing poverty levels make people unable to break out of the poverty cycle, especially as disaster recurrence occurs. Increased disaster risks such as those posed by climate change are expected to exacerbate poverty. Nevertheless, the effects of disaster on the poor is different across regions. In the ensuing sections, we briefly look at the different regions of Africa, showing how they are differently affected by disasters.

West Africa

According to Adger and Brooks (2003), the Sahel drought of 1972 and 1973 was the culmination of a downward trend in rainfall in West Africa that began in 1950, despite regionally receiving high rainfall. By 1972, a large number of Sahelians had already suffered the effects of several years of drought. The only previous year in which the average rainfall for the entire region was similarly deficient was in 1913. Current information shows that the Sahel region is still experiencing floods, desertification and drought. It is also pointed out by World Health Organisation (2004) that the Sahel region continues to be affected by a range of natural disasters which have caused various health problems and poverty in the region. For instance, in 2004 there were a number of epidemic diseases which spread across West Africa such as cholera, yellow fever, meningitis, and HIV/AIDS. The WHO considers the proliferation of these diseases as a new configuration of hazards (UNDP: 2004). The reason is simply that these epidemics are decimating communities in Sub-Saharan African countries.

Besides, in 2001, Ghana experienced torrential rain, which caused widespread floods in the capital, Accra. More than 100,000 homes were destroyed. Roads in the city were under water; others were completely washed away (BBC News: 2001). Moreover, Songsore *et al* (2008) postulates that floods in Ghana are more frequent in the rainy season but that flash flooding is prone to happen at any time. During the rainy season, between May/June and August, severe flooding of large areas of Accra has become a predictable seasonal occurrence. This situation has arisen because the capital was built on a flat terrain, and its drainage system is currently inadequate. In 2007 there was a similar situation in the neighbouring country of Nigeria where floods destroyed housing and other infrastructure, especially in poor areas. Disaster events were registered in nine federal states of Nigeria, namely Lagos, Ogun, Plateau, Sokoto, Nasarrawa, Bauchi, Yobe, Borno and Kebi. Other factors that contributed to the flood problem were poor drainage systems in those states and an overflow of water from a dam, which caused a major impact (Red Cross: 2007). The analysis presented by ENDA (2008) shows that the West African region is associated with hazards such as drought, desertification, flood, spread of disease and various other hazards. These occur not only in West African countries but are also found in other parts of Sub-Saharan Africa. In addition, in 2004 and 2005, Mali, Niger and Senegal registered drought, all of which caused extensive economic loss. Burkina Faso, like other countries of the West Africa sub-region faces similar hazards. According to the International Federation of Red Cross and Red Crescent Societies (2007), in 2007 Burkina Faso registered one of its heaviest rainfalls, which caused havoc throughout the country. The government reported that over 40,000 people were severely affected and were forced to live in miserable conditions. Together with international organisations, the government intervened, but economic losses and damage to housing and other infrastructure was extensive. According to government sources in Burkina Faso, no less than 8,412 houses were damaged. It is unclear whether these houses were ever rebuilt. The observation is that West African countries are exposed to natural disasters virtually every year. Another argument the paper suggested was that the growing incidence of hazards in the West Africa region could be linked to climate change. Nyong and Fiki (2005) opine that, it is anticipated that climate variability and change in West Africa will have an overwhelming impact on agriculture and land use; the ecosystem and biodiversity; human settlements; diseases and health; hydrology and water resources. They suggest that the region should have a better mechanism in place to try to combat the effect of climate variability.

Central Africa

Most countries in Central Africa have been affected by similar hazards. Since 2006, the region has registered significant floods in most countries in Central Africa (Red Cross; 2008). For instance, according to Ayanji (2004), in Cameroon the extensive and prolonged rainfall caused severe flooding in 2001. In the municipality of Limbe, the heavy downpours destroyed not only large areas of agricultural land but also urban property and homes in the surrounding suburbs, especially dwellings inhabited by the poor. The floods, thus, had a direct and indirect impact on human, environmental, and economic losses. The Republic of Congo experiences flooding virtually every year. According to the Red Cross Bulletin (2007), Brazzaville, the capital city of Congo, registered torrential rain which caused flooding in the central city area in 2007. One reason for the flooding phenomenon is the situation of the city on the banks of the Congo River, the boundary between the Democratic Republic of Congo (DRC) and the Congo Republic. Another reason is the poor drainage in Brazzaville, which makes it very vulnerable to flooding.

The DRC is considered one of the countries most affected by floods. It is at the mercy of the Congo River, which crosses it from East to West. The flooding of the river presents a serious threat to riparian communities, including the 12 million inhabitants of Kinshasa, the capital. The water level of the Congo River has been increasing steadily. This is a threat that the DRC government needs to take very seriously because a combination of cholera (which is recurrent in the country) and floods would complicate the situation immeasurably (Red Cross Bulletin; 2007). Beside the flood situation in the western DRC, in the eastern part of the country there is also the danger of volcanic eruptions.

According to the United Nations Disaster Assessment and Co-ordination (2008) the East African rift valley system is one of the most seismically active regions on the African continent. The Lake Kivu basin is among the most active areas in this rift and earthquakes frequently damage villages and towns situated there. The earthquakes also generate landslides on mountain slopes and hills surrounding Lake Kivu. Seismic studies and field observations indicate that since

1997 the Lake Kivu basin has become more active than usual. In 2007 the country experienced another earthquake registering 6.1 on the Richter scale, which struck the province of Sud Kivu (UNDAC; 2008). Significant damage was caused in Bukavu, the capital city of the province and in surrounding districts. Other countries of the central Africa region such as Gabon, Central African Republic and São Tomé and Principe also registered floods and landslides. According to the Red Cross Bulletin (2007), flood is registered as a disaster when occurring annually in these countries.

East Africa

The eastern part of Africa is recognised as one of the regions which has suffered severe drought for a number of years. Countries well known as being at high risk of drought conditions include Kenya, Ethiopia and Sudan. The drought has had a particularly negative impact on the poor because of lack of food. According to CRED (2009) climatological disasters in the form of drought have claimed many victims in the eastern part of Africa, with more than one third of the population affected in Eritrea, Djibouti, and Somalia. Then too, Kenya has suffered drought conditions for the past decade. In 2000, it experienced one of its worst droughts in 37 years. According to IFRC (2005) the Kenyan government needed international assistance in terms of food supplies for more than 2 million of its people. It is argued by Gadain *et al* (2005) that an impact analysis of the El Nino flood event clearly shows that the Kenyan government is inadequately prepared to mitigate the adverse effects of such disasters. The government has neither a flood disaster management policy nor an institutional framework to monitor and manage flood related disasters. Floods registered a significant impact in the West Kenya region and destroyed crops over a wide area. The country also registered a high death toll at that time. In the wake of this disaster the Kenyan government decided to strengthen its disaster capacity, and placed a major focus on preparedness and risk management. In April 2009, the government realised that there was another severe drought in western Kenya where a pastoral community had lost many head of cattle and crops had failed. Most

190

of the inhabitants of that part of Kenya needed government assistance.

Turning now to Ethiopia, according to the National Policy on Disaster Prevention and Management (1993) this country is severely threatened by disasters induced by drought and other natural hazards. In the last 20 years, disasters have, in varying degrees, occurred every year. These have cost the Ethiopian government heavily in terms of both human lives and resources. The Ethiopian government is determined to take every possible precaution to eradicate these persistent droughts. This is why the government decided to draw up the National Policy on Disaster Prevention and Management. The reality is that Ethiopia has faced drought conditions for decades. The areas worst hit have been on the border between Ethiopia-Djibouti, northern-Kenya, central and south Somalia and parts of Eritrea (Red Cross, 2006). It is argued by UNDP (2004) that Ethiopia shows high levels of vulnerability to drought and has recorded a growing number of droughts in the period 1980 to 2000.

The drought conditions in Ethiopia have a significant impact on food security in that country. It is argued by the International Red Cross Crescent (2006) that as many as 11 million people are affected by drought in the wider Horn of Africa region. Food insecurity in Ethiopia has left almost 2.6 million people in need of emergency assistance. The worst hits are the pastoralist or agro-pastoralists in the southern and the southern east part of Ethiopia, where most communities are dependent on the fertility of the land. When there is a drought these people are forced to relocate to other areas where the land is relatively fertile. The cause of the drought in this region is a scarcity of rain. Ababe *et al* (2008) argue that of those who are in immediate need of assistance, 69% reside in critically affected pastoral and agro-pastoral areas of the Afar region. Although the Ethiopian government has already established a policy on disaster prevention and management to deal with the problem of disasters, the reality is that the country still faces natural hazards every year. The impact of natural disasters as result of severe hazards drains the economy of the Ethiopian government. Ideally, the government should have a financial reserve to solve this problem. The situation in Sudan is not substantially different from that in Ethiopia, which

191

has faced drought and flood hazards for a long time. Sudan has registered drought for two decades.

According to Telku, Braun and Zaki (1991) Rainfall levels have declined in Sudan during the past three decades: mean annual rainfall declined by 6.7% between 1960–69 and 1970–79, and by 17.7% between 1970–79 and 1980–86. Drought has had severe consequences for the poor, and particularly those in the northern region of Sudan, many of whom faced hunger and even starvation. The low rainfall also had a negative effect on crop production, which dropped sharply. The same authors argued that a 10% drop in annual rainfall resulted in a decrease of 7.3% and 3.0% in sorghum and millet production respectively. A marked drop in rainfall levels at the end of 1970 meant that drought conditions became even worse. Hulme (1984) has shown that on the basis of observed rainfall data in the arid zone of Sudan, the years from 1979 to 1983 were as dry as the 1969–73 period. Following the same argument, the International Federation Red Cross Red Crescent (2001) noted that severe drought was reported in the western and the central parts of Sudan which affected at least 900 000 people, and that 600 000 people were at risk of famine. Sudan has also experienced severe flooding in past years. In 2007 the Sudanese government registered torrential rain across the country and the Nile and other rivers burst their banks in eight Sudanese states, resulting in widespread damage. According to an assessment of the situation by the government and to reports which appeared in the media, more than 30 people were killed, 100 were injured and more than 25 000 houses were destroyed by the floods. Villages were submerged and the raging floodwaters caused extensive damage to infrastructure, including roads and bridges (IFRCRC, 2007). The analysis provided in this article indicates that natural hazards still take place in virtually every country on the Africa continent. The relevant governments should be the main role player in attempts to offset these tragedies.

Southern Africa
The International Strategy for Disaster Reduction (2008) predicts that drought will continue to be a major concern for many African communities. The frequency of weather and climate related disasters

has increased since 1970 and the Sahel region and Southern Africa have become drier during the past three decades. Following this argument, in the future the African continent could face a reduction in water and this would impact on the agricultural sector leading to chronic poverty. From an economic point of view, most countries affected by disasters have had their economic development severely interrupted. For example, the flood in Mozambique in 2000 displaced approximately 4,000 people in Maputo alone and destroyed the road network which linked the city with other provinces (Christie and Hanlon, 2001). The economic recovery took years to overcome. There is also the case of a volcanic eruption in 2002 at Mount Nyiragongo in Goma, in the eastern part of the Democratic Republic of Congo, which destroyed the tourist town of Goma. Another example is the droughts in Kenya and Ethiopia, which had a devastating effect on the agricultural production of these countries. There are many other such cases from across Southern Africa.

As such, like its counterparts in the north, central, east and west Africa, the Southern Africa region also faces the impact of natural hazards. In South Africa's Western Cape Province, wildfires occur annually and the threat of natural hazards is frequent in many other countries in the region. Research indicates that southern African countries have suffered at least two debilitating droughts, triggering serious water-related imbalances and causing loss of crops (Unganai 1994). The shortage of water also led to loss of livestock, wildfires, famine and outbreaks of disease. Furthermore, the consequence of drought in Lukamba the 1994 and 1995 season caused a decline of cereal production by 35% compared to the previous years (Southern Africa Environment Outlook, 2008). Similar circumstances were experienced in countries such as Malawi, Zambia and Zimbabwe.

Further, the region also registered floods. Some analysts have linked the impact of flood s to climate change. It is argued by Singh (2006), for example, that climate change has a direct impact on rainfall. Scientists forecast that in the coming years, countries in the Sahel region will receive increased rainfall and the threat of floods will increase while southern Africa is likely to encounter persistent drought. In March 2000, flood caused by cyclone El Nino impacted heavily on the Southern Africa region, particularly in Mozambique, where more than 900 people were declared dead. Zimbabwe and Botswana were also affected.

As regards the threat of drought, Unganai (1994) reports that droughts have become a regular occurrence in southern Africa and also one of the most debilitating natural disasters in the sub-region. In fact, it is becoming increasingly unusual for drought conditions not to be experienced somewhere in southern Africa each year. This hazard impacts most heavily on the region's agricultural sector, which plays a major role in the economics of the sub-region. An analysis of statistics on droughts and floods in the Southern Africa region is presented below in the form of table. This is to show that the entire region has registered severe natural hazards over an extended period of more than 150 years. It suggests that most countries in the region have recorded natural disasters. Droughts and floods were the most frequent natural hazards in Southern Africa. On the basis of this information, it can be predicted that similar natural disasters will continue to occur in the region. The consequences of these hazards obviously differ in each country, depending on the magnitude of the particular disaster.

Disaster management measures

In order to reduce or avoid losses from hazard, there is need to ensure prompt assistance to victims and achieve rapid and effective recovery, the paper therefore recommends a disaster management measures that will not only prevent and mitigate but also prepare and response to disaster. The strategic action which usually presented as requirements before, during and after a disaster occurrence always put into consideration, the human element:

• The first thing to prevent disaster is to reduce poverty through various poverty alleviation programmes such as financial empowerment and provision of housing and necessary infrastructure.

• For flooding and rainstorm prevention, the requirements demand for the use of strong structural materials, provision of adequate open green space.

- The prevention of drought called for the use of drought tolerant and early maturing crop varieties by farmers.
- In term of preparedness; flooding and rainstorm equally called for concerted efforts that must be geared towards adequate city planning, policy formulation, enhanced public enlightenment programmes, integration of environmental planning and education into curriculum of schools at all levels, capacity building towards adaptation and mitigation of climate change.
- At the same time, for quick response to disaster in the Global South, governments at all levels should ensure proper and effective use of ecological fund; and encourage the integration of environmental disaster insurance to take care of the fall out of flood menace.
- Finally, national disaster and emergency policies should be strengthened to facilitate effective disaster response. This approach will not only save lives and livelihoods, but it will equally reduce vulnerability to disaster menace.

Conclusion

The Global South, just like other regions of the continent, is one of the most disaster-prone areas of the world. It experiences different types of natural disaster at a much higher frequency. These include flood, drought and cyclone. Natural disasters not only bring immense suffering and miseries to human communities but also triggers a whole set of mechanism that affect the economic and social life of the people. These have both short and long-term socio-economic and political implications. It is usually the poor who suffer the most because they lack the resources to overcome their financial losses. Their asset base and economic staying capacity is very low and therefore, cannot withstand the onslaught of such disaster making them utterly vulnerable. In most cases, the vulnerability derives from poverty itself. Poor people are more likely to live in disaster-prone areas. This vulnerability is further exacerbated because the poor who are forced to live in these areas cannot afford to undertake measures to reduce the risk of natural disaster. On the other hand, the rich and non-governmental organisations often view disasters as windows of opportunity for them to come in and make an impact in the affected areas.

References

Adamson, T. P. (1983). *Technical Report on Southern African Storm Rainfall, Republic of South Africa.* Department of Environment Affairs, Branch of Scientific Services.

Ariyanbandu, M. M. and Wackramasinghe, W. M. (2005). *Gender Dimension in Disaster Management: A guide for South Asia:* Sri Lanka.

Ayanji, E, N. (2004). *A critical assessment of the natural disaster risk management framework in Cameroon. An end-of- course case study submitted to the department of city management and urban development of the World Bank Institute in partial fulfilment of the requirements of the award of a certificate in natural disaster risk management.* Institute for Housing and Urban Development Studies (I.H.S,) Rotterdam.

Adger, W.N, and Brooks, N. (2003). *Does global environmental change cause vulnerability? Natural disasters and development in a globalising world.* Routledge, London.

Africa Union. (2006). *Report of the Africa Union Ministerial conference on disaster risk reduction: Africa Union,* Addis Ababa, Ethiopia.

Berloffa, G., & Modena, F. (2013). Income shocks, coping strategies, and consumption smoothing: An application to Indonesian Data, *Journal of Asian Economics,* 24, 158-171.

Borrows, P. and De Bruin, D. (2006). The Management of Riverine Flood Risk. *Journal,* 55: 5151-5157.

Carter, M., Little, P., Mogues, T., & Negatu, W. (2007). Poverty Traps and Natural Disasters in Ethiopia and Honduras. *World Development,* 35, 835-856.

Centre for Research on the Epidemiology of Disaster. (2009). *Annual disaster Statistical review 2008. The numbers and trends.* Universite Catholique de Louvain. Presses Universitaire de Louvain. Bruxelles

Cutter L. Susan, Barnesa Lindsey, Berrya, Melissa., Burtona, Christopher., Evansa, Elijah., Tatea, Eric., and Webba, Jennifer.

(2007). *A place-based model for understanding community resilience to natural disasters*, Global Environmental Change.

Coffman, M., & Noy, I. (2011). Hurricane Iniki: Measuring the long-term economic impact of a natural disaster using synthetic control. *Environmental and Development Economics*, 17, 187-205.

Dercon, S. (2004). Growth and shocks: Evidence from rural Ethiopia. *Journal of Development Economics*, 74, 309-329.

Ethiopia Government. (1993). *National Policy on Disaster Prevention and Management*. Transitional Government of Ethiopia. Addis Abeba.

ENDA. (2008). *Disaster Risk Reduction in West and Central Africa. Local perspective*. ENDA Tiers Monde. Dakar.

Gadain, H., Bidault, N., Stephen, L., Watkins, B., Dilley, M., and Mutunga, N. (2006). Reducing the impacts of floods through early warning and preparedness: A pilot study for Kenya. Natural disaster hotspots case studies. *Disaster risk management series No 6*. The World Bank Hazard Management Unit. Washington, D.C.

Freeman, P. (2000). Infrastructure, Natural Disasters, and Poverty. In A. Kreimer, & M. Arnold (Eds.), *Managing Disaster Risk in Emerging Economies* (pp. 55-61). Washington, D.C.: World Bank Publications.

Freeman, P. K., Keen, M., & Mani, M. (2003). Being prepared: Natural disasters are becoming more frequent, more destructive, and deadlier, and poor countries are being hit the hardest. *Finance and Development*, 40 (3): 42-45.

Hansson, k., Danielson, M. and Ekenberg, L. (2008). A Framework for Evaluation of Flood Management Strategies. *Journal*, 86 (3): 465-480.

Henderson, L. (2004). Emergency and disaster: Pervasive risk and public bureaucracy in developing nations. Public Organization Review: *A Global Journal*, 4, 103-119.

Hulme, M. (1984). "1983: An exceptionally dry year in central Sudan". *Weather 39*, Page 270-274.

International Federation of Red Cross and Red Crescent Societies (IFRC) (2006). *Ethiopia: Floods appeal No MORET 003*. Published by IFRC Geneva.

International Federation of Red Cross and Red Crescent Societies (IFRC). (2007). *West Africa: Floods focus on Burkina Faso.* Published by IFRC Geneva. Ouagadougou.

International Federation of Red Cross and Red Crescent Societies (IFRC) (2007). *Sudan: Floods. Emergency Appeal,* Published by IFRC Geneva. Khartoum

International Federation of Red Cross and Red Crescent Societies (IFRC) (2001). *Sudan: Drought. Information Bulletin No1.* Published by IFRC Geneva. Khartoum.

International Federation of Red Cross and Red Crescent Societies (IFRC) (2006). *Ethiopia: Drought. Emergency Appeal.* Published by IFRC Geneva. Addis Ababa

International Federation of Red Cross and Red Crescent Societies (IFRC) (2007). *Nigeria: Floods. Emergency Appeal.* Published by Nigerian Red Cross Society. Lagos.

International Federation of Red Cross and Red Crescent Societies (IFRC) (2005). Kenya: Floods. Minor emergency. *DREF bulletin No 05ME032.* Published by IFRC Geneva.

International Federation of Red Cross and Red Crescent Societies (IFRC) (2008). West and Central Africa: Flood preparedness. Focus on relief stock procurement and capacity building for response. *Emergency appeal No MOR61003.* Published by IFRC Geneva.

IPCC. (2007). Climate Change 2007: *Impacts, adaptation, and vulnerability.* Cambridge University Press, Cambridge.

IRIN. (2008). Kenya: Thousands affected as Floods Submerge Farms. *Humanitarian News Analysis,* 5 November.

Jakobsen, K. (2012). In the eye of the storm: The welfare impacts of a hurricane. *World Development,* 40, 2578-2589.

Khandlhela, M. and May, J. (2006). *A study on Poverty, Vulnerability and the Impact of Flooding in the Limpopo Province,* School of Development Studies, University of Kwazulu Natal, South Africa.

Lopez. (2008). *Adaptive capacity and resilience to floods in the Caribbean: A case study of two flood-prone communities in puertorico,* PhD dissertation submitted to The Pennsylvania State University.

Mechler, R. (2009). Disasters and economic welfare: Can national savings help explain post disaster changes in consumption? *(Policy Research Working Paper No. 4988)* Retrieved from World Bank website: http://econ.worldbank.org/WBSITE/EXTERNAL/EXTDE C/EXTRESEARCH/0, menuPK: 469435~pagePK: 64165236~piPK: 64165141~theSitePK: 46 9382,00.html Morris, S., Neidecker-Gonzales, O., Carletto, C., Munguia, M., Medina, J. M., &

Narayan, P. (2003). Macroeconomic impact of natural disasters on a small island economy: evidence from a CGE model. *Applied Economics Letters*, 10, 721-723

Nott, J. (2006). *Extreme Events: A Physical Reconstruction and Risk Assessment.* Cambridge University Press. New York.

OCHA. (2008). *Situation Report 5-Southern Africa Floods.* 31 January.

Oxfam. (2007). *Rethinking disasters,* Oxfam report, http://www.oxfarm.org.uk/resources/policy/conflict-disasters/downloads/oxfam-India-rethinking disasters.pdf.

Parker, J. D. (2000). Floods. *Tangler and Francis, National Academy Press*, Asian Disaster Preparedness Centre, Thailand

Sawada, Y., and Shimizutani, S. (2008). How do people cope with natural disasters? Evidence from the great Hanshin-Awaji (Kobe) earthquake in 1995. *Journal of Money*, Credit, and Banking, 40, 463-488

Singh, M. (2006). *Identifying and assessing drought hazard and risk in Africa. Regional conference on insurance and reinsurance for natural catastrophe risk in Africa.* Casablanca, Morocco, November 14/12/2005.

Shoji, M. (2010). Does Contingent Repayment in Microfinance Help the Poor During Natural Disasters? *Journal of Development Studies*, 46, 191-210.

Southern Africa Environment Outlook. (2008). *A report by the Southern African Development and Partner.* Southern African Research and Documentation Centre. Harare.

Teklu, T., Braun, J. V., Zakie, E. (1991). Drought and famine relationships in Sudan: Policy implication. *Research reports 88.* International Food Policy Research Institute. Khartoum.

Thanh, N., Hang, H., Chuc, N., Rudholm, N., Emmelin, A., & Lindholm, L. (2006). Does "the injury poverty trap" exist? A longitudinal study in Bavi, Vietnam. *Health Policy*, 78, 249-257.

Theron, M. (2007). *Climate Change and Increasing Floods in Africa: Implication for Africa's Development.*

Tompkins, E. Adger, N. Brown, K. (2002). Institutional Networks for Inclusive Coastal Zone Management in Trinidad and Tobago, *Environment and Planning* A, 34, 1095-1111.

Unganai, L, S. (1994). *Drought and Southern Africa: A note from the Harare regional office.* Drought Monitoring Centre. Harare.

United Nations Development Programme (UNDP) (2004). *Reducing Disaster Risk. A challenge for Development.* Bureau for Crisis Prevention and Recovery. United Nations Plaza. New York.

United Nations disaster assessment and Coordination (UNDAC) (2008). *Democratic Republic of Congo Earthquake in the Great lakes region. 10 to 22 February 2008.* UNDAC. New York.

Winsemius, H., B. Jongman, T. Veldkamp, S. Hallegatte, M. Bangalore and P. J. Ward. (2015). Disaster risk, climate change, and poverty: assessing the global exposure of poor people to floods and droughts, World *Bank Policy Research Working Paper series*, Washington, DC.

Chapter 8

The Emergence of the Cycle of Poverty and Traditional systems for Poverty Eradication in Yorubaland: Insights from the Biblical Ruth and Naomi

Caleb O. Ogunkunle

Introduction

In traditional Yorubaland of Nigeria, the expression "cycle of poverty" hardly existed, largely due to communal living and sharing guaranteed through the extended family system of mutual support. Today, however, the expression "cycle of poverty" is no longer a secret as this practically looms large in Nigeria due to several factors, including the effects of colonialism and neo-colonialism, and the advent of Christianity, Islam and westernization that have divided the people along near innumerable denominations, urbanization; new economic order based on money, salary and wages, and exploitative political elite as opposed to the impoverished and the wretched. Realization of such obtaining reality brings forth to the mind, the Biblical story of Ruth and Naomi, which teaches the importance of family support which does not only bring comfort but prevents people from sinking into the chasm of poverty. Based on personal knowledge of the Old Testament, this chapter interrogates the story of Ruth and Naomi exegetically, to x-ray its import and exemplary implication of the family support system that has almost broken down totally in Yorubaland. The purpose of the study is to promote the revival of the traditional African value of "I am because you are and since you are therefore I am;" and what the Yoruba express as Èniyàn ni aso mi (Human beings are my clothes- referring to protection and care). In the whole attempt, the historico- exegetical method is adopted. Historically, literature on Yoruba culture and poverty in Nigeria is reviewed while exegetical method is deployed to help explain key Hebrew words in the book of Ruth. The chapter advances the argument that Nigeria can draw inspiration and insights from the story of Ruth and Naomi which in itself demonstrates the extent to which the Old Testament Jews and traditional Africans have affinity. The chapter concludes that the principle of "we-feeling" and corporate social existence is paramount in Yorubaland as it is in the Christian World.

Yoruba Traditional Values

Nigeria has thirty-six states including the Federal Capital territory, Abuja. Major ethnic groups in the country include the Hausa, Fulani, Yoruba and Igbo among others. The Yorubaland is located in the south-western part of Nigeria. They are predominantly found in Oyo, Ogun, Ondo, Osun, Ekiti and Lagos States. A substantial population of Kwara and Kogi States is Yoruba. The Yoruba are regarded as one of the most advanced communities in West Africa especially in religion, agriculture, commerce, education, art, intelligence, government and warfare. The Yoruba people have a long history and they trace their ancestral home to Ile-Ife where they believe that the art of creation started. The Yoruba claim to have a common ancestor, Oduduwa. They speak the same language although there are dialectical variations. Among the dialectical groups are the Egba, Ekiti, Ibadan, Ife, Ijebu, Ijesa, Ikale Ondo, Owo and Oyo. The language is rich with almost over- supply of proverbs, folklore, folktales and pithy sayings (Awolalu & Dopamu, 1979).

The traditional Yoruba people in olden days lived in a compound setting called *agbo ilé* which is a collection of apartments for individual families. Each compound formed a square enclosing an open space in the middle. Also, each compound had a veranda, which opened on to the quadrangle and it was not divided by any partition as it gave room for intimate fellowship and for family members to walk from one end of the compound to the other. Children wandered from one part of the compound to another without restriction. And of course, they were jointly taught and educated together by the elderly people in the compound. Every compound had *baálé*, that is, the most elderly man in the compound whose duties were to preserve peace and order within his compound; and it is his duty to see that the members of

202

his compound were of mutual benefit to each other and interact with minimum friction. *Baálé* also maintained discipline in his compound. (Fadipe: 1970, 106). Fadipe further notes that:

> The *baálé* also punishes such anti-social behaviour as theft, incest and adultery. It is his duty to warn members of the compound to avoid being engaged in acts which would involve the family in a disgrace such as theft, burglary, or a charge of adultery emanating from outside (1970, 108).

The most elderly woman in the compound is called *ìyáálé*. Her duties were similar to those of *baálé* but among the women in the compound. The welfare of widows and orphans was taken care of through the mutual supports of family members in the compound. The community in general and members of the extended family of the deceased in particular take special interest in taking care of the widows and orphans. Young widows were encouraged to marry a brother of the deceased husband with the aim of protecting the woman socially and raising children in the family.

Poverty and vulnerability were alien in the Yoruba Traditional society. There was a deep sense of kinship among the people. Writing on kinship, Mbiti notes that "it is kinship which controls social relationship between people in a given community: it governs marital customs and regulations, it determines the behaviour of one individual towards another" (1970, 104). In other words, the communal lifestyle in Yoruba community did not allow poverty to strive. Apart from the fact that farming was the main occupation of the people and which made them to produce enough food; there was a team spirit among the people which made them to practice *Àárò*, *Òwè*, and *Èsúsú* or *Èésú* among others.

Àárò is the system where people of the same age group in the community come together to work on their farm, thereby moving from one farm to another. The number of individuals involved in *Àárò* is between four and eight and their farms are not too far from each other. They work on each farm until they go round all the farms. The purpose of *àárò* is to promote hard work among the individual group. In other words, what looks like an impossible task for an individual is done with ease when it is done through àáró. Àáró promotes love, fellowship and unity among the people in the group.

The traditional solidarity in which the individual says "I am because we are, therefore I am" (Mbiti: 1970, 224) is the same with the popular Yoruba saying *"Ènìyàn ni aso mi"* which literally means humans are my clothes. This saying is illustrated in *owe* which is one of the major ways the traditional people in the Yoruba community help one another. For example, unlike in the contemporary society when for a man to build a house, all that is needed is money to buy building the materials and then pay for labour in the traditional Yoruba society a man did not need money to buy any material or pay for labour. All that was needed was people around him. Thus, *owe* was used at every stage of the building: foundation, building and roofing of the house. Several individuals in the community were involved-men, women, the young and the old with each group doing specific assignments in the construction of the building. It was comparably easier for an average adult to have a building of his own without any physical and financial stress. *Owe* was also used when a family was about to do a major ceremony like wedding. Several people were involved in specific assignments voluntarily and thereby removing the financial burden from the responsible family.

Èsúsú or Èésú is another way of helping one another in the Yoruba society. Èsúsú or Èésú was the process whereby individuals of like minds came together to make weekly or monthly contribution of specified amount of money. At the end of the week or month such contribution was taken by a member of the group. A leader was chosen among the group whose duty was to coordinate the contribution. Usually, people arranged their own contribution to coincide with the ceremony such as wedding in the family. Also in times of emergency, arrangement could be made for an individual with special need to swap with another person so as to collect his own contribution at that particular point in time.

Furthermore, community work in the traditional Yoruba society was jointly done by every member of the community. For example, when a road in the community is bad, the *baálè* (the leader of the community) would simply inform each *baálé* (the leader of the compound)[1] that on a particular day in the coming week, such a road would be fixed. When the day came, everyone would be present at the site and the work was done jointly and gladly knowing that significant contribution was being made to the development of the community.

Poverty in Nigeria

Poverty can be defined as the lack of the basic necessities of life for any person or group. It is the condition of being poor and deficient in one form or the other. It is the condition of not having enough resources or income to meet basic needs of life. It is a lack of basic human needs, such as good nutritious food, clothing, shelter and health services. Chigbo (2011: 116) defines poverty as "a state of hopelessness, the inability to fend for oneself and his immediate dependent relatives."

Generally speaking, poverty is divided into three categories namely: absolute, relative and abject. Absolute poverty is the inability of an individual or a group to provide the material needs for physical, subsistence and protection of human dignity. These materials include shelter, water, health services, basic education, transportation, and work because the affected individual(s) have no job or income. Relative poverty is the inability of certain sections of the society to satisfy their basic needs. Abject poverty is a state in which an individual is not capable of utilizing resources around him to improve himself economically, socially, politically or otherwise (Lewu: 2008; Oni 2011; Chigbo 2011).

Poverty manifests itself in many ways in every society. Some of the most common include: prostitution, exposure to risks, corruption, robbery, street life, increased unemployment, living in squalor, shanties, shackles, high infant mortality, acute malnutrition, short life expectancy, human degradation, living in overcrowded and often poorly ventilated homes (Kunhiyop; 2008: 138). Akwara, et.al. (2013: 1-11) examine the relationship that exists between unemployment, poverty and national security. They argued that unemployment causes poverty and poverty causes insecurity. And for the achievement of national security, they recommend restructuring of the nation's socio-economic processes; making policies that will reduce poverty and unemployment; and accommodating the less privileged and unemployed members of the society.

Aiyedogbon and Ohwofasa (2012: 268-279) in their article entitled "Poverty and Youth Unemployment in Nigeria, 1987-2011" declare that for Nigeria to have been ranked 158th on the human development index is unacceptable as they make a strong connection of youth unemployment as the cause of poverty in Nigeria. They conclude that Nigeria is indeed a poor country with majority of her population wallowing in abject poverty. Also, they recommend a holistic effort by governments at all levels to create jobs and arrest unemployment. In addition, they both suggest that federal and state governments should endeavour to convince the citizens to adopt birth control and that the economic sector should be boosted to contribute meaningfully in reducing poverty in Nigeria.

Chukuemeka (2010: 54-67) examines a general review of poverty in Nigeria and various efforts of government to eradicate it. He argues that government should come up with policies that will indeed eradicate poverty besides that; credit scheme programme should be well articulated and strictly implemented; and most importantly, that the power sector be restructured since it would be difficult for small business holders to operate and break even without support from public power supply.

Lewu (2008) in her article entitled "A Critical Appraisal of Poverty Alleviation Programmes in Nigeria" highlights causes of poverty in Nigeria and different alleviation programmes that have been put in place by different governments through the history of the nation. She is of the view that all the factors that militated against the success of alleviation programmes in the past could be avoided. She recommends that focus should be on the educational and economic empowerment of women and youths, while agriculture should be promoted to make Nigeria self- sufficient in food production.

Oni (2011) in his inaugural lecture entitled "Man, Machine and Food Security" makes a strong connection between hunger, poverty and food security. According to him, poverty is the principal cause of hunger. Hunger is also a cause of poverty as it results in poor health, low levels of energy and mental impairment. Hence, hunger limits people's ability to work and learn. Describing the poverty in Nigeria, Oni (2011) states further that:

> Poverty in Nigeria is rated as absolute poverty for lack of any form of social security in place; no safety net of any sort. The incidence of poverty in Nigeria compares favourably with several other African countries that are not even blessed with the kind of natural endowment that Nigeria has. The incidence of poverty in Nigeria was in 1997 put at 70 percent, the same year that vision 2010 established for Nigeria a poverty line of 3,290.00 naira per capita… Although poor people are to be found in urban areas, the incidence of poverty is more dominant in rural Nigeria. (p. 6).

Ucha (2010: 46-56) identifies that unemployment, corruption, non-diversification of the economy, income inequality, laziness, and poor education system are some of the key factors contributing to poverty in Nigeria. He is of the opinion that all these factors must be properly tackled for any meaningful progress on poverty eradication in Nigeria.

Arogundade *et.al.* (2011: 42-52) examine various government policies on poverty alleviation in Nigeria. They discovered that each government in an attempt to introduce her own policy gradually abandoned the policy of the other governments which at the end of the day has not helped the targeted people. They recommended a harmonization of programmes by asking the federal government to establish an agency called- Poverty Alleviation Agency for Nigerians (PAAFN) for poverty policy continuation. This would guarantee that successive governments do not discard their predecessors' programmes on poverty. Rather, successive governments would be encouraged to add their own suggestions and all programmes would run concurrently to ensure that all targeted audiences are reached.

Unfortunately, in spite of wonderful recommendations by each of the researches carried out by the above mentioned researchers and scholars, poverty remains a major challenge in the Nigerian society as it is still the lot of the generality of the people. In addition, successive governments since the time of independence in 1960 have put in place different programmes with the aim of alleviating poverty.

Some of the programmes include: Directorate of Food, Roads and Rural Infrastructure (1986), Better Life for Rural Women (1988), Family Economic Advancement Programme (1993), Community Action Programme for Poverty Alleviation (1997), Family Support Programme (1998), National Economic Empowerment and Development Strategy (2007), among others. But each of these alleviation programmes failed and terminated with the government that set it up as a result egocentricism, greed, self-aggrandisement and corruption associated with people in each successive government. Many of the political leaders and government officials, instead of serving the people, are fond of diverting government monies into their pockets thereby causing untold hardship for ordinary citizens. Two recent cases include: the officials of Electricity Distribution Companies who were accused of corruption as they could not account for N213b power intervention fund (*Sunday Tribune,* December 18, 2016: 5); and the allegation of illegal withdrawal of N15m by the Speaker and two other officials of Ondo State House of Assembly (*Sunday Tribune,* January 29, 2017: 41). It is unfortunate that different allegations appear in the print media from time to time on government officials. Meanwhile, the Federal Government of Nigeria is set to invest some of the recently recovered funds on its social intervention programmes. The recovered funds, among others, are the §9m from Andrew Yakubu, a former group managing director of the Nigerian National Petroleum Corporation; and the §153m forfeited by Diezani Alison-Madueke, a former minister of Petroleum Resources (*Sunday Punch,* February 19, 2017: 4).

Why the Cycle of Poverty in Yorubaland

Attempt is made at this junction to examine the effects of colonialism, neo-colonialism and the advents of Christianity and westernisation on the African culture, especially the Yoruba culture. I intentionally do not attempt to look at the advent of Islam and its effect because generally Islam is closer to African system of life, especially in the area of polygamy.

In obedience to the commandment of Jesus Christ in Mat 28: 18-20, as the early Apostles went out from Jerusalem to the Gentile world, so also Western Christians over two hundred years ago came to the continent of Africa, including the Yorubaland. They came primarily to evangelize and educate the people of the "Dark Continent" (Akao: 1986). Unfortunately, their lack of understanding of the culture of the African people has had a negative impact on the people. Akao aptly comments on their action:

> Their preconceptions about Africa, its geography and the political and social conditions of the inhabitants, led them to taking decisions on their evangelistic methods and strategy, even before studying the people to know how to address themselves to their situation. Though the Gospel was preached, but it came in a packet with politics, commerce and culture. Some political and social analysts have come to look at the missionaries' activities as more of a curse rather than a blessing for the black man (p. 53).

In his research on the activity of the missionaries, Ayandele (1966: 329) pointedly observes that:

> Missionary activity was a disruptive force, rocking traditional society to its very foundations, denouncing ordered polygamy in favour of disordered monogamy, producing disrespectful, presumptuous and detribalized children through the mission schools, destroying the high moral principles and orderliness of indigenous society through denunciation of traditional religion, without an adequate substitute, and transforming the mental outlook of Nigerians in a way that made them imitate European values slavishly, whilst holding in irrational contempt valuable features of traditional culture.

Abioje (2014: 88) while discussing the disruptive force on family and social cohesion in traditional Africa made a reference to a quotation from Ablade (1976) saying:

> Nothing else has done more to destroy African socio-cultural values than did Christianity and capitalism those well-known allies of imperialism. The extended family system has almost broken down and

everybody is concerned only with himself. Africans are being corrupted by Western European capitalist ethics (p.88).

Consequently, Christianity which places emphasis on individual and his relationship to God has broken into the ethnic solidarity of the Yoruba traditional society which places emphasis on communal living where every member of the group or community from the highest to the lowest was no more than a unit in an organic whole controlled by an ironbound code of duties, taboos and rights. Thus, when a convert was made by the missionary, that convert was removed from an organic whole and thereby undermined the monolithic structure of the community: such a convert soon imbibed a new set of religious ideas and he began to nurse foreign ideas, economic ambitions and political aspirations of his own that was detrimental to the welfare and solidarity of the community (Ayandele, 1966: 330-1). One of the methods used by the early missionaries is the free Western education given to the children of some converts and church leaders as a means of enticing those outside the fold to come into it (Akao, 1986: 54).

Perhaps the root cause of the "cycle of poverty" in Yorubaland is connected with the activity of Protestant missionaries from Europe and America who came to evangelize but at the same time came with their denominational varieties and rivalries as succinctly put by Akao (1986):

> When the missionaries were leaving for Africa, it could be said that their aim was not to convert people into the "catholic Church" but to convert them into denominations. With this aim they came to Africa and started dividing it into religious districts, circuits, etc. In order to maintain the territorial integrity of each denomination, bickering and the spirit of petty jealousy that had riddled the home mission were imported and given expression here in Africa as the various denominations emerged (p.55).

Thus the concept of individualism and denominationalism planted by the early Western missionaries has germinated and grown to the point of causing serious havoc in the contemporary Nigerian society, especially in Yorubaland. Currently, the level of division in Christianity as represented by the Protestant, Pentecostal and Neo-Pentecostal Churches is alarming and the future looks very bleak.[2] Unfortunately, this individualistic tendency has gotten into the fabric of the majority of Christians in the Yorubaland. Everyone is after his/her own denomination and individuals are simply pursuing their own personal agenda. It is a known fact that adult Christian members of the same family in Yorubaland attend different Churches, especially in the cities and each one of them propagating the doctrines of his/her denomination. Unfortunately, some aspects of the doctrines are at variant with the Yoruba traditional value system. An example is dressing which has become controversial as the orthodox Churches frown at indecent dressing while the Neo-Pentecostal Churches accept it in the name of reaching the people with the gospel. Again, some individual Christians are much more committed to their Churches than the community they live and of course, this has led to their vulnerability.[3] Thus, it can be said that the loss of family solidarity is the real cause of the poverty predicament summarized as the "cycle of poverty."[4]

The intrusion into and destruction of the Yoruba family solidarity and values has brought about all kinds of evil and wickedness which have made many people vulnerable and at the risk of being attacked by the wicked individuals. Mbiti (1970: 224) aptly observes:

> Most of the problems of the emerging society are concentrated on people living in the cities. There are questions of housing, slums, earning and spending money, alcoholism, prostitution, corruption, and thousands of young people are roaming about in search of employment. Many people suddenly come from the country into the city where they have no roots or tradition to help them settle down. Others have hired most of their working life in the cities, and when they retire they do not quite know what to do there, and having lost their ties with country life they cannot easily return to it.

Indeed, the contemporary Nigerian society has shifted from the "we" of traditional corporate life to the "I" of modern individualism (Mbiti, 1970: 225). The logo in the contemporary society, especially in the cities is "I and my immediate family." This explains why today, egocentrism, self-aggrandizement, greed and all sorts of evil have taken over the hearts of humans. The poor masses in the society are being oppressed and marginalized by those in the political class. The politicians who are expected to serve the people are simply thinking and planning on wealth accumulation as reflected in their 'fat' salary and several allowances. Indeed, the level of atrocities being perpetrated in the contemporary Nigerian society is manifested in the current high rate of terrorism, kidnapping, and ritual killings among others, none of which was heard of in the Yoruba traditional society. Some recent cases of wickedness include: "An 18 year- old man has allegedly killed his mother in Plateau State for refusing to give him a 'disappearing' charm he claimed was his inheritance from his late herbalist father." (*The Nation*, August 6, 2017: 6); "An unidentified woman was shot dead by gunmen on motorcycles in Osogbo, Osun State." (*The Nation,* August 6, 2017: 8); "Gunmen have killed an Ado-Ekiti based businessman, Ifedayo Oladele Adeyemo in Ibadan in the presence of his daughter and wife." (*Sunday Punch,* June 11, 2015: 5); and "Kidnappers of six pupils of Igbonla Model College, Epe, Lagos State, have contacted some parents of the victims, demanding N1bn ransom to release them." (*Sunday Punch,* May 28, 2017: 2). Incidentally, the Chief of Army Staff, Lt. Gen. Tukur Buratai has "blamed the security challenge confronting Nigeria on poor upbringing of children," (*The Nation,* August 6, 2017: 6).

Biblical Ruth and Naomi

The book of Ruth derives its name from one of the main characters of the book, Ruth who was the daughter-in-law of Naomi and also a Moabitess. Other principal characters in the book are Naomi, the wife of Elimelech, who together with her husband left Bethlehem at the time of famine for Moab; and Boaz, who eventually served as kinsman-redeemer to Ruth and the father of Obed. The book of Ruth started with a crisis situation of poverty in the land of Bethlehem and which made Elimelech and his family vulnerable. Then, the book ended with a wonderful testimony which led to the birth of Obed. Canonically, many Hebrew manuscripts place Ruth in the *Megiloth* i.e. the five scrolls which were part of the third division of the Hebrew Bible.

Critical scholars are of the view that the book of Ruth should be dated sometime after the Babylonian captivity on accounts that the language of the book reflects Aramanism; legal customs are reflected, especially the explanation of the ceremony of the shoe in 4: 7 which presupposes a time when the practice was no longer understood; the interest in genealogies expressed in 4: 18-22, which recalls the 'priestly' genealogies in the Pentateuch and Chronicles, especially I Chr 2: 3-15; and the canonical placement of Ruth, not with the former prophets but among the Writings *(Hagiographa)*, on the assumption that those texts were gathered after the prophetic collection had been closed, among others (Block, 1999: 590-1).

Some other scholars argue for a period at the time of Josiah. One scholar that has made a strong case for this period is Block (1999: 596-80). He suggests that the reference to "the days when judges governed" and the book's interest in the Davidic house are the critical factors that determine the date of the book.

Obviously, the story of Ruth and Naomi started in a crisis situation which made the people to be vulnerable and helpless. Perhaps, it is possible to attribute the vulnerability of the people to human error. Elimelech led his wife, Naomi and their two sons out of Bethlehem, the house of bread to Moab as a result of poverty in the land. Unfortunately, Elimelech died shortly after his arrival in the land of Moab. This was the first serious disaster on the family. After the death of Elimelech, Naomi ought to lead his sons back to Bethlehem for them to marry and settle there. She, however, chose to stay in Moab where the sons married Moabite women which was forbidden for the Israelites (Deut 7: 1-4; Ezra 9: 12; 10: 2-3; I Kgs 11: 1). Again, disaster struck in the family as the two sons also died after living in the land of Moab for 10 years. This made Naomi to become even more vulnerable as well as her daughters-in-law.

The actions of Naomi and Ruth from this point on led to the breaking of the cycle of poverty in the family. Block (1999: 604) notes that one theme that is fully developed in the book of Ruth is "from emptiness to fullness." In other words, Naomi was initially emptied of all her resources such as food, home and familial support but at the end she experienced complete filling or fulfilment through a diligent and hardworking daughter-in-law who was in fact declared by the women of the town to be valuable than seven sons.

One verb that is repeatedly used in the book of Ruth is *subh* which means to turn back, go back or return. It means to go back and forth from gate to gate (Exod 32: 27); and it is a term used in returning to a leader or king (Jud 11: 8). Spiritually, it is used in turning back to God (Num 14: 43; Hos 6: 1; 7: 10; 14: 13; Jer 3: 7). In this context, the word is used of returning from foreign land (Ruth 1: 6, 7, 22; 2: 4; 4;3 cf. 2 Kgs 8: 3; 2 Chro 10: 2; Jer 31: 16; 40: 12; 43: 5; 44: 28; Ezra 6: 21; Neh 8: 17) (Brown, Driver & Briggs, 1979: 997).

Ruth's loyalty to Naomi was demonstrated in her choice of words while responding to her request of going back to her people. The Hebrew verb *pagha* which means to meet, encounter or reach has a number of meaning namely:

a). to meet or light upon (I Sam 10: 5; Exod 5: 20; Amos 5: 19);
b). to meet with kindness (Isa 64: 5);
c) to encounter with hostility (Jos 2: 16; Jud 8: 21; 15: 12; 18: 25; I Sam 22: 17, 18; 2 Sam 1: 15; I Kgs 2: 29,31,32,34 etc.);
d). to encounter with request, entreat (Ruth 1: 16; Jer7: 16; Job 21: 15; 27: 18); and
e). to strike, touch of boundary (Jos 16: 7). (Brown, Driver & Briggs, 1979: 803).

Ruth entreated Naomi not to discourage her from following her. The Hebrew word 'azabh means to leave, abandon, forsake, or let loose (Brown, Driver & Briggs, 1979: 736). Obviously, Ruth made up her mind to follow Naomi all the way and that she would not abandon her.

Ruth 1: 16-17 says:

> Don't urge me to leave you or to turn back from you where you go I will go, and where you stay I will stay. Your people will be my people and your God my God. Where you die I will die, and there I will be buried. May the LORD deal with me, be it ever so severely, if anything but death separates you and me.

The reaction of the people of Bethlehem to Naomi and Ruth is very instructive. The Hebrew verb used is *'hum'* or *'him'* which means to murmur, roar or discomfit. In this passage it is Niphil imperfect as everyone in Bethlehem stirred at them with unbelief (Brown, Driver & Briggs, 1979: 223).

Ruth 2 begins with the relationship between Naomi and Boaz, the son of Salmon (Ruth 4: 21) and the husband Rahab the harlot (Mat 1: 5) who had helped the spies prepare for the battle against Jericho (Josh 2: 1-21). Specifically, Ruth 2: 1 describes Boaz as the kinsman of Elimelech and a man of great wealth. The Hebrew word *go'el* means to redeem or act as kinsman. The word is used in three different ways in the Hebrew Bible. One, it is used of someone who acts as a kinsman, or taking the part of the next of kin as in Lev 25: 25; Num 5: 8; 35: 12; Ruth 2: 20; 3: 9, 12; 4: 1, 3, 6, 8, 14; I Kgs 16: 11. Two, the word is used of redemption whereby payment of the value assessed of consecrated things by the original owner is made (Lev 27: 13, 15, 19, 20, 31). Finally, it speaks of God as redeeming individuals from death (Psa 103: 4; Lam 3: 58), from bondage (Exod 6: 6) and from captivity (Isa 43: 1; 44: 22, 23) (Brown, Driver & Briggs, 1979: 145).

The turning point in the story of Naomi-Ruth begins with Ruth's initiative. Ruth said to Naomi "let me go to the fields and pick up the leftover grain behind anyone in whose eyes I find favour" (Ruth 2: 2). The Hebrew word *sadeh* is a masculine noun which means field. In this context it speaks of a definite portion of the land that has been cultivated (Gen 37: 7; 47: 24; Exod 22: 45; Lev 27: 16-17; Ruth 2: 2; 2 Sam 1: 21; etc.) (Brown, Driver & Briggs, 1979: 961). In other words, Ruth made herself available to change their pathetic situation. The Hebrew verb *laqat* means to pick, gather up or glean. Things that are gleaned include stones (Gen 31: 46), manna (Exod 16: 4, 5, 26), grapes (Lev 19: 10), arrows (I Sam 20: 38), firewood (Jer 7: 18). In Ruth, the verb is generally used in the Piel perfect as the lady was gleaning the grains after the reapers (Ruth 2: 3, 7, 15-19).

Ruth worked diligently on the field of Boaz who equally granted her favour. The Hebrew word *hen* is a masculine noun which means favour, grace or acceptance. This favour can be with God (Gen 6: 8; 18: 3; 19: 19; Exod 33: 12, 13, 16, 17; 34: 9; Num 11: 11,15; Jud 6: 17;

2 Sam 15: 25; Prov 3: 4, etc.) or with men, just as Ruth found favour in the eyes of Boaz (Ruth 2: 2, 10, 13, cf. Gen 30: 27; 32: 6; 33: 8, 10, 15; 34: 11; 39: 4; 47: 25, 29; 50: 4; Num 32: 5; Deut 24: 1; I Sam 1: 18; 16: 22; 20: 3, 29; 25: 8; 27: 5; 2 Sam 14: 22; 16: 1; I Kgs 11: 19; Est 5: 8; 7: 3 etc.) (Brown, Driver & Briggs, 1979: 336).

Apart from Ruth's diligence and hard work, she also listened to every instruction given by Naomi. Even the procedure that led to the marriage between Boaz and Ruth was as directed by Naomi. It all started with Naomi who told Ruth "my daughter, should I not try to find a home for you, where you will be provided for?" (Ruth 3: 1). Knowing the movement of Boaz, Naomi asked Ruth to wash and perfume herself and put on her best clothes and then go down to the threshing floor (Ruth 3: 3). The Hebrew verb *rahas* means to wash oneself with water, bathe (Exod 2: 5; 2 Sam 11: 2; 12: 21; I Kgs 22: 38; 2 Kgs 5: 10, 12, 13; Isa 1: 16; Ruth 3: 3; Ezek 23: 40, etc.) (Brown, Driver & Briggs, 1979: 934) while the verb *suk* means to anoint oneself or to pour in anointing oil (Ruth 3: 3; 2 Sam 12: 20; Dan 10: 3; 2 Sam 14: 2; Mic 6: 15; Deut 28: 40) (Brown, Driver & Briggs, 1979: 961). Thus, Naomi encouraged Ruth to make herself presentable to Boaz, the possible kinsman-redeemer.

One major concept that summarizes the book of Ruth is that of kindness or goodness. The Hebrew word *hesed* is a masculine noun which means kindness or goodness. The word is used to express the kindness of God towards men or the kindness of men towards men. For instance, in the first speech of Naomi (Ruth 1: 8), reference is made to Yahweh's kindness as emphasis is placed on the attributes of God such as love, mercy, grace and covenant faithfulness. In other words, God in His loving kindness redeems mankind from enemies and troubles (Gen 19: 19; 39: 21; Exod 15: 13; Jer 31: 3; Ezra 7: 28; 9: 9; Ps 21: 8; 31: 17, 22; 32: 10; 33: 22; 36: 8, 11; 42: 9; 44: 10; 59: 17; Ruth 1: 8; 2: 20, etc.) (Brown, Driver & Briggs: 1979, 338).

Speaking of the practical demonstration of *hesed* by Ruth, Block (1999: 613) says:

> She [Ruth] casts her lot with her widowed mother-in-aw (1: 15-18). She takes the initiative in providing food (2: 2); she expresses deep and humble appreciation for the kindness of Boaz (2: 10,13); she works

hard in Boaz's field (2: 17-18, 23); she follows her mother-in-law's counsel in approaching Boaz (3: 6-13); she sensitively listens to Boaz's concerns and patiently waits for a legal resolution (3: 14-18); she apparently lets her mother-in-law adopt her son as her own (4: 16).

Conclusively, the book of Ruth has so much to teach contemporary society on love and welfare. Smith (1981: 829) while highlighting the love exhibited by the principal characters in the book says:

> Throughout the book Naomi plans and acts for the welfare of her daughters-in-law. She urges them to leave her and to find husbands with their own people. She plans for Ruth's security in Bethlehem. Ruth acts always for love and trust of Naomi, "doing all that she bade her." Boaz from his first word, "The LORD be with you," to his final words at the gate, is the responsible landowner, great enough not to be limited by prejudice or by concern for his own inheritance.

The Yoruba Traditional Values Vis – à- Vis Biblical Ruth and Naomi

It is appropriate at this point to have a reflection on both the Yoruba traditional value system and the biblical Ruth and Naomi with a view of highlighting lessons for the contemporary Nigerian society. To begin with, the communal lifestyle in the Yoruba traditional society is a demonstration of love and concern which they had one for another. The lifestyle did not allow vulnerability and poverty to stand as the less privileged and vulnerable individuals are looked after by both immediate and extended family members. The same team spirit is exhibited in various other practices such as *Àárò*, *Òwè*, and *Èsúsú* of the Yoruba people where things are jointly done for the purpose of helping one another. This corporate and communal lifestyle is equally seen in the story of biblical Ruth and Naomi. Elimelech, his wife and children jointly left Bethlehem for a greener pasture in the land of Moab. Also, when the time came for Boaz to marry Ruth, everyone in the community was not only supportive but in the picture of the whole process.

Secondly, the Yoruba traditional values have their root in Yoruba ideology of *Omolúwàbí* which has the connotation of good and gentle character. An individual who is described as *Omolúwàbí* manifests principles of moral conduct in spoken word, respect and having good mind towards other people. In other words, an *Omolúwàbí* person is the individual who is deeply interested in the welfare of other people. Incidentally, each of the principal characters in the story of biblical Ruth and Naomi showed attributes of *Omolúwàbí*. For example, Ruth was very loyal to Naomi, her mother-in-law and she listened to her instruction. On the other hand, Naomi was not selfish as she properly counselled and mentored Ruth. Likewise, Boaz, though very rich yet, he was a responsible man who believed in due and legal process in marrying Ruth. Unfortunately, all these qualities enumerated in both the Yoruba traditional society and the story of biblical Ruth and Naomi, appear to be lacking in the contemporary society hence there are several challenges that are making the masses vulnerable.

Thirdly, *opó sísú* is one of the practices in the Yoruba traditional society perhaps to assist the widows who are most likely to be vulnerable. *Opó sísú* is the practice whereby one of the brothers of the deceased takes over the wife as his own with the aim of bearing children and taking care of both the woman and her children. Boaz's levirate marriage to Ruth is closely connected with *Opó sísú* in the Yoruba culture. Boaz was a responsible man who was aware of other people that were closer to Ruth than him. He did not take advantage of Ruth by exploiting her vulnerability. He followed due and legal process to marry Ruth. Perhaps, part of the major problems confronting the contemporary Nigerian society and which is making life vulnerable for the masses and people of the same standing as Ruth and Naomi, is lack of integrity among the rich and political leaders.

Finally, people in the Yoruba traditional society believe strongly in dignity of labour and they have high regard for hard work. Hence, the common saying in Yoruba:

Isé ni òògùn ìsè,
Isé ní ngbé ni dé ibi gíga.
Múra sí isé re òré mi,

Ojó nlo.

Hard work is medicine for poverty,
Hard work takes one to higher height.
Work diligently my friend,
Time is going.

Another Yoruba poem says:

Òle, a lápá má sisé,
Òle fi aso ìyà bora sùn,
Ení bí òle kò rómo bí,
Ewá w'ayé òle o,
Ó se o.

This literally means:

A lazy person has hand but cannot work,
A lazy person covers himself with clothes of affliction,
Anyone who gives birth to a lazy person does not have a child,
Look at the condition of a lazy man,
It is full of shame or pity.

Furthermore, the Yoruba saying *Bí oúnje bá ti kúrò nínú ìsé, ìsé bùse,* literally means "when the issue of feeding is taken out of poverty, such poverty is almost over." It is with this understanding that one appreciates the Yoruba traditional society that placed so much emphasis on farming, especially as it was the main occupation of the people. In fact, polygamy was encouraged with the aim of bearing many children who will eventually help on the farm. At the time of harvest, women and children, including widows and orphans take part and at the end of the exercise, everyone had something tangible to take home. Consequently, everyone is being taken care of through the extended family solidarity. The cycle of poverty was broken in the story of Ruth and Naomi as a result of the initiative and action of Ruth, the diligent and hard working woman who had the initiative of going to glean on the farm of Boaz, a prosperous farmer. It is highly

219

probable that the action of Ruth was the beginning of transformation that turned the fortune of Ruth and Naomi.

Conclusion

This chapter has demonstrated that both the Yoruba traditional values and the story of biblical Ruth and Naomi have much to teach contemporary Nigerian society on how to break cycle of poverty that is currently plaguing the nation. The communal lifestyle exhibited in the Yoruba traditional society was a plus for the then society. Also, the story of biblical Ruth and Naomi started in a crisis situation with one tragedy after the other but the story ended on a good and positive note as a result of corporate and selfless lifestyle that existed between Ruth, Naomi and Boaz. Therefore, the principle of "we-feeling" and corporate existence that is paramount in traditional Yoruba society which is also found in biblical Ruth and Naomi is highly recommended for the contemporary Nigerian society that is currently struggling with the effects of modern individualism.

Notes

1. The two words *baálè* and *baálé* look alike but they are not the same in accent and meaning. *Baálè* means the leader of the community while *baálé* means the leader of the compound.

2. I attended a funeral service in Offa, a major town in Kwara State on 29th of July, 2017. One of the groups that came out to pay tribute to the deceased was the 'Offa Christian Fellowship.' I observed that people that came out were elderly people- of 50 years and above. My discussion with other ministers on the altar who equally observed the group shows the influence of Pentecostalism or neo-Pentecostalism in the town as the younger generation Christians now belong to different other denominations and they do not believe in coming together to form a central fellowship. Every denomination is doing his "own thing" separately. Our fear is that in the next decade or two there will be no more of such central fellowship in the community and this will automatically lead to spiritual poverty in the town!

3. An example is the story of a Pastor a colleague shared with me. The said Pastor did not associate with the people in his community. He refused to

220

participate in community development. He refused to make contribution towards the payment of night guards salary claiming that the Lord was watching over him. Unfortunately, it was not too long when he became victim of robbers as he was robbed of his expensive car at gun point.

4. The other day I saw a post on my WhatsApp illustrating two different families. The first family that is made up of husband, wife and two children illustrate the communal way of living. They receive message from the landline together, listen to the message together, contributing, sharing and rejoicing together.

The second family was also made up of husband, wife and two children. Each member of the family though sitting on the same table but everyone of them had a cell phone and was busy doing things in his or her own way. This picture illustrates individualistic type of life where there is no communication or sharing.

The message is that landline unites the family while self-phone scatters the family.

References

Abioje, P. O. (2014). *African Ancestral Heritage in Christian Interpretations.* Cape Coast: Nyakod Printing Works.

Akao, J. O. (1986). "Is the Mission of the Church Still Understood in Western Terms?" In *The State of Christian Theology in Nigeria 1980-81.* Mercy Oduyoye (Ed.) Ibadan: Daystar Press.

Ayandele, E. A. (1966). *The Missionary Impact on Modern Nigeria 1842-1914: A Political and Social Analysis.* Harlow, Essex: Longman Group.

Arogundade, K. K.; Adebisi, S.O.; & Ogunro, V. O. (2011). "Poverty Alleviation Programmes in Nigeria: A Call for Policy Harmonisation." *European Journal of Globalization and Development Research, Vol. 1, No. 1.*

Aiyedogbon, J. O. & Ohwofasa, B. O. (2012). "Poverty and youth Unemployment in Nigeria, 1987-2011" *International Journal of Business and Social Science Vol. 3 No. 20.*

Akwara, A. F.; Akwara, N. F; Enwuchola, J; Adekunle, M; & Udaw, J. E. (2013). "Unemployment and Poverty: Implications for National Security and Good Governance in Nigeria" *International*

Journal of Public Administration and Management Research (IJPAMR), Volume 2, Number1.

Awolalu, J. O. & Dopamu, P. A. (1979). *West African Traditional Religion* (Ibadan: Onibonoje Publication Company.

Block, D. I. (1999). *The New American Commentary: Volume 6, Judges and Ruth*. Nashville: Broadman & Holman Publishers.

Brown, F; Driver, S. R.; & Briggs, C. A. (1979).*The New Brown-Driver-Briggs-Gesenius Hebrew and English Lexicon with An Appendix containing the Biblical Aramaic*. Peabody, Massachusetts: Hendrickson Publishers.

Chigbo, M. A. (2011). "The Menace of Corruption and Poverty in the Nigerian Society." *A Journal of Department of Sociology Abia State University, Uturu*. Volume 1, Number 1.

Chukuemeka, E. E. O. (2010). "Poverty and the Millennium Development Goals in Nigeria: The Nexus" *International Journal of Economic Development Research and Investment Vol. 1, No 1*.

Fadipe, N. A. (1970). *The Sociology of the Yoruba*. Ibadan: Ibadan University Press.

Kunhiyop, S. W. (2008). *African Christian Ethics*. Nairobi: Word Alive Publishers.

Lewu, M.A.Y. (2008). "A Critical Appraisal of Poverty Alleviation Programmes in Nigeria." In *Perspectives on Contemporary Socio-Political and Environmental Issues in Nigeria*. Babatolu, J. S. & Ikuejube, G. (eds). Ondo: School of Arts and Social Sciences, Adeyemi College of Education.

Mbiti, J. S. (1970). *African Religions & Philosophy*. London: Heinemann.

Oni, C. K. (2011). *Man, Machine, and Food Insecurity*. The Ninety- Four Inaugural Lecture, University of Ilorin, Ilorin.

Smith, L. P. (1981). "The Book of Ruth: Introduction and Exegesis." In *The Interpreter's Bible Twelve Volumes*. George Arthur Buttrick et al. (eds). Nashville: Abingdon Press.

Sunday Punch, May 28, 2017.

Sunday Tribune, December 18, 2016.

Sunday Tribune, January 29, 2017.

Sunday Punch, February 19, 2017.

The Nation, August 6, 2017.

Ucha, C. (2010). "Poverty in Nigeria: Some Dimensions and Contributing Factors" *Global Majority E-Journal, Vol. 1, No. 1.*

Chapter 9

Mwariology as Basis for Heritage Studies and Springboard for Africa's Development

Phillip T. D. Mazambara & Munyaradzi Mawere

Introduction: Understanding Mwariology within the context of heritage

Heritage is the root of any people or nation. Taking it from its French etymology, the term 'heritage' is a derivation from the word *heriter* which means something passed on from an earlier generation to the next (Mawere 2016c). As can be seen, this understanding of heritage relates it to history, which in itself owes its origins from a Latin term *historia* meaning inquiry (Fisher 2010). Nevertheless, Lowenthal (1998) underlines that history and heritage are two different worlds apart. He argues categorically that:

> History and heritage transmit different things to different audiences. History tells all who will listen what has happened and how things came to be as they are. Heritage passes on exclusive myths of origin and continuance, endowing a select group with prestige and common purpose [...]. History is for all, heritage for (us) alone (p. 128-129).

More so, heritage has been accused of being unscientific and an area that invests in emotions of, and allegiance to, imagined collective identities (cf. Grever, De Bruijn and Van Boxtel 2012). Lowenthal (1996) buying into the debate on the conceptualisation of heritage argues wittingly and convincingly that unlike history which is universally accessible and testable, heritage is "tribal, exclusive, patriotic, redemptive or self-aggrandising' and is not primarily concerned with 'checkable fact but credulous allegiance" (see, p. 120-121). He further argues that heritage embodies feelings of the past that shape identities and the historical materials that are harnessed to sustain them. For him, heritage's approach to the past is largely presentist and not particularly concerned with historical accuracy.

Trying to tell it all in tersest terms, Seixas (2014) has underscored the primacy of history as evidence and not authority given that heritage tends to be celebratory while history critiques the past. Put differently, heritage has been understood to underline the continuity from the past while history scrutinises and sometimes critiques or challenges the perceived links between the past and the present (Gadamer 1987). Whatever the compatibilities and incompatible divergences between heritage and history might be, it remains a fact that history and heritage converge, complement, and overlap.

Yet, studying heritage does not always entail that we go back to our roots (delving into *pasichigare* in Shona), but that in the power of our roots we can forge our today and tomorrow's well-being within our current environment as best as we can. Mwariology is derived from *Mwari* – a Shona term for The-Human-Being-Who-Is or one of the equivalent ethnic Zimbabwean words for the term '*Inzwi*' Voice-Ultimate-Concept. Other ethnic African equivalence are *Modhimo* (in Ndebele), *Mudzimu* (in Venda), *Xikwembu* (in Tsonga), *Nzambi* (in Lingala) *Zame* (variant in Karanga), *Mungu* (in Swahili), *Mulunghu* (in Nyasa), and *Umveling'api* (variant in Ndebele) (Personal Communications). All these words refer to the ethnic African Ultimate-Concept more or less identical among ethnic Africans in the central and southern parts of Africa.

A critical analysis of the concept of *Mwari* is not very different from the absolute monotheism of Islamic *Allah* or Jewish *Yaweh*, which, incidentally, many Zimbabweans call in perhaps its original Hebrew form when in jeopardy as '*Yowee!*' Yowee is a cry for help as saying; "Please deliver me U-Who-Hear-Me-Whom-I-Do-Not-See!" Whoever hears the cry is the *Yowe* (Yahweh in Jewish) and must do their best to deliver the victim or else they are also held accountable for the misfortune about to befall the victim in the *Nyikadzimu*, Shona for the Spiritual Realm. If the Zimbabwean *Yowe* is the Mosaic *JHWH*, then the Hebrew injunction: *You shall not call the name of the Ultimate Voice-All-in-All in vain* is adhered to by ethnic Zimbabweans who call it only when in jeopardy. This could be understood within the context that Moses is (and should be always) identified as an

226

African considering that most of the 70 ethnic groups of the Israelite League who were from Egypt travelled with him when they were delivered from Pharaoh's bondage. Note that in the bible, Yaweh – the Voice-God of the Israelites has to be distinguished from various Canaanite *Elohim* Hebrew plural/pantheon of gods.

Mwariology is a term that was coined at Great Zimbabwe University from a then Special Honours Religious Studies Student, Sunday Mavodyo. The student commented that all the written lectures for his Special Honours courses by the Lecturer concerned (Dr. Phillip Mazambara) and in other various courses he was custodian of were nothing but African Religious Tradition: be they New Testament, Biblical Languages, Religion and Ethics, Christianity in Africa and Religious Movements and the course on Selected Religious Texts. The student heard in all, the Afro-basis of thinking remaining shoutingly clear throughout the referred courses. At first this Lecturer felt it was a negative comment but as he realised that it is the 'Parliamentary State Niche' of the Great Zimbabwe University, he welcomed the comment as it was in tune with the national agenda and vision for Zimbabwe. Before this, the lecturer concerned called African Traditional Religion (ATR) African Religious and Cultural Traditions (ARCT) (see for example, Mazambara 1999). Religion is reduced to an adjective and traditionally promoted to the noun in place for religion. It is easier to define tradition(s) than religion(s). Ethnic Zimbabwean and other African nations' socio-cultural-religious and political developments, throughout history to present day, have never created a closed-up religious self-understanding to enclose themselves from the rest as the 'We-They' paradigm exclusively as missionary religions from Judaism or supposedly from Abraham (Israelite, European and Ancient Near East or Arabic traditions) have done. The term "Mwariology" was chosen to express the welcome generalisation remarked about the referred Lecturer and the lectures grouped as Mwariology Publications. Africa and African(-ness), from Cape to Cairo, is very difficult to define especially in the ethnic open-ended liberalness, pragmatism and accommodativeness. As Mawere and Mubaya (2016) have noted, considering the wave of the present-day globalisation as well as the fact that Africa is generally known as the cradle of mankind, distinguishing 'real' Africans from those that are not remains a mammoth task for any researcher who commits himself/herself to the task. We believe and accept the claim of the Hollandish Boers in South Africa that they are Africans in their own Dutch language: *Afrikaner*. Why not when they have left Holland for good, as the Zimbabweans have equally left Tanganyika (their 'first' place of origin) for good? The Hollandish Boers' apartheid common to European racism is something else not to blind this Author's conviction about the said Africanness. Whoever denies Africanness to the Hollandish Boers is unAfrican as all Zimbabwean *masvikiro* (spirit mediums) or highest beyond political borders advisors will consider every human being a *muzukuru* (grandchild) to them and each person or family is allowed to live its own religious culture and identity within any kingdom or village it migrates to.

As can be seen, the concept of 'Mwariology' has not only been used to refer to the 'The-Human-Being-Who-Is' or 'Voice-Ultimate-Concept' in terms of protection seeking. The concept has been viewed as influential in other spheres of human life such as education and development. When the ethnic Zimbabweans talk of the Voice-Ultimate-Concept, they do not seek protection but also guidance from their vulnerable situations, including situations of poverty. It is from this understanding that we also understand Mwariology as the springboard of development in Africa, and more specifically southern Africa. Thus, in this chapter we seek to demonstrate how Mwariology is linked to heritage studies and societal development in Africa.

What is it to see things from a mwariological point of view?

Mwariology is not a study of Mwari (God) as *Theology* implies in European concept. It is a study of Mwari's people from their own selves; their formations and self-understandings. Ethnic African religiosity is characteristic in its reservation to make and teach any dogmatic statements about unknowables. Seeing things from a Mwariological point of view therefore means doing one's best starting from the ethnic Zimbabwean/African roots besides the past

228

127 years – counting from Cecil John Rhodes' takeover of Zimbabwe –of being patterned to do otherwise. This calls for a starting from the African language/expression as the already given translations are from Eurocentric agenda. That is to say, the way indigenous Zimbabweans now understand themselves and their heritage is in part and sometimes in whole, what they have been led to believe about themselves and their heritage by the British. This is because since the advent of colonialism, many African indigenous groups were acculturated and sometimes made to believe to be what they are not (Mawere 2014b; Mawere 2016b). Yet, regardless of the acculturation that has taken place (and continue to do so), the indigenous Zimbabweans continue attached to their heritage in many ways. This is shouting in the area of their relationship to *Mwari* – The Ultimate and *vadzimu* the intermediaries. The following examples drawn from Shona ethnic group of Zimbabwe illustrate the point we are making here.

Example 1: *Mwari ndowemunhu wose* (The Ultimate is for all)

Zimbabwean heritage or *pasichigare* had it that The Ultimate is for everyone. No one can exclusively claim ownership or special relationship to God. This was contrary to the teachings of the early missionaries. The earlier missionaries stressed on the language play that the ethnic group had to become sons and daughters of God – a special relationship with God that would yield only benefits – by conversion to Christianity. In a similar tone, the American post-Second World War Religious Right Fundamentalism encouraged all who could to be popes of their own to the degree no Vatican has ever had in all the history of the Roman Catholic Church. The prophets, apostles or pastor popes of their own churches or ministries call themselves as "*munhu waMwari*" (person of God). In the 19th and 20th centuries or at least up to Ian Douglas Smith's Settler Regime, 1965-1980, ethnic Zimbabweans would question and dismiss forthwith this claim for the major reason that they understood God as for all and not as for specific individuals. Mwari is for all! How is the priest, pastor, preacher or self-acclaimed prophet "person of Mwari" as if s/he is the only one closer to the Ultimate? Are others therefore Satan's people? How come the 21st century

Zimbabweans have come to see the New Testament *Parousia* hope in the preacher who claims to be a person of God among them remains an enigma yet to be unveiled. We reason that this could possibly because the ethnic Zimbabweans have forgotten much about their heritage, their roots where no one – small or big, young or adult, man or woman – can claim such monopoly of Mwari.

Missionary religions, with their pride of being light to others and vain/false superiority over others, cannot swallow this basic Zimbabwean heritage, *pasichigare,* statement about universality of Mwari. But that is the fact of Mwariological perspective or concept of the Supreme Being/the Ultimate at least from an African point of view. The Ultimate has a great impact of respect in the lateral relationship of people living together. One finds the concept in the Judaeo-Christian scriptures in few texts like the canon-defining prophets such as *Amos, Hosea, Micah, Isaiah* and *Jeremiah*. The concept is also found in other literary constructs like *Jonah and individuals like in Jesus and Paul*. For example, whereas the Israelites thought of themselves as their Yaweh's elect and other nations their boot, Amos surprised them when he said to them:

> Yaweh was concerned about every nation around Israel, each in its own right without reference to Israel and to Israel also in particular in its own right. The book opens with proclamations of judgments on nations around Israel leading to the hearer herself. Judgment is proclaimed on the Israel's neighbours before Israel (Amos 1: 3-2: 5).

In *Amos* 9: 7, the text declares the clearest monotheism ever noting that Yaweh is God of all other nations in their migrations as Israel in her migrations. The story of Jonah (Jonah 1: 6-14) depicts gentiles very respectful of other human beings' perspectives and readiness to hear criticism from others. It further depicts that gentiles evoke; something exactly as *Chivanhu* or Zimbabwean *pasichigare*. Everyone is encouraged to do all they can calling to their God in case they have the solution: *chin'anga chinyepi chiedziwa* (proverbial Shona saying: prove a false diviner by trying him/her out first). Yaweh is for all (cf. Jonah 4: 11). This is further depicted in Jesus' ethic that centres around neighbourliness as sublime worship of Yaweh (Mat 7: 12),

230

and elevating the love command to equating it to the greatest Israelite law. The same applies to the enigmatic statement like the Pauline one to the Galatians that in The Redeemer Saviour Yaweh's Christ there is neither Jew nor Gentile, neither free nor slave, neither male nor female (*Galatians* 3: 28). These texts sound ethnic Zimbabwean Mwari as depicted in the expression '*Mwari ndowemunhu wose*' (universality of Yaweh), which in fact informs our theory of Mwariology and central to this chapter.

Example 2: *Tinopira kunaMwari nekuvadzimu* (We report to The Ultimate and or via the ancestors (and via our living elders)

The European Christian concept of a God to be *believed in or worshipped* is meaningless from a Mwariological point of view. There is no logic for anyone to preach to another to believe claims made about Mwari. One could say [indigenous] Zimbabweans revere or even fear The Ultimate in their lateral relations. But believing or not believing The Ultimate or ancestors is redundant from *pasichigare's* understanding of Mwari. It has no meaning at all. How does it come about to believe or not believe Mwari who is never elaborately described for Mwari is for all people whatever and whichever way? Trying a *chin'anga chinyepi* (Shona: "false diviner") saying underlined above, it is honestly or reluctantly the same as: one is trying it as the doctor's prescription, whose philosophy is based on a trial and error *modus operandi*. Ethnic Zimbabweans consult as many spiritual advisers as they can before they may settle for any suggestion or explanation to their own problems (or that of their relatives), which actually is informed and formulated by themselves basing on the many consultations made. Trying foreign providers of service or deliverance is typically ethnic Zimbabwean just as trying Catholicism, any other Christian prophet, an African traditional healer, an Islamic *imum* or any other religion's practitioner. One is still within the *pasichigare* Zimbabwean tradition when sojourning via any other route. One tries according to one's own assessment or as a small concerned group, that it might serve a specific purpose one understands.

The Christian gospel's hypothesis of *nyikadzimu* as heaven and hell is foreign to the *pasichigare* Zimbabwean tradition. Resurrection narratives are in ethnic Zimbabwean depicted as actually ghostly appearances needing some ritual to request the deceased to "rest" as others died before them. Their resurrection, according to Christian ethos, do not qualify as and can never be equated to the Biblical resurrection narratives. We find this very problematic as resurrection should be understood as resurrection whether it occurs in this or that context. If the deceased needed to come back to the living of his own people as others say in Christianity do through incarnating into one of the living to make them a *svikiro*, an ethnic Zimbabwe who seriously believes the basic Christian gospel will have to be in another world altogether. In fact, one just have to choose either to become a 'full' Christian and give up all his/her traditional beliefs or remain a staunch African traditional religionist who do not dine with Christians. There is no room for both for one and the same person. For the former, the ethnic logic has to be totally given up. A decision has to be made. No wonder Zimbabweans would not become Christians except after being disempowered, disposed and made destitute after Robert Moffat joined Cecil John Rhodes in the fall of the 19th century.

We should mention here that well before Robert Moffat converted indigenous Zimbabweans, the vocabulary *kunamata* was never used in respect to *vadzimu* or *Mwari*. *Kunamata* is total obedience: clink to something, as to one's saving thing like a *teve*, *zango*, *dumwa*, gona, *shavi*. This list is of various fetishes meant for protective powers supposed of medicine. All have an essence of power in them. *Dumwa* is from the verb "send" (*kutumwa*) in the passive. It is a thing send to protect or do something to someone about something. *Gona* describes the same *teve/zango* but has a meaning from the verb *kugona* (to be able). It enables the person to do something beyond their normal abilities. This is closer to *shavi* which refers to excellence in a skill, with or without any phenomena of the numinous (see also, Shoko 2016). It can be negative or positive depending on the consequences obtained on the victim and his/her relatives. *Wagutsa shavi rangu* (You have satisfied my craving desire) refers to a deep seated desire or craving which is not stigma at all. Zimbabweans who are reluctant to express this in its rightful context have been 'darkened' by the British stigmatisation. Artwell

Nhemachena (2014), among others, has discussed these survival strategies in ethnic Zimbabwe which have their springboard in Zimbabwean Heritage, *pasichigare*. Hence *shavi* is morally neutral; either of something bad as murdering others a *muroyi* (witch/wizard) is, or excellent artist/skilled as a hunter, singer or dancer. A person could say; *Unoda kuti ndikunamate here kuti undiitire chakuti?* (How do you want me to submit myself to you for you to do a favour to me?) Thus a person *anonamatwa* (is worshipped) and not God if we are to be analytic of the term *'kunamata'*, especially as viewed epistemologically and metaphysically.

Thus, *kunamata vadzimu* or *Mwari* is not an ethnic expression at least from an epistemological and metaphysical point of view. Basing on this understanding, one realises that Christians are very wrong when they allege that *VaZimbabwe vanonamata midzimu/Mwari* (Zimbabweans worship ancestors/God). The recycling of a misinterpreted term 'kunamata' have made many indigenous Zimbabweans to believe that Mwari is worshipped. Yet, the Shona vocabulary is very clear about it. The verbs used are different. Traditionally, *vainopira* (they reported) to the family eldest, *anova iye mubati wendiro, opiravo kuna* Mwari starting from the closest known to him who is late(The family eldest is the family priest to report to as the rest clap hands with boxed hands). Thus, Christianity would rather coin *kubhilivha nekuwoshipa* Mwari for "believing God and worshiping God" respectively because the use of the verb 'kunamata', was never used for Mwari. Used as such brings in a serious confusion in perspectives. Mwari never needed being believed in nor worshipped. Or else the word *Mwari* itself had to be avoided as the Roman Catholic Church tried to avoid it for *Yave* from the German pronunciation of *Yaweh*. European Christian concept of *God* can never translate to *Mwari*. The Zimbabwean concept of Mwari never supports/sanctions evil, racism, genocide, oppression of others or the defeated. The Judaeo-Christian Canaanite concepts of the Ultimate especially as *El/Elohim* supports such evils.

Example 3: *Mweya* (Spirit)

Mweya is consistently negative in ethnic Zimbabwean languages or dialects. *Une mweya* (You have a spirit) is never a positive remark

233

but something evil/bad. *Wabudisa mweya* (You have puffed), is likewise associated with negativity. So is *paita mweya* which the presence of evil spirit which may possess an individual. This traditional understanding of the word mweya makes us wonder when Christianity talks of *mweya mustvene* (holy spirit), which in fact, would not be quite appropriate translations for whatever the European Christians want to mean or express within ethnic Zimbabwe Mwariology. How come they take a consistently negative word to create need for qualification whenever used? That art of translation is unfortunate because it causes serious confusion as it always needs qualification. Whoever uses *mweya mustvene* or *mweya wesvina*, then, is speaking European culture and not African/Zimbabwean. *Mweya* and *mhepo* are ethnically the same and identical without qualification as *evil spirit* in English. "*Mweya uri pamusoro pangu*" (The spirit is upon me) would be negative, at least from a Shona point of view, as spirit is bad/evil.

Example 4: *Mudzimu* (Ancestor)

Mudzimu (Ancestor) is consistently virtuous, praiseworthy, positive and constructive (see for example the following, Gelfand 1977; Bosman 2010); Muzorewa 2014). *Kugadzira mudzimu kugara dare revapenyu votaurirana kugadzira mashoko pamusoro pemufi kuti veukama vake vapenyu vagare zvakanaka* (To make right/create an ancestor, is to have a council or seating or deliberation about the deceased settled so that the remaining relatives may live well in respect to the deceased). Critically said, the ancestor is created (*anogadzirwa*). There is absolutely nothing ever wrong with that deliberate action of verbal creation of something positive consistently, ritualised or not! The word for the ancestor is in some dialects or languages in Zimbabwe also the same for the Ultimate. In Venda, for example, *Mudzimu* is Mwari, God the Ultimate as ancestor is also *mudzimu*. So is *Modhimo* in Ndebele and *Xikwembu* in Tsonga. The context decides what one is talking about. Once in plural the names refer to ancestors but when singular they may be meaning God/Mwari. To associate *mudzimu*, whether as the Ultimate Ancestor, the supposed Universe/Human Creator Voice-Ultimate or the positive family multiple *vadzimu*/*midzimu* with something evil is unfortunate. It is generally

234

unAfrican and in particular unZimbabwean. When can a council be evil? *Musha matare* (Home/Village is made up of councils/meetings). *Mhosva dzinogurwa pamatare* (Crimes are settled at courts). *Mashoko anonyonganisa anogadziriswa pamatare* (Contentions are resolved at councils/meetings). Whoever and however one speaks of *mudzimu* as evil is therefore European stigmatisation of African culture and not African or Zimbabwean ethnic open mindedness to learning and new insights. Zimbabweans should therefore learn to reject the misinterpretations they have been used to for their springboard to self-realisation through rediscovering their heritage. Many of these usages and terminologies were deliberately intended to confuse them forever especially by missionaries!

Discussions on the intricate delicacy in stigmatisation of ethnic Zimbabwean *pasichigare* and the tragedy in borrowed mindsets are radio programmes such as *ChiKristu neTsika* (Christianity and Ethnic Traditions) and such newspapers as the weekly *The Patriot* which has its motto as "Celebrating Being Zimbabwean". These bring to the public masses of discussions in libraries and archives of scholarship from linguists, socio-anthropologists, historians and religionists.

Example 5: Racial stigmatisation and mystification

The British colonial agenda for Zimbabwe was frivolous and with far-reaching consequences. It involved the caricaturing and stigmatisation of ethnic culture as sin and European or particularly British deified as divine. European Christian missionaries have translated *sin* in the Jewish writings, the bible, as *chitema* for ethnic Shona Zimbabweans. The word *chitema* would 'strategically' but perniciously refer to the ways, cultures, traditions of the ethnic Africans as *vanhu vatema,* Black People. That word maliciously suggests that the Jewish writings were abrogative and indeed combating ethnic Zimbabwean culture at all costs. It suggests that the ethnic culture of the Zimbabwean people is *de facto* immoral (or what they call pagan) as was the European culture as seen by the Jews who compiled the bible. Yet it is the British saying this or who have this agenda to make the bible as fighting Africanness. Other words for wrongs done in Karanga are there like *chivi* (something evil/bad) or *chitadzo* (something done wrongly/mistakenly). The coining of a

235

new word for wrong done as *chitema* to mean "sin" is therefore inappropriate and unfortunate for Zimbabweans to continue using in their perpetual search for dignity and heritage as a springboard for their self-actualisation.

The word *muchena* referring to a human being, "white person" means a poor person of any race as in the saying; *chiri pamuchena chiri pamutsvedu,* a Shona Proverb meaning something possessed by a poor person gets quickly used up. In short, *muchena* is a poor fellow human being in ethnic Zimbabwe. This meaning is found also in some Christian hymns freely but wrongly translated forgetting that the British chose for the Shona the English "White" and not a "European". No European is "white" at all! As is the fact in the eyes of all. Munyaradzi Mawere (2013, 2016), among other critical scholars, have criticised the continued usage of the term "white" for Europeans audaciously and convincingly. They are not white as they want the world falsely believe. But they call themselves *Whites* not because they are colour blind but deliberately to figuratively mean an image of purity set against other complexions like dark, shades of brown or "red" and "yellow" as Europeans consider others even referring to those Africans whom Mawere call "Chocolate" skinned people. For the Europeans, this was meant to culturally stigmatise the rest other races setting themselves as The Ultimate's Chosen Race as Israelites once thought and claimed about themselves. Thus, it is figurative and in fact wrong for Europeans to call themselves "Whites" when in fact most of them are red and pink. It is not descriptive. Figurative language should never be translated verbatim into another language as it totally misses the original equivalent. Worse to take an already coined word for something and impose it to mean dual things in the new language! Something else should be said. The Shona never recognised ethnic European complexion as *vachena* but *vatsvuku,* "pink".

Most intriguing is the British taking for themselves the Karanga word for divine, *varungu/chirungu; zvenyikadzimu (of/from the ancestral realm).* The Europeans and the British in particular, thus, consider themselves *divine* and all theirs as *divine* to Zimbabweans in local language; *varungu/chirungu.* For us, that claim of the British sounds more blasphemous than saying Germans consider themselves a supper race as taught in history books to stigmatise the Germans, Britain's long-time enemies. Germans' self-esteem is something more or less common to any ethnic group on its own for its own and by its own. *Svikiro* Mukanga of Mabika Chiefdom in Bikita District of Zimbabwe, considered the British and/or Europeans in general as *zvitekedzi* (enemies, destroyers) just because the British themselves behaved immorally and destructively to the *vatangikugara* (the earlier inhabitants) of Zimbabwe. Svikiro Mukanga was said to be incarnated by the territorial Spirit called *Hanjikai:* a word exhorting people rather to revolt than accepting being ruled by foreigners. Mind boggling is that the Shona Language Committee to this day regard it as fact that *murungu* is a British, and divine culture/language is English when in fact the word refers to character as also the Tsonga have a proverbial statement that they are *varungu* for their ethnic self-esteem where the word is an adjective and anyone else may also use for themselves. But coining the word *murungu* to exclusively use it for the British is spurious and in fact a misnomer; and continuing to so use it as the Shona Language Committee still cherishes it in education and the public fora on the other side hoping to regain Zimbabwean dignity through Heritage Studies.

Example 6: Translating *vakuru vakati...*

Vakuru vakati ... is literally, "Elders have said ...," yet all elders also refer to the texts from experience and no one living elder is that elder referred to. Thus, proper translation to the growing open-ended body of authoritative texts gathered through experience should rather be translated as "Experience has taught that ..." no elderly Zimbabwean ever like to be addressed as *Vakuru* in ethnic Zimbabwean dialects referred to as Shona. They will say, *"Hakuna akakurira nzira kureba"* (No one is longer than the way of experience and exposure). It reinforces another proverbial saying; *"kudzidza hakuperi"* (learning does not end). They say this to deny the reference as to them but something more than them. One is addressed as either *Baba/Amai/Mai* (Father/Mother) when like one's parents; or *Sekuru/Mbuya* (Grandfather/mother) when like one's grandparents; or *Mukoma/Vakoma* (Senior Brother/Sister) when like one's senior siblings; or *Ba'mnini/Mainini* (Junior father/ brother/mother/sister)

237

when like one's younger siblings: or else the conglomeration of one's ancestry in the praise poems *Mutupo/Chidao* (Totem/Eulogy).

But currently, many people in the younger generations no longer know that *Vakuru*, is no welcome reference or address to the aged. There is a Europeanisation of the word in current usage, which in fact should be denounced and dropped off. Going back to the original will spur interest in readiness to learn more and be open for change. The arrogance of ignorance and holier-than-thou attitude taken from European Christianity will be reduced by attention to Zimbabwean *pasichigare* or Heritage.

In continual search for knowledge, ethnic Zimbabweans therefore never claimed absolute knowledge about unknowables, as said about *Mwari, vadzimu* and *Nyikadzimu* they did not. Nor did they use stories to make their postulations, if ever any, appear true to adults who must assess the situation they are always in. Inkosi Lobengula told Robert Moffatt that the good in his Catholicism/Christianity is all in the *Mwari* regarded here in Zimbabwe as "the Ultimate". Curious in Catholicism/Christianity is that stories are used to adults as if they were infants to make them accept as true claims about unknowables clear postulations of the clergy! Lobengula was using the ethnic posture that ethnic Zimbabweans are not mind-closed as European education closes them up within a box they must not freely move out. The said *Kura uone* in Shona is also in Ndebele as *Khula uzibonele*. Lobengula banned Moffatt from making his adult people like infants stressing that Moffatt should teach for which his Father Mzilikazi invited Moffatt from Nkulumane, Botswana (Bhebhe, 1979).

Robert Moffatt (1795-1883) recalled the ancient Zimbabwean resolute assessment of Christianity at the fruitlessness of Gonzalo da Silveira's (1526-1561) mission earlier than him. Hence, Moffatt resolved that unless these ethnic people in Zimbabwe be uprooted, disempowered, dispossessed and made destitute can they ever be converts to their "religion". When Europeans said, as in Karl Max, "religion is the opium of the people", they mean particularly their Christianity as they considered Africans not to be having any religion. So, Robert Moffatt joined Cecil John Rhodes to make *vatangigura* objects to be made destitute. Disempowerment, dispossession and subjection to destitution was a process along the colonial history of Zimbabwe from the company rule through the imperial rule and settler rule. In Zimbabwe as elsewhere in Africa, various acts were instituted to advance this agenda as the Native Land Apportionment Act of 1930, The Native Land Husbandry Act of 1951, and the Native Land Tenure Act of 1969 within the Chimurenga II phase. Progressively, ethnic Zimbabweans were impoverished to the extent that they saw the need to subject themselves willingly to both the colonial masters and their missionaries as Christians.

The interface of heritage with missionary religions

Words already coined in one culture and mean something definite within the cultural setting should be cautiously taken into another if not avoidable to reduce confusion. As one reads the tripartite missionary religions; Judaism, Christianity and Islam, one feels some sort of mafias or deliberate criminal sects to exploit others even the most current liberal 100% Papacy in Religious Right Personal Mysticism self-acclaimed prophets in Zimbabwe and Africa as a whole. Such would be rightly referred to as *mashavi* in Zimbabwean *pasichigare*. *Mashavi* can/may differ and compete among themselves. They are personal and selective. They can cooperate or fight each other just as Christian sects do on the basis of differences in doctrines. They can be benevolent or malicious. Hence, Judaeo-Christian and Islamic concepts of "the Ultimate" are in fact *mashavi* in Zimbabwean language or understanding or perspective. So, they fight among themselves although based on supposed one tradition; supposed one God; supposed one Saviour Christ; supposed one ancestor, Abraham; or supposed Holy Writ, the Bible. European Good Samaritanism/Human Rights Concern are skilful arts oft more of deceitful skills to exploit others. In fact, a Zimbabwean with the right Zimbabwean sense and sound heritage knowledge must self necessarily be cautious about them when s/he thinks autonomously. Zimbabweans *pasichigare* never depended on one spiritual advisor. They would inquire from five or more far apart until they are tired and they draw their conclusion from the findings and come up with their own intellectually resolved "voice of the spiritual world" in the matter they were seeking to resolve. No wonder widows were often taken as scapegoats as they would have no male resolute defenders to refuse to agree as the scapegoat. A married lady was advised to go to courts and consultations with her representative father. Still, the missionary religions are worse off than *mashavi* as each closes its adherents to itself. Zimbabwean mediums never closed their followers or family members to themselves exclusively as if they owned them. In fact the family having the *bira* invited as many spirit mediums as they could to their *bira* (consultation party). But the foreign contemporary missionary religious sects keep to their own preachers or clergy.

Mwariology and development

Mwariology, as understood in Shona metaphysics and epistemology, is not only linked to heritage as has already been demonstrated. It in fact informs development in its holistic terms, be it social, economic, political, moral, intellectual and cultural.

Development, just like its dialectical opposite poverty, is multi-dimensional (Sen 1999; Mawere 2017). It entails many things, though generally speaking, development involves a positive change where basic necessities are made available to the people. These normally include three core values: the satisfaction of basic physiological needs, self-esteem, and freedom from man's servitude to nature, ignorance, other men, misery, institutions, and dogmatic beliefs (Todaro 1992; Mawere 2017).

Now, it is worth noting that the concept of 'Mwariology' in Shona cosmology and epistemology has not only been used to designate the 'The-Human-Being-Who-Is' or 'Voice-Ultimate-Concept' – the one who should protect humanity and the earth in general. Mwariology can also be viewed as the springboard and in fact birth bed of African development. When the ethnic Zimbabweans talk of the Voice-Ultimate-Concept, they do not only seek protection from the evil – natural and moral. They also seek guidance on how they can navigate tumultuous situations of poverty and other related predicaments. This evocation is premised on the ethnic Zimbabweans' understanding of Mwari as the 'All Powerful' and the 'Ultimate Provider'. As a provider, Mwari is understood to have the powers to replace curse with blessings and misfortunes with fortunes. Where people believe that some malicious spirit is haunting their lives, wreaking havoc and causing a series of misfortunes and problems, the victims normally sought the assistance of diviners or traditional healer to exorcise the spirit haunting them. This is cleansing. Once cleansing is done, the curse is substituted by blessings in a manner that resembles renewal and invigoration of life. By virtue of having such powers to change [cursed] lives for the better, Mwari (and therefore Mwariology) is understood as the springboard of human development, without which development is impossible.

Conclusion

This chapter has argued that the current indigenous Zimbabweans are founded on a deep layer of sand (or false claims) created in the colonial, settler and postcolonial eras such that even they be speaking their own languages or foreign languages, they are trapped in a Bermuda mist they should operate out of. The language or terms, be they English or ethnic Zimbabwean, have to be reviewed first before any meaningful discussion. As such, heritage teachers of the nation of Zimbabwe are called upon to think twice as they teach the subject to build the nation of Zimbabwe on a solid foundation through citizens that know what it means to be a citizen: the lowest rank of the security system of a nation proud to be itself among others in the global village; who know they do not insubordinate their superiors but have the responsibility to challenge them as the sacredness of the offices they hold to the people, is in the officers embodying the citizens, each individually and all together; who do not insubordinate their fellow equals or juniors; but have the responsibility to express their opinion to them with honour and respect. The Heritage, *sui generis*, was very ideal for modern religious pluralism to make Zimbabweans work together be they Catholics, Protestants, Pentecostal Spiritual Fundamentalists, Zionists/Apostles, Moslems or ethnic Mwariists: *Mwari ndewemunhu wose: ari muna vose; anoshanda mune zvose uye vose* (God is for all, in all, through all). The basic sources of Mwariology, which is also Heritages Studies would liberate Zimbabweans from laming Christian doctrinal sectarianism for its inclusiveness and accommodativeness. It would also provide unfledging hope for the vulnerable and impoverished of the earth as keep their heads high looking forward for opportunities that one day Mwari would create for them. The open-endedness and absence of monopolising of the world of knowledge and unknowable is the basis for nation building. *Pasichigare* recognises initiative and greatness even in youths and novices *say as masvikiro* and various skills named *mashavi*. Thinking African would take serious from where we are back and forth to rebuild the past as a springboard for the future without any bitterness or revolt.

References

Bhebhe, N. (1979). *Christianity and Traditional Religion in Western Zimbabwe: 1859-1923,* Longman: London.

Bosman, M. (2010). 'Shona traditional religion,' Philadelphia Project, South Africa. Available at: www.philadephiaproject.co.za/

Fisher, J. L. (2010). *Pioneers, settlers, and aliens, exiles: The decolonisation of white identity in Zimbabwe,* Australian National University Press: Canberra.

Gadamer, H. G. (1987). The problem of historical consciousness, in: P. Rabinow and W. M. Sullivan, eds. *Interpretive social science: A second look,* Berkeley: University of California Press.

Gelfand, M. (1977). *The spiritual belief of the Shona: A study based on fieldwork among the east-central Shona,* Mambo Press, Gweru.

Grever, M. De Bruijn, P. and Van Boxtel, C. (2012). Negotiating historical distance: Or how to deal with the past as a foreign country in heritage education, in: *Paedagogica Historica,* Volume 46, Number 6, pp. 878.

Lowenthal, D. (1998). *The heritage crusade and the spoils of history,* Cambridge: Cambridge University Press.

Mawere, M. (2013). *Lyrics of Reason and Experience,* Langaa RPCIG: Mankon.

Mawere, M. (2014a). *Divining the Future of Africa: Healing the Wounds, Restoring Dignity and Fostering Development*, Langaa RPCIG Publishers: Cameroon.

Mawere, M. (2014b). *Culture, indigenous knowledge and development in Africa: Reviving interconnections for sustainable development*, Langaa Publishers: Bamenda.

Mawere, M. (2016b). 'Colonial heritage, memory, and sustainability in dialogue: An introduction,' In: Mawere, M. & Mubaya, R. T. (Eds). *Colonial heritage, memory and sustainability in Africa: Challenges, opportunities and prospect*, Langaa RPCIG Publishers: Bamenda.

Mawere, M. (2015). *Humans, other beings and the environment: Harurwa (edible stinkbugs) and environmental conservation in south-eastern Zimbabwe*, Cambridge Scholars Press: Cambridge.

Mawere, M. (2016c). *Heritage Practices for Sustainability: Ethnographic Insights from the BaTonga Community Museum in Zimbabwe*, Langaa Publishers: Bamenda.

Mawere, M. (2017). *Theorising Development in Africa: Towards Building an African Framework of Development*, Langaa Publishers: Bamenda.

Mawere, M. & Mubaya, R. T. (2016). *African philosophy and Thought Systems: A Search for a Culture and Philosophy of Belonging*, Langaa Publishers: Bamenda.

Mazambara, P. (1999). *The Self-understanding of African Instituted Churches: a study based on the Church of Apostles founded by John of Marange in Zimbabwe*, Verlag an der Lottbek: Aachen.

Muzorewa, G. H. (2014). *The African origins of monotheism: Challenging the Eurocentric interpretation of God concepts on the continent and in diaspora*, Thrift Books

Nhemachena, A. (2014). Knowledge, *Chivanhu and struggles for survival in conflict torn Manicaland*, PhD Thesis, University of Cape Town: South Africa.

Seixas, P. F. (2014). History and heritage: What is the difference? In: *Canadian Issues*, pp.12-17.

Sen, A. (1999). *Development as Freedom*, Oxford University Press: New York.

Shoko, T. (2007). *Karanga indigenous religion: Health and well-being*, Routledge.

Todaro, M. P. (1992). *Economics for a developing world: An introduction to principles, problems and policies for development*, 3rd Ed, Longman: New York.

Chapter 10

Disempowerment and Impoverishment of African Communities: Re-visiting the Effects of Land Grabbing by Foreigners in Africa

Tasara Muguti & Angeline Sithole

Introduction

This chapter seeks to interrogate land grabbing by wealth nations and multinational institutions in sub-Saharan Africa during the new millennium. Though land grabs have become a global phenomenon affecting Southeast Asia and Latin America, the Global South is the worst affected with 70% of the land grabs taking place in sub-Saharan Africa (Farmlandgrab.org). One of the key drivers for Africa's attractiveness to land grabbing by foreigners is the perception that Africa has an abundance of idle land. On this note, the present chapter examines the extent to which grabbing of African lands by these foreigners and at times in conjunction with the ruling African elites, has resulted in diminished agricultural sovereignty and exacerbated landlessness among rural communities.

The demonstrates how the land grabbing deals in Africa have negatively impacted on rural communities' access to land and water and how this has resulted in widespread poverty levels among the rural communities in the continent. Special emphasis is given on the impact of land grabbing on land held under customary tenure across Africa. The chapter further addresses how the contemporary land grabbing in Africa has a bearing on the productive sectors, employment opportunities of the indigenous people, natural resource use, compensation, investment partnerships and repatriation of profits, among others.

More importantly, the chapter unfolds by examining the experiences by the different selected African countries where land grabs have been witnessed on an unprecedented scale. It is mainly based on a review of related literature around issues of land grabbing in Africa and beyond.

The colonial experience

Land grabbing, which denotes the purchasing or leasing of vast tracts of land for various purposes from poor developing nations by more affluent but food insecure nations and private investors is as old as colonialism itself in Africa. The contemporary land grabs are a sad reminder of the unpleasant history of land seizures by Western imperial nations in colonial Africa. In essence, the scrambling and arbitrary partitioning of Africa by imperial nations such as Britain, Germany, Italy, Belgium, Portugal and France towards the last quarter of the 19th century heralded and accentuated the land grabs in Africa. This indeed remained the major distinctive feature of colonialism in Africa then. In colonial Africa, the European settlers appropriated and expropriated immeasurable quantities of land from the indigenous African people across the continent. At that time, the European colonialists did not pay anything for the dispossessed land from the indigenes since the colonies in Africa were their colonial prize and as such were under their direct control.

Land was acquired for settlement, infrastructural development, mining and farming purposes. It was also obtained in order to deny the indigenous people access to their traditional means of production and force them into wage employment. Large plantations were established in colonial Africa for the production of food and non-food crops largely for the export market. Furthermore, vast pieces of land were expropriated from the African people and turned into national parks/game reserves and tourist attractions. European missionaries also attained vast tracts of land which they turned into farms and mission schools. In most cases, the land acquisition throughout sub-Saharan Africa was achieved through legislative measures. For instance, after the colonisation of Zimbabwe in 1890, various pieces of legislation such as The Native Reserves Order in Council (1896), The Land Apportionment Act (1930), The Native Land Husbandry Act and The Tribal Trust Lands ACT (1965) were enacted and these resulted in the demarcation of land between the

European settlers and indigenous African people (http://www.gta/Land%20Issues/factsheet.htm). The racial division of land resulted in marked inequalities between 'commercial farmers' and an increasingly marginalised African peasantry. The various pieces of colonial land legislations alienated and segregated indigenous Africans and denied them ownership of land as they were pushed to unproductive, inaccessible and overcrowded areas such as Gwaai and Shangaan. In colonial Zimbabwe, for instance, the final demarcation of land between the races was achieved through the Land Apportionment Act of 1930 which formalised the separation of land between the indigenous African people and Europeans by law (Hallett, 1974, Moyana, 1984, Chinamasa, 2001). In South Africa, the legislatives included the Native Reserves Location Act of 1902, Crown Land Disposal Ordinance of 1903, Land Settlement Act of 1912, Native Land Act of 1913 and Native (Urban Areas) Consolidation Act 1945, among others (Lemon, 1991). The Natives Land Act of 1913 was very critical in that it severely limited the Africans' access to land by making it illegal for them to purchase land outside areas designated as reserves (Hallett, 1974). In the opinion of Hallett (1974: 640), "hundreds of black South Africans were uprooted from white-owned farms, forced to sell their stock and to seek a new livelihood either in the towns or the reserves or as full-time labourers". In the same vein, Plaatje (cited in Hallett,1974: 640) further observes that: "The next three decades were to see the almost total elimination of that class of rural African described by one contemporary observer as being 'fairly comfortable' and living in many instances like Dutchman". Thus, the Land Act limited the indigenous South Africans' options thereby forcing them into wage employment, which if anything led to their impoverishment.

In Nigeria there was the Native Lands Acquisition Ordinance of 1908 which sought to regulate the acquisition of land by 'Natives' (Ogiek, 2004). In 1901, the East African Lands Ordinance-in-council was enacted conferring on the Commissioner of the protectorate power to dispose of all public lands on such terms and conditions as he might think fit (Ibid). The Crown Land Ordinance of 1902 followed suit and empowered the commissioner to sell free holds in crown land up to 1000 acres to any person or grant leases of 99 years.

The Kenya Land Commission of 1932 and the Swynnerton Plan of 1954 are some of the Commissions that were set up to look into land cases in colonial Kenya. These Acts were intentionally designed to dispossess Africans of their land and force them into wage labour (Kimaiyo, 2002). In Mozambique, the situation was pretty much the same as the Portuguese settlers took over and occupied vast tracts of the country's fertile and arable lands (Isaacman, 1976).

In all the above scenarios, the indigenous African people were forcibly relocated to remote areas which were inaccessible, uninhabitable, and unproductive and above all, where they were overcrowded. This has persuaded Fay Chung (2006: 358) to postulate that in colonial Zimbabwe, the African people were relocated into reserves "where rocks grew more than crops". The land dispossessions resulted in the disempowerment and the impoverishment of the African people which eventually forced the able-bodied to leave the traditional peasant economies to go and seek wage employment in European farms, towns and mining settlements in order to sustain their families and also to meet their tax obligations. It is worth mentioning that land grabbing in Africa did not end with the demise of colonialism, but continued in post-colonial independent Africa.

Land grabs in New Millennia Africa

In post-colonial Africa, the former colonial powers have designed a new form of imperialism. Through the use of multinational companies and international financiers such as the World Bank and International Monetary Fund, they are continuing to siphon natural resources in the form of mineral and agricultural resources from countries such as Angola, Kenya, Ethiopia, Mozambique, Sudan, the Democratic Republic of Congo, Mozambique, Zambia and Zimbabwe (Graham, *et al*, 2011). The financial and energy crisis of 2007 and 2008, followed by the food price hike in 2008 paved the way for large scale land acquisitions and agricultural investment of farmland in different parts of the world in general and in sub-Saharan Africa in particular (Cotula, *et al.*, 2009). In reality, these large companies are making a significant contribution to contemporary land grabbing in Africa. Oxfam (2012) estimates that land acquisitions in sub-Saharan Africa between 2000 and 2010 had the potential to feed a billion people, "equivalent to the number of people who currently go to bed hungry each night".

The African continent is increasingly seen as a source of agricultural land and natural resources for the rest of the world. Leary (2009, cited in Mutodi, *et al*, 2011: 2) opines that "rich countries are buying poor countries' soil fertility, water and sun to ship food and fuel back home, in a kind of neo-colonial dynamic". Land grabbing in sub-Saharan Africa is now a fundamental feature of the rise of commercialisation within the content of globalisation. National governments and private companies are obtaining access to land across the continent to grow food and non-food crops and acquire bio fuels to meet the growing demand from mainly overseas countries that include Britain, China, German, France, Netherlands, Norway and Belgium. Some African countries such as Ethiopia, Madagascar, Mozambique, Sudan, and Tanzania believe that such endeavours will help increase foreign investment and decrease the unemployment rates (Murphy, 2008, Cotula, *et al*, 2009; Graham, *et al*, 2011).

These countries are of the conviction that, the African agricultural sector cannot develop in the long term without a transfer of foreign technology, experience and knowhow and the takeover of land for such developments. It is generally believed that foreign ownership of farms will enable local farmers to absorb innovative skills. However, Andersen (2010) argues that if the risks associated with land acquisitions remain unaddressed these could lead to failure to become development stimulators for host countries. These risks are natural resource degradation, loss of indigenous farming practices and increasing food insecurity and conflict (Andersen, 2010). Certainly, there is little doubt that many indigenous African farmers are being evicted from their ancestral lands which have been the source of their livelihoods from time immemorial. Looming like a malevolent shadow is a spectre of corruption in the whole process of land grabs where the ruling party officials enrich themselves. They clearly know that the transfer of land from poor farmers to the so-called foreign investors, multinationals at the forefront, cannot serve their interests, but rather the elite's and that of those who are in surrounding of the government. The land grabbing by foreigners in Africa involves 'illegal' acquisitions premised on secretive negotiations and hastily concluded binding legal contracts (Mutodi, *et al*, 2011). At times, the land acquisitions are accompanied by the use of force and violence by state agencies against the African peasantry. For example, when the Ethiopian government sold an estimated 42% of land belonging to the Anuak people of the Gambella province without their knowledge and consent to foreign investors in 2010, the Ethiopian soldiers and regional government officials forcibly moved the Anuak people into government sponsored villages (Human Rights Watch, 2012).

In new millennium Africa, land grabs are really spreading like veldfire. Indeed, it would not be an exaggeration to characterise them as a new form of modern imperialism as both former imperial powers and new players such as China and India are scrambling to acquire vast tracts of productive land in Africa. Selected examples from across the continent will suffice to demonstrate this new disquieting and unprecedented phenomenon.

Uganda has been a mark of this trend for land grabbing in Africa, mainly because the Ugandan government, reminiscent of most African postcolonial governments is desperate to attract foreign investment. While land grabbing is widespread in Uganda, it has resulted in catastrophic consequences on local people with customary land rights (Kalangala District Local·Government, 2012). As early as 2001, the Ugandan government leased land to a German coffee investor to establish a plantation under its subsidiary Kaweri Coffee Plantation Limited. The affected families were not adequately consulted when the land was leased. Houses were demolished; property destroyed and staple crops such as cassava and potatoes were confiscated by the army during the evections (Graham, *et al*, 2011). In Uganda, the worst areas affected by the unprecedented land grabbing are the Buliisa oil rich region in western Uganda, the Bukaleba Forest Reserve in eastern Uganda, the Mabira Natural Forest in the central region and the Kalangala Oil Palm Project in Lake Victoria (Mabike, 2011). Uganda has been consistently attracting the highest foreign direct investment in East Africa and the

Red Sea Region by attracting between $250- 300 million dollars in Foreign Direct Investments (FDIs) annually largely due to its stable and consistent macro-economic policies, liberalised business environment, proximity as a logistics hub within the Great Lakes Region and increasing regional trade (Mabike, 2011).

In Uganda, the majority of the community members do not have land titles and/or certificates. In fact, a large number of people owning land under customary tenure system are in rural areas and most do not know how to go about acquiring the certificates. Mailo land was traditionally land which was divided between the King of Buganda (known as Kabaka) and the Protectorate Government, but in 1967 Mailo Tenure was transformed into public land. In 1998, the Ugandan Government launched a Vegetable Oil Development Project (VODP), supported by the United Nations International Fund for Agricultural Development (IFAD) and World Bank, to increase domestic production of vegetable oils in partnership with the private sector (International Fund for Agricultural Republic of Uganda Vegetable Oil Development Project, 2010). This included the introduction of commercial oil palm production, as well as more traditional oil seed developments in eastern and Midwestern districts of Uganda. The Kalangala oil palm project aimed to plant 10,000 hectares of oil palm on Bugala Island in Kalangala district in Lake Victoria (Kalangala District Local Government, 2012). Bugala Island is one of the 84 islands in Lake Victoria which make up Kalangala district. The island has a population of around 20,000 people, who mainly depended on fishing, subsistence farming and tourism before the introduction of oil palm and the island had been taken over by a partnership between the government and a private sector consortium, Oil Palm Uganda Limited (OPUL), formed in 2003 (NAPE, 2006). OPUL brings together foreign investment from the Global palm oil giant, Wilmar International, one of the largest palm oil biodiesel manufacturers in the world. In 2006, the Kalangala Oil Palm Growers Trust (KOPGT), an association of local farmers, was established with support from IFAD, in order to promote local smallholder involvement in the palm oil project, joined the partnership, taking on a 10% holding in 2009 (Ibid). Besides increasing domestic production of vegetable oil, the project was also designed to improve the infrastructure on the island, increase rural incomes and reduce poverty levels, attract private sector investment and to stimulate economic development in the area (International Fund for Agricultural Republic of Uganda Vegetable Oil Development Project, 2010).

Ethiopia has not been spared from land grabs by multinational companies. With an average of 2.8million Ethiopian people needing food aid, the government still offers large hectares of its most fertile land to rich foreign nations and nationals to export food for their own populations (UNDP, 2010). Undeniably, Ethiopia is one of the poorest countries in the world, where about forty percent of its population is living below the poverty datum line of $1.25 a day and 46 % of the population is undernourished (IFAD, 2011). In 2010 the country ranked 157th out of 169 of the world's poorest countries according to the human development index (HDI (UNDP, 2010). Poverty is widespread both in urban and rural areas, but it is mostly prevalent in the rural parts of the country. The land grabs in Ethiopia have been very disastrous as they have increased the dependency of the country on food aid more than ever before. In Ethiopia, land grabbing has been ongoing since 1995 but there was a sharp rise in demand for agricultural land in the country from 2006 (Jaatee, 2016). Over one million hectares of land were transferred to 500 investors between 2003 and 2009 with the Indian Karuturi Enterprise being singled as the largest investor as it received 0.3 million hectares of land in Gambella and 11 000 in Bako district of Oramia. In actual fact, about 7 million hectares of agricultural land was transferred to foreign investor between 1995 and 2016 and this translated to 38% of the total land utilised by smallholder farmers in the country (Jaatee, 2016). Between 2000 and 2008 the European Union (EU) was the second largest investor in Ethiopia with investments in meat, agrofuels production and horticulture. The country also has bilateral investment treaties with countries such as Denmark, Italy and Netherlands (Graham, *et al*, 2011).

Dismissing critics of the government move to grant foreign investors land, then Ethiopian Prime Minister adumbrated that "we want to develop our land to feed ourselves rather than admire the beauty of the fallow fields while we starve". This was supported by

Essayas Kabede, the head of the government agency responsible for land leasing who pointed out that, "Ethiopia benefits in many ways from land deals that we will receive dollars by exporting food; the farms provide jobs; they import know how; they will help us to boost productivity; and therefore, we will improve food security" (Malkamuu Jaatee, Anywaa Survival Organisation, 2016). However, it was soon to be realised that institutionalised corruption by public officials and abusive multinationals corporations were to prevent the distribution of perceived investment benefits to the ordinary people as the country was to lose billions of dollars to illicit financial outflows. Consequently, in 2015 the Ethiopian government was forced to revoke one of its land deals with Karuturi Global limited. The deal had been entered into in 2010 when the company had been awarded a concession of 100 000 hectares of land to be developed for industrial agriculture for export in the Gambella region in southern Ethiopia which was home to the indigenous Mazenger, Nuer, Opo, Anuak and Komo peoples (Cultural Survival, 2016). Many of the land investment deals in the country have not benefited the Ethiopian people as the foreign companies largely produce for export.

For instance, the 10 000 hectare plantation acquired by a Saudi Arabian company in the fertile Gambella Region of South West Ethiopia in 2010 expanded the area under cultivation to 13 00 hectares in 2016 predominantly for export purposes (Cultural Survival, 2016). The rice produced from the region by the Saudi Star Rice company was exported to the Middle East and Saudi Arabia (Sidaway, 2014). The government embarked on a villagisation program in Gambella. According to Kadingo (2012: 9):

> When the investor showed up we were told to pack our things and go to the villages that were allocated for us by the government. If we had decided not to go, they would destroy our crops houses and our belongings. If you complain you were put in prison and they may even kill you. It's not our land anymore, we have been deprived of our rights.

When the Ethiopian government started the land leases, the official and primary assumptions for its policies were that Ethiopian farmers were not inherently entrepreneurial and productive and therefore needed to be taught how to farm by foreigners. However, these stereotypes about peasant entrepreneurship were predominantly unfounded as the Ethiopian peasants were in fact very entrepreneurial and oriented towards promoting innovation, hard work and generating profit (Reuter, 2010). Moreover, the government's perception that the land was idle was intrinsically spurious as it failed to understand the local farming culture and the importance of land as a primary source of sustenance.

In Ghana there are companies from Brazil, Italy, Norway, China, India, Germany, Netherlands and Belgium that are cultivating fields in the Volta, Brong Ahafo Ashanti, and Eastern and Northern regions of the country. The main non-food crop that these companies are planting is jatropha to be processed into biofuels for export. One of the companies, Agroils of Italy is cultivating jatropha on 10 000 hectares of land in Yeji in the Brong Ahafo region of Ghana for biofuels (World Bank, 2010). A Norwegian company, ScanFuel Limited started operations in the Asante Akim North district in Ashante region to produce biofuels. The company used heavy agricultural equipment to clear everything in its way including human settlements, crop farms and trees. According to Robertson *et al* (2015) all the fertile lands of the peoples of Efirise, Dukuse, Bamala and Brentuo have been taken over by ScanFuel and people are left with nothing but fear and uncertainty.

The amount of land in Ghana that is being taken to feed Europe's increasing Aikins Adusei (2010) highlighted shocking truths about land grabs in Africa in Ghana that were threatening food security in Ghana. An area of arable land the size of Denmark, around 5 million hectares, was acquired by foreign companies to produce bio-fuels, mainly for the European market, (Robertson, *et al*, 2015) In Ghana, development agencies reported that the spread of jatropha was pushing small farmers particularly women farmers off their land. Valuable food sources such as shear nut and *dawadawa* trees were cleared to make way for plantations. Between 2007 and 2010, a total of 769,000 hectares of lands were reportedly acquired across the country by foreign companies such as Agroils (Italy), Galten Global Alternative Energy (Israel), Gold Star Farms (Ghana), Jatropha

Africa (UK/Ghana), Biofuel Africa (Norway), ScanFuel (Norway) and Kimminic Corporation (Canada), (Ministry of Food and Agriculture (MoFA).

According to MoFA (2012), over 20 companies from around the world, including companies from Brazil, China, Germany, Italy, Netherlands and Norway acquired large tracts of land in the country to farm jatropha. The MoFA also estimated that just 16 percent of Ghana's total arable land was cultivated, despite agriculture employing 60 percent of the country's workforce. Consequently, there was every reason to believe that these multinationals were attracted to Ghana by the land availability, soil types and a lack of regulation on acquisitions, according to the Food Security Policy Advocacy Network (FoodSPAN), a CSO based in Accra. Media reports and other opinion pieces published between the period 2007 and 2010 suggested that foreign companies controlled 37 percent of Ghana's crop land. The farming of jatropha, an energy plant, by multinationals was said to have triggered land grabbing to the extent that the phenomenon pushed smallholder farmers including women off their land. Bakari Nyari, a rights activist noted that Biofuel Africa (Solar Harvest SA), a Norwegian company, in 2008 allegedly took advantage of Ghana's traditional system of communal land ownership and the climate and economic hardship at the time to claim large tracts of land in a village called Kusawgu in the northern region with the intention of creating the largest jatropha plantation in the world (IFAD, 2013). Bakari (2012) commended that by sidestepping local authorities and using methods that date back to the days of colonialism, Biofuel Africa claimed legal ownership of 38,000 hectares of land from an illiterate chief who was deceived to sign documents with mere thumb prints and by the time the community realized that they had been conned, 2,600 hectares of land had already been deforested (IFAD, 2012). Valuable food sources such as shea and *dawadawa* trees were cut down to make way for a jatropha plantation.

Cameroon is one of the African countries that is most exposed to land grabbing by multinational agribusinesses and foreign and local governments. According to a study conducted by Right and Resources Initiatives in 2011, 10 of the 22 million hectares of

Cameroon's forests have already been assigned for mining or agricultural exploitation. In Cameroon, in 2006, a subsidiary of the Shaanxi Land Reclamation General Corporation signed a US $120 million investment agreement with the government of Cameroon, thereby acquiring the Nanga-Eboko rice farm and a 99-year lease on a further 10,000 hectares, including 2,000 ha in Nanga-Eboko near the rice farm, and 4,000 ha in the neighbouring district of Ndjoré (Braun, 2011). The project covered 73,086 hectares of forest and farmland home to about 14,000 people (Ibid). Nevertheless, several scale small farmers and the local inhabitants were opposed to the plantation, fearing that it would deprive them of their farmland and access to forest products. Located in Southwest Cameroon, the Herakles plantations were expected to cover most of the land linking five important protected areas in the region, Korup National Park, Bakossi National Park, Banyang Mbo Wildlife Sanctuary, Nta Ali Forests Reserve and Rumpi Hills Forest Reserve (Robison, 2012). This region was part of the Guinean forests of West Africa, identified as a biodiversity hotspot – one of the world's top 25 critical areas for biodiversity conservation Borras (2013).

This region was part of the Guinean forests of West Africa, identified as a biodiversity hotspot – one of the world's top 25 critical areas for biodiversity conservation (Borras, 2013). A map compiled by Greenpeace showed that the plantation included 62,433 hectares of dense forest, almost 90% of the proposed concession (see map below). On top of that, Herakles demonstrated its total disregard for the country's laws when in 2010, without a presidential decree authorising the concession, Herakles started clearing forest to establish oil palm nurseries. It went further to violate a court decision, made in the town of Mundemba, to suspend all activities following a complaint filed by local people. Furthermore, the company was found guilty of illegal logging (Braun, 2011).

Herakles Farms Palm Oil Concession Area in the Southwest of Cameroon

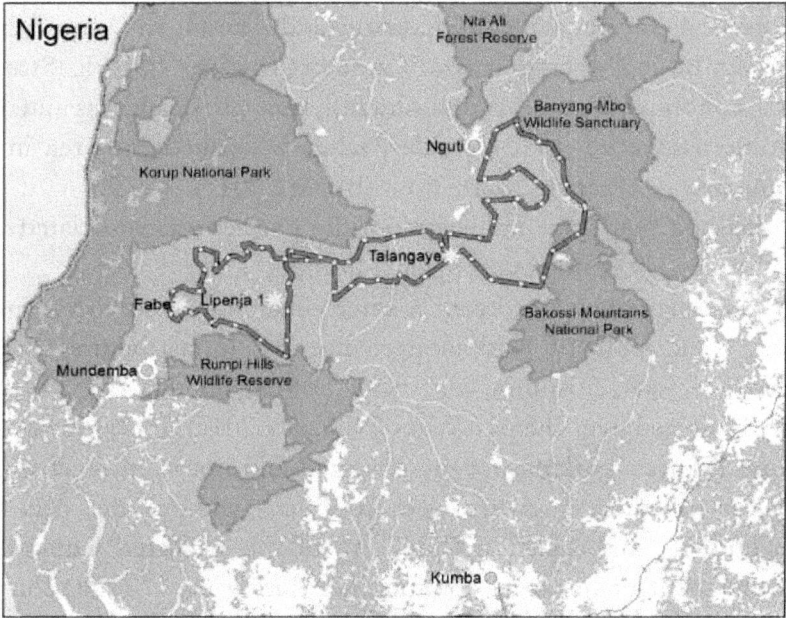

Source: Greenpeace, 2013

Another disconcerting characteristic associated with the company operations was that its environmental and social impact assessment was found to be inadequate as it acknowledged substantive negative potential future impacts on local people's

257

livelihoods but makes no provision for mitigation. Though residents complained that they were not consulted, farmland was demarcated without their consent and false promises were made orally. When residents protested against the plantation in the summer of 2012, the protests were met with intimidation and arrests. In August 2012, Nasako Besingi, the director of Cameroonian NGO SEFE (Struggle to Economise Future Environment), was physically assaulted by people associated with Herakles, while he visited the area in the company of French journalists (Braun, 2011). In 2016, it was established that since its inception, the project was associated with lawlessness, lies and abuses against farmers.

Although many ordinary Cameroonian inhabitants had given away their plots of land in exchange for infrastructure such as schools, roads, hospitals, electricity nothing in this direction was accomplished over the past years (Nhliziyo, 2015). It is also said that some farmers working for the company did not even receive their wages. In addition, many trees were cut without the necessary government authorization (Ibid). All of this occurred without the involvement of the local communities during the consultation and decision-making processes.

Bolloré Company has also been involved in land grabs in Cameroon. Borras (2013) observed that since the World Bank led privatisation of Cameroon's state owned companies in 2000, Bolloré has taken control of several rubber and palm oil plantations and this has also accompanied land grabbing in Cameroon. Bolloré is a French investment and industrial holding group headquartered in France. Bolloré subsidiaries manage large scale oil palm plantations throughout African countries like Ivory Coast, Nigeria and democratic Republic of Congo. The companies' agricultural ventures are largely criticised for deforestation, land grabbing, chemical pollution, poor working conditions, degrading the social and economic conditions of local and indigenous populations, industry monopolization and media intimidation (Hallam, 2012). Investigations were carried out and uncovered instances of child labour, forced evictions of peasant farmers within the plantations expansion area, trade union suppression, arbitrary dismissals, lack of protection from carcinogenic substances and the use of paramilitary forces for security purposes (Borras, 2013). The takeover has led to the evictions of local indigenous communities like Bagyeli. The communities' day-to-day activities have been increasingly become difficult due to the plantations' annual expansion rate of 1000 hectares per year (Ibid). The expansion programmes reduced the communities' access to their ancestral lands and vital resources such as water bodies and forests. Undoubtedly, this increased poverty levels considering that Bolloré offered limited job opportunities with abysmal living and working conditions leaving the people destitute with no alternative means of survival.

Furthermore, in 2011, nearly 6000 small farmers and their families in Cameroon had their livelihood wiped out by Socfin; a Luxemburg based company that grabbed their land for plantation agriculture (Borras 2013). Socfin group specialized in the development and management of oil palm plantations and rubber tree plantations (Ibid).

Zimbabwe is yet another African country that has been affected by widespread land grabbing in recent years. In Zimbabwe, people have been displaced from the Chisumbanje area which has been earmarked for ethanol production. The Chisumbanje Ethanol Project is a public-private partnership that started in 2009 when the Agriculture and Rural Development Authority (ARDA) signed a 20 year joint venture agreement with two private Zimbabwean companies to lease over 50 000 hectares of land (Thondlana, 2016). The objective was to establish 40 000 hectares of sugarcane plantations with the potential to develop additional 10 000 hectares as well as revive the irrigation infrastructure within eight years (Ibid). The surrounding communities claimed that the government only controls one tenth of the area and ARDA is grabbing the community land through encroaching outside the ARDA state boundaries. In Zimbabwe, it is interesting to note how the Fast Track Land Reform Programme (FTLRP) of 2000 has impacted on the lives of the African peasantry in country.

The Government of Mozambique, in similar fashion, has sought to attract this wave of foreign agricultural investment to its shores, particularly to the Nacala Corridor in the northern part of the country. Mozambique is among the countries in the world today where agro-fuels (ethanol and bio-diesel) are currently pursued with greater optimism and vigour by the transnational corporate sector, international development agencies and the national government (Sonja and Cotula, 2014). The government is partnering with foreign governments and donors, most notably Japan and Brazil, on a massive programme known as ProSavana, which aims to transform 14 million hectares of lands currently cultivated by peasant farmers serving local markets in this area into massive farming operations run by foreign companies to produce cheap agricultural commodities for export (Southern Africa Resource Watch (SARW, 2016).

The ProSavana plan in Mozambique has led to numerous land grabs. ProSavana is aimed at increasing production in the Nacala corridor, a 14,5m-hectare in central and northern Mozambique that has agricultural potential similar to the Cerrado region Brazil's savannah (SARW, 2016). In 2015, peasants in northern Mozambique made spirited efforts to retain their lands as the government and foreign companies moved aggressively to establish large-scale agribusiness projects.

In Nigeria, Wilmar an agribusiness company acquired around 30,000 hectares of land in Nigeria's Cross River State, an area rich in agricultural history and legacy (Jacobson, 2015). According to Jacobson (2015), the company evicted local farmers from their land, polluting local water supplies and destroying forest areas. Some of the affected communities were forced to sign up for a lawsuit seeking compensation or getting back their land. Nonetheless, given the high costs involved in litigation and the vagaries of the Nigerian justice system, some residents steered clear of the legal route as Wilmar denied responsibility to compensate the affected communities (Norman, 2015). Furthermore, the company claimed that its presence in the area should be viewed with a lot of optimism as it had the potential to turn around the fortunes of the people through its investment and development initiatives thereby creating abundant employment opportunities for the local inhabitants (Ibid).

In another incident of vast land grabbing in Nigeria, thousands of Nigerians were evicted from their land in the North-eastern Taraba State of Nigeria in 2015 when a US based food and agriculture company, Dominion Farms was allocated land by the government

(Robertson, 2015). The land offered to Dominion Farms was used by thousands of Nigerian families for agriculture, water resources, fishing ponds and grazing areas. Approximately 45 000 indigenous Nigerians were gravely affected by the large scale rice farm project (Robertson, 2015). The land grabbed was very fertile and the local people used to grow crops such as beans, guinea corn, cassava, soya beans, millet and yam as well as fish farming and the rearing of animals like goats, sheep and cattle before the company took over. When the Dominion Farms took over, the local people were asked to stop farming and evacuate their lands (Norman, 2015). According to Mallan (2016), some of the local people had been promised adequate compensation for their lands and that new schools, roads, hospitals and a farm training centre would be built but these promises remained a pipe dream as they were not fulfilled. Development of these agriculture projects began without community consent, while the affected Nigerians were not advised on how they were going to be compensated in future for losing their land. The frustration by the local people was plainly expressed by one local farmer, Mallan Danladi Jallo, who opined, "We were happy when we heard of the coming of the Dominion Farms not knowing it was for the selfish interest of some few members of the State, Federal Government and the foreigner in charge of the Dominion Farms" (Reuters, 2016: 3). Nigeria has been vulnerable to large land grabs since the government has prioritised attracting international investment in the country's agricultural sector. Both the Federal Ministry of Agriculture and the Federal Ministry of Investment pronounce that the investments would with time, inevitably increase national food production and make Nigeria a food exporting country (Norman, 2015). Conversely, this has not practically happened that way. If anything, this has amplified the risk of land grabs as local communities are displaced from their land getting nothing in return. In the process, as the locals lose land, their sources of livelihoods are diminished as they can no longer grow food to feed their families.

Land grabs in the DRC by the multinational companies has been largely propelled by the need to acquire agro products, besides the need to acquire abundant mineral wealth in the country. One of the biggest land acquisition deals involves the Italian Government which owns 30% of ENI's massive multi-billion land acquisition project in the DRC. The investment was meant to grow oil palm for biodiesel production (Graham, *et al*, 2011). In the DRC, numerous prominent development finance institutions (DFIs) are funding Feronia, a Canadian agribusiness company accused of land grabbing and human rights abuses in the DRC. Community leaders living within the 100,000 hectares covered by Feronia's oil palm concession areas say their land was taken from them illegally and that they never gave their consent for Feronia to operate there (Banchirigah, 2010). This leaves one in no doubt that the activities by Feronia are a direct contravention of the DFI policies that prevent companies from operating on lands that were acquired without the free, prior and informed consent of local communities. Feronia operates plantations and a large-scale cereal farm on 120,000 ha of land in the DRC (Bebbington, 2015). Its oil palm concessions were acquired from the transnational food company Unilever in 2009.The company is over 80 percent owned by the UK's CDC Group and a number of other DFIs – including the French Agency for Development (AFD) and the US government's Overseas Private Investment Corporation (OPIC) – through their investments in the Mauritius-based African Agriculture Fund (AAF) (Ibid). To receive a day's pay, workers on Feronia's Lokutu plantations underscore that they must complete tasks that are virtually impossible to complete in a day's work. While the company's directors are handsomely remunerated, plantation and nursery workers point out that their monthly wages are a far cry as they are around $1.50 per day (Bebbington, 2015).

In Madagascar, the 1.3 million hectares' land deal between the government and a South Korea company Daewoo Logistics attracted widespread media coverage as the land acquisition deal had the potential to displace thousands of rural inhabitants whose livelihoods entirely depended on land for their livelihoods (Daniel, 2011). The deal involved the acquisition of vast amounts of land in the east and west of the country to grow oil palm and maize predominantly for export to South Korea (Cotula, *et al*, 2009). The deal was eventually terminated by the government due to widespread resentment by the local citizens as it was likely to result in the massive displacement of the peasants as the company wanted to lease about half of all the country's arable land (Oliver, 2008; Reuters, 2008a). Another significant land acquisition deal in Madagascar involved the GEM Biofuels acquisition of close to half a million hectares of land in Sothern Madagascar to plant jatropha for biodiesel production (Reuters, 2008a).

Factors behind Land Grabs in Africa

In the contemporary times, land grabs from poor developing nations of Africa by wealthier, food-insecure nations and private investors such as United States of America, Brazil, Norway, China and Japan are gaining currency. For instance, foreigners sought to secure between 37 million and 49 million acres of farmland in sub Saharan Africa between 2006 and the middle of 2009 (Foreign land grabbing in Africa: Monitoring Report by European Civil Society Organizations of European Commission's proposal for Advancing African Agriculture, 2009). The land grabs in sub-Saharan Africa and other parts of the world accelerated during the 2008 financial and food crises as the food in-insecure wealth nations and private investor rushed to purchase or lease vast tracts of land from poor developing nations. Since then, this phenomenon has unfolded with increasing rapidity to the extent that it has received a lot of media coverage and in the process catching the attention of researchers, land rights, and environmental activists. Examples of the land and environmental activists in Africa include the Tanzania Land Rights, Pastoralist Indigenous NGOs Forum (Tanzania) and the Kenya Land Alliance (Loure & Nelson, 2016). These organisations, among several others across the continent, are affiliated to Friends of the Earth Africa which brings together different groups throughout the continent to participate in land and environmental programmes and develop initiatives to strengthen campaigning in the region (www.foei.org/membergroups). These organisations have been very critical in defending community threats to land rights as they invariably argue that land grabs across the continent have the potential to jeopardize worldwide food security as they simply amplify monoculture-based, export-oriented agriculture.

Proponents of the land grabbing exercise in Africa view it as a "win-win" situation in which while the rich but food in-secure nations gain access to food resources, the "host" African countries benefit from investments in the form of enhanced agricultural infrastructure and improved employment opportunities (Graham, *et al*, 2011). Indeed, some countries in sub-Saharan Africa such as Ethiopia, Mozambique and Kenya also view these land purchases or leases by rich nations and individual and corporate investors as a source of potential economic development. The modern day land grab phenomenon is multifaceted as it is motivated by, among other factors, the international food crisis, price unpredictability in the global markets, and elevated speculation. However, while the land grab phenomenon in Africa is multidimensional, the rush to secure food supply by increasingly food insecure nations, the surging demand for agro-fuels and other energy as well as the desire to acquire non-food stuffs in countries such as Ethiopia, Ghana, Madagascar, Kenya, Zimbabwe, Democratic Republic of Congo, Mozambique, Sudan, and Zambia seem to be the major drivers of this new phenomenon. Land grabbing in Africa has become an undisputable reality and a noteworthy threat to the livelihoods of small-scale farmers in Africa who fundamentally contribute to rural development as it also disregards the locals' property rights, exploits the natural resources of the host countries and impoverishes farmers not bringing about the pledged benefits.

Several countries both in the developed and developing world are looking forward to stabilize food supplies by acquiring foreign lands for food production in the hopes of averting potential domestic upheavals over food prices that may be triggered by food insecurity in their respective countries. Fears of a global food crisis are still widespread and well founded as food prices continue to remain high and food emergencies persist. For instance, the Gulf States such as Iraq, Qatar and Saudi Arabia, with scarce water and soil resources on which to grow food, but have an abundance of vast oil and cash reserves, have watched their dependence on food imports become increasingly uncertain and ever more expensive (World Bank 2010). Many European countries and private corporations are involved in the land grabbing exercise in sub-Saharan Africa as they endeavour to guarantee the food security of their own people (Graham, *et al*, 2011).

A surging demand for agro-fuels (biofuel produced from ethanol and sugarcane as well as biodiesel) and access to new sources of raw materials for manufacturing goods is also driving land purchases in post-colonial Africa. The rapidly growing consumption of fossil fuels, energy security concerns, as well as the requirement to reduce greenhouse gas emissions has pushed rich countries to diversify energy sources over the past decades (Reenberg, 2015). The European Renewable Energies Directive from April 2009 set a minimum 10% share of renewable energies in transport by 2020 as one mandatory target for Member States. The European Renewable Energies Directive is a European Union Directive which mandates levels of renewable energy use within the European Union; the Directive requires that 20% of the energy consumed within the European Union is renewable (Brooke, 2011). According to the Directive, about 10 % will be supplied mainly by biofuels and as much as two-thirds are likely to be imported, the majority from developing countries and meet the target alone, the total land area directly required to grow biofuels in developing countries could reach 17.5 million hectares, well over half the size of Italy (Ibid). The demand for agro-fuels has increased rapidly over the past several years as oil-dependent countries establish ambitious targets for agro-fuel production and for incorporating bio-diesel and bio-ethanol with traditional transport fuels. For example, the US Renewable Fuel Standard aimed to increase ethanol use by 3.5 billion gallons between 2005 and 2012, and the European Union (EU) aims to increase the proportion of bio-fuels used in land transport to 10% by 2020 (Boute, 2011). With these and other impetuses, the use and production of bio-fuels has skyrocketed in recent years such that the quantity of US corn used to produce ethanol increased by 53 million between 2002 and 2007 accounting for 30% of the total global growth in wheat and feed grains use (Ibid). Attracted by this big demand and market, investors mainly from the private sector and Organisation for Economic Cooperation and Development (OECD) member countries are targeting vast tracts of land to produce crops for agro-fuels in developing countries of Africa, which generally have

265

a comparative advantage in such production for example, due to low labour and land costs and, in some cases, land availability (Ibid). In this regard, countries such as the United Kingdom and Sweden have made it compulsory for their fuel suppliers to use a certain percentage of agro-fuels. European banks and firms have not been left out in the rush for land in Africa as they are also heavily promoting investments in agro-fuels production in the continent. This includes the German Deutsche Invetsitions-und Entwicklungsgesellshaft (GEG), British energy firm CAMS Group, growing sweet sorghum in Tanzania and another British firm, Sun Biofuels, growing jatropha in Tanzania. Sun Biofuels also has similar investments in Mozambique. German's Flora EcoPower has heavily invested in Ethiopia's Orama State for bio-fuels production (Graham, *et al*, 2011).

Land grabs are also driven by speculative activities. Since 2007, many foreign investors have turned their attention to agricultural acquisitions which they perceive to be a long-term bet. Montenegro (2009) argues that the shift to land markets and "soft commodities" since 2007 emanated from the fact that, the "soft commodities" began to surpass their "hard" counterparts as the major players in the commodities investment market (For a detailed discussion on the structural shift to investment in food and farming commodities, see Bidwells, 2007). Prospects of rising rates return in agriculture and land values are also major drivers of the contemporary land grabs in sub-Saharan Africa. These have been propelled by the food crisis of 2008 and the rising demand for agro-fuels in the developed world. Pension funds are also being invested in agricultural and commodity-related assets as business communities in Europe are progressively realising the clear value of investing in agricultural land in sub-Saharan Africa that has demonstrated the potential to offer superior returns to listed equities (Graham, *et al*, 2011).

The impact of land grabs on Indigenous African people

The selected case studies and examples herein clearly demonstrate that land grabbing by foreign investors in contemporary sub-Saharan Africa is rampant and that there is definite need to reflect on how this has variably impacted on the livelihoods of the indigenous African people across the continent. The unprecedented land grabs have resulted in the disempowerment and impoverishment of the indigenous African people since their socio-economic livelihoods are largely tied directly to the land on which they live. When Africans are forced to leave their land due to land grabs, they are also being forced to leave their livelihoods. Therefore, land grabs not only infringe upon Africans' property rights. They also infringe upon Africans' economic rights, leads to political conflicts, hunger and starvation, destitution, depletion of natural resources, dependency on foreign aid inaccessibility of basic services such as healthcare and education facilities, all of which attract poverty and underdevelopment. The struggle for economic rights has been the cornerstone of the modern African state since decolonisation in the 1960s. Aside from ending the racial discrimination that Africans suffered under colonisation, the push for decolonisation was also motivated by the right of Africans to reap the economic benefits of their own labour and the natural resources of their continent. Land grabs perpetuate the same economic disenfranchisement that Africans suffered under colonialism, making land grabs neo-colonial in nature and meant to exacerbate poverty levels among the indigenous African communities.

When MNCs take their operation to the developing world, the host societies generally suffer from weak infrastructure, poor governance, widespread poverty, illiteracy, health care problems, and disparities in income distribution, environmental degradation and depletion of resources. The so-called technology they claim to be transferring to host nations is absolute. MNCs have caused dramatic improvements in telecommunications, increased computing power and the development of information networks such as internet, and web-based commerce, among others. These technologies are helping to overcome the barrier of physical distance. However, Elaigwu (2014) argues that MNCs enterprises tend to bring down African economies overnight, a few clicks on a computer mouse can devalue a nations' currency very quickly wasting away the life savings of millions of bread winners. Ugwu and Tunde (2012) argue that MNCs provide finance for investment, provide employment, train and helps youth of the host nation to acquire skills and technology as well as contribute to government revenue through tax payments, fixed royalties and fees. However, Nwako (2014) refuted these claims in very strong terms. He argues that MNCs do in fact destroy jobs because they employ capital intensive technologies, their so-called technology being absolute, overpriced, inappropriate and inconsistent. Indeed, there are so many situations in post-colonial Africa in which MNCs have been used by their country governments to advance imperial needs and that's why they are viewed by some as the new colonisers in Africa (hptts://www.pambazuka/org). Besides, MNCs are driven by the need to maximise profits in their operations. MNCs such as France's Eif-Aquitane, Shell, British Petroleum (BP) and their counterparts in Europe and America offer bribes and makes improper payments in order to circumvent local regulations (hptts://www.pambazuka/org). The indigenes of the host country are not given the opportunity to occupy managerial positions in the giant corporations. These giant corporations exhibit the capitalist characteristics of exporting the raw materials to their mother countries. The characteristics of MNCs of control and ownership are capitalistic in nature. The apparent discriminatory appointment of indigenes of the host countries to managerial positions in the corporation is imperialistic. MNCs control the economy and dictate to the host countries products. These characteristics of MNCs have placed them in potential conflicts with host countries because they are not eager to improve the lives of the local people. The recent phenomenon of land grab has resulted in the sale of enormous portions of land in Africa. In 2009 alone, nearly 60 million hectares of land were purchased or leased throughout the continent for the production of export of food, cut flowers and agro-fuel crops source of food adequate for most families whose previous homesteads had at least four huts (Nwako, 2014). This same situation is most pronounced in countries such as South Africa, Malawi, Angola and Namibia (Nwako, 2014).

There is no denying that food security remains a dire problem rapidly rising prices for staple foods from 2006 to 2008 culminated in a worldwide food crisis, and while commodity prices have somewhat stabilised, millions especially among the poor are still suffering from hunger. FAO reports indicate that another 40 million people were pushed into hunger in 2008, primarily due to higher food prices, bringing the overall number of undernourished people in the world to 963 million compared to 923 million in 2007 (WB 2015). While supply shortfalls are a normal part of agriculture, and historically, a supply shortfall triggers increased production through higher prices, the current crisis is comprised of unique elements including uncontrolled financial speculation, new demand for agricultural commodities from the agro-fuels sector, mounting stress on the quantity and quality of soil and water available, and the uncertainty of how climate change will affect growing conditions.

No matter how convincing the claim that the global land grab will bring much needed agricultural investment to poor countries, evidence across the continent shows there is simply no place for the small farmer in the vast majority of these land grab situations. Most land deals consider the local population only to the extent that large-scale agriculture will create employment for subsistence farmers and rural land-dwellers. However, the extension of employment to local farmers to work on industrial, plantation-style farms effectively implies the forcing of subsistence farmers off their land to make room for large-scale farms producing food for other countries. Not only does land grabbing mean that farmers will lose their land, but these lands will be transformed from smallholdings or communal lands into large industrial estates connected to far-off markets (Elaigwu, 2014).

Another disturbing feature of the contemporary land grab movement is that commercial land deals are coming into direct conflict with land reform initiatives in some developing countries in Africa such as Ghana, Ethiopia, Kenya, Tanzania and Zimbabwe. In Ghana, for instance, the scramble for land between local African inhabitants and multinationals is very pronounced (Behnassi, *et al*, 2011). Mounting demand for land due to demographic and economic growth and resource depletion increasingly leads rural areas to be incorporated into market economies, and therefore governments often experience pressure to implement land reform policies that give the poor secure access to land, thereby allowing them to pursue their livelihoods without fear of harassment or eviction. The current land grab characterised by unprecedented pressures on land resources and increasing demand within land markets is placing new tensions on land tenure systems. Those at high risk of losing access to land are small-scale producers who do not have formal tenure over the land that they use, as well as women, indigenous people, pastoralists, and fisher-folks. Many indigenous vulnerable groups in countries such as Ethiopia, Mali, Zambia, Zimbabwe, Kenya, Madagascar, Mozambique, among others, have lost enormous quantities of land in recent years (Cotula, *et al*, 2009). Perhaps, a country by country perfunctory survey on how the land grabs in sub-Sahara Africa have disempowered and impoverished the indigenous African people suffices here.

In Uganda, some 85% of the population lives in rural areas and four in ten of the rural population predominantly in the north and north east of the country, are considered to be living in abject poverty (Kalangala District Local Government, 2012). It is further started that approximately 5 % of rural households in Uganda are affected by food insecurity (Kalangala District Local Government, 2012). Agriculture is pivotal to Uganda's economy, with 80% of all jobs in the agriculture and fishing sectors (National Association of Professional Environmentalists (NAPE), 2006). While some cash crops are grown for export (particularly coffee, tea, cotton and tobacco), many rural communities have traditionally relied on subsistence agriculture, growing cassava, corn, potatoes and millet, as well as plants for medicinal uses (NAPE, 2006). According to the Ugandan Constitution:

> Land in Uganda belongs to the citizens of Uganda and shall vest in them in accordance with the land tenure systems provided for in the constitution, and these are classed as customary, freehold, Mailo and leasehold (Kalangala District Local Government, 2012: 3).

The land grab in Bugala Island has resulted in numerous social and environmental challenges which have affected the island since then. An environmental impact assessment carried out there on behalf of the government established that the project would not have significant climate or hydrological impacts on the island, but that it was likely to reduce forest cover, resulting in a loss of endemic species, and that it would reduce windbreaks, increase siltation in Lake Victoria, increase logging, reduce the potential for ecotourism, increase the local population and increase the risk of HIV/AIDS, food insecurity, cultural erosion, loss of sacred places and cultural conflicts. Despite these threats identified by the Environmental Impact Assessment the project went ahead, with little evidence that the identified threats had been taken care of (NAPE, 2015).

The Business Industrial Development Corporation (BIDCO), a multinational consumer goods company headquartered in Thika, Kenya, signed an agreement with the Ugandan government to undertake an integrated palm oil project on the island in the year 2002. The project was supported by the International Fund for Agricultural Development (IFAD) and the World Bank. Under the terms of the 2002 agreement between BIDCO and the Ugandan government, the 10 000 hectares of land for the palm oil estate on Bugala was to be provided by the Government. Local people were not consulted (Matsiko, 2012). While most of this land has been provided to BIDCO, this has been at the expense of members of the community who did not hold formal land rights to the land they occupied often Mailo land, which is now officially recognized as public land; and at the expense of forests and the lakeshore buffer zone (Matsiko 2012). Land conflicts have arisen between members of the local community and BIDCO, following the allocation of land for the oil palm development, with reports of people being forcibly evicted from their homes in the forest to make way for oil palm. Because few rural dwellers hold official land titles for the land they lived on, they often cannot seek redress. Under the Constitution land tribunals are supposed to resolve land conflicts (Article 243) but these operated for only a short time before collapsing. Later, the tribunals were supposed to be replaced with Land Committees in the districts, but these have not yet become fully operational (Ibid). As a result there is little to prevent land grabbing, and indeed the government has appeared to sanction the process, giving land occupied under customary tenure to foreign investors. Some small holders have also said that they were effectively forced to sell land they owned after planting oil palm because they were not able to pay for the fertilizer and other inputs needed (Vidal, 2008).

271

Some people have reported that they were denied access to resources, including grazing lands, building materials and water, contravening their human rights. In Kulugulu village on the island, the path to the communal well which was the source of clean water for the community was blocked by BIDCO (NAPE, 2015). According to some governmental and nongovernmental reports, fertilizers and pesticides used in the oil palm plantation were also reported to have affected the community's water point (Uganda National Report, 2010, NAPE, 2011, 2012, Shively and Hao, 2012). The community sent a petition to Kalangala District Council Authorities asking it to exert pressure on BIDCO to reopen the path to the well, but the petition was ignored (Vidal, 2008). Wells in Kibaale–Jovu village were also reported to have been destroyed and animals found trespassing on former grazing lands in the palm oil project area have been confiscated and owners have been fined (Mabike, 2011). Hence, this discouraged people living in the area from raising animals, affecting their food supplies. Areas previously used for sand mining in Bukuzzindu have been allocated for palm oil, including accommodation buildings for staff and workers. This has meant that the local community no longer had access to the sand supplies, which are used for building leading to a conflict with the local community, with the community digging sand ditches along the roadside, creating a hazard for BIDCO vehicles and employees (Ibid).

The clearing of large areas by BIDCO has resulted in mounting pressure on the remaining forest resources, which traditionally provided building materials, boat-making materials, food and more importantly, firewood for the local people (NAPE, 2015). While one of the stated aims of the oil palm development was to create jobs for the local community, unfortunately most of the jobs on offer were for casual labourers and most of these were not from Kalangala (Matsiko, 2012). BIDCO owns 18 000 acres of palm oil plantation in Kalangala District and deliberately employs casual workers from the Northern and Eastern parts of Uganda so that there are fewer local workers to rally indigenous communities in protest of labour conditions and this has led to rising poverty on locals as they have been left with virtually no means for survival (Kalangala District

Local Government, 2012). Almost all of these are men and casual labourers are paid approximately one dollar a day for work on the project, and many say this is not enough to cover their living costs in Kalangala and as a result, there is a rapid turnover of casual staff, with casual workers remaining at the project for just three months (Ibid). Living conditions for the casual labourers in the BIDCO workers' quarters are overcrowded, with nine workers allocated to two rooms, many local people say that they can earn a better living fishing and prefer to do that, rather than work as labourers (Matsiko, 2012). Complaints by the local people of thefts of food crops and other items, with casual labourers being blamed are rampant. As a result of the increased demand for land on Bugala Island, land prices have increased considerably, from 70,000 shillings an acre in 2003 to between 800,000 – 2 million shillings in 2009 (NAPE, 2015). This increase in prices has attracted rich investors, encouraging poorer land owners to sell up. Some land owners who have refused to relinquish land have found that oil palm has been planted on their land anyway, making it difficult for them to continue farming and more than 20 families found themselves homeless as a result of oil palm plantation establishments (Matsiko, 2012).

The introduction of oil palm has affected the local economy, which used to be based around fishing, timber harvesting and food crops (NAPE, 2015). With land previously used for food production planted with oil palm, local food supplies have been reduced, and this means farmers who have lost access to their land have also lost their income. This has increased food insecurity, increased pressure on land and on forest products has pushed up. These changes in land use have increased poverty for some, resulting in an increase in crime and conflicts within the community. Members of the local communities around the shores of Lake Victoria used to derive their livelihoods from fishing, catching haplochromines, tilapia, Nile perch and lung fish. However, these fish have become scarcer or completely evaporated, possibly as a result of pollution from the agrochemicals used on the plantation (NAPE, 2015). Wilmar International and BIDCO operations are destroying forests with no regard for environmental regulations. Large areas of tropical forests and other ecosystems with high conservation values have been cleared to make room for vast monoculture oil palm plantations–destroying critical habitat for many endangered species, including rhinos, elephants and tigers (Ibid).

In some cases, the expansion of plantations has led to the eviction of forest-dwelling peoples. The establishment of vast monoculture oil palm plantations itself has a number of environmental impacts. The two most serious are, large-scale forest conversion, loss of critical habitat for endangered species, soil erosion, air pollutions oil and water pollution climate change. The project was accused of both clearing forest in violation of the terms of the country's environmental regulations and of polluting the lake with fertilisers and other agrochemicals. For instance, Sonja and Cotula (2009), purport that apart from massive application of fertilisers which washes into the lake causing over-production of algae and water weeds with knock-on effects on lake ecosystems, BIDCO has also encroached on national forestry land outside the 7,000 hectares it received from Uganda government, 40 percent of the natural forest cover on Bugala, the main island.

People living on Bugala Island used to grow beans, yams, peas, maize, and bananas and some of these crops were used to supply food to neighbouring islands (Sonja and Cotula, 2009). But the island now has been taken over by BIDCO and Wilmar International for palm oil production at the expense of food crops and now has to import almost all its supplies of bananas, rice, beans and maize flour from the main land (Sonja and Cotula, 2009). This has led to deterioration in living costs for the people on the island, making it difficult for some members of the community to be able to feed themselves.

In Ethiopian, the people's rights to farm were taken away and they were relocated and moved away from basic services such as healthcare and education Sonja and Cotula, 2009). The displacement of the people exacerbated hunger and starvation in the drought prone country. In a desperate need for shelter, some of the displaced Anuak people from Gambella were forced to relocate to the overcrowded refugee camps in South Sudan and Kenya were impoverished and were faced with food insecurity Sonja and Cotula, 2009). There are also documented occurrences of torture, rape and extrajudicial imprisonment which accompanied the displacements (http: www.theguardian.com).

The government of Ethiopia itself estimated that 50 million people were in need of food assistance in 2016 (Reuter, 2010). The socio-economic transformation that the people were promised was never realised as the indigenous people were moved in government sponsored villages. As one human rights activist from Gambella explained:

> People have been living on this land for generations. When I grew up we didn't have an office job to earn wages, people depend on land. Our supermarket is going to be the field. The field was our bank. When you take away our lands, you are taking away our livelihood, our futures (Cultural Survival, 2016).

One displaced villager lamented:

> In the old village there was a school under a mango tree. In the new village, donor money had paid for a new school building. The children, however, were too hungry to attend, roaming instead in the forest looking for food...but now the donor money had paid for a new school building. The children, however, were too hungry to attend, roaming instead in the forest looking for food...but now the government can show the world there is a school (http: www.theguardian.com).

The above clearly illustrates that the massive foreign investments on land traditionally exploited by small-scale farmers (95-98%) has significantly modified the land ownership structure with catastrophic consequences for the Ethiopian people. The introduction of wide-scale agriculture has failed to increase the local people's access to food supplies as most of the food produced is destined for the export market to the wealth food insecure nations (Graham, *et al*, 2011).

In Zimbabwe, the Chisumbanje ethanol project resulted in the displacement of an estimated 3 000 households. While in the past these people survived on cotton and maize production, after the displacement, the community was reduced to poverty (Mutondoro,

2016). The Green Fuel Company operating in Chisumbanje has privatised scarce water resources to the disadvantage of small scale farmers. It is also notable and interesting to highlight that the impacts of the people's displacement are highly gendered. With the land dispossession in the Chisumbanje area, a number of men have left for South Africa and Mozambique in search of jobs. This has further burdened women who have to shoulder more responsibilities and as a result a number of children have dropped out of school and some young girls have been forced into early marriage continuing a vicious cycle of poverty (Thondlana, 2016). The Green Fuel Company affected the local community in every aspect of their lives ranging from loss of livelihood strategies, dispossession, displacement and loss of social and economic status.

The Mozambique experience is very intriguing. Though the local inhabitants were made to believe that the investment in Biofuel projects would bring them immeasurable benefits the country's romance with foreign investors has been disastrous. A recent survey by Mozambique's National Farmers' Union (ANAC) and GRAIN demonstrated that a scramble for land reminiscent of the colonial model is under way in the country (SARW, 2016). AgroMoz (Agribusiness de Mozambique SA) a joint venture between Brazil, Mozambique and Portugal which produce soya, has evicted more than a thousand peasants at Wakhua, in Gurué district (Sonja and Cotula, 2014). Inspired by the technology for tropical agriculture developed in Brazil, small scale vegetable and grain production were threatened and water sources were polluted by the agrochemicals from the activity and become unsafe for human and livestock consumption. Above all, in 2015, the project displaced nearly 150 000 people (Nhancale, 2016). The company has been grabbing the best, most fertile land and moving people to areas that cannot grow anything. Viewed from this perspective, AgroMoz has wreaked havoc on the local peasant communities and their food systems.

There is also a global rush for minerals by large multinational companies in Africa. Mozambique has attracted two of the world's largest mining companies, Brazil's Companhia Vale do Rio Doce (Vale) and the Anglo-Australian multinational Rio Tinto to extract coal from the huge fields in Tete province (Nhancale, 2016). The coal

276

mining project relocated people from fertile soils to unproductive lands. For instance farmers resettled to Mualadzi received land with poor access to water and limited productivity. According to Muscati (2016: 7):

> The farming land we received is red, not black like we had before. I tried to grow corn and it died. Sorghum also failed. We were given houses as compensation but my question is, 'What is a house without food?' the houses given as compensation are already cracking and many promises which includes running water, ambulances, land for farming and employment have not been fulfilled.

The impact of these companies investment on local communities remains problematic as there seems to be no guarantee that the gigantic projects would benefit the people of Mozambique in the long run. What has been witnessed so far is that people have been displaced and in the process separated from their traditional sources of livelihoods.

Land grabbing in Nigeria by Wilmar, one of the world's largest agribusiness companies left many communities landless and vulnerable as this destroyed areas of high conservation value. The operations of Wilmar International have acted against the local people's interests. In May 2015, in the village of Igbo, the people saw their farmland being excavated. Before the company commenced operations in the area, the local inhabitants used to grow a wide range of crops for consumption and commercial purposes as well as acquiring firewood from the forests (Jacobson, 2015). They used to grow cassava, cocoyams, bananas, cocoa and vegetables as well as trees for timber but the forests have since disappeared as a result of massive deforestation spearheaded by the company. The people in the area became very vulnerable and poverty-stricken (Jacobson, 2015). Although the company has provided jobs to the local people, the jobs are unstable and lack job security as they are contract-free positions which are a far cry from the work of operating small scale farms of their own. As a result, as noted earlier on, the local communities have resorted to seeking legal recourse over what they perceived was unfair removal from their ancestral lands (Norman, 2015).

Conclusion

On the whole, this chapter has demonstrated that since the global food and financial crises of 2008, there has been a massive scramble by international governments, foreign individuals and companies to lease or purchase enormous areas of land in Africa for little money in order to produce food for the nutrition of wealthier peoples or for the production of bio fuels. Nonetheless, what cannot escape one's attention is that this has inevitably led to the disempowerment and impoverishment of the indigenous African people as they are driven away from their very small pieces of land that had enabled them to sustain their livelihoods. The chapter has also shown that in certain instances, the displacement of indigenous African people is accompanied by the use of force and violence. The displaced people are sometimes forced to work for the new investors under poor working conditions, receiving low wages or are displaced and relocated to uninhabitable areas where they struggle to eke out a living.

The chapter has also demonstrated that to a large extent, the interests of the foreign governments and multinational corporations are not tied with those of the nations they are operating within. They are therefore not in a position to assist the African nations in solving their economic problems as the foreign investors tend to encourage commercial activities at the detriment of productive activities thereby turning Sub-Saharan Africa into a trading outpost. They discourage local productive activities hence disempowering and impoverishing the local people. These actions by foreign governments and MNCs undermine sustainable development in African countries. The authors have, through the use of selected examples across the continent, established that the purported aid to the developing African nations to stimulate sustainable development is to a large measure a mere camouflage as it entrenches dependency of the recipients and the dictatorship of donors (MNCs). Viewed from this perspective, it can be argued that the aid which accompanies the land grabs in Africa is more of a dehydrating agent than an economic advancement catalyst as this has resulted in the disempowerment and impoverishment\ of the indigenous African people in the 21st century.

References

Andersen, P. (2010). Global Land acquisition: neo-colonialism or development opportunity? http://www.springerlink.com/content/2j8617q5p4477887/fullt ext.pdf [accessed August 2017].

Banchirigah, S. M. and Hilson, G. (2010). "De-agrarianisation, re-agrarianisation and local economic development: re-orienting livelihoods in African artisanal mining communities", *Policy Science* 43: 157-180.

Banro Corporation Technical report Twangiza Project. March 2015.

Bebbington, A., Hinojosa, L. Humphreys Bebbington, D., Burneo, M.L. and Warnaars, X. (2008). 'Contention and ambiguity: mining and the possibilities of development', *Development and Change* 39 (6): 887-914.

Behanassi, B, Shahid, S.A & D'Silva. (Eds). (2011) *Sustainable Agricultural Development: Recent Approaches in Resources Management and Environmentally- Balanced Production Enhancement*, Springer.

Bidwells (2007). *The 'bull run' in soft commodity cycle or structural shift in food and farming?* Bidwells Property Consultants, Cambridge.

Boute, A. (2011). The quest of regulatory stability in the EU Energy Market, *European law Review* 675-692.

Brooke, D. (2011). *Renewable Energy Road Map- Renewable energies in the 21st Century*, Sweet and Maxwell, London.

Campbell, B. (Ed.) (2000). *Mining in Africa. Regulation and development*, London and New York: Pluto Press: 1-24.

Chinamasa, M. (2001). *The Human Right to Land in Zimbabwe; The legal and extra-legal resettlement Processes*, Makerere University, Uganda.

Chung, F. (2006). *Re-living the Second Chimurenga: Memories from Zimbabwe's Liberation Struggle*, Weaver Press, Harare.

Cotula, L., Vermeula, S., Loenard, L & Keeley, J. (2009). *Land Grab or Development Opportunity? Agriculture Investment and international land deals in Africa*, IIED/FAO/FAD, London/Rome.

Cultural Survival. 2016. Ethiopia Cancels Concession for Karuturi Land Grab, (accessed 10 July 2017).

Daniel, S. (2011). "Land Grabbing and Potential Implications for World Food Security." In *Sustainable Agricultural Development: Recent Approaches in Resource Management and Environmentally-Balanced Production Enhancement,* (Eds). Mohamed Behnassi, Shabbir. A. Shahid & D'Silva, New York: Springer, 25-42.

Elaigwu, F. (2014). *African Political Economy*, McGraw Hill Enterprise, New York.

Geman, LA & Schonoveld, G. (2012). Biofuel Investments in Sub-Saharan Africa: A Review of the Early Legal and Institutional Framework in Zambia. *Review of Policy Research*, vol 29(4): 467-491.

German, L, Schoneveld, L & Mwangi, E. (2011). 'Processes of Large-Scale Land Acquisitionby Investors: Case Studies from Sub-Saharan Africa'. *Paper Presented at the International Conference on Global Land Grabbing,* University of Sussex, http://www.iss.nl/files/ASSETS/iss/Documents/ Conference papers, accessed 18 July 2017).

Graham, A., Aubry, Kunnemann & Sauerez, S. M. (2011). The Role of the EU in Land Grabbing in Africa – CSO Monitoring 2009-2010 Advancing African Agriculture (AAA): *The Impact of Europe's Policies and Practices on African Agriculture and Food Security*, Paper presented at the International Conference on Global Land Grabbing.

Hall, R. (2011). Land Grabbing in Southern Africa: The Many Faces of the Investor Rush, *Review of African Political Economy*, 36(128): 193-214.

Hall, R. (2012). The Next Great Trek? South African farmers move North, *Journal of Peasant Studies*, 39(3&4): 823-843.

Haralambous, S., Liversage, H., & Romano, M. (2009). The growing demand for land: risks and opportunities for smallholder farmers, *Discussion Paper prepared for the Round Table organized during the Thirty-second session of IFAD's Governing Council*, Rome, 18–19 February.

http://www.greenpeace.org/usa/Global/usa/planet3/PDFs/Fores
ts/HeraklesCrimeFile.pdf.

http://www.gta/Land%20Issues/factsheet.htm, Retrieved 27
September 2017.

http://www.theguardian.com/global-
dvelopment/2013/jul/17/ethiopia-rights-abuses-us-uk-aid-
agenices, Retrieved 25 June 2017.

Human Rights Watch, "Waiting for Death' Forced Displacement and
"Villagization" in Ethiopia's Gambella Region,
http://www.hrw.org/sites/default/files/reports/ethiopia0112w
ebcover_opdf, Retrieved 22 June 2017.

International Fund for Agricultural Development Republic of
Uganda Vegetable Oil Development Project
http://www.ifad.org/gbdocs/eb/ec/e/63/ugandavodp,
accessed 19 June 2017.

International Land Coalition, Land and vulnerable people in a world
of change. Commission on Sustainable Development Session 16,
New York, May 5–16 2008.

Isaacman, A. F. (1976). *The Tradition of Resistance in Mozambique*,
Heinemann, London.

Jacobson, P. (2015). *Nigerian farmers displaced by US company's Land
Grab*, Lagos State University, Nigeria.

Kalangala District Local Government (2012). District state of the
environment report
http://www.nemaug.org/district_reports/Kalangala_DSOER_
2004.

Kovalyova, S. (2009). *Win-win" farmland deals*, UN agencies Reuters,
London.

Li, T. 2011. Centering Labour in the Labour Debate, Journal of
Peasant Studies, vol 38(2): 281-298.

Loure, E. & Nelson, F. 2017. The global land rights struggle is
intensifying, https://www.theguardian.com Retrieved 02
October 2017.

Mabike, B. (2011). *Large-Scale Land Acquisitions for Investment in Uganda*,
Arusha, Tanzania.

Malkamuu Jaatee, Anywaa Survival Organization. 2016. Land
Grabbing and Violations of Human Rights in Ethiopia.

281

Marti. S. (2008). Friends of the Earth, Life Mosaic and Sawit Watch Losing Ground: The Human Rights Impacts of the Oil Palm Plantations in Indonesia, http://www.wrm.org.org.uy/countries/Indonesia/losinggroun d.pdf, accessed 26 June 2017.

Matsiko, H. (2012). *The great land grabs,* Foundation Press, New York, USA.

Mitchell, D. (2008). A note on rising food prices, *Policy Research Working Paper 4682 - Development Prospects Group*, The World Bank: Washington DC.

Montenegro, R. (April 2009). *Troubles in the delta,* Seed Magazine.

Moyana, H. V. (1984). *The political economy of land in Zimbabwe,* Mambo Press, Harare.

Mutodi, B., Havnevik, K. & Bevene, A. (Eds). (2011). *Biofuels, Land grabbing and Security in Africa,* Zeds Books, London.

Mutondoro, F. (2016). *An Analysis of the Impact of Land Related Corruption on Women; Case Studies from Ghana and Zimbabwe,* Washington DC.

NAPE. (2012). A Study on land grabbing cases in Uganda, https://www.nape+report+2012, Retrieved 25 September 2017.

National Association of Professional Environmentalists (NAPE) (2011). The Good and the Bad of REDD in Uganda. In: Daily Monitor New Internationalist, Uprooted, 2006 http://www.newint.org/features/2006/07/01/uganda/.

Nhancale, C. (2016). *Coal versus communities in Mozambique,* Southern African Resource, Mozambique.

Nhliziyo, C. (2015). *Zimbabwe new land crisis; Large Scale land Investments at Chisumbanje,* Institute for Poverty Land and Agrarian Studies University of Western Cape.

Norman, G. (2015). Wilmar accused of Nigerian land grab for palm oil, https//www.mordenghana.com/news/Landgrabing-manace-in-west-africa-help-nigerian.

Nwako, O. (2014). *Globalisation and Africa's Development,* Zed Books, London.

Oxfam Briefing note. 2012. 'Our land, our lives': Time out on the global land rush, www.oxfam.org, Retrieved 12 July 2017.

Oxfam, (2012). "The Hunger Grains", http://policy-pratcice.oxfam.org.uk/publications/the-hunger-grains-thefight-is-on-time-to-scrap-eu-biofuel-mandates-242997.

Principles for Responsible Agricultural Investment that Respects Rights, Livelihoods and Resources, (2010). Extended Version, FAO, IFAD, UNCTAD, World Bank Group: Washington DC.

Reenberg, A. (2015). Land grab in Africa: Emerging land system drivers in a teleconnected world, *GLP Report No. 1*, Copenhagen, Denmark: GLP-IPO.

Republic of Uganda, Ministry of Finance, Planning and Economic Development. (2010). *Uganda National Report for the Implementation of the Programme of Action for the Least Developed Countries for the Decade 2001-2010*, UNOHRLLS.

Robertson, B. & P, Andersen. (2015). Global Land Acquisition: neo-colonialism or development opportunity? *Food Security*, Vol. 2(3).

Robinson, D. (2010). Open letter sounds alarm on massive oil palm development in Cameroon, https://www.voices.nationalgeographic.org/2012/03.20, Retrieved 27 September 2017.

Schoneveld, G. C, German, L A & Nutakor, E. (2011). Land-based Investment s for Rural Development? A grounded Analysis of the Local Impacts of Biofuel Feedstock Plantation In Ghana, *Ecology and Society*, vol 16 (4): 10.

Shively, G. and Hao, J. (2012). A Review of Agriculture, Food Security and Human Nutrition Issues in Uganda, Working Paper, Dept. of Agricultural, Economics, Purdie University.

Sidaway, R. (2014). *Resolving Environmental Disputes: From Conflict to Consensus*, Cromwell Press Ltd, Trowbridge.UK.

Smalley, R. (2013). Plantations, Contract Farming and Commercial Farming Areas in Africa in Africa: A Comparative Review, PLAAS Institute for Poverty and Agrarian Studies, Working Paper 055, www.future-agriculture.org, Retrieved 25 September 2017.

Sonja, V. and Cotula, L. (2014). 'Over the heads of local people: consultation, consent and recompense in large-scale land deals for biofuels projects in Africa'. Paper under review, Journal of Peasant Studies.

Southern Africa Resource Watch. (2016). Coal versus communities in Mozambique, Maputo: Mozambique.

Thondlana, G. (2016). *The Local Livelihood Implications of Biofuel Development and Land Acquisitions in Zimbabwe*, CIGI, Ontario, Canada.

Ugwu, E. and Tunde, R. (2012). *The Concept of Appropriate Technology*, Inez Publishers, Nigeria.

Vidal, J. (2008). *The great green land grab*, Jubilee Insurance Exchange, Nairobi.

World Bank. (2010). Government's Role in Attracting Viable Agricultural Investment: Experiences from Ghana, Washington DC, April 26 and 27, 2010.

World, Bank. (2011). *Large-scale Acquisition of Land Rights for Agricultural or Natural Resource-based Use*, World Bank, Washington DC.

Chapter 11

Manifestations of the Symptoms of Poverty in the Electoral Behaviour of Nigerian Political Actors

Johnson O. Olaniyi

Introduction

Electoral behaviour as an area of study in politics and behavioural psychology depicts the summation of the activities of political actors during any electoral process. Principal among these political actors are; the electorate who by tradition, have the constitutional responsibility to determine who amongst the candidates in an election will be their representative, contestants who are usually fielded by political parties or, independent candidates - where the constitution makes provision for such, and godfathers who sponsor candidates for elections. These three sets of political actors usually inter-relate during electoral processes in Nigeria.

Electoral process may begin with delimitation of constituencies (where necessary) by the Election Management Body (EMB) or voter registration; and in all cases, ends with litigations regarding disputed election results – as is the case of Kenya's 2017 presidential elections – or any other issue that touches on 'party primaries' (a type of election in which a political party conducts a shadow or an in-house election to determine its candidate in an election)political actors usually exhibit diverse behaviours in any electoral process. The behaviours are usually informed by some factors which serve as their stimuli. One of such factors is the prevailing socio-economic condition of a society which touches on the well-being of people. This can take two different forms; 'affluence' and 'poverty'. When people's needs are regularly met by the government or other categories of policy makers, the tendency for them is to be ever-ready to participate in political activities of which electoral behaviour is a sub-set. On the other hand, where the living standard of a group of constituents in an electoral district is abysmally poor, the tendency is for them to become apathetic towards electoral activities. What often precipitates this is the insensitivity of the ruling class to the plights and rights of citizens of such societies. What will be paramount to them is how to survive the hardship created by the poor socio-economic condition of the constituency. Consequently, they will become a prey to anybody who can find an answer to their plight. Therefore, voters more often than not usually resort to 'settlement' before they can participate in electoral activities, which ordinarily, is a civic responsibility. Similarly, a candidate who is not economically buoyant might be forced to turn to a 'godfather' or 'money bag' who, in turn, will sponsor him or her for an election. Meanwhile, a godfather who sponsors a candidate for election expects returns, especially economic benefit to further enrich himself/herself. All these will have a negative effect on the election outcome because at the end of the day, the best political party or candidate may not be the winner of the election. The foregoing shows that there is a synergy between poverty and election.

Nigeria is a developing State. Consequently, poverty, as with corruption, is prevalent in the country. Elections in the past have been marred by 'electoral corruption' by competing political parties, electoral officers, political party agents, 'civil society, mass media, godfathers, and even election observers. This chapter is however, interested in how the poverty status of political actors and candidates in Nigeria have had a negative effect on the electoral process of the country. Apart from this major objective, the specific objectives of the chapter include: i) to examine the elements of poverty vis-à-vis the electoral behaviours of political actors in Nigeria; ii) to examine how and why some political actors in Nigeria often exploit the poverty status of an average Nigerian to their advantage; and, iii) to examine the extent to which electoral laws and constitutions have addressed the menace of electoral corruption as they affect political actors during any electoral process in the country.

The research methodology adopted for the chapter is historical-cum -comparative, while a number of research questions also guided the study. A theory of voting behaviour, namely; 'the rational choice theory', otherwise called 'economic theory of rational choice' formed the theoretical framework. The theory explains why an average political actor (especially those whose economic status are poor) usually give paramount consideration to what he or she stands to gain from supporting a political party or candidate in any election. This has been the experience of Nigeria since the era of partisan politics which began in 1922. However, although the problem was not so pronounced then, it has since graduated to becoming a recurring decimal in the Nigeria's electoral process.

This chapter is divided into the following sections; introduction, conceptual clarifications, poverty and the electoral behaviour of Nigerian political actors, and conclusion.

Poverty in the Nigerian State

When 'poverty' is discussed in relation to the status of a State, what it means is that the country is poor or underdeveloped. A poverty-ridden State will lack basic things that can ordinarily make its citizenry have a sense of satisfaction in every situation. In the comity of nations, it will be looked down by its contemporaries because of its inability to meet its obligations for its subjects. The implication of all these is that, a poverty-ridden State will leave and survive at the mercy of other nations that are well to do. Therefore, what will be paramount to such a country will be how to feed its citizens, provide security for them, provide them social amenities, give them jobs and above all, keep the machineries of the State moving.

The foregoing was what informed the decision of some of the then newly independent African States in the late 1950s and early 1960s, to shift allegiance from their former colonial masters to some of their perceived enemies. For instance, Ghana under Dr. Kwame Nkrumah jilted Great Britain its former colonial master and romanced with the East, the old Union of Soviet Socialist Republic (USSR), which was commonly known to be an arch rival of Great Britain in the comity of nations. To an ordinary mind, Ghana was an ingrate but for Ghana it was a survival strategy in view of the gargantuan socio-economic problems it inherited from its former colonial master. This explains why it is often difficult to brand the actions or policies of a State irrational. The same thing applies to the electoral decision of an average voter. For instance, apparently justifying Ghana's change of alliance from the West (the traditional base of capitalism) to the East (the seat of Socialism) after the country's independence, Dr. Kwame Nkrumah, its First Prime Minister and later the First President, posited that the only answer to the underdeveloped status of the African continent is 'industrialisation'. He however believed that this could only be come about through 'Socialism'". Consequently, he argued that Africa will only be free of neo-colonial tendencies (when a State that has attained political independence still have its economy being controlled by foreign powers) only "when the united power of the producer countries is harnessed by common political and economic policies and has behind it the united financial resources of the States concerned" (Nkrumah, 1974: 11). What this position portends is public ownership, control and distribution of goods and services in a State. These are some of the attributes of socialism which Nkrumah could not get answer to from Great Britain.

The understanding of poverty as it affects individuals is that poverty-ridden individuals are poor. They cannot meet their statutory responsibilities and therefore live miserable lives. Different thoughts usually come to the minds of poor individuals. Such thoughts provide lead ways to solving their problems. The way out do take two forms; exploring legal ways to addressing the menace or in the extreme cases, adopting unconventional method to solving the problem, for example, 'electoral corruption'. A voter who has economic challenges before coming to the voting arena on the election day can easily fall prey to the unsolicited gratification coming from a candidate contesting the election or, any of his or her vendors.

Similarly, it explains why a candidate cannot meet his or her financial obligations during among electioneering period always turn to money bags' who will bank-roll their campaign expenses. The foregoing sets the stage for the conceptual clarification of poverty.

Borrowing a leaf from the position of Ijaiya (2012) as it is customary of all concepts in social sciences poverty does not lend itself to an encompassing definition. According to Ijaiya (Ibid: 26) "earlier studies on poverty linked the concept to a situation where an individual is confronted with low income or low consumption-expenditure which is often used for the construction of the poverty line". This effort only links the understanding of poverty to economy; rather scholars from a 'wide spectrum of social sciences' currently argue that its scope is wider than this and that concentrating on, or emphasising economic variables alone is tantamount to missing the dynamics of the problem. According to Bello (2006) the group posits that the economic variables must be taken together with a host of other social, political and cultural factors.

Scholars of political economy and economy argue that there are two basic types of poverty; 'absolute poverty' and 'relative poverty'. The examples of the scholars include; Meier (1978) Ijaiya (2012); Alimeka (2001) Hoffman and Graham (2009). In their own perspective, Hoffman and Graham (2009: 59) identify two forms of inequality which they equate with poverty. They are 'absolute inequality' and 'relative inequality'. According to Ijaiya (2012: 27), when poverty is seen from the point of absoluteness, the experience is that "the total earnings of individuals/ families are insufficient to obtain the minimum necessaries for the maintenance of merely physical efficiency". Hoffman and Graham (2009: 59) also explain "relative inequality as a situation in which some people are not having their needs satisfied".

On the other hand relative poverty explicitly relates poverty to a 'reference group'. According to Ijaiya (2012: 27) "rather than referring to a supposedly objective standard it links poverty to a particular point in the distribution curve of a particular variable such as income" therefore, "people are judged to be poor if they are poor in comparison to those around them". For instance, if in a street there are ten Duplex buildings and one three bedroom bungalow. The individual who owns the bungalow will be deemed a poor man. But this judgment may not be totally correct because in actual fact, he may be richer than one of the owners of the duplexes. Therefore, his choice of having a bungalow may be a matter of interest.

Kankwenda (cited in Alimeka, 2001: 4) in his own view, posits that "poverty is a State of deprivation or denial of the basic choices and opportunities needed to enjoy a decent standard of living, to live a long, healthy constructive life and to participate in the cultural life of the community". What can be inferred from the above position is that any poor individual is not a complete being. He or she faces natural discriminations in all facets of life. But again, the definition gives an insight into the basic elements of poverty. This is also seen in the position of Sen (1985) who posits that; to be poor is to be incapable of being healthy, having a good job, being safe, being happy and having self-respect.

Manifestations of the Symptoms of Poverty in Nigeria

Different scholars on poverty reviewed in this chapter have given insights into what can be commonly regarded as the elements of poverty in Nigeria. Such positions cover the perspectives of scholars that include; Hoffman and Graham (2009), Sen (1985); Atineka (2001); and Narayan et al (2000). Some of the scholars' views on the elements of poverty are reflected in their definitions of the term. It is however imperative to note that their views are in no way contradictory. Consequently, this chapter will highlight the elements or manifestations of poverty as presented by them and elaborate on the few of them that have bearing with electoral discourse. They include the following; lack of decent housing; inability of the children of people to receive a proper education (Hofman and Graham, 2009); incapability of being healthy, not having a good job, being safe (insecurity) being happy and having self-respect (Sen, 1985); being exposed to agonizing choices because they are powerless and voiceless, lack of protection against violence, extortion and intimidation, lack of civility and predictability in interactions with public officials (Narayan et al, 2000). Other manifestations of poverty identified by Alimeka (2001) not covered by the scholars cited earlier include; lack of income and productive resources sufficient to ensure sustainable livelihoods, hunger and malnutrition, lack of access to basic services, increased morbidity and mortality from illness, social discrimination and exclusion, and lack of participation in decision making, in civil, social and cultural life.

The above positions on the manifestations of poverty as presented by some scholars give an insight into the scope of-poverty. Going by their postulations, poverty is encompassing. It covers every facet of life. In fact it can be argued that the very moment an individual cannot proffer solutions to his/ her challenges in life, regardless of his economic, social or political status, he/ she is poor. It is however, imperative to reiterate that not all the manifestations have direct impact on the electoral process in a society but it can be posited that they all have indirect, effect on it thus serving as inhibiting –factors to the effective performance of political actors in electoral process.

Incapability of an individual to having a good job may limit his/her participation in future electoral activities in his constituency. This is because unemployment may make him or her not to be in position of saving towards participating in electoral contest in the nearest future. Similarly, when he/she is not economically buoyant, he or she stands the risk of being bought over by candidates or their vendors when he/she is about to take voting decision on the political party or candidate of his choice when he gets to the polling station on the election day.

Limited or lack of access to education also inhibits the participation of individuals in electoral activities and makes them not to be conscious of their rights and civic responsibilities. This exposes them to the risk of having their electoral decisions influenced by some interested political actors. Nigeria being a predominantly illiterate society (about 70 per cent of the population does not either have access to education or lack the ability to receive education due to the poverty status of their parents or guardians) (Osundairo, 2015) falls under the category of States where lack of access to education is having negative effect on their electoral process. For instance, many citizens of the country do not appreciate the need to participate in electoral activities. Consequently, they see electoral contest or voting as other people's affairs. Political elites usually exploit this loophole to their advantage.

Hunger and Malnutrition expose some electoral stakeholders to electoral corruption. An individual who is unable to feed himself stands the risk of becoming the surrogate of the person who can put food on his table. Some rich politicians in the country had used the strategy of feeding the poor people to colonise them during electoral activities. Their examples included late Alhaji Lamidi Adedibu of Ibadan (the State capital of Oyo State in Nigeria) and late Dr. Abubakar Olusola Saraki of Ilorin, Kwara State Nigeria. Alhaji

Adedibu's brand of politics was tagged; 'Amala brand of politics'. Amala is a staple food among the Yoruba people of South-West. Amala is made from yam flour. Adedibu used to prepare Amala dish for his supporters and because of this, they used to frequent his house so as to be fed by him. Governor Ayodele Fayose of Ekiti State Nigeria, brands the system of using food items to woo supporters; 'Stomach infrastructure'.

Insecurity or unsafe environment is a manifestation of poverty which also have direct bearing with electoral process in Nigeria. Ordinarily, it is the responsibility of the State to protect the lives and properties of its citizens. For instance, Section 17 of the 1999 Constitution of the Federal Republic of Nigeria (as amended) on 'Social Objectives' touches on the obligation of the State to providing adequate security for its citizenry. However, when it fails to do this, political actors may seek help elsewhere. This explains why they often resort to private security arrangements or protection from political thugs (Olaniyi, 2006). Only the well –to-do among them can afford this. Consequently, electorate and contestants may seek cover under them. This has negative effect on the political stability of the country.

Social discrimination and exclusion; and lack of participation in decision-making as manifestations of poverty have direct bearing on the electoral process of Nigeria. Decision-making in the public sector should aim at promoting public (national) interest. Furthermore, every section of the polity to be affected by a public policy should be carried along before arriving at a final decision. Therefore, the failure of the government of a State to involve the necessary stakeholders in the decision-making process portends poverty of action. And if the trend continues unabated, it may precipitate agitation or apathy. This will threaten the political stability of the country.

Electoral behaviour is a sub-set of political behaviour, an area of study in political science which is a by-product of post-second world war behavioural revolution in political science. Behavioural revolution in political science was championed by a group of American Political Scientists and it is all about making the study of politics, scientific. The pre-Second World War study of politics was normative in nature which borrowed a lot from the historical method of analysis, descriptive method (Varma, 1982).

Political behaviour grew from 'behaviouralism' (a method of research in politics which provides scientific explanations to political actions by following scientific procedures and by adopting analytic tools from other disciplines. The bedrock of behavioural science is to deduce regularities about human behaviour and on the basis of this makes predictions. This connotes the scientific understanding of the political actions of man. Consequently, Eulau (1969: 15) concurs that "the political behaviour of the individual person is the central and critical datum of behavioural approaches to politics". This position explains why some political scientists (for example, Butler, 1958; Harris, 1979; Stanyer, 1954; and Roberts and Edwards, 1991) posit that the central idea of political studies is political behaviour. Butler (1958) who is one of such proponents argues that:

> The study of political behaviour is not distinct from the study of politics nor is it a sub-division of the subject. It merely denotes a particular approach. An approach that is more interested in the character of those in politics instead of studying institutions or events (p. 6).

The foregoing shows that any study in politics that has link with behaviouralism connotes the study of politics. Based on this notion, electoral behaviour can be explained as a sub-set of political behaviour and indeed an area of study in political science, concerned with the study of the behaviour of man in an electoral dispensation (Olaniyi, 2014). It can also be explained as the study of the totality of the behavioural patterns of the political actors of any named constituency during an electioneering period. Such political actors might include; electorate, election personnel, contestants (candidates), political parties, the sponsor of candidates, and the milieu. Political analysts will be interested in studying how the action or inaction of any of the afore-mentioned categories of individuals or groups has affected election outcomes in an area at any point in time.

The following research questions will further guide our efforts in this chapter:

1. What effect does the poverty status of an average political actor in Nigeria have on the country's electoral process?

2. What are the symptoms /elements/ manifestations of poverty in the electoral activities of Nigerian political actors?

3. In what ways do the Nigerian constitution and electoral laws address poverty related issues amongst electoral stakeholders in the country?

Voting Behaviour in Nigeria

This chapter is anchored on 'the rational choice theory' otherwise called 'economic theory of rational choice'. Downs (1957) has the credit of relating the rational choice theory to the discourse on electoral activities. The thrust of the theory is that a voter will cast his or her vote for a political party or candidate that will serve his ends. Similarly, an electoral officer or election official; and even godfathers, will do the biddings of a candidate who can give him or her economic benefits in return.

Earlier in this chapter an attempt had been made to examine the symptoms/ elements of poverty. To arrive at the symptoms, a review of different positions of some scholars (although in different language of expression) about the features of poverty was made. Furthermore, it was submitted that the symptoms are true of developing nations; and Nigeria being one of them, is having these symptoms prevailing in every facet of life. The concern of this chapter is to examine how these symptoms had affected (and still affecting) the electoral behaviour of an average political actor in Nigeria during electoral dispensations. The methodology of analysis to be adopted here is to examine the activities of the political actors individually, vis-à-vis the elements of poverty in Nigeria's electoral process. These actors include; voters, candidates, godfathers and election officials. Their activities in relation to manifestations of the symptoms of poverty in Nigeria are as discussed below.

i. Voters /Electorate /Elector and Manifestations of Poverty in Nigeria

Chaturvedi (2006: 101) defines electorate "as those citizens who are entitled to cast their votes; in any election". This definition shows that not everyone in a polity may have voting right, rather a would be

294

voter must meet certain requirements often stipulated in the Constitution of a country and/ or its electoral laws.

Voters are perhaps the most significant political actor during electioneering exercise. What informs this position is the fact that they have the responsibility to commute the activities of other political actors to action by way of determining their representatives through voting in any election. Therefore, they can be regarded as the final 'bus stop' or terminus of electioneering. Apart from this they enjoy the advantage of being in the majority as compared to other political actors. Therefore in view of their importance in any electoral dispensation other electoral stakeholders always lobby them by campaigning to them either directly or through other platforms like mass media and internet facilities. On their part, they have the responsibility to subject the campaign promises of candidates and manifestoes of various political parties to scrutiny and on the basis of that cast their votes for the candidate or political party that meets their aspirations.

Voters have constitutional responsibility in any electoral dispensation. Their roles are accorded recognition in both the Nigerian Constitution and the Electoral Act. This further stresses their importance in any electioneering exercise. For instance, Section 39 (1) of the 1999 Constitution of the Federal Republic of Nigeria (as amended) provides that; "every person shall be entitled to freedom of expression, including freedom to hold opinions and to receive and impart ideas and information without interference". This provision covers the right which a voter has to decide on who will represent him or her at any level of decision-making process. The Electoral Act 2010 (as amended) explains in details the qualifications and role of electorate in the electoral dispensation in the country. Section 13 of the Electoral Act 2010 (as amended) stipulates the requirements which an individual must meet before he can be registered as a voter. Sections 24 and 25 address 'offences of buying and selling voters' cards' and 'offences relating to registration of voters', respectively.

Some sections of the Electoral Act also address electoral offences affecting voters. Their examples include; Section 117 on 'offences in relation to registration'; Section 120 on 'improper use of voter's cards'; and Section 122 on 'impersonation and voting when not qualified'. All the sections cited here emphasise the important role played by voters in any electoral dispensation. But of concern to us is; to what extent do they assert their importance in electioneering? Findings have revealed that some electors more often than not betray the high expectation which the law and society have on them. This they do by setting aside decorum while participating in electoral activities. What is paramount to some of them is the economic aspect of their participation, that is, what they stand to gain from the participation.

In view of the fact that an average Nigerian is not comfortable economically, they are ready to sell their 'birth right', in this case voting right, for a plate of porridge. Some political elites usually cash on this. For instance, as earlier posited in this chapter, politicians like late Alhaji Lamidi Adedibu of Ibadan (capital of Oyo State, Nigeria) and Late Dr. Abubakar Olusola of Ilorin (capital of Kwara State, Nigeria) cashed on the poverty status of the people of their States to mobilise them for the political private interest.

Until recently when the country now shifts to electronic voting through the introduction of 'Card Reader' for verification of Voters claims, the tradition that prevailed among the rank and file of some electors was for them to trade their voters' cards for money or other materials like; Wrist-watches, telephone cells, bags or rice, semovita or groundnut oil. This used to take place before or during elections. The practice was for the politicians, candidates or representatives of political to send out their vendors and meet the representatives of voters at the ward level and settle them. Therefore they care less about who wins an election. In fact 'party loyalty' or 'party identification does not matter to them. Rather, what matters to them most is their stomach. Although, the justification some of them usually provide is that elected representatives will forget them as soon as they assume office, this is nonetheless, an aberration. Consequently, political parties or candidates who have settled accredited voters would have a field day by tump-printing the ballot papers meant for the 'settled' electorate Transition Monitoring Group (TMG) (2003) an election observer identifies this as a problem of Nigeria's electoral process during 2003 general elections. However, the effect this has on the election outcome is that the best candidate may not be the winner when the election result is declared. Instead, the highest bidder carries the day.

ii. Candidate / Contestant and Manifestations of Poverty in Nigeria

According Chaturvedi (2006: 36) a candidate is "person who puts himself forward for election". In order to avoid criticism of the definition, because except in situations where the law permits 'independent candidates' to contest for public offices, no contestant can circumvent the important role played by political parties in putting candidates forward for elections, in liberal climes, he later added that "each political party nominates its candidates for elections"

The first hurdle that confronts an aspirant in any electoral process, is the one internally created by his/her political party. One of the sources of party finance is through money realised from the sales of 'Nomination Forms' or 'Expression of Interest Forms'. Since there is no law that regulates this, political parties usually milk aspirants by imposing heavy rates on them. This usually make those of them who are not well to do to either run to godfathers for sponsorship or have their hopes dashed due to non-availability of money to buy 'Nomination Forms'. This is rampant in Nigeria since many youths who are vibrant and who could have sought elective offices are unemployed. Electoral contest is therefore left to the already rich politicians who can afford any amount as Nomination Form Fee. This scenario explains why the Nigeria's Upper Chamber, Senate, has become a haven for former State Governors. Consequently, what is being experienced in Nigeria is 'circulation of elites' (a political theory that explains how the same sets of people are succeeding themselves in the government circle).

During the Presidential parties' primaries that preceded 2015 elections, the two major political parties in the country then (still relevant till now), Peoples Democratic Party (PDP), and All Progressives Congress (APC) imposed high nomination forms' fees on their aspirants. For instance, APC made her Presidential aspirants to pay N27.5 million (about $63,750) as 'expression of interest and nomination form fee'. This limited the number of aspirants who came forward to bid for the office. Only three Party members (Muhammad Buhari, Atiku Abubakar and Rabiu Kwankwaso) were able to make it. Even Muhammad Buhari (now the President of the country) who made it claims that he had to take loan in order to make it. This claim irked some commentators. For instance, a human rights lawyer in the country, Femi Falana (Senior Advocate of Nigeria-SAN) in his reaction to the claim of Buhari posits; "is he going to obtain another loan during his campaign, because in Nigeria, it costs billions of Naira to run a presidential campaign?" (Femi Falana SAN, while speaking at the Nigeria Union of Journalists, Paramount FM chapel press week, The Punch, October 24, 2014: 12).

The foregoing gives an insight into why aspirants are not always many or not available at all, during party primaries. A case in point was a less popular party in the country, United Progressive Party (UPP) which originally zoned its Presidential ticket to South-West geopolitical zone and made its nomination form N15 million (about $37,500). No aspirant came forward from South-West. The party had to jettison its zoning arrangement before an aspirant, Chekwas Okorie, from South-East geopolitical zone emerged as the party's flag-bearer in the 2015 Presidential election. Again, it can be posited that what scared aspirants away was their poor economic status but on the other hand, it can be argued that it might be the unpopularity of the party in the country.

Candidates of political parties for elections usually emerge through the process of 'Party Primaries' (a type of an in-house election in which accredited members of a political party vote for the candidates to be fielded for an election). This is where the commitment of financial resources to an election begins. Those to vote in the in-house election are representatives of the various wards in a constituency. In Nigeria, experiences have revealed that party members always lobby party officials or their ward members to be picked as one of those delegates to the 'party primaries'. What is responsible for this is their desire to make money out of the exercise. For an aspirant to win 'the election', he must be prepared to settle the delegates. In fact, the vendors of contestants usually bargain with delegates and part with huge sums of money. More often than not they also make provisions for their accommodation and feeding of the delegates.

In view of the 'expensive' nature of party primaries, 'capable' aspirants who are poor may not have their ways. For instance, during the last All Progressives Congress' party primaries that produced the gubernatorial candidate of the party in 2016 in Ondo State, it was widely reported that monies changed hands. Snap-shots of vendors distributing money to delegates on behalf of an aspirant were made and circulated. It was reported that one of the candidates had the expenses bank-rolled for him by a reputable party member. The danger inherent in this is that he will become the stooge of his sponsor when he assumes office.

The financial commitment of a candidate does not terminate with winning party's ticket but becomes gargantuan during electioneering campaigns. Although it is possible for a buoyant political party to fund part of the election campaign expenses of its candidate, more often than not he or she carries a greater burden. The Nigerian Electoral Law recognises this though not helping the situation) when it pegs the campaign expenses of candidates into various public offices. Section 93 of the Electoral Act 2010 (as amended) on 'Limitations on Election expenses' provides as follows; the maximum of election expenses shall be;

  i.   Presidential election (N500,000,000) (about $1.2 billion)
  ii. Governorship election (N100,000,000) (about $250,000)
  iii. Senatorial election (N20,000,000) (about $50,000)
  iv. House of Representatives (N10,000,000) (about $25,000)
  v.   State Assembly (N5,000,000) (about &12,500)
  vi. Chairmanship   of   Local   Government   Area (N5,000,000)(about $12,500)
  vii. Councillorship Election (N500,000) (about $1,250) (Federal Republic of Nigeria, 2010).

The above election campaign expenses though described as the maximum by the Act are not feasible. In fact they can be described as mere templates because one, candidates and political parties usually spend unquantifiable amount on electioneering campaigns. Second, the amounts can no longer stand the test of time caused by the economic melt-down in the country. In fact political parties usually organise fund-raising for their presidential candidates and what they usually realise are always far above the limit set by the law. The same thing is true of what is usually realised from sales of nomination forms. For instance, from the sales of forms alone, it was reported that PDP realised about N3 billion (about $7.5 million) which is in multiples of the maximum campaign expenses set by law for presidential candidates (The Punch, November 5, 2014: 1-2).

From the above case studies, it is glaring that a fresh university graduate or a low income earner cannot contest election on his own volition. Even, the gratuity to be paid to a Director in a Federal Ministry who retires from public service after thirty-five years (the maximum number of years a government employee can spend in service in Nigeria) is not enough to contest for election into House of Representatives. This shows that the plight of a School Certificate holder (the minimum educational qualification set by Section 65 (2) (a) of the 1999 Constitution of the Federal Republic of Nigeria as amended) is even worse. Therefore, before a determined aspirant can bribe his way through, he or she must enjoy the sponsorship of a money bag. Consequently, it can be posited that the system is also adding to the already prevalent problem.

iii. Godfathers and Manifestations of Poverty in Nigeria
Unlike voters and candidates majority of who have economic challenges that often propel them to seek help from well-to-do individuals for the sponsorship of electoral contests, godfathers can be described as rich individuals in the society who sponsor some candidates for elective offices in a State. Apart from money, they also make available material resources to them. But the question that arises is, do they render such 'assistance' without an undertone? The answer to this will be addressed after explaining whoa godfather is from the perspectives of some scholars. However, it needs be reiterated that it is always the poverty status of candidates that usually drag them to godfathers.

According to Anakwense (2004) the concept of 'godfatherism' has its origin in Christianity. In the religion (Catholic denomination in particular) 'godparents' are chosen as surrogates to help biological

300

(or adopted) parents raise a Christian child to become a God-fearing, law-abiding adult. He goes further to add that the meaning of godfather has been twisted in the modern age because members of organised climes, politicians and powerbrokers now use the term, 'godfather', to refer to their relationships with subordinates. He states further that the main difference between the godfather as in the Christian faith and godfather as it is known today is that "the former provides counselling and guidance that benefits the godchild, whereas the latter views himself /herself as the beneficiary, and gives favour only when he feels that it advances his selfish interests and ideology; political, economic, or otherwise" (Anakwense, 2004: http://www.kwene.com/ lectures/anakwenze_godfatherism.htm). This is the prevailing guiding principle of godson-godfather relationship currently in Nigeria.

The idea of godfatherism in politics stems from power configuration in which there is political power inter-play between two groups with each group struggling to have an upper hand on the other so as to be in position of controlling the resources in a society. This informs the position of Omotola (2007: 135) who posits that; "godfathers are those who have the security connections, extended local links, enormous financial weight, and so on, to plot and determine the success or otherwise of a power seeker at any level of a supposedly competitive politics". He added that "the complex processes of doing this from 'womb to womb' is famously known as godfatherism".

Tobechukwu (2008) in his own view posits that godfatherism is a lingering factor in the Nigerian political scene. He thereafter describes it as politics of sponsorship to political positions, control of political power, political patronage and the ultimate control of state treasury, personnel and resources.

The interests of godfathers are usually political and economic. For example, Ogbonwan (2007) and Nnamani (2003) capture this in their positions. Ogbonmwan (2007) in his submission posits that:

The modus operandi of the Nigerian godfather is clear even to the blind. The godfather or the godson occupies an exalted position in government, rather than spending the available fund to establish a factory or set up a process that will employ youths like school leavers and university graduates, the money is diverted to Swiss or other European or American banks. School leavers and University graduates are therefore made jobless and provide fertile ground for recruiting foot soldiers that will do the evil bidding of these godfathers (p. 5).

Ogbonmwan (2007) concludes his argument by asserting that "godfatherism is an evil building block for corruption, retrogression underdevelopment, mediocrity, backwardness and perpetual poverty of the people" (p. 5).

In his own view, Nnamani (2003: 20) posits that; "the overriding essence of godfatherism in Nigeria consists in mercantilism, clientelism and prenbendalism". According to him, poverty often drives people to seek for sponsorship of a protégé during elections. This is because the cost of putting a government in power in Nigeria is usually enormous, often times beyond the resources of the individual power seeker thereby making him to lean on certain individuals who are ready to finance and pay for the mobilisation of electorate. Nnamani (2007: 10) added that the few who can finance the emergence of government "usually constitute themselves to monopolists of the values of the outcomes of governance".

Nnamani (2007: 10-11) considers the effect of poverty on the electoral behaviour in two main dimensions; 'psychological' and 'physical'. According to him, the 'psychological dimension' is rooted in the poverty of awareness which fore closes the ability of the poor citizens to appreciate the dangers inherent in the abdication of civic responsibilities as they often engaged in. This lack of awareness also provides the root for reservation on relationship with government. They see government as an enterprise of elite. The 'physical dimension', Nnamani posits, consists of the capital short-fall in the access to the means of adequate livelihood which impairs their energy to take an active part in the making and substances of government.

The idea of godfatherism is not new to Nigerian politics. The likes of Dr. Nnamadi Azikwe, Chief Obafemi Awolowo, Sir. Ahmadu Bello, Joseph Tarka, Ibrahim Waziri, Michael Okpara and Denis Osadebe were known to be godfathers in the colonial days and First Republic. They assisted in raising godsons who assisted in their nationalist struggle most of who later occupied positions of authority

302

in the country's post-independence period. What however, marks them out from the contemporary godfathers in the country is that they were not after monetary and/ or financial benefits. Anakwenze (2004) posits that the godfathers then "put the interests of their people before personal gain" (p. 7). He concludes that godfatherism is then seen as "a positive practice that benefits the godchildren and the larger society" (p. 7). Perhaps, the only publicised fall-out between a godfather and godson in the First Republic was the internal crisis that rocked the founder and leader of Action Group (AG) Chief Obafemi Awolowo and his deputy Chief S.L. Akintola caused by the failure of the latte to take directive from the later. The same cannot be said of the experience of the people of the country in the Second Republic (1979-1983) when there were records of crises among godfathers and godsons in some States. A case in point was the fall-out between the then Governor of Ondo State, Chief Adekunle Ajasin and his godson who was his deputy, Chief Akin Omoboriowo. The unresolved crisis led to Omoboriowo dumping Unity Party of Nigeria (UPN). He later contested the 1983 governorship election in the State against his boss under the platform of National Party of Nigeria. Furthermore, the failure of Mallam Balarabe Musa the then governor of Kaduna State, who was a godson of Mallam Aminu Kano, the founder and leader of Peoples Redemption Party (PRP) generated unresolved internal wrangling between the duo the end-result of which was the impeachment of Mallam Balarabe Musa as the governor of Kaduna State in 1981. What led to the crisis between the godfather and godson was that after riding on the popularity of Mallam Aminu Kano to become a governor, Balarabe Musa refused to be teleguided by his boss.

In the Fourth Nigeria's Republic, one issue that has been charactering political /electoral issues since 1999 when the Republic came on board is godfather-godson political inter-play. This cuts across political parties and states of the Federation. This is however, not unconnected with the expensive nature of politicking in Nigeria earlier addressed in this chapter. Records of crises between godfathers and godson abound in the Republic.

Examples of catalogue of godfathers-godsons in the Fourth Republic are numerous. They include Chris Uba versus Chris Ngige;

Chris Uba Versus Chinwoke Mbadinuju (Anambra State); Mallar Kachalla versus Ali Modu Sheriff (Borno State). Jim Nwobodo versus Chimaroke Nnamani (Enugu State) Ganiyu Dawodu versus Ahmed Bola Tinubu, Ahmed Bola Tinubu versus Batatunde Raji Fahsola (Lagos State). Dr. Olusola Abubakar Saraki Versus Mohammed Alabi Lawal; Dr. Olusola Abubakar Saraki versus Olubukola Abubakar Saraki (Kwara); Rabiu Kwankwaso Versus Abdullahi Umar Ganduje (Kano State) and Godwin Akpabio versus Udom Emmanuel (Akwa Ibom State). In fact, experiences have revealed that there is hardly any State Governor in Nigeria who did not get to power through a godfather. Getting to power, most of them usually assert their authority by turning their backs against their sponsors. This is because as Nnamani (2003) observes, although "the deciding terms of paymaster (Godfather) (bracket mine) is always high" but poverty and lust for power will make a power seeker to enter into an agreement with the client (godson) (bracket mine). Gboyega (2004: 11) similarly notes that "when a godfather provides the financial resources for, a candidate to win an election he will have high expectations that the governor (that is the godson) would deliver some benefit to him". According to him, such benefits could be:

1. The right to choose some or a majority of the people in the cabinet and;

2. to have the final words on contracts.

Gboyega (2004) however, notes that when the candidate provides the financial resources to the godfather (which happens rarely) to ensure that he won the party primaries; "then he would be entitled to assume that he paid his way to walk into power and therefore he has no overriding obligations to defer to the godfather"(Gboyege, 2004: 11).Whichever way, Gboyega opines that; "it is anomalous for governmental powers to be wielded by a man who is not directly accountable to the public".

Breach of agreements between godfathers and godsons had precipitated crises in the past between the duo. The first of such crises was recorded between a former Governor of Anambra State, Dr. Chris Ngige, and his godfather, Chris Uba in 2003. It was alleged that before Chris Uba could agree to sponsor Ngige, the duo took oath at 'Okija Shrine' (the Shrine of an oracle in Okija town, Anambra State). This bordered on the amount Dr. Chris Ngige, would be remitting to Chris Uba, monthly. The crisis reached its peak on July 10, 2003 when Ngige a serving Governor was abducted by a team of policemen led by an Assistant Inspector-General of Police Mr. Raphael Ige (Okereke, 2009). Chris Uba later swore an affidavit in an Enugu High Court that the election was rigged in favour of Ngige. It was the crisis that led to the removal of Ngige as the Governor of Anambra State in 2004.

Another case that can be cited was Dr. Olusola Abubakar Saraki versus Muhammed Alabi Lawal, a onetime Governor of Kwara State. Lawal, a retired Naval Admiral in the Nigerian Navy with little or no political experience had to ride on the popularity of Dr. Saraki to win the 1999 governorship election but the duo fell-out shortly after Lawal became the Governor of Kwara State. The unresolved crisis however, cost Lawal second term as he lost to the son of his godfather Dr. Olubukola Saraki, who contested the 2003 election under the platform of another party, PDP. Furthermore, currently, there is a face-off between the immediate past Governor of Kano State, the godfather; and his successor in office, his godson, Abdullahi Umar Ganduje, whom he sponsored for the 2015 governorship election. The cause of their misunderstanding borders on how to share the spoils office and issues relating to award of contracts in the State by the godson.

In all the cases bordering on godfathers –godsons crisis in Nigeria, Nnamani (2003) noted that ignorance and poverty are responsible for the high incidence of godfatherism in Africa. He however, later noted that "when the godson attempts to satisfy the godfather, the interest of the larger society is savagely undermined" (Nnamani, 2003: 11). In apparent defence of godsons, Nnamani posits that availability of limited resources may force the godson not to meet some of the demands of the godfather. When this happens, the godfather will remind the godson of the earlier agreement as was the case between Chris Uba and Dr. Chris Ngige of Anambra State in 2003. When the godson fails, Nnamani noted, the godfather exercises his 'pound of flesh' or 'power of influence' by precipitating crisis. In all these, it is the common man who bears the brunt.

Election Officials/ Election Managers and Manifestations of Poverty in Nigeria

Election officials are the employees of an Election Management Body (EMB) who are saddled with the responsibility of organising and conducting elections in a State at any point in time. This explanation shows that the employees of an EMB who are desk officers but who are in no way engaged in the actual management of election are not election officials but administrative or clerical staff.

Election officials also include ad hoc Electoral officers who are usually recruited by a country's EMB for the purpose of conducting election and laid-off, as soon as the election is concluded.

In Nigeria, election personnel include; Presiding Officer (PO), Poll Clerk (PC), Poll Assistant (PA), Supervisory Presiding Officer (SPO), Electoral Officers (EO), Resident Electoral Commissioner (REC), and Poll Orderlies (INEC, 2003). The election officials have their duties in the electoral process clearly defined in the manual for election officials. The manual also defines the ethics of election officials. It states that the electoral process is to be undertaken in a transparent manner. Therefore, election officials must:

(a) Be transparent and neutral;

(b) exhibit a high level of integrity;

(c) respect the secrecy of the vote; and

(d) conduct their duties according to the law and INEC guidelines (INEC, 2003: 5).

In view of the important role performed by election officials in any electoral process the Electoral Act 2010 (as amended) also addresses the issue of persons qualified from acting as election officials. Section 152 of the Act provides that:

No person holding an elective office to which this Act relates or a registered member of a political party shall be eligible for or be appointed to carry out the duties of a returning officers, an electoral officer, presiding officer or a poll clerk; and any officer appointed to carry out any of those duties shall be ineligible for nomination as a candidate for election while he continues to hold any such appointment (p.71).

In order to be sure that election officers are not in any way engaged in any form of electoral (electoral) malpractice, the Electoral Act 2010 further makes them to subscribe to "Oath /Affirmation of Neutrality' in which they will pledge to perform their duties strictly in line with the constitution of the Federal Republic of Nigeria, the Electoral Act and guidelines issued by the INEC. They will also pledge to be neutral to political parties and candidates and not to be allowed to be influenced by whatever means. Section 117 of the Electoral Act 2010 (as amended) also stipulates electoral offences which concern different categories of electoral stakeholders, election officials inclusive.

Furthermore, in its report on the 2003 General Elections in Nigeria, Transition Monitoring Group (TMG) which was one of the Election observers that monitored the elections identified a number fraudulent election practices' perpetrated by different categories of electoral stakeholders then. Those that concerned election officials /electoral officers are of interest to us. They include the following:

i. corrupt inducement of electoral officials;

ii. depriving the electorate of voting opportunities to opposition /opponents and their supports through inadequate supply of voting materials, delay in commencing voting and early termination of voting at polling centres located in opponents stronghold; and

iii. falsification of election results (TMG, 2003: 108).

The above observed election frauds perpetrated by some election officials during the 2003 general elections reported by TMG (2003) could not have been perpetrated because the beneficiaries enjoyed the good will of the perpetrators. Rather they (election officials) must have acted on inducement. This position is anchored on the belief that it would be fool-hardy for an individual to stake his job and reputation without anything substantial in return. Instead experiences have revealed that political parties usually vote huge sums of money for the settlement of election officials in Nigeria any time electoral dispensation is on course. There have been expositions in the ongoing trial of the former Chief Security Adviser to ex-President Goodluck Ebele Jonathan, Colonel Sambo Dasunki (rtd.) over

$2.2bn security vote scam. About N450 million (about $1.12 million) was voted to the each state chapter of the PDP part of which was used to settle Independent National Electoral Commission (INEC) personnel of the state. Consequently, majority of them betrayed the 'Oath /Affirmation of Neutrality'. They took from onset not minding the fact that the system took adequate care of them while performing their statutory responsibilities.

While performing their duties, election officials are usually paid allowances these include the regular staff of an EMB who are engaged in the election management. But more often than not there are always reported cases of electoral corruption affecting them during the performance of their sacred duty. Such cases include; diversion of registration or voting materials in exchange of money, manipulation of election results after receiving bribes from candidates or political parties; deliberate late arrival of voting materials at voting centres, and posting of electoral officers in a way to facilitate election outcomes/ results. In all cases, money or valuable materials always change hands between some election officials/ electoral officers and political parties or candidates. The concern which this raises is why despite the fact that they are paid good allowances for conducting any election they are still engaging in unwholesome acts? The reply to this concern centres on their poor mindset and the desire to find solutions to their economic problems. They therefore betray the confidence other electoral stakeholders have in them on their ability to organize and conduct elections that will be devoid of sentiments. Few of their involvement in electoral corruption will be cited here.

In its post-2003 General Elections' reports, TMG (2003) gave accounts of incidents of election frauds that affected some election officers across the nation. Few of them include that;

1. In Imo State some election officials colluded with agents of one of the political parties and took ballot boxes to Owerri Plaza Hotel where they were stuffed with already thumb-printed ballot papers. The same thing was observed in Taraba State

2. At Eziama Autonomous Community in Ngo Okpala Local Government Area of Imo State, the INEC supervisor carted away

the materials for elections and took them to somebody's house with the result that election did not take place in the community (TMG, 2003: 121).

Apart from the report of TMG (2003) on the elections of 2003, similar incidents characterised the General Elections of 2007, 2011 and 2015. For instance, prior to the conduct of the 2015 General Elections, it was reported on November 11, 2014 during the distribution of Permanent Voters Card (PVC) by election officials, that 4,658 voter cards were stolen in Edo State. The incident was made public by the Resident Electoral Commissioner (REC) (the head of a State INEC office) for Edo State, Mr. Baritor Kpagih (Okere, 2014: 20). It is our submission that such an electoral fraud of the highest (because it may disenfranchise the affected registered voters who are the owners of the card stolen) could not have materialised without the connivance of the election official designated to distribute the PVCs to their accredited owners. Money or material items must have changed hands between perhaps, a member of an opposition or less popular party in the area and an election official as a way of watering down the chance of a leading political party winning election in the area. Worst still, when the affected election official is arrested by the police, politician(s) whose bidding he has carried out know(s) how to free him or her. At any rate, the compromised election official must have staked his job and most importantly, reputation because of his/her poverty status or mindset.

The most orchestrated and publicised electoral fraud in the Fourth Republic that affected some election officials so far, occurred during the December 2016 by-election held in Rivers State to elect Senators that would represent the State in the Senate. The bye-election was held because of the annulment of the previous one held in May 2015 by the Supreme Court. At the end of the poll, PDP, (the ruling party in the State) captured two (2) seats while APC which is the main opposition party in the State won one (1) seat. Owing to allegation of bribery and corruption that characterised the election, the Inspector-General of Police, Idris Mohammed, constituted an investigating panel in January 2017. The Panel submitted its report to the Inspector-General of Police on February 7, 2017. The report revealed that the Panel recovered N111.3 million (about $278,250) from twenty-three (23) officials of INEC who participated in the Senatorial election. The report further revealed that the Rivers State Government spent N360million on election officials to 'rig'- the elections. This claim was attributed to the affected personnel. The allegation was however denied by the River State Government, which instantly described it as "being politically motivated" and described the Nigeria Police Force as "an extension of the APC"- the political party currently in power at the centre in Nigeria (The Punch, February 8, 2017: 1-2). Although commenting on the matter is tantamount to being prejudicial, since it has become Court litigation because the twenty-three election officials had been arraigned in Court by one of the country's anti-graft agencies, the Economic Financial Crime Commission (EFCC) the scenario can still be assessed on its merit. The controversial monies were displayed in the full glare of mass media and later tendered in Court as evidence. The election officials can also be taken up on their public confessional statement- that they received bribe. For them to have admitted and confessed that they took bribe from 'State officials portray them as individuals who want to elevate their economic statuses to higher levels. Therefore, they were poor in thought and action. If they were to be comfortable in thought, they would have not resorted to an embarrassing action.

Conclusion

This chapter has addressed the manifestations of the symptoms of poverty in the activities of Nigeria's political actors during political executions. It starts with introduction, then conceptual clarifications followed by an analysis of how the symptoms of poverty reflect in the activities of political actors in Nigeria which was discussed in relation to how electorate (voter) candidate godfathers and election officials fare during electoral processes. The methodology of analysis adopted was historical cum comparative methods while a number of research questions which guided the study were raised.

The conclusion of the chapter has given insight into the following:

1. The elements or symptoms of poverty are prevalent in Nigeria's electoral process. This usually makes electoral stakeholders, voters, candidates, godfathers and election officials in particular to get enmeshed in fraudulent acts.

2. Political actors usually exploit the poverty status of Nigerians to their advantage during electoral processes. It was revealed that they always capitalise on their financial needs, hunger and illiterate mind-sets to impose their electoral wishes on them.

3. Although provisions are enshrined in the Nigerian constitution and Electoral Act in particular to address electoral corruption, they have not been made functional. For instance, it is on rare occasions election officials who betray their Oath /Affirmation of neutrality are brought to book by the appropriate authorities

4. The high cost of 'Nomination forms' or 'Expression of Interest Forms' for would-be candidates who are of low economic status in the society usually make them to shop for well-to-do individuals who can bank-roll their election expenses.

In order to reduce the incidence of electoral corruption in Nigeria caused by the poverty status of an average citizen of the country, the study recommends that;

i. Political executives and other categories of policy makers in Nigeria should address the problem of the well- being of the poor masses of the country through pragmatic economic programmes that can reduce the gap between the classes of the 'rich' and 'poor'. The current monetary policy of the country where a dollar exchanges for about N400 is to say the least, abnormal. Therefore in order to bridge the gap between the well to do citizens and the rich individuals, the economic policy of the country should be taken to the 'economic laboratory' for necessary therapy.

ii. The Federal Government of Nigeria should make the welfare of election officials a topmost priority before and during elections. There should be a difference between their welfare packages and other public servants in the country. They should be paid 'special salaries' just like Judges and Medical Doctors who render essential services. This will go a long way to reduce the incidence of corruption among them. Towards this end, INEC should be granted financial autonomy and its funds charged to the consolidated fund as contained in the Section 3 of the Electoral Act 2010 (As amended) on the establishment of the Independent National Electoral Commission Fund.

iii. Candidates in elections should be made not to depend on godfathers before they can get their parties' tickets and win elections. To strengthen this recommendation, political parties should desist from imposing high fees on 'Nomination Forms' or 'Expression of Interest Forms'. This should be addressed by the country's Electoral Act by pegging nomination forms' fees just like the way campaign expenses were pegged by it'. Again, in order to reduce the high cost involved in open campaigns, candidates and political parties alike should utilize the advantage of electronic media through which they can reach people cheaply.

iv. 'Godfathers' should play their role in mentoring and advisory capacities as was done by the godfathers of the First Nigeria's Republic. The current 'warlord-clientele' relationship that exists between a godson and godfather is antithetical to democratic norms.

References

Alimeka, C. (2013). Poverty, Social exclusion and social dislocation in Nigeria'. *Paper Presented at the National Conference on Law and Poverty in Nigeria*, Kaduna: Nigeria.

Anakwense, N. (2004). 'Kwenu! Our Culture, our future: Godfatherism'. A paper presented on behalf of Enyimba N.A; a pan-Igbo think tank, during the Convention of Anambra State Association USA, Oklahoma, October 31. http://www.kwenu.com/lectures/anakwenze_godfatherism.ht m. Retrieved on 3/4 /2008.

Bello, M.L. (2006). 'Reflections on Poverty-Reduction Strategies'. In Saliu, H.A; Ogunsanya, A.A, Olujide, J. O. And Olaniyi, J. O. (Eds.) Democracy and development in Nigeria, Volume 2:

Economic and environmental issues. Lagos: Concept Publications Limited. 86-106.

Butler, D. E. (1958). *The Study of Political behaviour*, Hutchinson.

Chaturvedi, A. K. (2006). *Dictionary of Political Science*, New Delhi: Academic (India) Publishers.

Downs, A. (1957). An economic theory of democracy, New York: Harper and Row.

Dudley, B. J. (1982). *Introduction to Government and politics*, London: Macmillan.

Eulau, H. (1969). *Micro-Macro Political analysis*. Chicago: Aldine Publishing Company.

Federal Republic of Nigeria. (2010). 'Electoral Act 2010'. Lagos: 'The Federal Government Printer.

Federal Republic of Nigeria. (2011). Amended Constitution of the Federal Republic of Nigeria Abuja: National Assembly.

Gboyega, A. (2004). 'Godfatherism in politics will son die'. Sunday Punch, August 8: 11.

Harris, P.B. (1979). Foundations of Political Science.

Hoffman, J. and Graham, P. (2009). *Introduction to Political theory*, Harlow: Pearson Longman Education Limited.

Ijaiya, G. T. (2012). 'Poverty and development Survey'. In Bandara, H.M. (Ed.) *Issues in development*, Pannipitoya: Stamford Lake (pvt) Ltd. 24-50.

Independent National Electoral Commission (INEC) (2003). 'Manual for election officials'. Abuja: INEC.

Meier, G. M. (1978). *Leading Issues in economic development*, New York: Oxford University Press.

Narayan, D., Chambers, R., Shah, M.K. and Petesch, P. (2000). Voices of the Poor: Crying out for change. New York: Oxford University Press.

Nkrumah, K. (1974). *Neo-Colonialism: The last Stage of imperialism*, London: Panaf Books Ltd.

Nnamani, C. (2003). 'The godfather phenomenon in democratic Nigeria: Idea, Silicon or Real?' 2003 Edition of Pre-Inaugural /Transition Lecture Series of the Source Magazine, Lagos and Udi Hill (centre for Public Affairs and Research Development),

Enugu, at the Nigerian Institute for International Affairs, Lagos, Nigeria, May, 20.

Ogbonmwan, S. (2007). 'The Nigerian Political godfather: Edo State as a case study'. http://www.dawodu.com/ogbonmwan1.htm.Retrieved on 3/4/2008.

Okere, A. (2014). '4 658 Voter Cards Stolen in Edo. The Punch, November 12: 20.

Okereke, C. N. (2009). 'Between Corruption and integrity: An appraisal of judicial activism in democratic consolidation in Nigeria (1999-2004). In Jega, A.M. Wakili, H. and Zango, I.M. (Eds). *Consolidation of democracy in Nigeria: Challenges and Prospects,* Kano: Aminu Kano Centre for Democratic Research and Training: 140-141.

Olaniyi, J. O. (2006). 'Political thuggery and electoral context in Nigeria; Implications for democratisation process and political development'. The Resurging India *(Journal of Polities and Development)* Volume III No. 2, July; 85-105.

Olaniyi, J. O. (2014). 'Theories of Voting behaviour: An appraisal of their relevance to Nigerian experience, *Dutse International Journal of Humanities and Social Sciences,* Vol. 1.

Omotola, J. S. (2007). 'Godfathers and the 2007 Nigerian elections', *Journal of African Elections,* Volume 6 No.2: 134-154.

Osundairo, G. (2015). *Developmental Stages in Nigeria's educational system,* Lagos: Citadel publishing House.

Sen, A. (1985). *Commodities and Capabilities,* Amsterdam: North Holland.

The Punch, February 8, 2017: 1-2.

The Punch, October 24, 2014: 12

Tobechukwu, E.N. (2008). 'The Nigerian Press coverage of political conflicts in a pluralistic society'. Maindiy2k 2000@yahoo.com. Retrieved on 3/4/2008.

Transition Monitoring Group (TMG) *(2003). Do the Votes Count? Final report of the 2003 General Elections in Nigeria,* Lagos: Transition Monitoring Group.

Varma, S.P. (1982). *Modern Political Theory,* New Delhi: Vikas Publishing House, PVI Ltd.

Chapter 12

Witchcraft, Development and Politicking: The Zimbabwe African National Union Patriotic Front (ZANU-PF) Power Struggles and their Poverty Implications in Zimbabwe

Fidelis Peter Thomas Duri

Introduction

Witchcraft is a belief in the use of magic and charms or any other substances such as toxins to cause illness, injury, disability, death or other misfortunes to a person while privileging the perpetrator with fortunes such as wealth (Daneel, 1971; Chavunduka, 1980; Golooba-Mutebi, 2005; Mawere, 2011). Evans-Pritchard (1937), a British anthropologist, distinguished between 'witchcraft' and 'sorcery' by their technique. He defined the former as the innate, inherited ability to cause misfortune or death. To many pre-colonial African societies, witchcraft involved the unconscious use of magical and psychic powers. By contrast, sorcery is largely viewed as the performance of rituals, the uttering of spells, and the manipulation of organic substances such as herbs, with the conscious intent of causing harm. Unlike in the case of witchcraft, as Evans-Pritchard (1937) notes, a person can learn to practise sorcery. Thus, a witch is "born into his/her position and harms by means of psychic powers" while a sorcerer is "not born into his/her position and uses material substances such as medicines and charms" (Ball, 1994: 6). In this case, what 'modern' science regards as 'poisoning' is in actual fact 'sorcery' in the indigenous African sense. In this chapter, the term 'witch' is used in the broader sense to refer to sorcerers, witches and wizards. This is because, in most African societies, there is no clear distinction between witchcraft and sorcery since they are both viewed as representations of evil, and their operations overlap (Bourdillon, 1998; Chireshe, Chireshe and Shumba, 2012; Tatira, 2014).

Despite being an age-old tradition, many witchcraft beliefs have survived counter influences from developments such as westernisation, urbanisation and globalisation. In fact, witchcraft discourses continue to shape various aspects of life in contemporary Africa and many other parts of the world. This chapter explores the struggles for power and counter-productive wrangles within the Zimbabwe African Union Patriotic Front (ZANU-PF), a party that dominated Zimbabwe's political landscape since independence in 1980 under the leadership of Robert Mugabe, paying particular attention to the trading of witchcraft accusations by rivals in an effort to discredit each other and monopolise political space. It argues that, far from being an institution of rural Africa's past, witchcraft beliefs, particularly witchcraft accusations, are sometimes instrumentalised as a transformative dynamic in contemporary political contestations, much to the detriment of socio-economic development.

Most importantly, this chapter contends that power struggles constitute one of the major causes of poverty and underdevelopment in contemporary Zimbabwe for a number of reasons. They divert the attention of the ruling elite towards political survival instead of addressing the urgent socio-economic needs of the majority of Zimbabweans. Much of the time, energy and resources at the disposal of the ruling elites, which could have been utilised in developing the country and improving the living standards of many ordinary citizens, is devoted to political feuds. Political squabbles and related witchcraft allegations create societal tension and bring about an environment that is not conducive for development. It should be added that witchcraft accusations are difficult to prove and are tantamount to scapegoating. Instead, the ruling elites should be more practical in diagnosing the root causes of the major socio-economic challenges experienced by their people and come up with viable solutions of alleviating them. It is also cogent to note that witchcraft allegations, whether real or imagined, psychologically affect both the accused and the 'bewitched' resulting in them not contributing meaningfully towards their own development and that of the community at large. It is, however, not within the scope of this chapter to establish the authenticity of witchcraft as an institution but to examine its implications on development.

Ironically, the power struggles and related witchcraft accusations within the ruling ZANU-PF party have been taking place in dire times when the country desperately needs urgent interventions to mitigate the severe socio-economic crisis that has eroded the livelihoods of the majority of the population, especially from the onset of the new millennium. The crisis was sparked off in the year 2000 when the ZANU-PF government sanctioned the invasion of commercial farms, mostly white-owned, with the intention of redistributing them to landless indigenous Zimbabweans in an effort to regain political legitimacy in the face of serious challenges from the opposition Movement for Democratic Change (MDC) that had been launched in September 1999 (Alexander, 2003; Bond and Manyanya, 2001). The political gamble backfired as the country was plunged into socio-economic doldrums. Zimbabwe became isolated from the greater part of the international community (Duri, 2016b; Raftopoulos, 2003). Investor confidence waned and many companies closed resulting in unprecedented unemployment levels (Richardson, 2005). Commercial agriculture collapsed and shortages of food and many basic commodities became the order of the day (Duri, 2016b; Hammar and Raftopoulos, 2003; Richardson, 2005). Severe droughts, for example, in 2001-2002 (Richardson, 2005), 2007 (*Reuters Alert*, 20 March 2017), and 2014-2015 (*Thomson Reuters Foundation*, 18 January 2016) aggravated the plight of most ordinary Zimbabweans. Farm invasions, investor flight, international isolation, deindustrialisation and the drastic fall in the production of export crops resulted in serious foreign currency shortages and loss of revenue inflows into government coffers. The government increasingly became bankrupt and incapacitated to provide basic services and infrastructure to most citizens. Instead of coming up with concrete remedies to address the socio-economic catastrophe which it largely contributed in bringing about though political expediency, the ruling ZANU-PF elites are largely preoccupied with power struggles during which witchcraft allegations are often traded and political opponents scapegoated, leaving many ordinary Zimbabweans in a sorrowful state of neglect and abject poverty.

It should be noted from the onset that most of the major internal squabbles, particularly from the late 1990s, had more to do with the vice-presidency of the ZANU-PF party and the country rather than the presidency itself. This is because with Mugabe as the supreme leader of the party, the ascendancy to the vice-presidency was "a possible indicator as to what might happen when the next vacancy arises" (Matyszak, 2014: 3). Thus, such struggles within ZANU-PF were more pronounced following the death of a vice-president, for example, Joshua Nkomo (1999), Simon Muzenda (2003), Joseph Msika (2009) and John Nkomo (2013) (Ibid). Counter-productive infightings have always been rampant towards national and local government elections and ZANU-PF's national annual conferences as some members jostle for various positions (Matyszak, 2014; Newsday, 5 November 2011), without even considering their suitability to the posts.

This chapter illustrates how witchcraft accusations are sometimes utilised as a political resource to taper democratic space by demonising and silencing rivals during ZANU-PF's intra-party struggles and the manner in which they derail development efforts while promoting poverty and underdevelopment among the general populace. These allegations can best be understood as "a political ploy" against opponents "in order to make them look disreputable" (NewsdzeZimbabwe, 17 January 2014: 1), but at the same time they can be interpreted as credible from the indigenous African perspective and result in impoverishment and untold suffering of political adversaries and the general population.

Situating witchcraft in academic and development discourses

The analysis of data in this chapter is considerably informed by psychological and sociological theories of witchcraft. As will be noted later on in this section, however, the political dimension of witchcraft is proposed to complement the psychological and sociological perspectives. The interaction of these three tools of analysis, it is hoped, will enhance one's understanding of the dynamics of ZANU-PF's power struggles and their impact on the socio-economic wellbeing of targeted political opponents and the general population.

Psychological theories generally regard witchcraft beliefs as unsubstantiated imaginations. Evans-Pritchard (1937), in his study of the Azande people of the present Democratic Republic of Congo, for example, illustrates how witchcraft beliefs are part of imaginative or speculative dynamics. He contends that human beings sometimes advance presumptions to account for the incidence of calamitous and/or unfortunate events. Kluckhohn (1944) added more insights into the psychological theory of witchcraft basing his arguments on the Navaho, the Native American people of the south-western United States. He asserts that the institution of witchcraft, particularly witchcraft accusations, act as a medium to articulate emotions/anxieties and desires. Thus, by attributing misfortunes to the machinations of witches, the Navaho psychologically absolved themselves from blame. He concluded that people besieged by challenges sometimes scapegoat witches for their plight. Similarly, Kapferer (2003) suggests that despite their far-reaching implications, witchcraft beliefs are usually imaginative and unscientific. These psychological perspectives offer useful insights in the study of poverty in Zimbabwe and ZANU-PF's internal political dynamics from the onset of the 21ˢᵗ century. As this chapter demonstrates, political rivals within ZANU-PF often raise witchcraft accusations towards elections or when a vacancy exists in the party hierarchy, most probably in order to defame each other's characters with the major aim of winning popularity among the electorate at the expense of their counterparts who may actually be more competent in spearheading the country's development agenda. It is also prudent to note that the tendency to scapegoat other human beings and even supernatural phenomena such as witchcraft for socio-economic and political challenges is one of the major obstacles to development in many African countries. Instead of seeking realistic solutions to the challenges of governance, poverty and development bedevilling many communities in developing countries such as Zimbabwe, this chapter illustrates how some African political elites fail to acknowledge their failures and instead, find fault in their competitors whom they seek to defame through unsubstantiated witchcraft allegations.

From the 1960s, sociological theories of conflict made significant contributions to the study of witchcraft. Marwick (1965), for instance, propounds that witchcraft accusations are reflections of problematic social relations that are not susceptible to judicial processes. Drawing examples from the Chewa of Zambia, he notes that witchcraft allegations often arose when matrilineages grew beyond the size that locally-available resources could sustain. As a result, members of some matrilineages often clashed over increasingly shrinking resources. Duri (2017) also made similar observations in Zimbabwe during the socio-economic crisis from the onset of the new millennium when fierce struggles for livelihoods among the ordinary people were often accompanied by the trading of witchcraft accusations.

During the 1970s, neo-Marxists broadened the sociological theory by articulating the instrumentalisation of witchcraft accusations in socio-economic contestations. In his study of the Hewa of Papua New Guinea, Steadman (1985), for example, observed that witchcraft accusations and the killing of witches were part of the fierce struggles over scarce resources. By killing people who competed against them in the scramble for shrinking resources, the witch hunters safeguarded their material well-being by instilling fear into their contemporary and potential adversaries. Ritchken (1989: 14) reiterates that witch-hunts and witchcraft accusations become common "in the context of a society competing for scarce resources and riddled with potential points of conflict." As Golooba-Mutebi (2005: 939) also observed in post-Apartheid South Africa, suspicions and accusations of witchcraft can be triggered by socio-economic challenges. He argues:

Social and economic differentiation, now firmly entrenched in rural South Africa, provides fertile ground for suspicion and accusation. Wide socio-economic disparities cause social tensions, when the well-to-do fail to fulfil the expectations of poorer neighbours and kin for support. Tensions may lead to suspicion which often erupts into open accusation of witchcraft. The better-off accuse the poorer of bewitching them, while the latter accuse the former of having prospered through witchcraft.

Similarly, as Nyamnjoh (2001) noted in Cameroon, socio-economic hardships such as unemployment and chronic poverty enriched witchcraft discourses within communities as jobless youths blamed witches for their plight while the relatively well-off were

320

envied. Nyamnjoh's observations on Cameroon are also true for Zimbabwe. Duri (2017), for example, noted an upsurge in witchcraft accusations in Zimbabwe from the onset of the new millennium as many marginalised sections of the population, particularly those worst affected by socio-economic challenges, often accused those who monopolised economic resources of bewitching them. This chapter shows how witchcraft allegations became a critical political resource of mobilising supporters against opponents in the struggles for power and material resources among ZANU-PF elites when, in actual fact, the majority of the population expected the government to urgently address pressing socio-economic challenges such as food shortages, health ailments such as the HIV/AIDS pandemic, unemployment and poverty.

Although the psychological and sociological frameworks offer useful insights to this study, they are rather silent on the interaction between witchcraft discourses and political dynamics. This chapter goes beyond the psychological and sociological interpretations by proposing the political-economy dimension of witchcraft accusations. In an effort to articulate witchcraft discourses in a political-economy context, the chapter illustrates how witchery accusations are sometimes presented by some individuals and institutions as a veil to conceal their selfish political and material interests. Thus, witchcraft accusations should not be viewed only in sociological and psychological contexts, but also in economic and political terms. In Zimbabwe, as is the case in many other African countries, political ascendancy enhances one's chances of accumulating wealth through corruption, tender manipulation, low-interest bank loans and exorbitant allowances, among other things (Ayittey, 1998; Moyo, 4 November 2014). As this chapter demonstrates, ZANU-PF officials often trade witchcraft allegations against each other during times of fierce contestations for party posts and in many cases, those who fall out of favour with powerful political figures and institutions become paupers overnight. Examples include Amos Midzi, a former ZANU-PF Member of Parliament, Cabinet Minister, and ambassador to the United States (Mambo, 19 June 2015); Olivia Muchena, a former ZANU-PF Minister of Higher and Tertiary Education (*Internet Zimbabwe*, 13

August 2015; *Nehanda Radio*, 14 August 2015); and Didymus Mutasa, the former ZANU-PF Minister of State Security and Secretary for Administration (*Daily News*, 10 July 2017; *Herald*, 18 July 2017; Tafirenyika, 10 July 2017).

Given that political authority and patronage are important avenues of accumulation in Zimbabwe, many politicians are obsessed with harnessing power and accumulating wealth without paying due attention to the developmental needs of ordinary citizens, most of who are languishing in poverty. As Vince Musewe, a Zimbabwean political analyst, cited by Jakes (25 May 2007: 1), explained in May 2017 why Zimbabwe had become a crumbled state both socially, economically and politically:

The question is what must we do to create the Zimbabwe we want? First, we must understand why we are where we are now…The fundamental cause is that of predatory leadership. We have a political leadership that is clearly concerned with the accumulation of personal power and wealth at the expense of development. Until that changes, we are bound not to witness any significant allocation and efficient use of state resources for infrastructural development.

Mudslinging, sometimes punctuated by witchcraft accusations, becomes the order of the day as political entrepreneurs struggle for power in order to gain access to resources. Thus, in many post-independent African states such as Zimbabwe, power struggles are largely spurred by what Bayart (2009) termed 'the politics of the belly' during which the subaltern are the major casualties in political and socio-economic terms. As this chapter illustrates, both psychological and sociological perspectives, together with the proposed political-economy analytical framework, point to the instrumentalisation of witchcraft discourses by rivals in an effort to monopolise socio-economic and political space while the ordinary people continue to wallow in poverty.

Internal rivalries in ZANU-PF from the mid-1980s

This section examines some of the major internal struggles that rocked the ruling ZANU-PF party from the mid-1980s. This brief account provides as useful background against which witchcraft discourses were later articulated by various protagonists in the struggle for political space within the party.

Internal dissent within the ruling ZANU-PF party during the post-colonial period can be traced back to the mid-1980s when Edgar Tekere, one of Mugabe's closest lieutenants during the liberation struggle, expressed disgruntlement over corruption by government officials and the party's plans to establish a one-party state, among other things (Tekere, 2009). Mugabe accused Tekere of dissent and subsequently fired him from the party (Tendi, 2016). Tekere went on to form the Zimbabwe Unity Movement (ZUM) and contested against Mugabe during the 1990 presidential elections but garnered only 16.75% of the vote against the incumbent's 83% (Matonhodze, 31 July 2013). The obsession with power on the part of the ZANU-PF leadership, at the expense of democracy and development, largely explains the expulsion of Tekere from the ruling party. Despite Tekere's expulsion, there remained a considerable number of senior officials who were critical of dictatorial tendencies of governance within the party. These included retired Air Marshall Josiah Tungamirai, retired General Vitalis Zvinawashe and cabinet ministers such as Edison Zvobgo (Tendi, 2016).

During the late 1990s, some critics within the ruling ZANU-PF party accused the ageing Mugabe of dictatorial tendencies and urged him to retire. In 1997, for example, Dzikamai Mavhaire, a Masvingo legislator, urged the 73-year-old Mugabe to resign for failing to address the country's socio-economic meltdown caused by austerity measures recommended by the World Bank and the International Monetary Fund (*New Zimbabwe*, 28 August 2017). In retaliation, Mugabe referred to Mavhaire as a witch bent on destroying the party. Mugabe went on to reprimand Cyril Ndebele, the then Speaker of Parliament, for entertaining people like Mavhaire during parliamentary debates (Ibid). The castigation of Mavhaire by President Mugabe is perhaps one of the earliest instances in which witchcraft discourses were articulated within ZANU-PF as a ploy to defame the characters of political opponents. Mavhaire was immediately suspended from ZANU-PF and subsequently lost his parliamentary seat (Braid, 3 May 1998; *New Zimbabwe*, 25 June 2016). There is no doubt that democracy and good governance in a country's socio-economic and political fabric are indispensable factors for meaningful development to take place. Mavhaire's case demonstrates how some politicians are victimised and demonised, to the extent of being labelled as witches, for freely expressing themselves about solutions to prevailing socio-economic and political challenges. It should be noted, therefore, that the betrayal of democracy in all spheres of life is an impediment to development and a prescription for socio-economic hardships for many ordinary people.

As Mugabe grew older, a leadership succession dispute began to brew within ZANU-PF during the late 1990s with two rival factions emerging under the leadership of Solomon Mujuru and Emmerson Mnangagwa. While Mnangagwa began harbouring ambitions of succeeding Mugabe, Solomon Mujuru settled for his wife, Joyce, in the power struggle (Matyszak, 2014; Tendi, 2016). Soon after the death of Vice-President Simon Muzenda in 2003, the pro-Munangwa faction began angling itself for the vacant post. Under the guidance of Jonathan Moyo, a ZANU-PF cabinet minister, the faction secretly met in the town of Tsholotsho in 2004 and came up with proposals of reforming the party. In a document that came to be known as the Tsholotsho Declaration, the faction, with a view to having Mnangagwa, then Minister for Rural Housing, elevated to the vice-presidency, proposed that the country's four major ethnic groups (Karanga, Manyika, Zezuru and Ndebele) should be represented in the ZANU-PF Presidium (which comprised the President, two Vice-Presidents and the National Chairman); the post of President should not be monopolised by one ethnic group but should rotate among the four major ethnic groupings; the filling in of positions in the Presidium should not be imposed but elected through a secret ballot by party structures; and these posts had to be filled according to the party's constitution (Matyszak, 2014). In 2004, General Mujuru's faction gained an upper hand in the succession race when, through Mugabe's influence, Joyce, the wife of General Mujuru, was appointed as one of the two Vice-Presidents of both ZANU-PF and the Republic of Zimbabwe (Matyszak, 2014; Tendi, 2016). Solomon Mujuru died on 15 August 2011 during a fire that gutted his farmhouse in circumstances that were suspected to be an assassination by his political rivals (Tendi, 2016; *Zimbabwe Daily*, 23 February 2016).

After her husband's death, Joyce Mujuru took over the leadership of his faction and continued with the succession contest against Mnangagwa. Her political ambitions were shattered from mid-2014 when Grace Mugabe, the First Lady, during countrywide campaigns, began to denounce her for treason, corruption and witchcraft (Tendi, 2016). On 8 December 2014, Mugabe fired Joyce Mujuru from the Vice-Presidency of both the party and the government, together with eight ministers believed to be her allies, on unverified allegations of treason (*Newsday*, 3 March 2015). She was replaced by Mnangagwa who, together with Phelekezela Mphoko, became the two Vice-Presidents of both ZANU-PF and the country (Tendi, 2016).

After the ousting of Joyce Mujuru, a ZANU-PF faction known as Generation 40 (G40) emerged to frustrate Mnangagwa's ambitions of succeeding President Mugabe. The G40 is believed to be in favour of the First Lady, Grace Mugabe, succeeding her husband (Byrne, 30 August 2017). Fierce clashes often took place, and continue to erupt, between the G40 and the pro-Mnangagwa faction which calls itself Lacoste (*New Zimbabwe*, 28 August 2017; *Zimbabwe Standard*, 27 August 2017).

This section has provided an overview of ZANU-PF's internal struggles from the mid-1980s. It was in this context of fierce internal squabbles that disparaging witchcraft allegations were often traded in an effort to win public sympathy and support in politics at the expense of discredited foes. In African indigenous beliefs since the pre-colonial period, witchcraft accusations severely damage one's social standing. The next section examines the content and logic of these beliefs in order to establish their impact on human progress in both socio-economic and political terms.

African witchcraft beliefs since the pre-colonial period

In many African societies since the pre-colonial era, the belief in witchcraft "constitutes part of the traditional religion," while the practice of witch-hunting has always been "a form of traditional religious expression" (Igwe, 30 August 2011: 1). Witches have always been viewed as "social deviants" and "traitors to the social solidarity of the community" (Ball, 1994: 1) as well as the socio-economic development of the general population. In actual fact, the belief in witchcraft constitutes a demonology, an "idea of treason against the kin group itself" and "an attack on the very basis of the social structure, which makes witchcraft activity such a heinous offence" (Hammond-Tooke, 1974: 337). Consequently, as Igwe (30 August 2011: 1) notes, "Witches and sorcerers are the most hated people in their community" who are widely regarded as enemies of development and prosperity of the generality of the population. This is partly because of the commonly held belief that the bewitched can be incapacitated to make progress in both political and economic life.

Witchcraft beliefs have remained pervasive in the post-colonial period in various parts of the African continent despite the influence of Western education, science and technology (Chireshe, Chireshe and Shumba, 2012). According to the Pew Research Centre Survey of 2010, Zimbabwe ranks 15th in Africa in terms of witchcraft beliefs, behind such countries as the Democratic Republic of Congo, Ethiopia, Nigeria, Zambia and Rwanda (Majaka, 4 December 2016). As will be noted in this chapter, witchcraft beliefs have several negative implications on many aspects of socio-economic and political development in some parts of the contemporary world, including Zimbabwe.

In Zimbabwe, the Shona term for a witch, wizard or sorcerer is *muroyi*, plural *varoyi* (Tatira, 2014), while the Ndebele equivalents are *umthakathi* and *abathakathi* respectively (Chireshe, Chireshe and Shumba, 2012). The Shona generally regard a *muroyi* as "anyone who is hard-hearted or who has evil intention, or an antisocial being" who can, among other means, use spiritual power to harm others and retard human progress and development (Tatira, 2014: 114). Among the Ndebele and Shona people of Zimbabwe, as in many other African societies, a broad range of hardships were, and are still, sometimes linked to the machinations of witchery (Bucher, 1980; Chireshe, Chireshe and Shumba, 2012; Essein, 2010; Rodlach, 2006; Mawere 2011). These include poverty, bad harvests, failure to bear children, mysterious deaths of people and livestock, and diseases, particularly those that Western medicine fails to explain or cure. The

Shona also believe that witches use animals such as hyenas, owls, ant bears and snakes on nocturnal errands to harm other people. Even some lightning strikes are believed to be orchestrated by witches (Mawere, 2011). Witches are also believed to eat human flesh, for which they can open up graves to get it (Bourdillon, 1998; Mawere, 2011). It should also be noted that the Shona and Ndebele people also use the term 'witchcraft' in a broader sense to refer to various forms of evil and anti-social behaviour (Howman, 1948; Nhemachena, 2014; Thorpe, 1991). Thus, *muroyi* or *umthakathi* can be used to swear at someone who is greedy, selfish, jealous, bullish, unpopular, or who uses foul language (Bourdillon, 1998). In addition, people who are accused of violating taboos are sometimes referred to as witches (Ibid, 1998). Broadly, witches are regarded as social outcasts who retard human progress and development.

Witchcraft beliefs are also prevalent in other parts of the African continent. In Nigeria, for example, it is generally believed that witches can use magic to disguise themselves as animal species such as cats, ants, rats, bats and butterflies in order to inflict harm on others (Igwe, 19 August 2011). In Gambia, it is commonly held that witches can change into owls at night (Ibid). Many Senegalese believe that witches reside inside the pawpaw fruit which they also use as a nocturnal springboard to cause harm (Ibid). In Malawi, there is a widespread belief that witches fly at night in magic aeroplanes while in Burkina Faso, many people believe that they devour human flesh and suck people's blood (Ibid). In countries such as Tanzania, Burundi and Nigeria, albinos are often accused of witchcraft on grounds that their skin can be used to make harmful magical concoctions (Igwe, 30 August 2011). It can be noted that many witchcraft beliefs are not scientifically verifiable and this has serious negative implications on the development of communities by causing individual stress, general animosity and social discord among people who could otherwise have collectively worked towards improving their living standards.

Some witchcraft accusations arose from general conflicts, class differentials, and jealousies within neighbourhoods and communities. In many African societies since the pre-colonial period, it was common practice for the less-privileged people to accuse their wealthy neighbours of witchcraft while others made similar allegations against those with whom they had longstanding disputes (Brinkman, 2003). Some African rulers devised strategies of eliminating political foes by accusing them of witchery, an offence that was usually punishable by death. Lobengula, the Ndebele king during the period 1870-1893, for example, would "so frequently...remove any of his principal councillors whom he thought was becoming too popular or too powerful, which might make him a possible rival. It was a simple matter to have the offender 'smelt out' on some pretext or other of witchcraft, and put to death" (Gale, 1960: 145).

This chapter will illustrate that in contemporary Zimbabwe, as is the case in some crisis-ridden communities around the world, some people besieged by socio-economic and political challenges sometimes attribute their plight to the works of witchcraft. Such scapegoating tendencies derail development prospects by either overlooking or deliberately circumventing the real causes of societal challenges such as poverty, wealth differentials and conflicts as well as the viable strategies of mitigating them.

In many African societies, it is also believed that witches can also use magic or 'medicine' to seek unfair advantage over others in activities such as gambling, farming and retail business (Bourdillon, 1998; Mawere, 2011). In some cases, the relatively wealthy people are suspected to have attained such status through the use of magic (Chireshe, Chireshe and Shumba, 2012). Without despising African indigenous beliefs and practices, this chapter asserts that such witchcraft discourses are not progressive as they fail to acknowledge the skill and genuine effort that some people apply in order to succeed in ventures they undertake. Instead, great strides can be made towards poverty alleviation and sustainable development by many impoverished societies around the world through learning from other people's success stories and acquiring the necessary skills to maximise productivity.

Another retrogressive aspect is that the institution of witchcraft has always been largely mediated by gender in many African societies (Krige, 1976). Among the Shona people in pre-colonial Zimbabwe, as was the case in many parts of the continent, witches were almost exclusively women (Gelfand, 1964; Schmidt, 1992; Thorpe, 1991). It was common for women who failed to bear children to be accused of witchcraft (Crawford, 1967), the explanation being that "a witch is supposed to be fond of destroying her children, and also because a childless woman is expected to be jealous of those who have children" (Bourdillon, 1998: 177). Similarly, among the Chopi people of southern Mozambique, women were believed to be "particularly associated with the mystical forces carrying sickness and death and were often accused of witchcraft and named in cases of contamination" (Young, 1977: 69).

These gender dimensions of witchcraft in particular and the negative patriarchal stereotypes towards women as partners in development in general are quite evident in independent Zimbabwe. In 2014, as will be discussed in more detail later in this chapter, Joyce Mujuru, the then Vice President of ZANU-PF and the Republic of Zimbabwe, for example, was deposed on unproven allegations of treason, corruption and witchcraft, among other things, as power struggles rocked the ruling party (Duri, 2016a). These political feuds, together with the damaging witchcraft accusations, took place at a time when the country was in urgent need of concrete solutions from the ruling elite to mitigate the debilitating socio-economic and political crisis in the country. Most ordinary Zimbabweans were left to wallow in abject poverty while the ruling party elites were at each other's throat in fierce power struggles largely characterised by violence, mudslinging and character assassinations.

Witch-hunting and cleansing rituals were held frequently in many pre-colonial African societies "to ensure that witches do not terrorise people and that their powers are kept under control" (Igwe, 30 August 2011: 1). By far the most widespread, but unscientific, procedure of 'detecting' witches in many parts of pre-colonial Africa involved the accused person being compelled to undergo an ordeal administered by a diviner to prove whether he or she was guilty Bourdillon, 1998). The most common ordeal was to have the accused person to drink some bitter medicine. Vomiting was believed to show innocence while a running stomach was regarded as an indication of guilt (Ibid).

In many pre-colonial African societies, people found 'guilty' of witchcraft were punished severely by their secular leaders. The punitive measures included being beaten to death or permanent banishment from their communities or polities (Bourdillon, 1998; Brinkman, 2003). In the Ndebele state, for example, people found guilty of witchcraft were taken to Sizinda where they were killed (Dube, 6 May 2014). Among the Nguni, Tsonga and Sotho in Southern Africa, death was also the common penalty (Hammond-Tooke, 1974).Thus, many people accused of witchcraft committed suicide rather than suffer from psychological stress and social ostracisation after which they underwent painful ordeals and subsequent penalties (Crawford, 1967). The justification for killing alleged witches is quite problematic given that witchcraft accusations themselves are difficult to prove. Even the arbitrary ordeals that were conducted to ascertain whether one was guilty of witchery or not lack scientific substance. It is quite possible that many innocent people lost their lives during the ordeals and the subsequent death penalties that were often passed, thus the loss of human capital that could otherwise have been actively involved in the development of the community in various capacities.

During Zimbabwe's liberation war (1966-1979), guerrillas and some sections of the civilian population regarded people accused of witchcraft as enemies of the revolution and a threat to social cohesion. In fact, the terms 'witch' and 'traitor' were often used interchangeably by many guerrillas and civilians in many parts of Zimbabwe during the armed struggle (Bourdillon, 1987; Kriger, 1992). As a result, many people accused of witchcraft were, in many cases, arbitrarily killed by the guerrillas (Werbner, 1991). According to Lan (1985), many local civilians regarded the killing of 'witches' by the guerrillas as a commendable effort to restore societal order that had been ruptured by colonial rule. The guerrillas also used the execution of alleged witches as one of the strategies of enforcing and legitimising their control over the civilian population (Ibid). Thus, as Kriger (1992) noted, the killing of alleged witches was often used as an instrument of mobilisation and coercion by the guerrillas. Similarly, as Brinkman (2003: 303) noted about Angola's liberation struggle (1977-1975), there were "many links between treason and witchcraft," and some civilian communities believed that treason accusations were usually instrumentalised by the Movimento Popular de Libertac͜a͡o de Angola (MPLA) guerrillas "to get rid of political or personal rivals and/or to control the population." MPLA guerrillas usually used firing squads to execute civilians accused of witchcraft (Ibid). In the realm of human progress and development, it becomes evident that witch-hunts raise a surfeit of controversies than they endeavour to resolve. When witchcraft accusations are made, problems arise in seeking to distinguish between fact and fiction, truth and jealousy, and fabrications and realities. Human progress can be impeded if people are demonised and eliminated without concrete evidence being provided. There is no doubt that in theory, the activities of witches are retrogressive to human progress but unsubstantiated witchery accusations can cause more harm than good to social-economic organisation and development.

In some post-colonial African societies, harsh penalties are also meted out on people found 'guilty' of witchcraft. In Nigeria, the Democratic Republic of Congo and the Central African Republic, for example, many children accused of witchcraft are flogged, killed, abandoned or chased away from their homes (Igwe, 30 August 2011). In Malawi, women accused of witchcraft, even on the basis of hearsay, are often harassed and tortured (Ibid). In Kenya, Tanzania and Uganda, women facing the same accusations are sometimes beaten up and killed (Ibid). After being accused of witchcraft, some African women fled their homes to seek protection in refugee camps for fear of reprisals from their local communities (Ibid). In August 2011, for example, such refugee camps existed in Burkina Faso and northern Ghana (Ibid). Besides inflicting untold misery on the accused individuals, some of whom may be innocent, such arbitrary penalties have the potential to destabilise societies through conflicts, displacements, injuries and even deaths thereby creating an environment unconducive for human progress. This partly explains why colonial and post-colonial governments passed some laws in an effort to curb the incidence of extra-judicial penalties meted out on people accused of witchcraft. In colonial Zimbabwe (Rhodesia), for instance, the Witchcraft Suppression Act of 1893 did not recognise the existence of witchcraft. The Act criminalised witchcraft accusations (Southern Rhodesia Government, 1939).

Upon attaining independence in 1980, the Zimbabwean government acknowledged the existence of supernatural powers but outlawed the use of magic to cause harm on others (Majaka, 4 December 2016). In 2006, the Zimbabwean government amended the colonial Witchcraft Suppression Act and enacted the Witchcraft Suppression Act, Chapter 9: 19, that made witchcraft a criminal offence as long as there was evidence to that effect (Zimbabwe Government, 2006). In particular, Section 5 of the 2006 Act outlawed the practice of witchcraft as follows:

Any person who employs or solicits any other person (a) to name or indicate any other person as a wizard or witch; or (b) to name or indicate by means of witchcraft or by application of any of the tests mentioned in the paragraph (b) of Section 8 or by the use of any non-natural means any person as the perpetrator of any alleged crime or other act complained of or (c) to advise him or any other person how, by means of witchcraft or by any non-natural means whatsoever, the perpetrator of any alleged or other act complained of may be discovered; shall be guilty of an offence and liable to a fine not exceeding fifty dollars or, in default of payment to imprisonment for a period not exceeding six months (Zimbabwe Government, 2006: Chapter 5).

The revised Act, however, criminalises any accusations of witchcraft that are not backed up by evidence (Chireshe, Chireshe and Shumba, 2012; *Sunday Mail*, 11 December 2016). This statute was reinforced by the Criminal Law (Codification and Reform) Act, Chapter 9: 23 which reiterated that it was an offence to accuse someone of witchcraft. Section 99 (1) of this Act specifically criminalises groundless accusations of witchcraft (Nkomo, 26 January 2011; Nyamayaro, 7 December 2016; Saunyama, 30 January 2017). Under this law, a person found guilty of practising witchcraft is liable to a fine or a five-year jail term (Nkomo, 26 January 2011).

Despite these legal provisions, there was an upsurge in witchcraft accusations and witch-hunts since the onset of the new millennium as ZANU-PF officials were engulfed in internal power struggles owing to Mugabe's advanced age, among other things. Ironically, the most publicised witchcraft accusations were made by senior government officials, the very people who should lead by example in safeguarding the country's laws and spearheading development. This clearly demonstrates how the law was sacrificed by individual pursuits of political survival. The next sections examine the upsurge in witchcraft accusations in the context of ZANU-PF's power struggles during the 21st century and the manner in which they severely compromised the country's development prospects.

Witchcraft accusations in the downfall of Joyce Mujuru

The First Lady, Grace Mugabe, burst onto Zimbabwe's political scene in 2014 amid rumours that she harboured ambitions to succeed her husband as President of both ZANU-PF and the Republic of Zimbabwe (Tendi, 2016). She began by accusing Joyce Mujuru, then one of the two Vice-Presidents of both ZANU-PF and the country, of corruption and conspiring to topple President Mugabe, among other things (Ibid). From October 2014, the First Lady went on a nationwide campaign denigrating Mujuru and pressuring her to resign as Vice-President (*Newsday*, 3 March 2015).

Witchcraft allegations were levelled against Mujuru in an effort to discredit her. In addition, these accusations were also meant to mobilise support against her. On 30 October 2014, for example, a rented crowd of ZANU-PF supporters congregated at the party headquarters in Harare just before a politburo meeting that was to be held on that day, to denounce Joyce Mujuru and her sympathisers such as Jabulani Sibanda, the then Chairperson of the Zimbabwe National Liberation War Veterans Association (ZNLWVA) (*Newsday*, 3 March 2015). During the demonstration, the crowd chanted: "Witch, old woman from Dotito, witch," in apparent reference to Joyce Mujuru who came from the Dotito area in the Mount Darwin District (Ibid: 1).

President Mugabe was at the forefront in articulating witchcraft discourses meant to denigrate Joyce Mujuru. It should be noted, however, that Mugabe's witchcraft allegations against Mujuru came in a series of different versions which make one to doubt their authenticity. While addressing the ZANU-PF Central Committee on 3 December 2014, Mugabe said that Ray Kaukonde, the former ZANU-PF Mashonaland East Provincial Chairman, was sent by

Mujuru to look for a *sangoma* (witchdoctor) in Nigeria to perform rituals that would enhance her prospects of becoming the President of Zimbabwe. Mugabe continued:

> One of the *n'angas* said look for two tadpoles of different colours. One should be named Mugabe and the other should be called Mujuru and put them in water. That is what happened. They were made to fight and if Mugabe's tadpole died then she would rule. Now if mine won against yours, it seems that is what happened then (Matenga, 4 December 2014: 1).

In another "fanciful witchcraft tale," Mugabe charged that Mujuru had attended ceremonies in Mashonaland East Province where sheep were slaughtered and rituals performed in an effort to kill him (*Zimbabwe Standard*, 3 September 2017: 1).

On 28 February 2015, while addressing ZANU-PF supporters in the town of Victoria Falls, Mugabe alleged that Mujuru conducted witchcraft rituals bare-breasted with the intention of killing him. He claimed that Mujuru slaughtered 10 chickens, each one representing a ZANU-PF official she wanted to kill. Mugabe added that he and his wife, Grace, were top of the list of people who Mujuru wanted dead (Muponde, 4 March 2015; *South African Press Association*, 3 March 2015). Other ZANU-PF officials who were on the list, Mugabe alleged, included Vice-President Emmerson Mnangagwa and Local Government Minister Ignatius Chombo (*News24*, 3 March 2015). There is no doubt that these unsubstantiated claims were meant to politically isolate Mujuru by creating animosity between her and ministers in the so-called hit list yet, as senior government officials, both were supposed to work together to solve the country's socio-economic challenges. This clearly shows how President Mugabe tore his cabinet apart for purposes of political expediency. If the accusations were true, then Mugabe should have taken Mujuru to court to answer charges of contravening the Witchcraft Suppression Act, Chapter 9: 19 and the Criminal Law (Codification and Reform) Act, Chapter 9: 23, which he never did.

On 2 March 2015, Mujuru dismissed Mugabe's witchcraft and treason allegations as baseless and blatant lies. In her defence, she argued:

> I am at a loss as to how I continue to be the subject matter of presidential conjecture and fantasy based on outright lies. I was born into the Apostolic Faith and once at school, became a member of the Salvation Army. I am a committed Christian and was the leader of Apostolic Churches as patron, and I have been committed to Christian life and values, all of my life. It is disturbing that the allegations that I tried to, or was part of a conspiracy to, assassinate the President have now been reduced to allegations of witchcraft, whose versions change on a daily basis. I am sure even the ordinary Zimbabwean has become tired of this story in its various guises. It is a charade which has lost steam (*Newsday*, 3 March 2015: 1).

In late March 2015, Rugare Gumbo, a war veteran and former ZANU-PF Information Secretary, who was fired together with Mujuru, claimed that Mugabe was a man of double standards who publicly denigrated spirit mediums and traditional healers (the so-called witch doctors) but secretly consulted them (*Bulawayo 24 News*, 26 March 2015. He argued: "Mugabe has been consulting *sangomas* (witch doctors) and all who have belonged to his inner circle know that. It is surprising that he now wants to talk as if *sangomas* are an unfamiliar thing to him. That is utter hypocrisy" (Ibid, p.1).

These ZANU-PF succession struggles were raging at a time when the country was in socio-economic doldrums that needed urgent redress from the ruling party. The power struggles and witchcraft accusations were taking place in a country struck by a debilitating liquidity crunch, where capacity utilisation had tumbled from 57.2% in 2011 to 34.3% in 2015 (Ibid). In the year 2013, over 800 companies closed in Harare alone (*Zimbabwe Independent*, 13 October 2014). Between 2011 and 2014, more than 4 600 companies closed countrywide, resulting in 55 443 job losses (Kuwaza, 18 December 2015).

Mugabe's witchcraft allegations against Joyce Mujuru clearly contravened the Witchcraft Suppression Act, as amended in 2006, and Section 99 of the Criminal Law (Codification and Reform) Act (Chapter 9: 23) which criminalise the act of accusing anyone of being a witch and/or of practising witchcraft or sorcery (Muponde, 4 March 2015). However, in terms of the provisions of Section 98 of the Zimbabwean Constitution, a sitting president is immune from prosecution. This means that Mujuru can only sue Mugabe after he leaves office (Muponde, 4 March 2015; *News24*, 3 March 2015). The fact of the matter here is that President Mugabe himself violated the law since he neither provided any evidence to prove the witchcraft allegations, nor did he institute legal proceedings against Mujuru. This may suggest that the accusations were mere politicking in order to mobilise the electorate against Mujuru and terminate her political career. Should this be the case, then the President's actions constitute a gross violation of democratic ethics and the rule of law, which a developing country like Zimbabwe cannot afford to risk if it is to attract investors and donors to assist in the development of the country.

In addition, the unsubstantiated allegations of witchcraft, treason and corruption levelled against Mujuru, and her subsequent ousting from the Vice Presidency, severely undermined the status of women as equal partners to their male counterparts in Zimbabwe's socio-economic and political development. With Mujuru's exit, ZANU-PF power struggles became even more protracted as Mugabe remained tight-lipped over who would succeed him. Such turbulent developments, which will be discussed in the next section, repel investors and donors and further shatter the country's hopes for a relatively stable socio-economic and political environment. As Alex Magaisa (5 May 2015: 1), a Zimbabwean political analyst, aptly noted: "Investors do not throw their money into zones of insecurity, unfairness and instability."

After being ousted, Joyce Mujuru launched a new opposition political party, the Zimbabwe People First, on 1 March 2016 whose leadership included other fired ZANU-PF officials such as Rugare Gumbo and Didymus Mutasa (Machipisa, 1 March 2016; *News24*, 2 March 2016). During party's launch, she claimed that President Robert Mugabe must have been "drunk" after taking "intoxicating substances" when she accused her of being a witch (*News 24*, 2 March

2016: 1). Mujuru dismissed the witchcraft accusations as "imaginative allegations" and added: "... I know others said those things under the influence of toxic substances, so it is not anything that pays anybody to repeat certain things. We have more important things to talk about and take the country forward" (*News24*, 2 March 2016: 1). She also sought to clear her name from the witchcraft allegations when she declared, "I am neither a witch nor an assassin" (Machipisa, 1 March 2016: 1).

Joyce Mujuru's case illuminates the instrumentalisation of witchcraft accusations in ZANU-PF's internal power struggles. While President Mugabe levelled witchcraft allegations against his former deputy as part of a strategy to politically liquidate her, Rugare Gumbo also made counter-accusations in defence of Mujuru in order to clear the air as they prepared to launch a new opposition political party. Mugabe's witchery accusations are hard to believe for three reasons. Firstly, they came in a series of different versions which make one to doubt their authenticity. Secondly, they were neither substantiated, nor were their sources acknowledged. Thirdly, it boggles the mind why Mugabe did not take Mujuru to court to answer charges of practising witchcraft as provided for by the law. Mujuru herself could have sued Mugabe for making unsubstantiated witchcraft allegations but the futility of such as exercise was written on the wall given the constitutional provisions of presidential immunity from prosecution.

Lamentably, these power struggles and related witchcraft allegations were very costly to Zimbabwe in terms of socio-economic and political development. Politically, internal democracy within ZANU-PF itself was sacrificed as supporters were mobilised in the ouster of Joyce Mujuru and other senior officials. In addition, the internal feuds also dented the prospects of the country's economic recovery in the near future as ruling party officials wasted time jostling for posts and discrediting each other through witchcraft accusations. As Herbert Moyo, a *Zimbabwe Independent* correspondent, aptly put it in April 2014:

> The concern is that the succession issue has become an all-consuming issue of ZANU-PF party stalwarts who will stop at nothing

to fight their opponents to gain advantage in the race to succeed Mugabe, even if this means sacrificing the people and the country's interests…Even the fight against corruption has been sacrificed on the altar of factionalism and political expediency (Moyo, 3 April 1014: 1).

A report by the International Crisis Group, published in October 2014, illuminated Zimbabwe's inexorable socio-economic catastrophe:

> Zimbabwe is an insolvent and failing state, its politics zero sum, its institutions hollowing out, and its once vibrant economy moribund. A major culture change is needed among political elites, as well as commitment to national as opposed to partisan and personal interests (*Zimbabwe Independent*, 13 October 2014: 1).

It should be noted that these ZANU-PF feuds were escalating at a time when the country desperately needed a viable national development agenda to address the problems of unemployment and widespread poverty that were being experienced by most Zimbabweans, particularly from the onset of the new millennium. The power struggles within the ruling party were therefore retrogressive towards the national cause of resuscitating the economy and providing basic social services to the majority of ordinary Zimbabweans who were reeling in poverty.

Witchcraft discourses in the rivalry between Lacoste and G40 factions and their negative implications for development in Zimbabwe

The rivalry between G40 and Lacoste factions, reportedly led by Grace Mugabe and Emmerson Mnangagwa respectively, started soon after the ouster of Joyce Mujuru and filtered into most levels of the ruling party's structures where some officials often articulated witchcraft discourses against each other. The feud, which gained much publicity from early 2015, compromised the country's development trajectory at a time when the majority of Zimbabweans were wallowing in poverty. In December 2015, for instance, Kudzai

Kuwaza, a *Zimbabwe Independent* journalist, bemoaned how ZANU-PF's succession struggles had "taken precedence over an imploding economy marked by company closures and job losses on a massive scale" (Kuwaza, 18 December 2015: 1).

When Shuvai Ben Mahofa, the then Minister of State for Masvingo Province, mysteriously fell ill in 2015, for example, she claimed that ZANU-PF was replete with witches who wanted to kill her. She openly alleged being bewitched ahead of the ZANU-PF Annual Conference that was held in Victoria Falls in December 2015 (Chaota, 13 May 2017; Mawawa, 19 May 2017). Mahofa left the 2015 annual conference and was rushed to seek treatment in South Africa after allegedly eating poisoned food. She spent close to three months in South Africa receiving medical treatment (Chitagu, 21 December 2016). Ironically, Mahofa, a Mnangagwa apologist and prominent member of the Lacoste faction, had verbally attacked the First Lady, Grace Mugabe, publicly just a few days before the conference. In December 2015, Mahofa had described the First Lady as "a little girl incapable of leading the ruling party" (Mawawa, 19 May 2017: 1). During the 2016 conference held in the City of Masvingo, Mahofa avoided eating food that was served for fear of being poisoned again by her political rivals (Chitagu, 21 December 2016).

While addressing a ZANU-PF Masvingo Provincial Coordinating Committee meeting on 14 May 2017, Mahofa reiterated that witches within the ruling party had tried to kill her but failed. She charged: "This party is full of witches. They disabled my legs and hands but I am still around. They know what they did to me. They really wanted to kill me but I am more powerful than ever" (Mawawa, 19 May 2017: 1). She went on to castigate G40 members for refusing to accept the provincial election victories of party members who were not in their faction (Chaota, 13 May 2017; Mawawa, 19 May 2017).

Mahofa died on 17 August 2017, reportedly after suffering from a number of ailments which many Lacoste members believed had been aggravated by her poisoning during the 2015 ZANU-PF Annual Conference (Chidza, Manayiti and Mhlanga, 21 August 2017). Chaos erupted at the National Heroes' Acre on 20 August 2017 during Mahofa's burial which was presided over by Phelekezela Mphoko, one of the country's two Vice-Presidents, who allegedly belongs to the G40 faction (Ibid). During the burial, Lacoste youths "occasionally disrupted the proceedings by singing and chanting slogans denouncing their rivals, while scores walked out on Vice-President Phelekezela Mphoko, who presided over the event" (Ibid: 1).

Mahofa's case illustrates that ruling party elites were largely preoccupied with politicking at the expense of the country's development. Instead of devoting their time, energy and resources towards addressing Zimbabwe's socio-economic problems, ZANU-PF officials became bogged down in witchcraft accusations and counter-accusations. Even some ordinary Zimbabweans were made to believe that some government officials, such as Mahofa, had failed to address their plight of poverty because of the machinations of witchcraft. In addition, even if it is really the case that Mahofa was bewitched/poisoned, it shows that some ruling ZANU-PF officials had abandoned their constitutional mandate to serve the people as they engaged in battles to ensure their political survival as individuals.

First Lady Grace Mugabe also levelled witchcraft allegations against her political opponents within ZANU-PF for her personal misfortunes, such as the accident in which her foot was crushed by the presidential armoured vehicle she was about to board at the Harare International Airport on 22 July 2017 (*ZimEye*, 24 July 2017). The First Lady had just landed at the airport from Singapore. As she was getting into the presidential car, in which President Mugabe was already aboard, their driver set the vehicle in motion resulting in her foot being crushed by one of the rear wheels. The First Lady blamed the accident on the driver for negligence and her political adversaries, most probably the Lacoste faction, for casting witchcraft spells (Ibid). This case demonstrates the politicisation of witchcraft by rival parties in an effort to discredit each other. There is no doubt that the First Lady deliberately articulated witchcraft discourses in order to demonise her political adversaries by scapegoating them for an accident that had been caused by a negligent driver.

The politicisation of witchcraft was also witnessed in the City of Kadoma in Mashonaland West Province on 17 August 2017 during the burial of Joan Tsogorani, the ZANU-PF Mashonaland West Proportional Representation Member of Parliament and also a

Lacoste apologist. Tsogorani died on 14 August after succumbing to hypertension-related complications which had resulted in her becoming blind, in addition to having respiratory challenges. During her burial, some Lacoste supporters alleged that she had been bewitched by fellow party members, suspected to belong to the G40 faction, who were jealous of her political rise (*News Anchor*, 18 August 2017). This incident demonstrates how witchcraft accusations and counter-accusations can bifurcate the society and jeopardise development trajectories.

Some Lacoste officials and their supporters also accused the G40 faction of witchcraft after Vice-President Mnangagwa had eaten an ice cream, allegedly laced with poison in August 2017. He allegedly ate the ice cream during a reception held at a ZANU-PF rally in Gwanda Town that was addressed by President Mugabe (*Zimbabwe Standard*, 27 August 2017). Mnangagwa started vomiting and experiencing severe diarrhoea after eating the ice cream. He had to be airlifted from the rally to a Midlands hospital before being whisked to Johannesburg, South Africa, for emergency treatment (Dube, 2 September 2017; *Zimbabwean*, 4 September 2017; *Zimbabwe Standard*, 27 August 2017). Christopher Mushohwe, the Minister of Information, suggested that Mnangagwa had eaten stale food (Ncube, 28 August 2017). However, evidence from South African medical practitioners at the Johannesburg hospital where Mnangagwa was admitted confirmed that he had been poisoned. During their diagnosis, they identified traces of a toxic substance known as palladium, which had damaged his liver. Palladium, a rare metal mined in Russia and South Africa, is combined with platinum to make catalytic converters (Byrne, 30 August 2017).

A week after Mnangagwa had been airlifted to South Africa, ZANU-PF youths from Midlands Province chanted slogans suggesting that the Vice-President had been poisoned by the G40 faction which is aligned to the First Lady, Grace Mugabe (*Zimbabwe Standard*, 27 August 2017). An intelligence report submitted to Mugabe confirmed that some senior ZANU-PF officials believed that the source of the poisoned ice cream that almost killed Mnangagwa was Gushungo Dairies, a company owned by President

Mugabe and his wife (Gonye and Ncube, 27 August 2017; *Zimbabwe Standard*, 27 August 2017).

On 26 August 2017, while addressing mourners at the National Heroes' Acre during the burial of two national heroes, Maud Muzenda and George Rutanhire, President Mugabe prioritised witchcraft issues over the country's pressing developmental needs. He exonerated the G40 faction and rubbished allegations that Mnangagwa had been poisoned or bewitched. In a tirade seemingly directed at the Lacoste faction, most of whose supporters were from the provinces of Masvingo and Midlands, Mugabe warned:

During the armed struggle, we never had weak cadres like what we are seeing today. This is not the Masvingo tradition that we know. Now the talk of witchcraft is the order of the day. Some are even saying the president is a witch, how many did I kill? We have travelled a long journey together and why kill today? This is coming from Midlands going to Masvingo. So if you have your witch doctors who are telling you about being bewitched, down with your witchcraft issues. During our days, we never knew that someone had been bewitched. People can go and consult witch doctors but use your own beliefs against people. It is common to be sick. We often hear that when a leader falls sick he would have been bewitched, no! When did this culture of accusing other people of witchcraft start? That is why we say please, please go to doctors and hospitals for constant check-ups. This is not the Masvingo that we know. Masvingo should be ashamed…Their support to the struggle was number one. It had people who were straightforward unlike these days. It is not the tradition of the Masvingo that we know. Now they are busy seeing witchcraft and…now everyone is being accused of being a witch; even the president is now a witch (*Zimbabwe Standard*, 27 August 2017: 1).

It is quite ironic that in his address at the National Heroes Acre, Mugabe was dismissing witchcraft accusations as a primitive practice yet a few years back, he had accused his political opponents such as Dzikamai Mavhaire (1997) and Joyce Mujuru (2014-2015) of being witches. These inconsistencies clearly illustrate that witchcraft allegations can be employed as instruments to assassinate the characters of political opponents. Thus, as Tendi (2016: 221) noted, such witchcraft accusations are "an effective, time-honoured means of vanquishing political rivals" (Tendi, 2016: 221).

In their reaction to the allegations of Mnangagwa's poisoning, the Zimbabwe Republic Police said they could not investigate the case because no official complaint had been submitted (Byrne, 30 August 2017). Instead, Mugabe threatened to summon the police to apprehend those who accused him of witchery. Addressing thousands of people at a ZANU-PF Youth League Interface Rally in the City of Gweru on 1 September 2017, Mugabe said that people accusing him of witchcraft should be hauled before the courts to answer charges of contravening the Witchcraft Suppression Act (Dube, 2 September 2017).

Mugabe's threat to have those who allegedly accused him of witchcraft prosecuted are quite ironic considering that he had previously accused some of his political opponents within ZANU-PF of witchcraft as stated earlier on in this chapter. In addition, the threat is illustrative on the manner in which Mugabe abused constitutional provisions of presidential immunity to prosecution by accusing political foes of witchcraft and then threatening to take to court those people who levelled similar allegations against him. This clearly shows that he could not stomach the bitter taste of his own medicine in Zimbabwe's political landscape.

As the fierce rivalry between G40 and Lacoste factions escalated during 2017, with the First Family actively involved, Zimbabwe's socio-economic meltdown persisted unabated as the ruling elites seemed to have abrogated their constitutional mandate to serve the people. In April 2017, for example, unemployment was over 90% and industrial utilisation capacity had plunged to below 15% (Dzamara, 23 April 2017). Alarming poverty levels were being witnessed, with 96% of the rural inhabitants surviving on less than US$1 per day and 72% of Zimbabweans living below the Poverty Datum Line (Ibid). The country's life expectancy of 46 years for men and 45 years for women was the highest in the world (Ibid). By engaging in endless squabbles during such dire times, the ZANU-PF elite demonstrated beyond doubt that "their insatiable love for power causes them never to respect the will of the people" (Ibid: 1).

Whether Mnangagwa was bewitched/poisoned or not, the witchcraft case had serious negative implications for Zimbabwe's development, particularly the socio-economic hardships which most people were experiencing. If it is true that Mnangagwa was 'bewitched' by his political opponents, then the point is that politics takes precedence over development issues in Zimbabwe, a country that has been in the throes of a debilitating socio-economic crisis, particularly from the onset of the new millennium. Vice President Mnangagwa temporarily suspended his government duties as he was admitted in a South African hospital. As ZANU-PF government officials, factions and supporters were bickering over witchcraft allegations, their attention was diverted from the country's pressing socio-economic challenges. President Mugabe himself prioritised the witchcraft case during public rallies at a time when famished Zimbabweans eagerly expected him to rescue the country from the dungeons of poverty.

Witchcraft allegations and rivalry within ZANU-PF structures and factions

ZANU-PF factions and localised structures also experienced internal struggles during which witchcraft accusations were traded by rivals in an effort to outwit each other in the struggle for political dominance while the majority of the population languished in poverty. In 2011, for example, witchcraft accusations were traded by political foes within ZANU-PF structures in the Buhera District of Manicaland Province and the case ended up in the courts (*Newsday*, 5 November 2011). The rivalry involved Zvenyika Machokoto, the 42-year-old ZANU-PF Buhera District Coordinating Committee Chairman who was reportedly eyeing the Buhera Constituency senatorial seat, and Judith Muodzeri, his 46-year-old wife, on one hand, and five Buhera-based senior party members on the other. The five Buhera-based senior ZANU-PF members were Joseph Chinotimba, a war veterans' leader; Kumbirai Kangai, former Minister of Agriculture; William Mtomba, Buhera North Member of Parliament; Kenneth Mwanditurira and Tapiwa Zengeya (Ibid). The five politicians reported Machokoto and his wife to the police on

344

charges of contravening Section 98 (1) of the Criminal Law (Codification and Reform) Act by hiring Jimmy Motsi, a traditional healer from the Mount Darwin District, to kill them using witchcraft (Nkomo, 26 January 2011; *Newsday*, 5 November 2011).

In his testimony at the Mutare Magistrate's Court in November 2011, Motsi stated that he was approached by Machokoto and his wife for assistance to use witchcraft to kill the five Buhera-based senior ZANU-PF officials and was paid US$7 000 and fertiliser (Ibid). He said the couple drove him from his rural home in Mt Darwin to Dorowa Mine, near the Buhera District, where a ritual ceremony to kill the five politicians was to be conducted. On the day of the ritual, Motsi said he prepared bottled water and asked Machokoto to call out the names of the five officials and state exactly the fate that he wanted to befall on them. According to Motsi, Machokoto called out the names of the five officials whom he accused of frustrating his political ambitions and expressed his wish that they die through road accidents or mysterious deaths (Ibid). He described the proceedings of the alleged ritual as follows:

> The names of the five were being called as a way of placing them in the bottle. They were supposed to die from that ritual had it not that I omitted some of the important elements of the ritual. I am not a traditional healer or a wizard, but I know that with the powers invested in me, I would be able to kill all of them though I realised it was not proper. Even Moses caused death of the Egyptians while Elijah caused serious droughts and what would you call that? (*Newsday*, 5 November 2011: 1).

The inconsistencies in Motsi's testimony are quite apparent and it is most probable that he had been hired by the five senior politicians to fabricate the story as part of a political agenda to tarnish the image of Machokoto. From his 'evidence,' Motsi exposed himself when he denied being a traditional healer and cooperating in the ritual. This leaves one wondering why he accepted the cash and fertiliser as payment when he did not wish to take part in the witchcraft conspiracy. It was not surprising that the case was dismissed at the Mutare Magistrate's Court on 5 April 2012 (*Newsday*,

9 April 2012). This case illustrates how ZANU-PF power struggles ate into the time and resources that could otherwise have been utilised in addressing the plight of Zimbabwe's marginalised people.

Another example can be drawn from Masvingo Province in January 2014 when the pro-Mnangagwa faction led by Josiah Hungwe, the Minister of State for Liaising on Psychomotor Activities in Education, was also rocked by infighting during which rivals traded witchcraft allegations as a political ploy to discredit each other. Hungwe himself threatened to quit the faction after his adversaries accused him of witchcraft. Hungwe reacted to the witchcraft allegations as follows: "I am a man of God and for some people to accuse me of having done a wrong thing without proving it is very disgusting. There are some within the party who hate my success and the best way is just to stop working with such people" (*NewsdzeZimbabwe*, 17 January 2014: 1). Taken at face value, Hungwe's sentiments are quite educative to the ruling elites to avoid wasting valuable time and resources on politicking and squabbling and instead, seriously consider addressing the plight of the ordinary people who voted them into power.

Conclusion

Even though the belief in witchcraft in Africa in particular and many other parts of the world in general dates back to ancient times, it is very much alive in contemporary Zimbabwean politics and development discourses where it is often used as a critical resource during contestations for political hegemony and to impoverish opponents. It was not within the scope of this chapter to interrogate the scientific authenticity of witchcraft as an institution. Rather, the chapter was primarily preoccupied with the manner in which witchcraft beliefs shape human relations in the realm of political dynamics within ZANU-PF as the majority of Zimbabweans were engulfed in a socio-economic crisis particularly from the onset of the new millennium. The chapter, therefore, was not concerned with ascertaining whether particular witchcraft allegations were true or false, but examined their intention in the context of prevailing political conflicts within ZANU-PF circles and the socio-economic meltdown that most ordinary Zimbabweans had to endure. As has been noted, most witchcraft accusations were articulated in the context of power struggles in ZANU-PF.

Broadly, the chapter noted that indigenous African cosmology since the pre-colonial period generally views the practice of witchcraft as retrogressive to human development in many aspects of life. This is because witches are associated with magical and harmful powers which are believed to have the potential to privilege the 'self' with wealth and other fortunes at the expense of acquaintances, relatives, neighbours and the general community. Thus, in contemporary political dynamics of many African countries and other parts of the world, witchcraft accusations can be a powerful tool employed by some politicians to mobilise sections of the electorate against rivals. Unfortunately, besides fuelling societal discord, such propagandistic machinations sacrifice valuable time and material resources that ruling elites could otherwise utilise to address urgent developmental challenges affecting the ordinary people such as food insecurity, homelessness, health ailments such as HIV/AIDS, unemployment and poverty.

References

Alexander, J. (2003). 'Squatters, veterans and the state in Zimbabwe,' in: B. Raftopoulos, A. Hammar and S. Jensen (Eds.) *Zimbabwe's unfinished business: Rethinking land, state and nation in the context of crisis*, Harare: Weaver Press, pp.83-117.

Ayittey, G. B. N. (1998). *Africa in chaos*, New York: St Martin's Press.

Ball, J. (1994). 'The ritual of the necklace,' *Research report prepared for the Centre for the Study of Violence and Reconciliation*, Johannesburg: South Africa

Bayart, J. F. (2009). *The state in Africa: The politics of the belly*, Cambridge: Polity Press.

Bond, P. and Manyanya, M. (2001). *Zimbabwe's plunge: Exhausted nationalism, neoliberalism and the search for social justice*, Asmara: Africa World Press.

Bourdillon, M. (1987). 'Book review of *Guns and rain*: Taking structural analysis too far?' in: *Africa*, Volume 57, p.273.

Bourdillon, M. F. C. (1998). *The Shona peoples: An ethnography of the contemporary Shona, with special reference to their religion*, Gweru: Mambo Press.

Braid, M. (3 May 1998). 'Zimbabwe tells Mugabe he must go,' Available at: www.independent.co.uk/news, Accessed 3 October 2017.

Brinkman, I. (2003). 'War, witches and traitors: Cases from the MPLA's eastern front in Angola, 1966-1975,' in: *Journal of African History*, Volume 33, pp.303-325.

Bucher, H. (1980). *Spirits and power*, Cape Town: Oxford University Press.

Bulawayo 24 News (26 March 2015). 'Mugabe consults witchdoctors,' Available at: http://bulawayo24.com/index-id-news, Accessed 22 September 2017.

Byrne, P. (30 August 2017). 'Robert Mugabe denies being a witch and poisoning rival with toxic ice cream,' Available at: http://www.mirror.co.uk/news/politics, Accessed 16 September 2017.

Chaota, U. (13 May 2017). 'ZANU-PF full of witches: Mahofa,' Available at: http://www.tellzim.com, Accessed 17 May 2017.

Chavunduka, G. L. (1980). 'Witchcraft and the law in Zimbabwe,' in: *Zambezia*, Volume VII, Number ii, pp.129-147.

Chidza, R. Manayiti, O. and Mhlanga, B. (21 August 2017). 'Mystery deepens over Mahofa's death-night calls,' Available at: https://www.newsday.co.zw, Accessed 17 September 2017.

Chireshe, E. Chireshe, R. and Shumba, A. (2012). 'Witchcraft and social life in Zimbabwe: Documenting the evidence,' in: *Study Tribes Tribals*, Volume 10, Number 2, pp.163-172.

Chitagu, T. (21 December 2016). "Poisoned' Mahofa avoids conference food,' Available at: https://www.newsday.co.zw, Accessed 17 September 2017.

Crawford, J. R. (1967). *Witchcraft and sorcery in Rhodesia*, London: Oxford University Press.

Daily News (10 July 2017). 'Mutasa hits hard times,' Harare: Zimbabwe.

Daneel, M. L. (1971). *The background and rise of southern Shona independent churches*, The Hague: Mouton.

Dube, G. (2 September 2017). 'Mugabe: Police should arrest people accusing me of witchcraft,' Available at: https://www.voazimbabwe.com, Accessed 16 September 2017.

Duri, F. (2016a). 'Presentism, contested narratives and dissonances in Zimbabwe's liberation war heritage: The case of Joyce Mujuru,' in: M. Mawere and T. R. Mubaya (Eds.) *Colonial heritage, memory and sustainability in Africa: Challenges, opportunities and prospects*, Bamenda: Langaa Research and Publishing Common Initiative Group, pp.11-32.

Duri, F. (2016b). 'Defining the Zimbabwean crisis during the New Millennium,' in: F. Duri (ed.) *Resilience amid adversity: Informal coping mechanisms to the Zimbabwean crisis during the New Millennium*, Gweru: Booklove Publishers, pp.22-49

Duri, F. (2017). 'African indigenous belief systems on the crossroads: The *Tsikamutanda* and witchcraft-related disputes in the 21st century Zimbabwe,' in: M. Mawere and T.R. Mubaya (eds.) *African studies in the academy: The cornucopia of theory, praxis and transformation in Africa?* Bamenda: Langaa Research and Publishing Common Initiative Group, pp.41-78.

Dzamara, P. (23 April 2017). 'Zimbabwe's make or break moment,' Available at: www.thezimbabwean.co, Accessed 4 October 2017.

Evans-Pritchard, E. E. (1937). *Witchcraft, oracles and magic among the Azande*, Oxford: Oxford University Press.

Gale, W. D. (1960). *Deserve to be great: The story of Rhodesia and Nyasaland*, Bulawayo: Stuart Manning.

Gelfand, M. (1964). *Witch doctor: Traditional medicine man in Rhodesia*, London: Harvill Press.

Golooba-Mutebi, A. (2005). 'Witchcraft, social cohesion and participation in a South African village,' in: *Development and Change*, Volume 36, Issue 5, pp.937-958.

Gonye, V. and Ncube, X. (27 August 2017). 'Mugabe wades into Vice-President 'poisoning' saga,' Available at: https://www.thestandard.co.zw, Accessed 20 September 2017.

Hammar, A. and Raftopoulos, B. (2003). 'Zimbabwe's unfinished business: Rethinking land, state and nation,' in: A. Hammar, B.

Raftopoulos and S. Jensen (Eds.) *Zimbabwe's unfinished business: Rethinking land, state and nation in the context of crisis*, Harare: Weaver Press, pp.1-47.

Hammond-Tooke, W. D. (Ed. (1974). *The Bantu-speaking peoples of Southern Africa*, London: Routledge and Kegan Paul.

Herald (18 July 2017). 'Mutasa loses assets,' Harare: Zimbabwe.

Howman, R. H. G. (1948). 'Witchcraft and the law,' in: *The Native Affairs Department Annual (NADA)*, Number 25, pp.7-18.

Igwe, L. (19 August 2011). 'Belief in witchcraft in Africa,' Available at: http://www.butterfliesandwheels.org, Accessed 28 March 2017.

Igwe, L. (30 August 2011). 'Witch hunts and the New Dark Age in Africa,' Available at: http://www.butterfliesandwheels.org, Accessed 28 March 2017.

Internet Zimbabwe (13 August 2015). 'Ex-Minister Olivia Muchena now homeless,' Available at: www.izimbabwe.co.zw, Accessed 3 October 2017.

Jakes, S. (25 May 2017). 'Zimbabwe has a leadership concerned only with accumulation of power,' Available at: www.bulawayo24.com/index, Accessed 4 October 2017.

Kapferer, B. (2003). *Beyond rationalism: Rethinking magic, witchcraft and sorcery*, New York: Oxford Berghahn Books.

Kluckhohn, C. (1944). 'Culture and personality: A conceptual scheme,' in: *American Ethnologist*, Volume 46, Issue 1, pp.1-29.

Krige, E. J. (1976). 'The Lovedu of Transvaal,' in: D. Forde (ed.) *African worlds: Studies in the cosmological and social values of African peoples*, Plymouth: Oxford University Press, pp.55-82.

Kriger, N. (1992). *Zimbabwe's guerrilla war: Peasant voices*, Cambridge: Cambridge University Press.

Kuwaza, K. (18 December 2015). 'ZANU-PF sacrifices economy on political expediency,' Available at: www.theindependent.co.zw, Accessed 3 October 3017.

Lan, D. (1985). *Guns and rain: Guerrillas and spirit mediums in Zimbabwe*, Harare: Zimbabwe Publishing House.

Machipisa, L. (1 March 2016). 'Zimbabwe's Joyce Mujuru forms ZPF to oppose Mugabe,' Available at:

http://www.bbc.com/news/world-africa, Accessed 16 September 2017.

Magaisa, A. (5 May 2015). 'Telecel saga: The problem of primitive accumulation in Zimbabwe,' Available at: www.newzimbabwe.com/columns, Accessed 4 October 2017.

Majaka, N. (4 December 2016). 'Sorcery and witchcraft in Zimbabwe,' Available at: https://www.dailynews.co.zw/articles, Accessed 30 March 2017.

Mambo, E. (19 June 2015). 'Events preceding Midzi's fateful day,' in: *The Zimbabwe Independent*, Harare: Zimbabwe.

Marwick, M. G. (1965). *Sorcery in its social setting: A study of the Northern Rhodesian Cewa*. Manchester: Manchester University Press.

Matenga, M. (4 December 2014). 'Mujuru tried juju on me: Mugabe,' Available at: https://www.southerneye.co.zw, Accessed 17 September 2017.

Matonhodze, C. R. (31 July 2013). 'Multimedia: A history of Zimbabwean elections,' in: *The Newsday*, Harare: Zimbabwe.

Matyszak, D. (2014). *The mortal remains: Succession and the ZANU-PF body politic: Report produced for the Zimbabwe Human Rights NGO Forum by the Research and Advocacy Unit*, Harare: Zimbabwe Human Rights NGO Forum.

Mawawa, T. (19 May 2017). 'ZANU-PF witches nearly killed me: Mahofa,' Available at: https://www.zimeye.net, Accessed 17 September 2017.

Mawere, M. (2011). 'Possibilities for cultivating African Indigenous Knowledge Systems (IKSs): Lessons from selected cases of witchcraft in Zimbabwe,' in: *Journal of Gender, Peace and Development*, Volume 1, Number 3, pp.91-100.

Moyo, H. (11 April 2014). 'Power struggles reign as country bleeds,' Available at: https://www.theindependent.co.zw, Accessed 3 October 2017.

Muponde, R. (4 March 2015). 'Mugabe in witchcraft boob,' Available at: https://www.southerneye.co.zw, Accessed 19 September 2017.

Ncube, X. (28 August 2017). 'I did not poison Vice-President Mnangagwa: S.K. Moyo,' in: *The Zimbabwe Standard*, Harare: Zimbabwe.

351

Nehanda Radio (14 August 2015). 'Former ZANU-PF minister now homeless,' Available at: www.google.com.zw, Accessed 3 October 2017.

New Zimbabwe (28 August 2017). 'Political analysts accuse Mugabe of double standards: He believes in both witchcraft and Christianity,' Available at: http://www.myzimbabwe.co.zw, Accessed 16 September 2017.

News Anchor (18 August 2017). 'Grace misled by ZANU-PF witches,' Available at: www.newsanchor.co.zw, Accessed 19 September 2017.

New Zimbabwe (25 June 2016). 'Mavhaire says if people had supported his 1997 call for Mugabe to go, the President would be history now,' Available at: www.newzimbabwe.com/news, Accessed 3 October 2017.

News24 (3 March 2015). 'Mujuru wanted to use Nigerian witches to topple me - Mugabe,' Available at:
http://www.news24.com/Africa, Accessed 18 September 2017.

News24 (2 March 2016). 'Mugabe must have been drunk when he accused me of witchcraft: Mujuru,' Available at: www.news24.com/Africa, Accessed 18 September 2017.

Newsday (5 November 2011). 'Chinotimba 'marked for death' in ZANU-PF witchcraft case,' Available at:
https://www.newsday.co.zw, Accessed 17 September 2017.

Newsday (9 April 2012). 'Chinotimba loses witchcraft case,' Available at: https: //www.newsday.co.zw, Accessed 22 September 2017.

Newsday (3 March 2015). 'Timeline: Mugabe's allegations against Mujuru,' Harare: Zimbabwe.

NewsdzeZimbabwe (17 January 2014). 'Zimbabwe official accused of witchcraft in political ploy,' Available at:
http://doubtfulnews.com, Accessed 16 September 2017.

Nhemachena, A. (2014). 'Knowledge, *chivanhu* and struggles for survival in conflict-torn Manicaland, Zimbabwe,' *D.Phil. Thesis*, University of Cape Town.

Nkomo, N. (26 January 2011). 'Couple in court over witchcraft plot,' Available at: www.newzimbabwe.com/news, Accessed 19 September 2017.

Nyamayaro, A. (7 December 2016). '*Tsikamutanda* humiliates elderly people,' Available at: http://hmetro.co.zw/tsikamutanda-humiliates-elderly-people, Accessed 28 March 2017.

Raftopoulos, B. (2003). 'The state in crisis: Authoritarian nationalism, selective citizenship and distortions of democracy in Zimbabwe,' in: A. Hammar, B. Raftopoulos and S. Jensen (eds.) *Zimbabwe's unfinished business: Rethinking land, state and nation in the context of crisis*, Harare: Weaver Press, pp.217-41.

Reuters Alert (20 March 2007). 'Zimbabwe says drought will worsen food shortages,' Available at: http://www.ReutersAlertNet.org, Accessed 12 July 2014.

Richardson, C. J. (2005). The loss of property rights and the collapse of Zimbabwe, *Cato Journal*, 25 (3): 541-565.

Ritchken, E. (1989). 'The meaning of rural political violence,' *Seminar Paper,* Johannesburg: Centre for the Study of Violence and Reconciliation.

Saunyama, J. (30 January 2017). '*Tsikamutanda* shenanigans exposed,' Available at: https://www.newsday.co.zw, Accessed 26 March 2017.

Schmidt, E. (1992). *Peasants, traders and wives: Shona women in the history of Zimbabwe, 1870-1939*, Harare: Baobab.

South African Press Association (3 March 2015). 'Joice Mujuru says Mugabe lewd, rejects witchcraft,' Available at: http://www.news24.com/Africa, Accessed 14 September 2017.

Southern Rhodesia Government. (1939). *The statute law of Southern Rhodesia Volume 1*, Salisbury: Southern Rhodesia Government.

Steadman, L. (1985). 'The killing of witches,' in: *Oceania*, Volume 56, Number 1, pp.106-123.

Sunday Mail. (11 December 2016). '*Tsikamutanda*: Hunting the hunters,' Available at: http://bulawayo24.com/index-id-news-sc-national-byo-100941.html, Accessed 29 March 2017.

Tafirenyika, M. (10 July 2017). 'Didymus Mutasa falls into poverty: Begs for food, school fees,' Available at: www.zimnews.net, Accessed 3 October 2017.

Tatira, L. (2014). Shona belief systems: Finding relevancy for a new generation, *The Journal of Pan African Studies*, 6 (8): 106-118.

Tekere, E. (2009). *A lifetime of struggle*, Harare: SAPES Books.

Tendi, B. M. (2016). 'State intelligence and the politics of Zimbabwe's presidential succession,' in: *African Affairs*, Volume115, Number 459, pp.203–224, Available at: https://academic.oup.com/afraf/article, Accessed 15 September 2017.

Thomson Reuters Foundation (18 January 2016). 'Baobab, food aid on the menu as drought bites,' Available at: www.newzimbabwe.com/NEWS, Accessed 19 May 2017.

Thorpe, S.A. (1991). *African traditional religions: An introduction*, Pretoria: University of South Africa.

Werbner, R. (1991). *Tears of the dead: The social biography of an African family*, Edinburgh: Edinburgh University Press.

Young, S. (1977). 'Fertility and famine: Women's agricultural history in southern Mozambique,' in: R. Palmer and N. Parsons (Eds.). *The roots of rural poverty in Central and Southern Africa*, London: Heinemann.

ZimEye (24 July 2017). 'Grace speaks on horror witchcraft that triggered her car accident,' Available at: https://www.zimeye.net, Accessed 17 September 2017.

Zimbabwe Daily (23 February 2016). 'Mujuru claims her husband was shot dead and his body burnt,' Available at: https://www.thezimbabwedaily.com/news, Accessed 18 September 2017.

Zimbabwe Government. (2006). *The Witchcraft Suppression Act, Chapter 9*, Harare: Government Printer.

Zimbabwe Independent (13 October 2014). 'Economy bleeds as ZANU-PF feud escalates,' Available at: http://www.zimbabweonlinenews.com, Accessed 3 October 2017.

Zimbabwe Standard (3 September 2017). 'Mugabe getting a taste of his medicine,' Available at: https://www.thestandard.co.zw, Accessed 21 September 2017.

Zimbabwean (4 September 2017). 'Which is witch?' Available at: http://www.thezimbabwean.co, Accessed 17 September 2017.

Chapter 13

Corruption and Failures of Various Poverty Alleviation Programmes to Eradicate Poverty: Historical Appraisal of Nigeria from 1985-2015

Orji Boniface Ifeanyi

Introduction

Poverty is currently one of the most serious problems in Nigeria and many other countries of Africa. Sadly, the poverty level in Nigeria contradicts her immense wealth and resources that the country has at its disposal. Nigeria is tremendously blessed with remarkable human and economic resources- underground and aboveground resources. Despite all these natural resources and blessed assets, it is really lamentable to see a great number of Nigerians living in abject poverty. Nigeria happens to be one of the 24th poorest countries of the world, with more than 50% of its population living on less than one US dollars per day. The incidence of poverty has been on the increase since independence in 1960 and both local and international data show that the majority of the Nigerians are not doing well, despite the series of poverty alleviation programmes, with the major victims of poverty being women, children and youths (Maggaji, 2005). The 2000 World Bank research reveals that "only 50% of Nigerian population has access to safe drinking water, about 38% of the population does not have access to the primary healthcare, and most Nigerians consume less than 1/3 of the minimum required protein and vitamins, due to low purchasing power" (Ibid, 2005: 33).

One needs not to be an economic expert to know that the majority of Nigerians are poor and the economy is stagnant. This is because the general signs of poverty and economic stagnation, namely; low purchasing power, unemployment, low productivity, low consumption, low investment, poor health system, poor education system, poor network of transportation system, unstable power supply and so on are visible to everyone with "eyes" to see.

As spelt out by the United Nations (1998), poverty is a denial of choices and opportunities, a violation of human dignity. According to Sen (1999), poverty must be seen as the deprivation of basic capabilities, and relative deprivation in terms of incomes can lead to absolute deprivations in terms of capabilities (e.g. being poor in a rich country: in a rich country more income is needed to buy the commodities to achieve the same social functioning). This is the case of Nigeria who is richly endowed but have poor citizens. Amartya Sen went further to see poverty as the lack of basic capacity to participate effectively in society. It means not having enough to feed and clothe a family, not having a school or clinic to go to; not having the land on which to grow one's food or a job to earn one's living, not having access to credit. It means insecurity, powerlessness and exclusion of individuals, households and communities. It means susceptibility to violence, and it often implies living on marginal or fragile environments, without access to clean water or sanitation.

In Nigeria, widespread and severe poverty is a reality. It is a reality that depicts a lack of food, clothes, education and other basic amenities. Severely poor people lack the most basic necessities of life to a degree that it can be wondered how they manage to survive. There are several effects and deficiencies associated with poverty in Nigeria. One of the main effects of poverty is poor health, as is reflected in Nigeria's high infant mortality and low life expectancy. Poor people in Nigeria face several health issues as they lack basic health amenities and competent medical practitioners (Adigun, Awoyemi and Fabiyi: 2015). Most children do not have the opportunity of being immunized and this leads to certain physical defects in some of the children (Ucha: 2010). Their health has become low priority and as they have little or no choices, they live with whatever they are provided with, whether healthy or not.

Poverty reduction remains one of the major priorities of successive governments in Nigeria since political independence in 1960, yet no meaningful improvement seems forthcoming. Some policy framework and incentive plan such as National Poverty Alleviation Program (NAPEP), National Directorate of Employment; Better Life for Rural Women; Family Economic Advancement Programme and the most recent poverty reduction schemes include The Youth Empowerment Schemes (YES), The Rural Infrastructure Development Schemes (RIDS), The Natural Resources Development and Conservation Scheme (NRDCS), and The Social Welfare Service Scheme (SOWESS), and other, that are aimed at alleviating poverty in Nigeria have been put in place. Unfortunately, corruption has been the bane of success of the provision of the incentive plans which have not been followed with effective implementation and monitoring mechanisms to the target areas.

Corruption has been identified as one of the factors responsible for poverty in the country. In its Annual Report for 2012, the Economic and Financial Crimes Commission (EFCC) (2012: 10) observed that:

> Corruption in the public sector remains a sore spot in Nigeria's quest to instil transparency and accountability in the polity. The failure to deliver social services, the endemic problem of power supply and the collapse of infrastructure are all linked with corruption ... Unfortunately, the will to combat corruption in all tiers of government is still very weak. In some cases, especially in the states and local governments, the political will to fight corruption is non-existent, as the workings of the polity are intricately connected with corruption activities ... It is no surprise therefore that most of the predicate offences to money laundering are connected with corruption within the officialdom.

Corruption by the Nigerian leaders and other government officials saddled with the responsibility of administering the eradication schemes is catastrophic and has continued to contribute to the poverty scourge ravaging the nation. Through corruption, money meant for education, health and other productive sectors are siphoned for private uses, denying the poor the basic necessities of life they deserve. Systematically, corruption promotes poverty, but the poor promotes corruption in Nigeria. Sadly, such people amassing wealth through unscrupulous means are even entitled to honours in the churches such as Deacons, Elders, and Knights among others; at the community level, they are giving traditional titles

357

such chieftaincies, while many of them uses the corrupt money to campaign and contest for Councillorship, Local Government Chairman, Governorship, State Houses of Assembly, House of Representatives and Senate positions at the detriment of the poor. Unfortunately, the poor worship these people in the society, which is an indication that the poor in particular promotes corruption (Abdulsalami: 2006).

This chapter examines the effects of poverty in Nigeria, the failure of the Nigerian government and the country's leadership to reduce poverty rate as a result of corruption and other such unethical and unprofessional practices. The justification for this chapter emanates from the fact that in spite of these poverty alleviation programmes instituted by various administration, Nigeria still ranks 54th in Human Poverty Index (HPI), and is among the 20 poorest countries in the world with 70% of the population living below the poverty datum line as of 2003 (World Development Report; 2005). This chapter adopts a qualitative research methodology and adopted the elite theory to explain why poverty alleviation programmes fail in Nigeria bearing in mind some of the failed programmes in the past. The chapter concludes that poverty has not been tackled in Nigeria because those that are saddled with the responsibility of implementing the various programme, see it as opportunity of enriching themselves, thereby inflicting more poverty on the Nigerian populace.

The historicity of Poverty in Nigeria

After gaining political independence in 1960, Nigeria failed to recognize economic development machinery which is the basis of poverty eradication. On the contrary, the country divided itself along ethnic cleaver age, with the three major ethnic groups (Hausa, Igbo and Yoruba) trying to achieve supremacy over each other. This resulted in wars, lack of trust, disharmony and wanton destruction of life and properties. Suffix it to say that the problem of disunity and ethnicism in Nigeria can be traced to colonialism which through their division of Africa into states (or countries) bunched together people of totally different ethnic origins, some who were hostile to each other before the partition of Africa at the 1884-85 Berlin Conference was forcefully forced together. Instead of Nigerians to use their differences to achieve economic development, they have been using the differences to achieve economic destruction.

Poverty, between the 1960s and early 1970s, was minimal as few people were below the poverty line in Nigeria. During this period, Nigeria enjoyed steady economic growth and relative stability (Nigeria Economic Society, 1975). The economy and per capita income grew steadily as the agricultural, industrial and even public sector absorbed most of the labour force. The poverty incidence started rising in the late 1970s and early 1980s when the economy experienced difficulties as a result of oil shock, deteriorating terms of trade, debt overhang and macroeconomic instability (Bello, Toyebi, Balogun and Akanbi: 2009). In the mid-80s the poverty rate in Nigeria started rising. For instance about 34% of the Nigeria's population was living below poverty line between 1985 and 1986 (Ibid). It rose to 53% and 67% in 1996 and 1997 respectively. By 1999, about 67% lived below poverty line, making Nigeria the 54th in the Human Poverty Index (HPI) and among the twenty poorest nations in the world (CBN Bullion 2003).

Table 1. Incidence of Poverty in Nigeria

Year	Poverty Incidence (%)	Estimated Total Population (in Millions)	Population in Poverty (in Millions)
1980	28.1	65	18.26
1985	46.3	75	34.73
1992	42.7	91.5	39.07
1996	65.6	102.3	67.11
2004	54.7	126.3	69.09
2010	69.0	163.0	112.47
2016	70.1	180	126.13

Source: National Bureau of Statistics, 2017

Before the commercial mining of oil in early 1959, the Nigerian economy was mainly dependent on agricultural products for its domestic food supply and foreign exchange earnings. This was soon to change with the coming of the oil boom which led to the neglect of the agricultural sector, leading to deterioration in agricultural production. This on the other hand, led to massive importation of food. Many attempts have been made to correct this problem through agricultural programmes such as Operation Feed the Nation, Agricultural Credit Guarantee Scheme Funds and the Green Revolution, but they have not achieved the desired objective of food security for the masses (Forae, 2005).

With the oil boom of the mid-1970s to the early 1980s, the Nigeria's economic policies of that period wittingly neglected other viable areas of the economy such as agriculture and the non-oil export sector. The country, according to Atoloye (1997), depended heavily on oil for meeting her international commitments and executing domestic economic programmes. By 1982 Atoloye added, when the volatility of the oil market became a stark reality, the economy was already caught in the throes of a depression.

To reverse this condition, the Structural Adjustment Programme (SAP) was adopted in 1986. The most important of the various policies under the programme was the restructuring of the production as well as the export base of the economy with a view to restructure and revamp the ailing economy and breaking the mono-product nature of Nigeria's export sector. The programme was however, plagued by a lot of contradictions and distortions that inhibited its full implementation and was subsequently abandoned after six years (Forae 2000). Worthy of note, was its haphazard implementation which brought about problems of greater dimension; that of debt overhang and its attendant rescheduling and forgiveness proposals which President Olusegun Obasanjo achieved in 2006, after protracted negotiations with the Paris Club.

In 1986, a mass mobilization approach which included integrated rural development and basic needs strategies, were adopted in Nigeria. Programmes that were created in this macro approach included; the Directorate for Food, Roads and Rural Infrastructures (DFRRI); the National Directorate of Employment (NDE); Mass Mobilization for Social Justice and Economic Reconstruction (MAMSER); Better Life for Rural Women; the People's Bank, Community Banks; Rural Health Schemes; and the Expanded

Programme on Immunization (EPI). The ADPs were also strengthened. The Directorate for Foods, Roads and Rural Infrastructures (DFRRI) was expected to provide basic amenities like access roads, rural electrification and portable water to ease the living conditions of the rural people as it was noted that poverty is widespread in both rural and urban areas in Nigeria. The rural areas, however, record a higher incidence, depth and severity of poverty than the urban areas.

Table 2. Relative Poverty by Sector - Urban and Rural (%)

Year	Urban	Rural
1980	16.2	28.3
1985	37.8	51.4
1992	37.5	46.0
1996	58.2	69.3
2004	43.1	63.8
2010	61.8	73.2

Source: National Bureau of Statistics, 2017

The National Bureau of Statistics (2007) attributed the high incidence of poverty in the rural areas to their dependence on low-productive agriculture, lack of access to opportunities and poor social and economic infrastructure. This was part of the reasons that led to the introduction of National Directorate of Employment (NDE) to help provide self-employment opportunities for unemployed youths in rural and urban areas. They were to do this by training the youths in different arts and crafts and by providing them with soft loans and equipment.

The 2000s saw the emergence of the Universal Basic Education (UBE) Schemes, Mass Adult Literacy Programmes and Primary Health care Programme. With these schemes, the government was determined to create more jobs for about 200,000 unemployed persons and stimulate production within a period of one year. Within the same period, the government recognized that about 70 percent of Nigerians are poor in real terms and earmarked 50 percent of Poverty Alleviation Programmes (PAP) jobs for youths; 25 percent for women and the remaining 25 percent for the men, with special

361

preference for the destitute and disabled persons. The jobs thus created were spread among states at (5000 persons each) while the balance of 15,000 was shared among thickly populated cities (Forae: 2011). In addition, PAP participants were paid monthly stipends of N3500 each (Ibid). In most cases, the stipends and incentives never got to the participants. However, the original outlay of the Poverty Alleviation Programme (PAP) that was introduced in 1999 immediately the Obasanjo administration came in was amended and renamed National Poverty Eradication Programme (NAPEP) in 2001 to address the problems of rising unemployment and crime wave, particularly among youths. It was ultimately aimed at increasing the welfare of Nigerians. Its major components are the Mandatory Attachment Programme (MAP), the Youth Empowerment Scheme (YES) and the Capacity Acquisition Programme (CAP).

Worth noting is also the fact that poverty in Nigeria has a regional dimension. Statistics show that people living in the northern part of the country are more likely to live in poverty than those living in the rest of the country. More specifically, NBS reports that in 2004 the poverty incidence was highest in the North-East zone (67.3%) and lowest in the South-East zone (34.5%), with similar figures for 2016.

Table 3

Zone	1980	1985	1992	1996	2004	2010	2016
South-South	12.2	45.7	51.1	58.2	51.3	37.6	38.4
South-East	12.9	30.4	41.0	52.5	34.1	34.3	34.5
South-West	12.4	38.6	42.2	60.9	43.2	42.0	43.4
North-Central	32.2	50.8	46.0	64.7	63.4	62.3	65.8
North-East	32.6	54.9	54.0	70.1	67.6	63.0	68.5
North-West	37.7	52.1	36.5	77.2	63.9	62.9	65.4

Source: National Bureau of Statistics: 2017

Perception on the causes of poverty in Nigeria

There seems to be narrow disagreement on the causes of poverty as against the difficulty encountered in arriving at a universally accepted definition of poverty. Although researchers and scholars tend to discuss causes of poverty mostly from their areas of profession, region or gender, there are basic factors that enable the prevalence of poverty. These basic factors, including macro-economic distortions, effects of globalisation, governance, corruption, debt burden, low productivity, unemployment, high population growth rate and poor human resources development etc., may differ from country to country depending on the level of economic development (Oyemomi: 2003). There are however, many issues involved when looking at the causes of poverty. Some are fundamental while others are not.

While the CBN (1999: 12) grouped causes of poverty into two categories "namely low economic growth and market imperfections", the World Bank (2001: 34) reasoned that "one route of investigating the causes of poverty is to examine the dimensions highlighted by poor people" namely:

- Lack of income and assets to attain basic necessities – food, shelter, clothing, and acceptable levels of health and education;
- Sense of voicelessness and powerlessness in the institutions of state and society; and
- Vulnerability to adverse shocks, linked to an inability to cope with them.

On the other hand, the Federal Office of Statistics in its publication: Socio- Economic Profile of Nigeria (1996: 109) was definite in categorizing the causes of poverty in Nigeria into problems of access and endowments such as:

- Inadequate access to employment opportunities for the poor. This is often caused by the stunted growth of economic activities or growth with labour saving device;
- Lack or inadequate access to assets such as land capital by the poor: this is often attributed to the absence of land reform and minimal opportunities for small-credit;
- Inadequate access to the means of fostering rural development in poor regions: the preference for high potential areas and the strong urban bias in the design of development programmes is often assumed to be its primary cause;

- Inadequate access to markets for the goods and services that the poor can sell: this is caused by their remote geographic location or other factors;

- Inadequate access to education, health, sanitation and water services. This emanates from inequitable social service delivery which consequently results in the inability of the poor to live a healthy and active life and take full advantage of employment opportunities;

- The destruction of the natural resources endowments, which has led to reduced productivity of agriculture, forestry and fisheries. This often resulted from the desperate survival strategies of the poor as well as inadequate and ineffective public policy on natural resource management;

- The inadequate access to assistance by those who are the victims of transitory poverty such as drought, floods, pests and war. This is brought about by lack of well-conceived strategies and resources; and

- Inadequate involvement of the poor in the design of development programmes. This is often exacerbated by the non-involvement of the representatives of the poor communities or beneficiaries in the discussion, preparation, design and implementation of programmes that will affect them.

A careful assessment of the above alleged causes indicates the multidimensional nature of poverty. This indication no doubt, provides basis for a better approach for effective attack on poverty. Aliyu (2002: 30) in his own contribution cited other factors as effects of globalization, governance, corruption, debt burden and low productivity, as causes of poverty. What Aliyu fail to understand that all the above mention factors takes place as a result of corruption. The World Bank (2016) in its study: Consultation with the Poor, posits that, "the impact of a range of possible shocks, trends and cycles were seen to be important influence on local vulnerability and helped to differentiate the vulnerable from the more secure". The report went further to state that "the risks people face were linked to a number of key aspects of security that affected the poor at different levels of social organization, from the individual to the household to entire communities". Specifically, the report linked poverty in many instances to some perceived pathologies such as reckless spending and distaste for farming, laziness, over population, bad government and non-payment of compensation for land acquired by government. This to an extent can be said to be the picture of Nigeria scenario.

The causes of poverty as the CBN (2009) suggested a summary of the causative factors of poverty, which tried to capture all the pertinent issues raised as: The stage of Economic and Social Development; Low Productivity; Market imperfection; Physical or Environmental Degradation; Structural Shift in the Economy; Inadequate Commitment to Programme Implementation; Political Instability; and Corruption.

Corruption and policy failures in poverty alleviation

There are several causes of the failure of poverty alleviation policy in Nigeria in which corruption played a greater part. Corruption related factors responsible for the failures of most of these policies are associated with deliberate wrong policy design, implementation and policy acceptability which include: misunderstanding of the policies made for the people by the policy makers, misplaced priorities, favouritism and benefit capture, which breeds contempt for the policies.

There are always situations where the supposed change agents or policy makers are incompetent in driving and implementing poverty eradication programme, and at the same time do not know the people they make the policy for, especially their felt perceived needs. But because of who they know in government, they are given these opportunities, and at the end they will want to either overestimate or underestimate the problems of such people and are also likely to misplace priorities. Due to their corrupt intentions, these corrupt agents tend to make the prevailing public policy on poverty alleviation to be at variance with the people's perception of what constitute their development (Amundsen: 2010).

It is obvious from the above assertion, that this action makes the poor not to share government's enthusiasm for poverty alleviation. In most cases, these corrupt officials do not adopt the availed poverty alleviation proposals, programmes and projects that are espoused in the official national development programmes. They therefore undertake other types of projects that are inferior that they think will bring more money into their individual pockets at the detriment of the poor masses (Owasanoye: 2014). For instance, there were cases in Ebonyi, Imo and Abia States where hospital and water projects under the MDG that are sited in the middle of bushes where the people cannot have easy access them(This Day: 2014). They hurriedly commissioned them and they have never functioned after the commissioning.

Poverty alleviation policies in Nigeria have continued to be directed at unemployment as part of the solution to the problem of poverty in the most rural areas. However, the corrupt officials will call for the submission of Curriculum Vitae (CV) from the unemployed citizens, use their data to register them for the poverty alleviation programme, but at the end, the money released for this category of people will never get to them. This is because the corrupt officials, who are supposed to pay the stipends, end up diverting the money into their private pockets.

There is no doubt that the Nigerian government has made different attempts alleviate poverty in the country, as evidenced by the introduction of different poverty alleviation programmes and projects such as Roads and Rural Infrastructure (DFRRI) in 1986; Better Life Programme (BLP) in 1987; National Directorate of Employment (NDE) in 1987; Family Support Programme (FSP) in 1993; Family Economic Advancement Programme (FEAP) in 1997, and others. Unfortunately, the wide spread of corruption, fiscal indiscipline, political and policy instability that characterized the nation always make these programmes fail to achieve the set goals.

When Nigeria transited from military rule to civilian government under Obasanjo in 1999, there were a lot of expectations by the citizens to address the issue of poverty in the country, which many blamed the long years of military rule as being responsible for that. The new government having recognized the expectations saw the need to introduce another poverty alleviation programme following the continuous increase in the poverty level and mass unemployment of youth. In 2000, poverty Alleviation Programme (PAP) was launched. The programme was designed to provide employment for about 200,000 people, and the sum of NI06 million was set aside for the programme (Ejikeme: 2014). Owing to its failure which was attributed to corruption and irregularities by the officials, PAP was replaced with the National Poverty Eradication Programme (NAPEP) in the following year (Aliyu: 2002), which has the responsibility of coordinating and monitoring the activities of the core poverty eradication ministries and Agencies, such as health, education, power and steel, water resources, work and housing among others. Unfortunately, the same factor (corruption) which made all the various poverty alleviation Programmes not to succeed in Nigeria, equally did not allow NAPEP and other subsequent ones to succeed.

Recommendation

Nigeria is a country blessed with enormous human and natural resources, yet well over two-third of about 180 million of her population are wallowing in poverty. This is as a result of a compound of factors, the major ones being corruption, mismanagement and illegal embezzling of public funds by public officials and a few others instead of distributing this wealth across every strata of the country. This has left many poor and unemployed youth to roam the street, making them an easy prey for use to instigate political and social unrest. The following recommendations are therefore suggested:

1. Government and its agencies should develop a multi-dimensional approach to poverty reduction strategies and implement along that line.
2. The poverty alleviation programmes should not be politicized and there should be proper scrutinizing and supervisory Machinery to ensure that every plan is well implemented. The officials should not see the programme as self-seeking activities that involve cake sharing rather; they should see it as cake baking.
3. Poverty reduction programmes should be given its pride of place through adequate budgeting and prompt release of funds to them;

4. Efforts should be made to effectively target the poor in all considerations and at all levels of articulation, implementation, monitoring and review of the poverty reduction strategies;

5. The government's anti-corruption efforts should be stepped up and seriously upheld in dealing with matters concerning poverty reduction programmes/agencies and even beneficiaries;

6. The National Poverty Eradication Programme should be strengthened for its coordination and monitoring mandate;

7. Issues concerning policy inconsistency should be resolved through the approval and faithful implementation of the National Policy on Poverty Reduction

Conclusion

It is often posited that the various successive governments in Nigeria cannot be said to be oblivious of the depth of poverty in the country which necessitated the introduction of some programmes to better the lots of citizenry. Poverty has various dimensions such as lack of adequate food and shelter, education and health, vulnerability to ill health, natural disasters and economic dislocation as well as lack of voice in matters concerning them. Until the adequate understanding of all the multi-dimensional nature of poverty is put into place and brought into play, all strategies may end up addressing only one dimension or, at best, some dimensions of poverty. To be able to effectively achieve the objective of reducing poverty to a considerable low level, efforts or strategies formulated and directed towards poverty reduction need to be holistic in nature.

References

Abdulsalami, I. (1998). Inaugural Lecture Series No.9 on Development Administration: As Approach to Nation Building Nigeria; the Illusion of a Country on the horns of Dilemma. *ABU Zaria* Tues. 28th May

Adeniyi, J. P. (1998). *Poor Quality of Rural Life in Nigeria: Implication for a United Nations Statement*, which was signed by the heads of all UN agencies. June.

Adigun, G. T., Awoyemi, T. T., and Fabiyi, E. F. (2015). "Analysing Poverty Situation in Rural Nigeria". *Journal of Agricultural Science and Engineering* 1 (4): 178-188.

Aliyu, A. (2002). Re-Structuring of the Poverty Alleviation Activities of the Federal Government of Nigeria. *National Poverty Eradication Programme Report*. Abuja.

Amundsen, I. (2010). *Good Governance in Nigeria: A Study in Political Economy and Donor Support*, Michelsen Institute, Project number: 10013, Project title: Study of Norwegian Support for Good Governance in Nigeria, 24 August.

Bello, R. A.; Toyebi, G. O. A; Balogun, I. O. and Akanbi, B. S. (2009). "Poverty Alleviation Programmes and Economic Development in Nigeria: A Comparative Assessment of Asa and Ilorin West Local Govt. Areas of Kwara State, Nigeria". *Journal of African Research Review*, Ethiopia.

Bullion. (2003). An Appraisal of Federal Government's National Poverty Eradication Programme (NAPEP), *CBN Research Department*.

Central Bank of Nigeria. (2009). "Nigerian Development Prospects Poverty Assessment and Alleviation Study", p. 12.

EFCC. (2012). "Ongoing Corrupt Cases in Nigeria", Abuja: Nigeria.

Ejikeme, J. N. (2014). "Unemployment and Poverty in Nigeria: A Link to National Insecurity". *Global Journal of Politics and Law Research* 2 (1): 19-35

Federal Office of Statistics (1999). *Poverty Profile of Nigeria 1980 -1996*, Lagos, FOS.

Forae F. O. (2011). An Appraisal of Poverty Alleviation Programmes in Nigeria, *JORIND (9)1* June.

Forae, F. O. (2000). 'Structural Adjustment Programme and Development in the Third World: An Appraisal, *Nigerian Journal of Economic History*, Vol.2.

Forae F. O. (2005). The Food and Agricultural Crisis in Africa: An Appraisal of Capitalist Agriculture in Nigeria, *African Journal of Economy and Society*, 2(5).

Magaji, D. (2005). "The Mystery of Poverty Eradication" *Weekly Trust*, August 2005.

National Bureau of Statistics. (2012). *'The Nigerian Poverty Profile 2010 Report'*, Abuja, p12-14.

National Bureau of Statistics. (2007). *Nigeria Poverty Assessment Report*, Abuja, p7.

National Poverty Eradication Council. (2000). *"Nigeria: Poverty Reduction Plan, 2001 to 2004"* – A Report of Inter-Ministerial Group of Officials, Coordinated by the Economic Policy Coordinating Committee Abuja.

Owasanoye, B. (2014). Justice or Impunity? High Profile Corruption Cases Crawling or Gone to Sleep, Lagos, *Human Development Initiatives.*

Oyemomi, E.O. (2003). *Unpublished Ph.D. Thesis in the Department of Management*, St. Clement University.

Sen, A. (1999). *Development as Freedom,* Oxford University Press: New York.

Ucha, C. (2010). Poverty in Nigeria: Some Dimensions and Contributing Factors, *Global Majority E-Journal,* 1 (1): 46-56.

United Nations Development Programme. (1998). *Human Development Report1997*, New York.

World Bank. (2016). *"Consultation with the Poor"*, Washington DC: New York.

World Bank. (2005). *"Voices of the Poor"*, World Development Report, Washington D. C.

Chapter 14

'A Prophet for the Poor?' A Contextual Reading of the Book of Micah vis-a-vis Poverty Alleviation Efforts in Zimbabwe

Nyasha Madzokere

Introduction

The identity of Micah, like that of Amos, raises controversy of epic proportion in the Old Testament prophetic studies. It remains mired in mystery, which prompts the necessity for more research to be done around issues of his prophetic message and cause of existence. This study examines whether Micah should safely be designated a prophet for the Poor or a neutral prophet. The chapter raises a number of questions in a bid to unravel Micah's identity and the gist of his prophetic message, thus: Who was his father or mother? What was known about his family and his personal life? What was the connection between his rural background and his message? Was Micah a true or a false prophet? What was his social status?

Due to lack of consensus on the identity of Micah as compounded by lack of clarity by the superscription leading to the above questions, this chapter makes deductions based on the internal testimony of the book of Micah and insights from scholars. While focusing on a contextual understanding of Micah, the chapter draws insights from his identity and message to the effect that it examines whether it befits that Micah of Moresheth be considered a prophet for the Poor or for the rich. On this note, this chapter interrogates Micah's identity and his message to the people of Judah who were experiencing serious social, political, economic and religious injustices and tries to apply Micah's prophecy to the current Zimbabwean context. The chapter is a daring attempt to juxtapose Micah's message in light of the prevailing socio-political and religious-economic factors which fuel poverty among the general populace in Zimbabwe.

371

Drawing on the critical analysis of the Biblical texts on Micah, the chapter argues that social justice is a promoter of peace, abundance, equality and tranquillity whilst social injustice is a promoter of chaos, inequality, poverty and hunger. In order to make a convincing argument, the chapter is organised as follows: Firstly, it examines the poverty situation in Zimbabwe in the 21st century. Secondly, the chapter critically investigates the identity of Micah which takes two parallel positions namely: Hans Walter Wolf's Thesis which designates Micah as one of the elders of Moresheth and the rebuttal of Hans Walter Wolf's Thesis which tags Micah as the prophet for the Poor. Thirdly, the chapter interrogates Micah's radical shift of his social standing from a victim of an oppressive system to an advocate for change in Judah. Fourthly, a contextualisation look at Micah closes the chapter paving way for the conclusion. Taking it from the fourth task here proposed, the chapter examines the poverty situation in Zimbabwe in the 21st century by drawing lessons from Micah the prophet who through inspiration from his poor peasant identity championed a message of justice (*mispat*) to quell prevalent inequalities and injustices in Judah in the 8th century.

The Poverty Situation in Zimbabwe in the 21st Century

Poverty is one of the most topical and controversial issues in the world to date. It is controversial at both theoretical and practical levels. As Madzokere and Machingura (2015-) concur, the problem of poverty and hunger has continued to be the number one enemy of humanity and directly affects Africa's economic development. For them, economic development in any country cannot be realised when people are visibly poor and hungry. Annual statistical data for Zimbabwe in 2015 shows that a sizable number of people are always in need of food assistance to the effect that eight out of every ten people are presently unemployed and poor (http://www.fao.org/docrep/013/i1683e/pdf). This is despite the fact that the Zimbabwean government is still promising to work towards fulfilling the eight goals of the UNDP-MDGS whose goal number one is: Eradicating extreme poverty and hunger.

Unfortunately, the first goal of eradicating poverty and hunger which is in tandem with this study has remained a nightmare for the general majority of Zimbabweans. Some of the seven out of the eight goals of the UNDP-MDGS are: Achieving universal primary education, Promoting gender equality and empowerment of women, Reducing child mortality rate, Improving maternal health, Combating HIV and AIDS, malaria and other diseases, Ensuring environmental sustainability and lastly Developing a global partnership for development (Mangena and Chitando 2011). These seven of the eight goals are worth mentioning though they are beyond the scope of this study. According to the 2016 Global Hunger Index, the factors which have exacerbated Zimbabwe's food security situation over the years are a plethora. The list ranges from widespread poverty to HIV and AIDS, limited employment opportunities, liquidity challenges, recurrent induced climate shocks and economic instability, which all contribute to limiting adequate access to food.

From the list given above, it is not coincidental that poverty is recorded as number one of the problems affecting Zimbabwe. It is ironic for Zimbabwe because it is generally referred to as 'the jewel in Africa's crown' because of its natural resources (Good 2002).However, the jewel status of Zimbabwe has long been lost due to misuse of the natural resources by political elites exacerbating poverty and hungry in the country(Matanda and Madzokere 2017). For Raftopolous (2009), years of political, social and economic crises from the period 2000 to 2008 threw many people into abject poverty in Zimbabwe. Now in 2017 as this book chapter is being written, many Zimbabweans have not yet recovered from the crises noted above. If anything, the levels of poverty in the country seem to be worsening day in day out to prove beyond doubt that the zeal to eradicate poverty and hunger in the country has become a pipedream for the majority of the "ordinary" Zimbabweans.

Paradoxically, Zimbabwe is one of the countries in Africa south of the Sahara with abundant resources especially minerals-almost every mineral in this world is found in Zimbabwe (Madzokere 2017, Madzokere & Matanda 2014) but its people are experiencing worst situations of artificialized hunger and abject poverty. At independence in 1980, Zimbabwe inherited one of the most powerful economies in Southern Africa, which however, got ruined by Robert Mugabe and his cronies (Madzokere 2017). Taking from this obtaining reality, it is beyond doubt that poverty's chief propeller in Zimbabwe is not the natural cause but the artificial one. The Zimbabwe Catholic Bishops' Conference (ZCBC) pastoral letter of 14 January, 2011 entitled: "Let Us Work for the Common Good: Let Us Save Our Nation" (available at http://relzim.org/tag/zimbabwe-catholic-bishops-conference/page/2), made the following observations about Africa, including Zimbabwe:

> Africa is rich in human and natural resources, but many of our people are still left to wallow in poverty and misery, wars and conflicts, crisis and chaos. These are very rarely caused by natural disasters. They are largely due to human decisions and activities by the people who have no regard for the Common Good…but then we urge political leaders to prioritize poverty eradication by using proceeds from the natural resources like diamonds, land and others, for the development of the whole nation and its citizens.

Instead of blaming God who has control over the natural disasters for the evil and suffering prevalent in Zimbabwe, human beings especially those in leadership hierarchies should be singled out as the chief perpetrators of evil and suffering. One needs to ask man not God for corruption, hunger and poverty ruining Zimbabwe. Madzokere and Machingura (2015) scholarly sentiments hold water that poverty and hunger are mostly man-made, self-inflicting and artificial disasters where the greedy, egocentric and corrupt leaders abuse resources to the peril of the "ordinary" majority. The perpetration of poverty and hunger in Zimbabwe by those in leadership positions typifies the 8th century Judah whose political, social, economic and religious leaders fuelled gargantuan injustices to the peril and detriment of the majority poor peasant classes. Such a situation in Judah triggered Micah the prophet from the rural village of Moresheth to attack injustices championed by the various political leaders of his time. What then follows below is an interrogation of Micah's identity.

Unravelling Micah's identity

Micah of Moresheth was one of the canonical eighth century prophets who championed social justice (6: 8) like Amos (5: 24) and Isaiah of Jerusalem (1: 17). He prophesied in Judah during the reign of Ahaz, Jotham and Hezekiah as evidenced by the superscription (Mason 1991). Micah's prophetic message to the people of Judah was greatly influenced by the political, economic, social, and religious evils of a highly stratified society, which prevailed during his time. The identity of Micah is pivotal in this regard because identity comprises of a myriad facets of who a person is, why his message addressed these and no other human problems, and the link between the prophet's persona and his message. It covers the historical background of a person (origin), language, culture, customs, and traditions, the social, economic, political and religious environmental factors. These facets contribute a lot to the overall character and personality of a person. Human beings are products of their own environments which shape them to be who they are and how they behave (Madzokere 2011).

The identity of Micah in this scenario has a lot of bearing to his message. As argued by Mason (1991), Micah's place of origin was to be identified with the village of Moresheth-Gath mentioned in Micah 1: 14. Moresheth-Gath was located in the *shephelah (*low land*)* .The internal scriptural evidence of the book of Micah shows that Micah's hometown was a small village located about twenty-five miles south-west of Jerusalem just outside the Philistine City of Gath. There was nothing substantial known about Micah's family and about his personal life. James Luther Mays (1976) says that Micah's identification as a Moreshite indicates that Micah was someone who lived outside the city of Jerusalem. In a comparative view, Mason (1991) observed that Isaiah of Jerusalem was identified as of high social status, since he had access to the King and mixed freely with leading priests and other officials of aristocratic orientation. This presents Micah of Moresheth as an exact opposite of Isaiah of Isaiah of Jerusalem in terms of their social status. It also implies that Micah travelled a long way on foot from his rural peripheral village called

Moresheth to convey Yahweh's message to the residents of the city of Jerusalem.

Although there were some traditional modes of transportation (horse riding, chariots, ox-drawn carts), Micah walked twenty-five miles on foot (with or mostly without sandals) to the cosmopolitan Jerusalem to proclaim the message to the Jerusalem urbanites. Since the internal textual evidence of the book is silent about Micah's father and that he was only identified by his village of origin, most scholars (Mason 1991, Mays 1976, Van Der Woude, 1982) would like to believe that he was a peasant who was highly concerned with the plight of the suffering poor of Judah and those who were powerless, a person of less importance in his village, who was commissioned by Yahweh to herald an urgent message on behalf of the oppressed poor in Judah. Unlike the depiction of Micah as a man of high social status (as given by Mays), this chapter, basing on the concern and message of Micah to the people of Judah, views the prophet otherwise. Such a scholarly standpoint is commonly referred to as an 'underdog' perspective. It is motivated by the fact that Micah identified himself with those who were poor and oppressed in a typically oppressive stratified Judean society. To further substantiate this view, Mason (1991) argues that Micah should have been a poor countryman (peasant class) who appears to have known about oppression from the bottom of the heap, from the margins of society. He knew exactly how the overbearing policies of the leaders bore down on the day to day life of ordinary peasants, and his attacks are all against what the contemporary times should be called the political and religious 'Establishment' (3: 1-3;9-12). These were torch-bearers of power. It is the policies of these groups he attacks, not the ordinary people (general populace).The oppressive structural system of the powerful political-cum-religious clique wanted to be uprooted for social justice to be realised in such a society. For this reason, it is highly probable that Micah came from the despised peasant classes and was horrified by what he saw in his own vicinity in Moresheth and also in a typically urbanised Jerusalem. Mason, as he intensifies his argument, reiterates that perhaps it was such a sense of outrage which Micah understood to be God's call to prophesy against the leaders in the land, rather as the later Jeremiah seems to have been appalled by what he saw when he moved from the village of Anathoth to the city (Jeremiah 5: 1-5).

Kojo (2015) states categorically that Micah rose in the midst of the pitch-dark condition of a nation, where corruption and wickedness pervaded the entire society. He condemned the leaders of society and encouraged the poor to look up to God who will save them from their oppressions. Such scholarly sentiments are also shared by Buono (2000) who refers to Micah as, "the prophet of divine justice" because of his burning passion to address social inequalities and injustices experienced by the oppressed poor classes in Judah. But was Micah a prophet at all or a mere politician? He is not called such, although the superscription brings him into line with similar editorial notes about Amos (1: 1) and Isaiah of Jerusalem (1: 1; 2: 1; 13: 1).Was Micah a prophet or an elder of Moresheth? What exactly was his social status? Why was he taking sides with the peasant poor in Judah? Was it mere coincidence or he was acting in solidarity with his own poor peasant fellows? There are many theories, perspectives derived from these questions as scholars continue grappling with the identity and message of Micah to the people of Judah. In the sections below, I reflect on these questions further as I quest to uncover the identity and message of Micah.

'Micah as one of the Elders': Hans Walter Wolff's Thesis

Hans Walter Wolff (1990) argue that Micah was not a prophet, but that he was one of the elders of Moresheth whose responsibility was for administering true justice in the community. An elder here refers to an ecclesiastical title given to someone who is well grounded in the tradition, culture, and customs of a religious community but not based on age. There is no account of the prophetic call of Micah though that is not unusual because most of the canonical prophets' calls do not follow the definite call narrative which we witness on the pre-canonical prophets like Moses (Exodus 3: 1ff). Only rarely does Micah use the prophetic formulae to introduce or conclude oracles which show a rare characteristic of Micah. They appear only twice (2: 3 and 3: 5) and they might be redactional additions by the redactors not Micah himself. For Wolff, God is usually only named when

Micah is quoting his opponents (2: 7; 3: 4, 11). His name is strangely absent, for example, from 3: 12, the climax of Micah's pronouncements against leaders of the city. In 3: 8 also, apart from the phrase, 'the Spirit of the Lord' often seen as an addition, there is nothing of name, Yahweh. Wolff developed his argument further by stating that the 'And I said' of 3: 1 is in contrast to the words of the false prophets and is somewhat akin to the use of the first person 'I' by Wisdom in Proverbs 8 and Sirach 24.1. It is a remnant also of the old "clan" wisdom style (Proverbs 8: 12, 14, 20). Micah does not use the term, 'king' but rather the title, 'heads' descriptive of the heads of the old clans, and 'rulers', used of the 'judges'(3: 1,3;9,3: 11). His concern is above all for 'justice'. All of this suggests, according to Wolff, that Micah himself was one of the elders who were guardians of the 'wisdom' tradition and who were responsible for administering justice in the community. It was because he saw the leaders of Jerusalem failing to maintain this responsibility towards the ordinary people in the Judean countryside that he went to the city to challenge them. Wolff's thesis is based on Jeremiah 26: 16-20, where the elders of the land were familiar with Micah's words and used them to defend Jeremiah. Jeremiah 26: 16-20 reads:

> Then rose up certain of the elders of the land, and spoke to all the assembly of the people, saying, Micah the Moreshite prophesied in the days of Hezekiah king of Judah, and spoke to the people of Judah, saying, "Thus says the Lord of hosts; Zion shall be ploughed like a field, and Jerusalem shall become heaps, and the mountain of as the high place of a forest." Did Hezekiah king of Judah and all Judah put him at all to death? Did he not fear the Lord and besought the Lord, and the Lord repented him of the evil which he had pronounced against them? Thus might we procure great evil against our souls.

According to Wolff's argument, since Micah was an elder in Moresheth, the elders of Judah preserved Micah's words because he was one of them. In addition, Wolff contends that as an elder in Moresheth, Micah was welcomed by the assembly of elders in Jerusalem and was given the platform to present his case against the religious and political authorities of Judah and decry their abuses of power. What follows is the rebuttal of Hans Walter Wolff's thesis here elaborated.

'Micah as a prophet for the Poor': Hans Walter Wolff's Thesis Rebuttal

Although Wolff's thesis on Micah's identity raises powerful arguments, unfortunately it has not been widely adopted by Old Testament scholars. The only disciple of Wolff is Carrera (1982) who argue along the same line of thought that Micah belonged in the stream of Old Testament wisdom, but Weiser (1985) places Micah firmly among the prophets as does Van Der Woude (1982), who strongly dismisses Wolff's arguments. He argues that Wolff was writing at a time when scholars were tending to find 'Wisdom' traditions everywhere, whereas in the contemporary times scholars should be cautious to establish close links between a particular prophet and the wisdom teachers. Perhaps we might be less sure that village 'elders' were the guardians of such Wisdom traditions.

To substantiate his argument further, Van Der Woude (1982) categorically argues that it was clear both from the present form of the book as well as from Jeremiah 26: 16-20, where it is specifically stated that Micah had 'prophesied', that tradition remembered him as a prophet. The unusual form of Micah's 'prophecies' should be noted; but this may only serve to remind us that Micah did not belong to the 'mainstream' of Old Testament prophets, and the Old Testament Prophecy was a varied phenomenon. Van Der Woude observes that Wolff's arguments do, however, have the value of underlying the truth that Old Testament prophets were passionately concerned with justice in society.

Whatever else Micah may or may not have been, he was clearly aflame with a sense of burning indignation at the unjust system in which so many ordinary people suffered at the hands of the powerful and the wealthy. He was the prophet who championed the cause of the poor and the downtrodden masses in Judah. He seems to have been more of a prophet of the market place and the town square than the sanctuary. For him, Yahwism was nothing if it did not affect the political, social, economic and religious life of society (Van Der

Woude1982). He apparently set little store by the great 'institutions' of the nation and its religion, whether that meant the temple, the palace or the 'chosen' city. In the same line of thought, Mason (1991) asserts that God could and would dispense with all of these if necessary (3: 12); and this if the passage comes from him, is also the implication of Micah 6: 6. If Micah saw any hope beyond such a total catastrophe as he believed was coming on a nation and temple; it must have been a future with a new set of institutions and a new line of leaders. What follows below is a scholarly intensification of the above scholarly position to argue that Micah was a prophet for the Poor who was a victim of an oppressive system which oppressed the peasant classes in Judah. His attack of the Affluent classes in Judah was done not as mere coincidence but he was acting in solidarity with his own poor peasant fellows who were underdogs in Judah.

For my own critical and textual analysis, the superscription of Micah (1: 1) and the content of his message indicates that Micah was a person of humble historical origin and most probably an individual who was a victim of the oppressive policies of the aristocracy of Judah. As a victim of oppressive structures in Judah, Micah experienced every bitter ingredient of the political, economic, social and religious injustices prevalent during his time. Experience was the best teacher to Micah and all victims of various forms of domination in a stratified Judean society. While the question on why should Yahweh call a typically rural personality to be a messenger to a diametrically opposite cosmopolitan Jerusalem population remains topical even today, it should be noted that this was not accidental in Yahweh's *modus operandi* in recruitment of prophetic figures as we also see the same in the call of Amos of Tekoa-a dresser of sycamore trees and a mere shepherd boy (Madzokere 2011).

Amos like Micah attacked the affluent classes who were perpetrating political, social, economic and religious injustices in Judah. He called prophetic luminaries with controversial historical upbringing characterised by complexity as was Moses-the deliverer of the Hebrew slaves (Madzokere 2010). Moses like Micah was sent by Yahweh to liberate a bunchy of Hebrew slaves who were exploited politically, economically, socially and religiously in Egypt under the most notorious Pharaohs. The prophetic mission of Micah as dictated by Yahweh was to attack the powerful rich classes who championed injustices in the political, social, religious and economic fabric of the downtrodden poor classes in Judah (2: 1-3, 3: 1-12). There was an enormous gap between the affluent rich classes and abject poor classes – the rich ones getting richer and richest whilst the poor were getting poorer and poorest each day. His attack was done in solidarity with his own poor folk living in doldrums for birds of the same feathers perambulate in close proximity. The language of Micah points to his identity as more of a poor peasant farmer than an elder.

To substantiate this point further, it is argued that Micah speaks the language of a personality from the countryside. To be more specific, Micah speaks the language of a shepherd on one hand and language of a farmer on the other hand. His identity also speaks loud to support his rural peasantry background. The following textual examples give evidence of the claim. In Micah1: 13, Micah makes reference to "bind the chariots to the swift beast" and also "baldness as an eagle" (Micah 1: 16). Micah was also identified by the name of his village-Moresheth so was now a Moreshethite which is evident of his alien identity in the city of Jerusalem. This was a simplest way of identifying a foreigner through tagging him to the name of his place of origin. In Micah 1: 6, Micah also speaks of "a heap of a field and as plantings of a vineyard" and "they covet fields" (Micah 2: 2) shows that he was a personality from the countryside who is well conversant of the rural environment. Micah also speaks of "the flock in the midst of their fold" (Micah 2: 12) and who "pluck off their skin" (Micah 3: 2).The verb, 'pluck' is generally used to refer to the harvesting of crops by farmers especially cereal ones such as rapoko, sorghum or millet.

In Micah 3: 12, Micah uses a chain of words that points to his rural peasantry background when he says, "therefore shall Zion for your sake be plowed as a field, and Jerusalem shall become heaps, and the mountain of the house as the high places of the forest". In Micah 4: 3-4, Micah also points to his poor peasantry identity by the following, "they shall beat their swords into plowshares, and their spears into pruning hooks: nation shall not lift up a sword against nation, neither shall they learn war anymore. But they shall sit every man under his vine and under his fig tree…".Another evidence in (5: 8) which reads, "…as a lion among the beasts of the forest, as a young lion among the flocks of sheep: who if he go through, both tread down, and tear in pieces, and none can deliver." To substantiate further, in Micah 6: 15, he avers, "You shall sow, but you shall not reap; you shall tread the olives, but you shall not anoint yourself with oil; and sweet wine, but shall not drink wine."

To conclude the support for Micah's peasantry background, we take a leaf from the last chapter of Micah (7: 1-2) which says: "Woe is me! For I am as when they have gathered the summer fruits, as the grape gleanings of the vintage: there is no cluster to eat: my soul desired the first ripe fruit…they hunt every man his brother with a net." We cannot expect such kind of language from a typically cosmopolitan personality whose life revolves around the corridors of the city of Jerusalem or the so-called "born in locations or *salalas*" from the writer's own contextual understanding of the word. Micah was a prophet of a rural poor peasant orientation who championed social justice (*mispat*) in a stratified oppressive system in Judah where there was prevalence of political, social, economic and religious injustices. He did this in solidarity with his peasantry crew oppressed by the powerful aristocratic clique in Judah. His attack of the affluent class in Judah was not a mere coincidence but it was done in tandem with his identity.

'From a Victim of an Oppressive System to an Advocate for change': A radical shift of Micah's prophetic career

Micah of Moresheth's attack of the rich oppressive class was done to fulfil Yahweh's mandate of seeing social justice (*mispat,* c.f. Micah 6: 8) prevailing in Judah among the *goyim* (people of God). It was also influenced by his impoverished peasantry background of Moresheth characterised by human suffering of highest order. Mason (1991) in agreement with Madzokere (2011) reiterates that Micah was a passionate personality for justice towards the underdogs of society who were in a dungeon of an affluent oppressive system. For Mariottini (2014), such an impoverished condition of Micah and most of his peasantry background was perpetrated by the aristocracy,

382

merchants and the clergymen. The stinking poverty experienced by the poor class was artificialised by the powerful classes hence a cry for social justice (*mispat*). Micah strongly criticised those who oppressed the poor and deprived them of their rights. Notwithstanding these political crises, the first part of the eighth century B.C.E in Judah was a time of economic prosperity. Archaeology gives evidence that a wealthy class of citizens emerged in Judah (Limburg 1988; Mason 1991).

According to the prophets, Isaiah of Jerusalem and Micah of Moresheth, this group of people became wealthier by exploiting the poor people who lived in the many villages of Judah. This exploitation of the poor became even worse after the fall of Samaria and during the many years Judah became subservient to Assyria as a vassal state. As such, Judah had to pay a yearly tribute to Assyria and the money for the tribute was raised by taxing the people who were least able to pay the exorbitant taxes collected by the government and by the landlords. The rich and powerfully connected elites turned to the poor powerless classes for payment of taxes whilst they exempt themselves. Micah preached against those who were greedy for money: In Micah 7: 3-4, Micah notes that "Officials and judges altogether demanded bribes. The people with influence get what they want, and together they scheme to twist justice. Even the best of them is like a brier; the most honest is as dangerous as a hedge of thorns". The Shona idiom applies here, "*Kakara kununa kudya kamwe*" translated in English, "*An animal survives on devouring the other*", which if we are to draw parallels with Zimbabwe it happens to be the exact situation currently obtaining in the country.

Mariottini (2014) makes a powerful reflection on the prevalence of social injustices in Judah which triggered Micah to burst into attack of the affluent powerful class who were perpetrators of such evils. The poor class were an easy prey for the rich at this moment because the annual payment of tribute by all citizens to the government was strictly mandatory at this juncture and that jeopardises the lives of the poor class who were now economically doomed. The poor peasants could not even afford a daily meal. They were now living like rats cornered by a cat. The result was the oppression of the poor by the wealthy and the powerful, such as the seizing of land from those unable to pay their debts (Micah 2: 1-2), the eviction of people from their homes (Micah 2: 9), the taking of bribes (Micah 3: 11), merchants and wealthy businessmen cheating people by using inaccurate weights and measures (Micah 6: 10), and people becoming rich through extortion and violence (Micah 6: 12).Constable (2016) shares the same sentiments with Mariottini when he asserts that Micah was so unhappy with the political, economic, social and religious conditions of Judah at this time, hence he uttered, "the godly people have all disappeared; not one honest person is left on the earth. They are all murderers, setting traps even for their own brothers" (Micah 7: 2). Micah's message condemns the oppression of the poor, the political corruption of the leaders of Judah, and some of the religious syncretism that was common during the reign of Ahaz. The reference to Micah in Jeremiah 26: 17-19 states that Micah prophesied "during the days of King Hezekiah" (Mason 1991; Van Der Woude 1982). Micah's message was one of the factors that prompted Hezekiah to initiate the religious reforms that removed some of the pagan practices that had been introduced into the religious life of Judah. In his oracles, Micah claims that his message about the sins of the people and his call to justice came because of the endowment of the Spirit of God (Hebrew-*ruach*, Greek-*numa*), "But as for me, I am filled with power, with the spirit of the LORD, and with justice and might, to declare to Jacob his transgression and to Israel his sin" (Micah 3: 8).

Drawing on this analysis, it is possible that Micah, as a poor peasant, living in the small village of Moresheth as argued above had personal experiences of the worst and evil policies that promoted social injustice in the Judean society. Constable notes further that Micah was familiar with the political, economic, social and judicial corruption that deprived the poor of their day in court: "Woe for those who devise wickedness and evil deeds on their beds! They covet fields, and seize them; houses, and take them away; they oppress householder and house, people and their inheritance" (Micah 2: 1-2). Limburg (1988) also observed that Micah was familiar with the widespread idolatry rampant in Samaria and Judah: "All her images shall be beaten to pieces, all her wages shall be burned with fire, and all her idols I will lay waste; for as the wages of a prostitute she gathered them, and as the wages of a prostitute they shall again be used" (Micah 1: 7). The sins of Israel and Judah had a profound effect in the sensitive soul of Micah: "For this I will lament and wail; I will go barefoot and naked; I will make lamentation like the jackals, and mourning like the ostriches" (Micah 1: 8). In the same vein, Constable (2016: 10) asserts that Micah attacked the political and religious leadership of Judah for it was responsible for the perpetration of injustice against the powerless people. The political leaders of Judah, the religious leaders in the temple, the judges in the court, and the merchants were not only oppressing the people, but were feeding off of them like social cannibals: "Listen, O heads of Jacob, and rulers of the house of Israel! Should you not know justice?–you who hate the good and love the evil, who tear the skin off my people, and the flesh off their bones; who eat the flesh of my people, flay their skin off them, break their bones in pieces, and chop them up like meat in a kettle, like flesh in a caldron" (Micah 3: 1-3). According to Cornell (2014), social cannibalism is a predatory form of behaviour that can be found in any culture and class of people. It tends to be more prevalent among refined and ostensibly religious people. The Germans call the behaviour *schadenfreude*. The word refers to a twisted kind of pleasure in the misfortune of others. Social cannibals threaten good relationships and destroy wholesome community hence were condemned by Micah. What follows now is the contextualization of Micah's message to Zimbabwe.

Reading Micah in the context of poverty in Zimbabwe

Although Micah of Moresheth prophesied in Judah in the 8th century BCE, there is some sound rational justification to tap some lessons to enable Zimbabwe address her poverty stricken quagmire. The prevalent injustices which took place during the 8th century in Judah triggered Micah's attack of the perpetrators of and such share striking similarities with Zimbabwe although the two are separated by the cultural gap, geographical remoteness, worlds apart factor and historical gap (Hayes and Holladay 1987). Reading Micah to the context of poverty in Zimbabwe enables one to draw parallels between Micah's time and the contemporary Zimbabwe on four key aspects: political, social, economic and religious.

Politically, the leaders (kings) of Judah according to Micah were corrupt, evil and greedy for money (Micah 2: 1ff, 3: 1ff, 6: 12). According to Constable (2016), Micah's picture of false authority of the leaders of Judah is clearly shown in 3: 11: "Israel's leaders pronounce judgment for a bribe, her priests instruct for a price and her 'prophets' divine for money." Micah identified all three major types of Judean rulers as corrupt: civil leaders (the princes), religious leaders (the priests), and moral leaders (the prophets). The judges were judging according to who paid them best. The priests were teaching the people, but for what they could get out of it. The 'prophets' were not really prophesying messages from the Lord hence were false prophets. They were practicing sorcery and witchcraft for money and passing these revelations off as the word of God. The judges (princes) were passing judgment in legal cases because they hated good and loved evil (see Micah 3: 1-3). They should have "known" judgment (cf. Micah 3: 1). That is, they should have practiced justice (*mispat*), ruled justly, and shown no partiality. Instead they were, as Micah described them, tearing the skin off the people, eating their flesh, and chopping up their bones like butchers (Micah 3: 2b-3). They were robbing the people, like soldiers who took the spoils of war. They were not impartial. They did not represent God, the true Judge of His people. They were corrupt. The priests were no better (Micah 3: 11). When we think of Israel's priests, we probably think of them offering the sacrifices that the people brought to the temple. But one of the primary responsibilities of the priests in Israel was to teach the people the Word of God (Deut. 17: 8-13). This was really a more important ecclesiastical duty than cutting up animals. For Constable (2016), this man-ward duty was more significant than their God-ward duty. God scattered the priests in Israel, rather than giving them one geographic region to inhabit, so they could teach the Judeans Yahweh's statutes and ordinances. Yet the priests in Micah's day were just telling the people what the Judeans wanted to hear, not what God had said typical of blind nationalist prophets the world over. And they were doing it for generation of money which is typical of 'gospreneurship' in the contemporary world (Vengeyi 2011; Chitando 2013,Madzokere and Machingura 2015-JCSS).This way they are no longer fit to be called prophets but profiteers. They distorted their messages to get a favourable response to their messages. Even the priests (false ones) and the prophets (false ones) were not immune to dishonest practices in order to get money. According to Micah, the priests who taught God's laws did so for a price. The prophets who were responsible for revealing God's message to the people would not prophesy unless they were paid (Micah 3: 11).

The prophets claimed to have received fresh messages from the Lord for the people, but most of the prophets in Micah's day delivered favourable "words from the Lord" only if they received adequate compensation. If the people did not pay them well, they either gave a message of gloom and doom, or no message at all. They were getting messages for the people all right, but they were messages from the wrong source. Their "prophecies" amounted to sorcery and witchcraft. Micah wrote of them in 3: 5: "When they have something to bite with their teeth, they cry, 'Peace.' But against him who puts nothing in their mouths, they declare holy war." The people had to pay for good prophecies. Otherwise, they would get prophecies of disaster. In other words, such prophets were blind nationalists who prophesied peace where there was war, who prophesied prosperity where there was rampant exploitation of the poor by the rich, who prophesied blessings of Yahweh where there was disobedience to Yahweh's statutes and ordinances. They were typically money mongers who manipulated the political, economic and social crises in Judah to enrich themselves at the expense of the vulnerable impoverished poor peasant population in Judah. Constable (2016) argues that wherever you find distressed and suffering people, the cause is usually their leaders. If the leaders are out of harmony with God, if they love evil and hate good, if they are selfish rather than servants, the people suffer. This is true no matter what form of government exists. Every form of government has the equivalent of kings, princes, priests, and prophets: civil, religious, and moral leaders.

They were characterized by misgovernance and maladministration. Corrupt authorities rule for their own benefit, not for the benefit of the people. This is the opposite of "servant leadership" (Greek-*dulos*)-a type of leadership which is *pro-populo* (Latin-for the people). It is the contrast between selfish leadership and selfless leadership. Leaders condemned by Micah were selfish ones who were geared to further their egocentric desires not the needs of the general populace. In Micah 5: 2, Micah prophesy of a true leader who would arise from the obscure town of Bethlehem in Judah, whose rule would usher a new era that would mark the destruction of all that the people's false rulers had encouraged them to trust in: horses, chariots, cities, strongholds, treaties, witchcraft, images, and idols. For Constable (2016), if the motive of leaders is self-aggrandizement, self-service, and self-glory, their leadership is corrupt and pernicious. This is exactly what Micah condemned in his prophecy whose topos was social justice (*mispat*).

They were spectators as the powerful elite of Judah exploit the poor yet they were expected to see to it that people live in peace and harmony. This is a true replica of Zimbabwe where the President of the country-Robert Mugabe, his wife Grace and children are the most corrupt, most evil and greediest in Zimbabwe (Madzokere 2017, Matanda and Madzokere 2017).He owns fourteen farms instead of one against the country policy of one man one farm. Most of his adherents in the ruling party-ZANU-PF own each of them more than one farm (details check in The Zimbabwean 16 October, 2009).Socially, during the 8th century in Judah Micah observes that there was a massive gap between the rich classes and poor ones. The rich owned large tracts of land because they had money to buy as much as they could. They had money to lend to the peasants who in turn would pay back with an interest. The rich landowners (landlords) could take advantage of the poor who failed to pay back the debts by taking away their pieces of land. Most of the peasants were losing their land because of such evil machinations by the rich elites. Some of the peasants who failed to pay back were enslaved forever which is typical of the Fast Track Land Reform Programme (FTLRP) in Zimbabwe which was instituted to redress the colonial injustice but at the end benefitted the powerful political elites in the country. In Zimbabwe, most of the peasant farmers those who were working under the white commercial farmers suffered the worst because they were either given the option to leave the farm with the white farmer or agree to work under a new indigenous farmer with less pay and benefits (Todd 2007, Msipa 2015).The FTLRP in Zimbabwe had long term effects to the country. Raftopolous (2009: 284) observes:

> The Fast Track Programme had adverse effects on the agricultural sector in several ways: concerns about the capacity and ability of the beneficiaries; large amounts of vacant and underutilized land; vandalized and deteriorating infrastructure; decline of specialized production systems; drastic decline in seed maize production-exacerbated by drought-that resulted in the need for food assistance to about five million people by the end of 2008; the loss of skilled farmers; the breakdown in production linkages between the agricultural and other sectors; and the lack of security of tenure with its associated implications for financial investment on the land.

What we have now with the FTLP in Zimbabwe is exactly the fast tracking of poverty and hunger in country suffering from multiple crises-political, social, economic and religious (Madzokere and Machingura forthcoming, Sachikonye 2003, Manzungu 2004).Most of the commercial farmers who were displaced by Robert Mugabe and his cronies went to neighbouring Zambia, South Africa and Mozambique where they are performing wonders in the farms boosting agriculture. Ironically, the government of Zimbabwe is following up on the same displaced commercial farmers to buy grain from them at exorbitant charges. Through the implementation of the FTRLP, the government of Zimbabwe and its leadership of the tyrant Robert Mugabe fast tracked food crisis in the country. Although the motive behind the FTLRP in Zimbabwe was a noble one, it ended up impoverishing instead of empowering the marginalized peasant folk. Overall, the FTLRP had adverse social and economic effects to the general Zimbabwean populace which deprived them of holistic lives.

Conclusion

This chapter interrogated Micah's identity and message in a bid for a contextual application to Zimbabwe-a country bedevilled with poverty and hunger. The historical context of Micah characterized by political, economic, social and religious crises shaped his message. His message was targeting the leadership hierarchy of Judah that comprised of kings, princes, merchants, priests and prophets who were championing the political, economic, social and religious injustices in Judah. It was not coincidental for Micah to attack this target group but he was doing it in solidarity with his own people who were living in the dungeons of abject poverty hence the prophetic message of social justice-*mispat* (cf. Micah 6: 8) was boldly proclaimed by the prophet for the Poor. Micah's message revolves around political justice, social justice, economic justice and religious justice which was lacking in Judah. Political justice promotes peace, abundance, equality and tranquillity in the country whilst political injustices propel chaos, inequality, suffering, poverty and hunger. Micah attacked all political heavy weights who perpetrated political injustices in Judah so the political leaders in Zimbabwe who are fuelling injustices should be attacked across the political divide to quell poverty and hunger ruining the country. Social justice promotes peace, abundance, equality and tranquillity in the country whilst social injustices promote chaos, suffering, inequality, poverty and hunger. Micah attacked all the powerful social players who perpetrated social injustices in Judah so the powerful social players in Zimbabwe who are championing social injustices should be condemned across the social divide without favour to thwart poverty and hunger devastating the country. Economic justice promotes abundance, freedom, peace, equality and harmony in the country whilst economic injustices escalate suffering, starvation, malnutrition, poverty and hunger. Micah castigated those who were behind economic injustices in Judah so the economic giants in Zimbabwe who are propelling economic injustices should be challenged to stop the evil to thwart the poverty and chaos in the country. Religious justice is crucial for the promotion of peace, harmony, love, equality and abundance in the country whilst religious injustices fuel chaos, confusion, disunity, suffering and poverty. Micah attacked vehemently the ecclesiastical personalities-priests, bishops and prophets who were propagating religious injustices in Judah so the evil members of the clergy in Zimbabwe who are propelling religious injustices should be castigated strongly to quell such hypocrisy and injustices committed in the pretext of religion in the country (Madzokere forthcoming).A contextual application of Micah enabled the study draw four crucial lessons for Zimbabwe namely the vitality of political justice, social justice, economic justice and religious justice which serve as promoters of peace, equality, abundance, love and tranquillity in the country against the backdrop of political, social, economic and religious injustices which bedevilled the nation from 2000 to date.

References

Buono, A. M. (2000). Micah, Prophet of the Divine Justice, *Pastoral Life* 49: 42-47.

Chitando, E. (2013). 'Introduction' in Chitando, E, Gunda, M.R & Kuegler, J. (Eds). *Prophets, Profits and the Bible*, University of Bamberg: Bamberg.

Carrera, J. N. (1982). '*Kunstsprache und Weisheit bei Micha. Biblicher Zeitchrift*, Freiburg, Paderborn. 26: 50-74.

Constable, T. (2016). *Commentary on Micah*, John Knox Press: Westminster.

Good, K. (2002). 'Dealing with Despotism: The People and the Presidents', In: Melber, H. (Ed) *Zimbabwe's Presidential Elections 2002: Evidence, Lessons and Implications*, Nordiska Afrikainstitutet Discussion Paper 14, Uppsala.

Hayes and Holladay. (1987). *Biblical Exegesis-A Beginner's Handbook*, John Knox: Atlanta.

Kojo, O. (2015). Prophetic Action against Injustice: An Exegetical Reading of Micah 3: 1-4.*Trinity Journal of Church and Theology* 18/4: 121-135.

Leschow, T. (1972). 'Redaktiongeschtliche Analyse von Micha 6-7, Zeitchrift fur die alttestamentliche, Wissenschift, Geissen& Berlin 84: 182-212.

Limburg, J. (1988). *Hosea-Micah,* John Knox Press: Westminster.

Madzokere, N. (2011). *Amos'attack of the Affluent Classes: A Reflection of his Social Status,* Lambert Publishing: Saarbrucken.

Madzokere, N. (2010). *The Divine Preferential option for the Oppressed: the Liberation topos behind the Exodus,* Verlag Doctor Muller: Saarbrucken.

Madzokere, N. (forthcoming). Prophets or Profiteers?: An Interrogative Study of the contemporary Pentecostal Prophets in Zimbabwe, *A Paper presented at an Annual International Conference at Multi-Media University,* Nairobi, Kenya on 29 June, 2017.

Madzokere, N. (2017). "'Let my People Go!" A Contextual Reading of the Book of Exodus in Light of Political and Economic Crisis in Post-independent Zimbabwe', In: Mawere, M.(Ed).*Underdevelopment, Development and the Future of Africa.* Bamenda: Langaa.

Madzokere, N & Machingura, F. (forthcoming) 'Impoverishing the Marginalized Poor': A Critique of the Plight of the Commercial Farm Workers in the Fast Track Land Reform Programme (FTRLP) in post-independent Zimbabwe in light of Micah 5: 2. *A Paper presented at ATISCA Zimbabwe Chapter conference,* Harare: Rainbow Towers Hotel.

Madzokere, N. and Machingura, F. (2015). Re-Reading the Parable of the Rich-man and Lazarus in light of Poverty and Hunger in Zimbabwe in Mangena, F, Mabiri, and Chimuka, T. (eds). *Philosophy, Tradition and Progress: An African Perspective,* Council for Research in Value and Philosophy: USA.

Madzokere, N. and Machingura, F. (2015). True and False Prophets/esses in Light of Prophets/esses and Wonders in Zimbabwe, *Journal of Critical Southern Studies,* Volume 3, Winter.53-71.

Madzokere, N. and Matanda, E. (2014). 'A Progressive or Failed State?': A Critique of the Economic Status of Zimbabwe since independence in Amutabi, M. (Ed). *Africa and the Challenges of Globalization: Opportunities and Prospects,* USA Africa Series. Kenya.

Mangena, F. and Chitando. E. (2011). Millennium Development Goals in Zimbabwe's "Decade of Crisis," *Journal of Sustainable Development in Africa*, 13(5): 233-24.

Manzungu, E. (2004), 'Environmental impacts of the Fast- Track Land Reform Programme: a Livelihoods perspective' in Barry, H.D. (Ed). *Zimbabwe: The Past is the Future*, Weaver Press: Harare.

Mays, L. J. (1976). *Micah: A Commentary*, Old Testament Library. The Westminster Press.

Mason, M. (1991). *Micah, Nahum, Obadiah*, T&T Clark: London.

Mariottini, C. (2014). The Prophet of the Poor accessed from claudemariottini.com/2014/02/21-1400hrs.

Mariottini, C. (2013). Studies on Micah the Prophet accessed from claudemariottini.com/2013/12/07-1500hrs.

McKeating, T. (1971). *Amos, Hosea & Micah*, The Syndics of the Cambridge University Press: New York.

Msipa. G. C. (2015). *In Pursuit of Freedom and Justice: A Memoir*, Weaver Press: Harare.

Raftopolous, B. (2009). 'The Zimbabwe Crisis' in Mlambo, A. and Raftopolous, B. (Eds). *Becoming Zimbabwe*, Weaver Press: Harare.

Sachikonye, L. M. (2003). *Land Reform for Poverty Reduction? Social Exclusion and Farm Workers in Zimbabwe*, Manchester University: London.

Thomas, D. W. (1962). 'Micah' in Black. M & Rowley, H. H. (Eds). *Peakes Commentary on the Bible,*

Todd, J. (2007). *Through the Darkness: A Life in Zimbabwe*, Struik Publishers: Cape Town.

Vengeyi, O. (2011). 'Zimbabwean Poverty is man-made!' Demystifying Poverty by Appealing to the Book of Amos, *Scriptura 107*: 223-237.

Weiser, A. (1985).*Die Propheten Hosea, Joel, Amos, Obadja, Jona, Micha Alte Testament* Deutsch, Gottingen 24, 6th Edition.

Wolfe, R. E. (1956). '*The book of Micah*', New York: USA.

Wolff, H. W. (1990). *Micah: A Commentary*, Minneapolis: Augsburg.

Woude, V. D. (1982). 'The Three Classical Prophets', In: R. J. Coggins and Others (Ed). *Israel's Prophetic Tradition,* Cambridge University Press: Cambridge.

Websites

http://www.fao.org/docrep/013/i1683e/pdf) accessed 15.08.2017-1300hrs.

http://www1.wfp.org/countries/zimbabwe accessed 15.08.2017-1400hrs.

http://relzim.org/tag/zimbabwe-catholic-bishops-conference/page/2accessed15.08.2017.